# Living Your Best Life After 50

## ALL-IN-ONE

### by The Experts at AARP and For Dummies

A Wiley Brand

## Living Your Best Life After 50 All-in-One For Dummies®

Published by: **John Wiley & Sons, Inc.**, 111 River Street, Hoboken, NJ 07030-5774, www.wiley.com

Copyright © 2024 by AARP. All rights reserved. AARP is a registered trademark.

Published simultaneously in Canada

For general information on our other products and services, please contact our Customer Care Department within the U.S. at 877-762-2974, outside the U.S. at 317-572-3993, or fax 317-572-4002. For technical support, please visit https://hub.wiley.com/community/support/dummies.

Wiley publishes in a variety of print and electronic formats and by print-on-demand. Some material included with standard print versions of this book may not be included in e-books or in print-on-demand. If this book refers to media such as a CD or DVD that is not included in the version you purchased, you may download this material at http://booksupport.wiley.com. For more information about Wiley products, visit www.wiley.com.

This and other AARP books are available in print and e-formats at AARP's online bookstore, www.aarp.org/bookstore, and through local and online bookstores.

Library of Congress Control Number: 2024930742

ISBN 978-1-394-23696-1 (pbk); ISBN 978-1-394-23697-8 (ebk); ISBN 978-1-394-23698-5 (ebk)

# Contents at a Glance

# Recipes at a Glance

# Table of Contents

# Introduction

Have you turned 50 yet, or will you be turning 50 soon? Reaching this milestone means that you're heading into an exciting second act of your life. If you're ready to make the most of your new chapter, *Living Your Best Life After 50 All-in-One For Dummies* is here to help.

## About This Book

*Living Your Best Life After 50 All-in-One For Dummies* is chock-full of tips for taking charge of your finances — including investing and getting Social Security benefits — so that you can pay your bills and still have money to do the things you enjoy. This book will help you get the work you *really* want, whether paid or unpaid. You'll also find loads of pointers for downsizing and decluttering, and even hitting the road for weeks or months at a time as you consider a nomad lifestyle. And experts offer advice on eating healthy (yummy recipes included) and staying active. Have you thought about trying yoga or pickleball? Now is your chance!

A quick note: Sidebars (shaded boxes of text) dig into the details of a given topic related to living your best life after 50, but they aren't crucial to understanding it. Feel free to read them or skip them. You can pass over the text accompanied by the Technical Stuff icon, too. The text marked with this icon gives some interesting but nonessential information about making the most of your later years.

Within this book, you may note that some web addresses break across two lines of text. If you're reading this book in print and want to visit one of these web pages, simply key in the address exactly as it's noted in the text, as though the line break doesn't exist. If you're reading this text as an e-book, you've got it easy — just click the address to be taken directly to the page.

# Foolish Assumptions

This book assumes that you want to explore new opportunities as you make the most of the decades ahead. You can find help in these pages if you want to do any of the following:

>> Manage your money, invest for the long term, collect Social Security benefits, and put together a will or a trust

>> Find a new job and negotiate for what you want (and deserve)

>> Downsize from your current home

>> Travel around the country or the world and try a nomad lifestyle

>> Whip up delicious and nutritious recipes (including some that are gluten-free)

>> Boost your health by trying new activities like pickleball and yoga

# Icons Used in This Book

Icons are those fun drawings you see in the page margins now and again. Here's what they mean.

**REMEMBER**

The name says it all! This icon indicates something *really* important to take away from this book.

**TECHNICAL STUFF**

Information marked with this icon is interesting but not crucial to understanding how to live your best life in your 50s and beyond. Skip it or read it; the choice is yours.

**TIP**

This icon highlights helpful strategies for handling your finances, downsizing, eating healthy, and much more.

**WARNING**

This icon indicates potentially territory when it comes to making the most of your later decades. Skip this information at your own peril.

# Beyond the Book

In addition to the material in the book you're reading right now, this product also comes with some access-anywhere info on the web. Go to www.dummies.com and type "Living Your Best Life After 50 All-in-One For Dummies Cheat Sheet" in the search box to discover some additional life-after-50 pointers.

# Where to Go from Here

You don't have to read this book from cover to cover, but if you're an especially thorough person, feel free to do so! If you just want to find tips in a specific subject, take a look at the table of contents or the index, and then dive into the chapter or section that interests you. For example:

>> Want to get a better grip on your finances so that you can afford the lifestyle you choose? Start with Book 1.

>> Eager to find a new job? Check out Book 2.

>> Thinking about downsizing? Want to declutter? Book 3 shows you the way.

>> Curious about traveling more and even living like a nomad, either domestically or abroad? Get the scoop in Book 4.

>> Interested in eating healthy, trying new recipes, and staying active in your later years? You'll find lots of tips in Books 5 and 6.

The future is bright — good luck!

# 1

# Handling Your Finances

# Contents at a Glance

# Chapter **1**

# Managing Your Money

A budget is the first step to living within your means and, even more important, living the life you choose. Knowing your expenses, your income, and your financial goals is the foundation. In this chapter, you grab a notebook — or create an easy spreadsheet on your computer — to find out just where you stand financially so that you can move forward with financial awareness and stability.

Start by taking a look at expenses. How much do you spend each month? What are fixed expenses — those bills you pay regularly? What about variable expenses — those that fluctuate? Think about the difference between basic necessities and luxuries — needs versus wants.

The next step is looking at income. How much do you earn? Do you have investments? Other streams of income? Do you have retirement income?

The final step is setting your sights on the future. What are your financial goals? Going out to dinner more often? Fixing the roof? Visiting family more often or going on that dream vacation?

These are the types of questions you look at in this chapter. And, with the answers to these questions, you can begin to create a budget. When you become financially aware, your life can change in ways small and big. You can make room for things that matter so you're living life on your terms.

# Seeing Where Your Money Goes: Your Expenses

Tracking your expenses for a month or longer can show you exactly where your money is going. Write down what you spend in cash, by check, and through payment services such as CashApp, PayPal, and Venmo. Review your debit and credit card expenditures. Then look at periodic — including quarterly and annual — expenditures such as taxes, homeowners or renters insurance, and vacations. You'll most likely discover spending patterns, some of which may surprise you. Perhaps you realize you're spending way too much in a category, like takeout meals or multiple streaming services. Or maybe you find that your medications are depleting your income, and you want to look at discount cards or different insurance options.

## Identifying fixed expenses

*Fixed expenses* are approximately the same amount of money every billing period, such as your rent or mortgage and car payments. Fixed expenses are paid weekly, monthly, quarterly, or annually. For example, you may pay for your car registration every year or two and your car insurance monthly or quarterly. Weekly fixed expenses may include things like a parking or commuter pass. Figure 1-1 shows various examples of fixed expenses.

## Allowing for variable expenses

*Variable expenses,* or *variable costs,* unlike fixed expenses, vary from month to month and may be items you regularly purchase or ones you buy only occasionally (see Figure 1-2). Common variable expenses include areas like the following:

>> Groceries

>> Gas for your car

>> Food for your pets

>> Items for any hobbies

>> Personal care items like hygiene products or makeup

## Fixed Expenses

**Housing**

- Rent
- Mortgage
- Property taxes
- Homeowners association or condo fees
- Internet
- Electricity
- Water
- Landline
- Gas
- Lawn maintenance

**Work**

- Public transportation
- Parking
- Professional association fees

**Personal**

- Gym and other memberships
- Newspaper and magazine subscriptions
- Streaming services
- Cellphone
- Car payments
- House of worship

**Insurance Premium**

- Disability insurance
- Health insurance
- Life insurance
- Renters or homeowners insurance
- Vehicle insurance

**Children**

- Childcare
- Tuition
- 529 and Coverdell savings accounts
- After-school activities

**FIGURE 1-1:**
Spending categories that are considered fixed expenses.

**Medical**

- Flexible spending account
- High-yield savings account

© John Wiley & Sons, Inc.

Variable expenses can be more challenging for you to track. Depending on the time of year or stage of your life, your spending in these categories can fluctuate. You may spend nearly nothing in a category like household items one month and then easily spend a few hundred dollars there the next month. You may spend a lot more money during the holiday season between vacations and gifts.

Once you've tracked variable expenses for a few months, you'll have an easier time assigning a monetary value to them. A category may occasionally spike, initially throwing everything you had planned off course. You're going to figure this all out.

**Variable Expenses**

**Food**
- Groceries
- Dining out
- Lunch (work and school)
- Coffee

**Transportation**
- Gas
- Tolls
- Oil changes and other maintenance
- Car repairs
- Bus and train fare
- Parking

**Leisure**
- Concerts
- Movies and museums
- Books
- Hobbies
- Games for family
- Vacations

**Household**
- Pet food and supplies
- Veterinary care
- Cleaning supplies
- Decor
- Home maintenance and repairs

**Miscellaneous**
- Clothing
- Haircuts
- Charitable contributions
- Gifts
- Medical co-pays and out-of-pocket expenses
- Sports, lessons, tutors, school field trips

**FIGURE 1-2:** Spending categories that are variable expenses.

© John Wiley & Sons, Inc.

## Calculating your total spending

**REMEMBER**

After you know your fixed and variable expenses, you're ready to evaluate what you spend every month. Grab your notebook or open up your spreadsheet and follow these steps:

**1. Make a list of your fixed expenses.**

In addition to your housing expenses, list car payments and fun things like gym memberships, subscription boxes, and streaming services. Divide these into categories. For instance, under housing you'd put mortgage or rent, homeowners or renters insurance, and utilities.

**2. Make a list of your variable expenses.**

Just as you did for fixed expenses, put your variable expenses in categories.

**3.** **Add up the total monthly costs for fixed expenses each month.**

You now clearly see how much you spend every month on your fixed expenses. Once you've done this for a few months, compare your fixed expenses month over month.

**4.** **Add up the total annual costs for variable expenses.**

Because these are periodic, not monthly, you'll need to gather your expenses over time to see your annual costs. To get a monthly estimate, divide by 12.

**5.** **Evaluate whether you need those expenses.**

Consider whether all your expenses are necessary. Do you need to spend money on a gym membership every month, or can you find a cheaper way to work out, such as walking on local trails? If you've signed up to get monthly items or deliveries, do you have the option to pause them and work through your current supply instead?

TIP

Assess your larger expenses, too — not just the minor ones. For example: You realize rent may be costing you more of your take-home pay than you're comfortable with. Moving can be expensive, but make a note to research other living arrangements when you get closer to the end of your lease.

## Understanding needs versus wants

REMEMBER

Fixed and variable expenses can include both needs and wants:

» Generally speaking, *needs* include categories such as rent or mortgage payments, food, gas to get to and from work if you commute, and healthcare, including medicine.

» *Wants* are things like eating out, getting a new cellphone when your current one works fine, and going to concerts and movies.

TIP

Consider ways to save on both needs and wants. For instance, on needs, look for weekly specials at the grocery store. For wants, get on listservs for discounts on entertainment.

The difference between needs and wants can get murky quickly, especially because one person's want may genuinely be another person's need. Spending money on your wants is perfectly okay; you just need to figure out how to budget for them.

Be realistic when determining your wants and needs. Suppose you have a specific life situation that requires you to spend a bit more on your variable expenses. If so, budget for it. Perhaps you have a busy, stressful job. Maybe getting a massage once a month and ordering takeout a few times a week makes your own and your family's life manageable. Perhaps you pay more in a specific category, like eating out, than people say you should. But being realistic about your spending will help keep you on budget.

# Knowing Where Your Money Comes From: Your Income

Your *income* is an essential component of your budget. Knowing how much money you have coming in helps you make sure your expenses don't exceed your income. It can also help you set realistic goals for all areas that relate to your finances and perhaps even quality of life. When tracking your income, you may realize you have more than you initially thought you had. On the other hand, when you look at your income and expenses, you may find you have a spending deficit, which means you need to find ways to either cut back or earn more.

**REMEMBER**

When discussing your work income, one dollar amount you need to keep in mind is your *net pay*. Net pay is the amount of money left after any withholdings you may be subjected to, such as federal and state taxes, FICA taxes (supporting Social Security and Medicare), health insurance, and any wage garnishments you may be paying off. Your net pay is the money you have to pay your fixed and variable expenses and put toward savings and your goals.

Your income may also include earnings from your investments and other sources such as retirement income.

The most important type of income you should consider is what you earn monthly to cover all your expenses. *Monthly income* can come from various sources. While it can be consistent, it can also be different from month to month. Here's a list of different types of monthly income you can earn:

>> **Income from full-time and/or part-time employment:** This is income you receive from an employer that has you on its payroll. Some jobs pay a *salary* — a flat amount of money per paycheck — and others pay an hourly *wage*. Unlike a salary, hourly income can fluctuate because the number of hours you work may vary.

>> **Income as a self-employed freelancer or consultant:** Freelancers and contractors are considered self-employed, but the main difference is that *freelancers* generally balance more than one client and work on projects with a short timeline. *Contractors* often work with one main client on a longer time frame. (For tax purposes, there is no distinction between the two. Both should

pay estimated taxes quarterly because they are not deducted from paychecks automatically.)

>> **Pensions and other paid retirement plans:** A *pension* is a type of retirement program that an employee, an employer, or both pay into. The plan pays a fixed sum to the employee at regular intervals upon retirement. Some pensions require you to work for the company for a certain number of years before you're eligible (or *vested*). Federal, state, and local government or other public sectors also allow for paid retirement plans.

>> **Self-funded retirement plans:** Outside of traditional pensions or government-paid retirement plans, you may receive payments from retirement accounts, such as 401(k)s, 403(b)s, and IRAs. These types of retirement accounts allow you to save for retirement by investing.

>> **Social Security retirement benefits:** When people talk about receiving Social Security, they're usually referring to retirement benefits. Every year you remain in the workforce, you can receive up to four work credits. After you've earned 40 credits, you're eligible to collect benefits. When you can start receiving Social Security retirement benefits depends on when you were born. The longer you wait to receive benefits, up to age 70, the larger your payments. For up-to-date information, visit www.ssa.gov/retirement or see AARP's *Social Security For Dummies* (published by Wiley). Chapter 3 in Book 1 also has information on Social Security retirement benefits.

>> **Social Security Disability Benefits, Supplemental Security Income, and survivors benefits:** Social Security has three other benefits. If you're disabled, you can receive two different types of benefits:

- *Social Security Disability Insurance (SSDI)* benefits are granted when you meet the Social Security Administration's definition of having a disability and you have earned enough workforce credits, depending on the age you become disabled.

- If you've never worked due to a disability, you can qualify for *Supplemental Security Income (SSI)*.

Last but not least, if you're a child, spouse, or parent who relies on someone in the workforce to support you and that person dies, you may be eligible for *survivors benefits*.

**TIP**

You can create a Social Security account at www.ssa.gov/myaccount. Doing so allows you to check your workforce credits and the money you've paid into Social Security and to get an estimate of your retirement benefit payment. You can also check to see what other Social Security benefits may be available to you, such as disability insurance or survivors benefits, along with the amount you or a loved one would qualify for. This information can help you budget better for life circumstances and save for retirement.

# You Gotta Have Dreams: Financial Goals

You'll want to set aside money for emergency expenses. But you'll also want to set financial goals. Goals can be simple, like going to a concert once a month. They can be moderate, like treating the family for dinner every Sunday or saving enough so you can retire comfortably. They can also be ambitious, like taking a dream vacation. After you're clear on your financial goals, figuring out the steps to get you there is easier.

Setting financial goals can help you live a better quality of life, which can mean the difference in where you can afford to live, what you do in your free time, whether you can take a leave of absence due to a life-changing emergency, and when you can retire.

## Saving for your future

Life is short, and putting money aside for your future sets you up for long-term financial security — and happiness. In addition to retirement accounts, you may need a new car. Maybe the perfect home of your dreams hits the housing market, and you see yourself establishing some roots! You may have kids or grandkids heading off to college — or you may want to go back to school yourself to pursue a passion or make more money so you can have an even sounder budget than before. Somedays can turn into your current day, so you may as well plan for them.

Saving for the future can also include fabulous trips you want to experience, like visiting a national park. Maybe it's establishing a scholarship fund in someone's name at a local nonprofit, or taking an art or music class. Your future can include fun, and your budget helps you do just that.

REMEMBER

Make sure your goal is actually yours. You may hear, for example, that the way to make the most money is to become your own boss. It may not be as easy as some people claim. Many people quit their jobs to become entrepreneurs but don't have a clear plan or realize they aren't suited for self-employment at all. Make sure whatever financial goal you choose is one that you want to achieve, so you'll put in the hard work to make it your reality.

## Paying down your debt

Another financial goal you may want to set is paying down your debt. Debt isn't evil if you use it strategically. But having even strategic debt can cost thousands of dollars in interest and financing fees. Setting a financial goal to pay your debt down, no matter how slowly, can help in the long run. Because as soon as you pay off that debt, you have more cash flow to do things that are important to you.

## Putting your financial goals in place

Setting financial goals doesn't have to be complicated. Just follow these steps:

1. **Establish what your goals are.**

   For example, maybe you want to buy a house.

2. **Make the goal as clear as can be.**

   Decide precisely how much money you'll need to buy that house and when you want to be able to make the purchase.

3. **Take actionable steps toward completing it.**

   Examples of actionable steps may be slowly paying off your credit card so that eventually you can open a high-yield savings account for the house you want. Every little bit adds up, so don't be discouraged if you have to start small. With every action, you move the needle closer to your goal.

# Creating Your Budget

After you've set out your expenses, income, and financial goals, it's time to put it all together. In your notebook or on your spreadsheet, you've set out your three components:

>> Expenses (how much money you spend), both fixed and variable

>> Income (how much money comes in)

>> Financial goals (things you want to accomplish, such as retiring, paying down debt, and saving for something in the future)

Now you probably see that all three are equally important. Your expenses can affect how much income you need to bring in, which determines whether you can accomplish your goals by working one regular full-time job or also getting a side gig. Your income determines how much money you can spend on your lifestyle or put toward your future, like vacations or retirement. It's all related, so the sooner you figure out what you need to pay and what you want to accomplish, the faster a budget will work for you.

Add up your income and subtract your expenses. Perhaps as you see your budget in full, you realize your net pay doesn't cover all your monthly expenses or the goals you've set for yourself. In these cases, you have to either cut your spending or increase your income.

## Finding ways to cut your expenses

TIP

Here are some ideas for trimming your expenses:

>> See whether you can get a better rate by paying for certain things, like insurance, annually rather than monthly.

>> Call your providers, such as cellphone or internet, to see whether you qualify for any discounts or loyalty rates. Sometimes saying that you're preparing to move to another provider will prompt the offer of a discount.

>> Research competitors for insurance policies: healthcare, automobile, renters or homeowners, and life.

>> Consider switching to different tiers of subscription services, such as home streaming networks.

>> Discuss options with your landlord or mortgage company.

Nothing is off the table; the more money you can free up, the more you have to save for your goals or spend on things that bring value to your life. For more ideas, see *500 Great Ways to Save For Dummies* (John Wiley & Sons, Inc.)

# Identifying additional sources of income

The economy can be volatile. A job may be here one day and outsourced the next. Or your needs and circumstances can change. This section offers a few ways you can earn additional income.

## Earning rental income

Renting out a room is a common way to break even on your living expenses. Collecting the monthly payment from a roommate is considered rental income. You can also earn rental income if you're a landlord or have investment properties you collect earnings on.

Another way people earn this type of income is by renting their residences as short-term vacation rentals. With websites such as Airbnb and Vrbo, you can rent out a room in your home or the entire house for a nightly fee.

## Taking part-time gigs

TIP

You can earn extra income by doing odd jobs or selling stuff. Here are some common side hustles:

>> Shop and deliver groceries or restaurant meals.

>> Sell items you have laying around or buy items for a lower price and then sell them for a profit on sites like Amazon, eBay, and Facebook Marketplace.

>> Create content online as a writer.

>> Make crafts and sell them on a site like Etsy, Handmade Artists, Facebook Marketplace, or other social media.

>> Put together furniture.

>> Babysit kids.

>> Be a companion for older people.

>> Dog-walk and pet sit, either at your house or theirs.

>> Drive for rideshare services.

## Setting aside money for taxes

Income from side gigs may be considered earned income depending on the source, so check with the IRS to see whether you need to put money aside for taxes. If so, save 25 to 30 percent of any income earned from side hustles in a checking account. Pay your estimated taxes quarterly and save anything left over for business expenses. You may be able to deduct certain expenses on your taxes. For more information on self-employment taxes, visit www.irs.gov.

Like anything in life that you're trying to improve, things may feel uncomfortable in the beginning. Finding out you spend far more than you earn, for example, can be discouraging. But keep this in mind: Knowing your expenses and income and creating a realistic budget can have a cascading effect and improve all areas of your life.

Celebrate the small wins, and know your future is more financially stable every day.

# Chapter **2**

# Investing for the Long Term

When considering investment advice, keep in mind that your financial situation is unique. The tips in this chapter may suit your circumstances, but consult an expert for individualized guidance. Here, you find out about working with financial advisors, adding different funds to your portfolio, and preparing for your later years with retirement accounts.

**TIP**

Use AARP's free online tools to estimate your income taxes, find out how to maximize your Social Security benefits, see whether you're saving enough for retirement, and more. Visit www.aarp.org/tools.

## Finding the Right Advisor

Just as there's a medical specialist for most every ailment, there's a financial specialist for most every money-related problem or need. The Financial Industry Regulatory Authority (FINRA), Wall Street's self-regulatory organization, lists more than 200 different credentials or designations, ranging from AAI (accredited advisor in insurance) to WMS (wealth management specialist). All those abbreviations can confuse more than inform. Bottom line: You want someone who can help you protect and grow your money.

When the time comes to seek professional help to rethink investments, plan retirement finances, deal with debt, or take on any other money-related task, your first move is to find the right expert. How?

**WARNING**

>> Check that the advisor is permitted to sell securities or give investment advice and has a clean record. Visit brokercheck.finra.org or call FINRA at 800-289-9999. Insurance sellers need a state license.

>> If the advisor uses a title, find out who awarded it and what it required. Some titles take little effort to obtain. FINRA has a directory of designations at www.finra.org/investors/professional-designations.

>> Watch for red flags when you first meet, such as promises of above-market returns or risk-free investing, a hard sell on certain products, or failure to ask about your specific financial needs and goals.

>> For help in finding a financial advisor, use AARP's Interview an Advisor tool at www.aarp.org/interviewanadvisor.

# Making the Most of Your Investments

You have a wealth of investment choices (pun intended!): mutual funds, stocks, and more. The following sections give you the scoop on funds and show you how to steer clear of fraud.

## Looking at different funds

Where should you begin when you want to invest in funds? Consider the following to maximize your profits:

>> **Keep investing costs low.** This is one of the most important things you can do to boost your returns. That's why index funds are good. What's more, Standard & Poor's research indicates that over time, index funds consistently outperform actively managed accounts.

>> **Buy mutual funds, not individual stocks.** Have both stock funds and bond funds in your portfolio to balance growth and safety.

>> **Sell what isn't working for you.** If you've got some old dogs — investment losers, that is — sitting in your portfolio, selling them for a loss could provide a tax benefit.

>> **Buy a target-date retirement fund.** These funds are especially useful for those who are confused and intimidated by the prospect of investing. They're a simple way to own a diversified portfolio of stocks and bonds that gradually gets more conservative as you near retirement. Choose funds with low fees. You can find low-fee choices at major brokerages, including Fidelity, Schwab, T. Rowe Price, and Vanguard, or do some comparison shopping at www. morningstar.com/target-date-funds.

>> **Use FINRA's fund analyzer to check the fees in your mutual funds and compare the costs.** Just a 1 percent annual fee on investments can cost you thousands by the time you retire. Visit tools.finra.org/fund_analyzer.

# Watching out for fraud

The phone rings, and a friendly, energetic-sounding stranger is on the line asking if you have a minute to discover how to triple your money in just six months by investing in gold and silver mines. Or maybe you get an email urging you to buy shares of a company whose stock price is sure to go through the roof. It sounds too good to be true — because it *is* too good to be true.

Each year, fraud siphons billions from investors, according to the North American Securities Administrators Association. This isn't new. In the early 1920s, to name one famous example, a con artist named Charles Ponzi fleeced scores of Americans by promising lavish returns from a strange scheme to speculate in international coupons used by people in different countries to send each other return postage. In reality, Ponzi was using new investors' money to pay off existing investors.

It's a trick that criminals still employ. But in today's world, they have more — and more powerful — ways to reach ordinary people (robocalls, email, TV, social media) and convince them to hand over their money.

**WARNING**

Fraud criminals target people of all ages, education and socioeconomic levels, gender, and racial/ethnic backgrounds with phony investment schemes. Watch for the following warning signs:

>> A caller who pressures you to send money right away to take advantage of a supposedly once-in-a-lifetime opportunity.

>> A caller who uses phrases such as "incredible gains," "breakout stock pick," or "huge upside and almost no risk!" The U.S. Securities and Exchange Commission (SEC) says such claims suggest high risk and possible fraud.

>> Recommendations of foreign or "offshore" investments from someone you don't already know and trust. Once your money is in another country, the SEC cautions, it's more difficult to keep watch over it.

Protect yourself with these do's and don'ts:

>> Do ask plenty of questions before you make any investment, including the following: Is the financial product registered with the SEC or state securities agencies? What are the fees? How does the investment company make money? What factors could affect the value of the investment?

>> Do your homework. If you're considering investing in a publicly traded company, look up information about its finances and operations in the SEC's EDGAR database (www.sec.gov/edgar/searchedgar/companysearch).

>> Do get advice from a person you trust and respect before making any decisions.

>> Do know who's handling your investment. Conduct a background search in BrokerCheck, an online database maintained by FINRA. Visit brokercheck.finra.org/.

>> Do be wary of free investment seminars, especially ones that include free meals. The SEC says scammers often figure that if they do you a small favor, you'll feel obligated to invest.

>> Do have an exit strategy. FINRA recommends rehearsing some stock lines to cut short a caller's high-pressure pitch, such as "I'm sorry, I'm not interested. Thank you."

>> Don't make investment decisions based on ads, TV commercials, phone calls, or email solicitations.

>> Don't believe anyone who guarantees returns on your investment, quick or otherwise. Con artists like to dangle the prospect of fabulous wealth to distract you from realizing the whole thing is a scam.

>> Don't jump on "inside" information posted to social media, chat rooms, or forums promoting shares of a company that are certain to go up. It may be a "pump-and-dump" — a ploy to drive up the price artificially, enabling scammers to sell their shares for a big profit before the stock crashes and the remaining investors take a loss.

>> Don't believe someone claiming to represent FINRA who offers an investment guarantee — the organization says its officers and employees never do this. Some particularly audacious scammers pose as FINRA executives to create a false sense of security about an investment and secure an advance fee.

>> Don't judge an investment opportunity by a company's professional-looking website. These days, crooks can easily create a convincing online facade.

>> Don't make an immediate impulse-buying decision. Wait at least 24 hours to allow emotions to subside before making a purchase.

# Participating in Retirement Accounts

Invest in your company's retirement accounts, such as a 401(k), a 403(b), or, for federal workers, a Thrift Savings Plan. Your employer will deduct your pretax contributions from your paycheck, and your savings will be tax-deferred until you take withdrawals during retirement. (The exception is Roth accounts, which are funded with after-tax dollars and from which withdrawals in retirement are tax-free.) As of 2023, the contribution limit is $22,500, or for people aged 50-plus, $30,000.

If you can't afford to contribute the maximum, invest what you can and then try to increase that amount each year. You may find that putting pretax money into your account doesn't affect your paycheck as much as you'd think, because of the tax savings.

TIP

Be sure to contribute enough to take advantage of your employer's match. Many employers automatically match a percentage of your contributions, which is essentially free money and can make a big difference in the amount of money in your account at retirement.

Say you're 50 years old and you earn $50,000 a year. You put 5 percent of your salary a year into your 401(k), and you get 3 percent raises each year until you retire at 65. You'll have $87,376 in your account when you retire, factoring in a 7 percent annual rate of return. Now say your employer matches 50 percent of your contribution up to 5 percent of your salary. You'll have $131,064 in your account, according to AARP's 401(k) calculator. Visit www.aarp.org/calculators.

TIP

Finally, consider tax diversification in your retirement account. Many plans have added Roth options — which allow you to contribute dollars you've already paid taxes on and then withdraw the money in retirement tax free. If you think your tax bracket will go up in the future, stashing some contributions here can be smart.

# Chapter **3**

# Collecting Social Security Retirement Benefits

Y ou probably know people who are sick of their jobs, fed up with the demands of the work world, and ready to begin collecting Social Security the very first day they can get it. You probably also know people who love their jobs, see themselves as forever young, and are pained even to think about collecting retirement benefits. Where do *you* fit on the spectrum?

Of course, the decision on when to start collecting Social Security is personal. Your priorities and needs, your spouse's needs, your financial resources, your health, and your expected longevity all can shape your attitude about collecting Social Security.

Your decision on when to begin collecting Social Security retirement benefits may be the most important financial decision you ever make. Starting too early can cost you tens of thousands of dollars. Worse, jumping the gun may hurt the most in your final years, when it's too late to do anything about it.

This chapter fills you in on the most important factors to consider in order to make the right decision for you. There is no one right answer. The goal here is for you to make the decision about when to collect Social Security fully armed with all the information you need.

# Paying Attention to Your Full Retirement Age

A key consideration in choosing a start date for collecting Social Security is something called your *full retirement age.* The Social Security Administration (SSA) gives you a window of several years before and after your full retirement age in which to begin collecting your retirement benefits, starting at 62. In the following sections, you find out how to determine this age (based on your year of birth) and how it affects the amount of your monthly benefit.

## Determining your full retirement age

Your first question is probably this: How much Social Security am I going to get? The answer: It depends. The first step is knowing your full retirement age. If you collect Social Security *before* reaching your full retirement age, you'll get less each month — potentially a lot less, for the rest of your life. If you collect Social Security *after* reaching your full retirement age, you'll get more each month.

REMEMBER

Your full retirement benefit is the amount you get if you wait until your full retirement age to begin collecting. But what the SSA calls your full benefit is not the biggest benefit you can get. You can actually get a lot *more* than your full benefit by waiting until you're 70 to begin collecting — 32 percent more if your full retirement age is 66, and 24 percent more if it's 67. The SSA uses your full benefit as the starting point when it decides how much you or your dependents will receive (see the next section for details).

The earliest age at which you can start collecting retirement benefits is 62, and the latest is 70. Your full retirement age falls somewhere in between. Table 3-1 shows a person's full retirement age based on their year of birth.

## Estimating how much you'll get each month based on when you retire

After you figure out your full retirement age (see the preceding section), you can get a ballpark idea of your monthly benefit. Currently, the average retirement benefit is over $1,800 per month (at the time of writing), but benefits go much higher, depending on your earnings history and when you begin collecting.

TABLE 3-1

## Full Retirement Age Based on Year of Birth

| Year of Birth* | Full Retirement Age |
|---|---|
| 1937 or earlier | 65 years |
| 1938 | 65 years and 2 months |
| 1939 | 65 years and 4 months |
| 1940 | 65 years and 6 months |
| 1941 | 65 years and 8 months |
| 1942 | 65 years and 10 months |
| 1943–1954 | 66 years |
| 1955 | 66 years and 2 months |
| 1956 | 66 years and 4 months |
| 1957 | 66 years and 6 months |
| 1958 | 66 years and 8 months |
| 1959 | 66 years and 10 months |
| 1960 and later | 67 years |

*\* If you were born on January 1, refer to the previous year. Full retirement age may be slightly different for survivor benefits.*

**TIP**

It's easy to get at least a rough estimate of your retirement benefits. Just use one of the SSA's online calculators — the Social Security Quick Calculator at www.ssa.gov/oact/quickcalc or the Retirement Estimator at www.ssa.gov/estimator. They can give you projected amounts for retiring at different ages, such as 62, waiting for your full retirement age (according to Table 3-1), or delaying all the way until 70. You also can get estimates customized to your personal situation by using AARP's Social Security Benefits Calculator at www.aarp.org/calculators.

If you use the SSA's Retirement Estimator, you'll see roughly how much Social Security you could get, especially if your earnings don't skyrocket or crash between now and the time you retire. If you haven't yet done so, you can use the Retirement Estimator as a starting point to think about how much money you can count on in retirement.

**TIP**

Online calculators are not the only tools you can use to get an idea of your benefit amount. You also can sign up for a personal "*my* Social Security" account with the Social Security Administration at www.ssa.gov/site/signin/en/. This online statement offers estimates of your future benefits for retirement, for your survivors, and for disability.

Whether the Social Security numbers look small, large, or in between, remember that Social Security is meant to be just *one part* of your financial foundation.

As mentioned earlier, you stand to get much more money each month if you can delay collecting Social Security past your full retirement age. For example, if you were born between 1943 and 1954, your Social Security payment at 62 is 25 percent lower than if you wait until 66 (your full retirement age). If you hold off until age 70 — four years past your full retirement age — the benefit balloons by 32 percent.

These differences can add up to real money over the years — or decades. Consider the following example:

> Elisa was born in 1957 and wanted to know how she would be affected by choosing different dates to retire. She went to SSA's Quick Calculator (www.ssa. gov/OACT/quickcalc/index.html) and plugged in the $160,000 she earned last year. If Elisa started collecting benefits at her full retirement age of 66 years and 6 months, she would have gotten about $2,881 per month. She decided to wait until 70 to collect benefits, so she'll get about $3,756 per month.

> Elisa knows that longevity runs in her family, so she wants to find out how much she'll collect from Social Security if she lives to 90. To get the answer, she calculates the number of months she would receive benefits in three different cases: starting at 62 (336 months), starting at 66 and six months — her full retirement age — (280 months), and starting at 70 (240 months). Then she multiplies the number of months by the estimated benefit provided by the online tool.

> If Elisa starts the benefit at 62 and lives to 90, she can end up with more than $686,784 over her lifetime, not even counting increases for inflation (336 months between 62 and 90, multiplied by the estimated benefit of $2,044 per month for benefits starting at 62). If she starts at 66 and 6 months, her lifetime collection will exceed $806,680. And if she starts the benefit at 70, she ends up with more than $901,440. The difference between starting benefits at 62 and at 70 comes to $214,656 for Elisa.

Figure 3-1 shows that your decision on when to begin retirement benefits makes a real difference in your monthly income. The numbers here are based on a retirement age of 66 and a monthly benefit of $1,000. They may differ based on your year of birth and other factors.

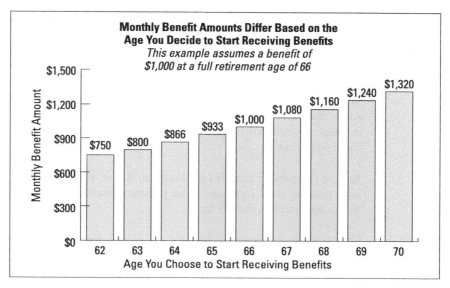

**FIGURE 3-1:** The amount of your monthly benefit depends on the age you start receiving it.

**Monthly Benefit Amounts Differ Based on the Age You Decide to Start Receiving Benefits**
*This example assumes a benefit of $1,000 at a full retirement age of 66*

Monthly Benefit Amount

| Age | Amount |
|---|---|
| 62 | $750 |
| 63 | $800 |
| 64 | $866 |
| 65 | $933 |
| 66 | $1,000 |
| 67 | $1,080 |
| 68 | $1,160 |
| 69 | $1,240 |
| 70 | $1,320 |

Age You Choose to Start Receiving Benefits

*Source: Social Security Administration*

TIP

Waiting to take retirement benefits beyond your full retirement age could prove especially important for Baby Boomers and, right behind them on the age ladder, members of Generation X. For people born in 1943 or later, the retirement benefit expands at a rate of 8 percent per year (or ⅔ of 1 percent per month) for each year you delay claiming (up to age 70) after reaching full retirement age. Check out Table 3-2 for the numbers.

**TABLE 3-2**

## Increase for Delayed Retirement

| Year of Birth* | Yearly Rate of Increase | Monthly Rate of Increase |
|---|---|---|
| 1933–1934 | 5.5 percent | $^{11}/_{24}$ of 1 percent |
| 1935–1936 | 6.0 percent | ½ of 1 percent |
| 1937–1938 | 6.5 percent | $^{13}/_{24}$ of 1 percent |
| 1939–1940 | 7.0 percent | $^{7}/_{12}$ of 1 percent |
| 1941–1942 | 7.5 percent | ⅝ of 1 percent |
| 1943 or later | 8.0 percent | ⅔ of 1 percent |

*\* If you were born on January 1, refer to the previous year.*

# Looking at Life Expectancy When You Claim Benefits

When figuring out how much to reduce people's benefits if they take the benefits early, the SSA considered average longevity. But you could live a lot longer than average — and that makes your decision on when to claim benefits that much more important.

No one can predict exactly how long you'll live. You should also consider how old your parents lived to be and your personal health, including chronic conditions that may shorten your life span.

**TIP**

You can use an online calculator to assess your life expectancy. Go to www. livingto100.com and click on "Take the Calculator" or take the Longevity Test at www.bluezones.com, and you'll be given an estimate. The Longevity Illustrator, developed by the American Academy of Actuaries and the Society of Actuaries, highlights how long you might live at different ages of retirement; visit www. longevityillustrator.org.

The following sections cover two topics related to longevity and Social Security: completing a break-even analysis and handling the possibility of exceeding your projected life expectancy. Neither is as complicated as it sounds.

## Doing a break-even analysis: The payoff from different retirement dates

A *break-even analysis* compares what you get in your lifetime if you pick different dates to collect Social Security. It's a way to estimate your total payoff from retiring at an earlier date (with reduced monthly payments) and retiring at a later date (with higher monthly payments). This approach gets some criticism, because it can lead to a costly decision if you end up living longer than expected. Factors such as your health and other financial resources also should be weighed in deciding when it makes the most sense to claim retirement benefits.

But many people care — understandably! — how much Social Security they may get in a lifetime. In general, if you die before reaching the break-even age and you started collecting benefits at the *earlier* date, you come out ahead. If you live beyond your break-even age but started benefits at the *later* date, you also come out ahead, because those bigger payments add up over time. Where you lose out is if you die before reaching the break-even age and you started collecting larger benefits at the later date, or if you die after your break-even age and you started smaller benefits at the earlier date.

The break-even approach is a common tool recommended by financial planners, and it can provide perspective. But it's just one consideration. The more you care about how your benefits add up over a lifetime, the greater weight you may give a break-even calculation. The more you care about ending up with the biggest monthly benefit, the greater weight you may give to delaying your claim for Social Security.

TIP

Your break-even age will vary based on your earnings record and date of birth, but estimating it isn't too difficult. Here's how to compare how you'll come out over your lifetime if you start benefits at age 62 versus your full retirement age:

1. **Determine your full retirement age (refer to Table 3-1).**

   For example, say your full retirement age is 66.

2. **Determine your full retirement benefit at that retirement age by going to www.ssa.gov/estimator.**

   For example, say your full retirement benefit at 66 is $1,500 per month. (***Note:*** The estimator assumes you keep working until age 66.)

3. **Determine your benefit at 62 by going to www.ssa.gov/estimator.**

   In this example, if you claim benefits at 62, your monthly payment is $1,125.

4. **Figure out how much you would take home in the 48 months between age 62 and your full retirement age (66) if you were to start collecting at age 62.**

   In this example, you're taking home $1,125 per month, and you're doing that for 48 months, so multiplying $1,125 by 48 months gives you $54,000.

5. **Now figure out how many months you would have to survive beyond age 66 in order to break even.**

   In this example, the difference in monthly payments taken at age 62 ($1,125 per month) and 66 ($1,500 per month) is $375. So, divide the amount from Step 4 ($54,000, in this example) by the difference in monthly payments ($375, in this example), and you get the number of months you'd have to survive beyond age 66 in order to break even (in this case, 144 months, or 12 years). So, in this example, if you live past age 78, you come out ahead by starting your benefits at the full retirement age of 66.

If doing all that math doesn't appeal to you, and if you were born between 1943 and 1954, here are some general guidelines:

» **If you're comparing retirement at 62 with full retirement at 66, your break-even age is typically around 77 or 78.** In other words, if you die earlier, you could end up with more money by claiming early retirement benefits. If you live longer, you could be better off taking your benefits at 66.

» **If you're comparing full retirement at 66 with delayed retirement at 70, your break-even age is typically several months after your 82nd birthday.** In other words, if you die before 82 or so, you could end up with more money by beginning benefits at 66. If you live past 82, you could be better off delaying your retirement benefits until you turn 70.

Social Security provides a kind of insurance against running out of money for however long you live. The guarantee of inflation-protected income makes Social Security different from a typical investment. For many people, a range of considerations affect the timing of a claim. The break-even analysis is just one piece of information.

## Considering what'll happen if you live longer than you expect

Half the people in any given age group will exceed their life expectancy, in some cases by a lot. Does longevity run in your family? For older couples in decent health, the odds that at least one spouse will survive to a ripe old age are very high. Life expectancy may be higher if you have a good education, if you make a nice living, if you're closely connected to your friends and family, and if you're careful about keeping in shape.

The possibility of living a very long life can be a big factor when you're deciding when to start Social Security. You could live a lot longer than you expect. That means your price tag for retirement will keep going up, while financial resources may dwindle. How much will the cost of living be 20 or more years down the road? What about doctors' bills or long-term care needs? How long can you realistically expect your savings to last? The bigger Social Security payment you get by delaying benefits until you're 70 could come in very handy in those later years.

Here's some food for thought: A man who turned 65 in 2023 can expect to live about another 17 years. A woman who turned 65 in 2023 can anticipate another 20 years. At age 75, he can expect another 11.2 years, and she can expect another 13. If that man and woman make it to 85, each is projected to live past their 90th birthday. Among today's 65-year-olds, one in three will make it past 90.

**REMEMBER**

Knowing your life expectancy isn't enough. You also need to know what gives you peace of mind when it comes to money. What do you think is worse: living longer than you expected and running short of money, or living shorter than you expected and feeling secure until the end (even if you didn't max out your lifetime Social Security benefits)?

To illustrate, here are Eager Edgar and Steady Betty, two pre-retirees who are thinking about the next phase of their lives in very different ways. Both are 61 and have had virtually identical earnings in their careers.

Eager Edgar dreams of retiring from his job as a warehouse manager and trekking through the wilderness while he still has the energy. His parents died young, and he views early retirement as his last sure chance to really live. He has a couple hundred thousand dollars in an individual retirement account (IRA), and his rent is modest. The month after he turns 62, Edgar collects his first Social Security payment of $1,600.

Steady Betty sees the world differently. She likes her accounting job, even though the commute is increasingly stressful. But Betty doesn't want to worry about money when she's older, and she knows her mother lived until 90. Betty decides to wait until she reaches 66 (her full retirement age) before claiming Social Security. The prospect of getting a bigger monthly payment and building her nest egg further gives Betty peace of mind.

Fast-forward a few years. Eager Edgar's arthritis is getting worse, and his medications are costing more and more. After a couple of adventures in the Rocky Mountains, his hiking equipment begins to gather dust. Unplanned costs for healthcare, a loan to his unemployed son, and the rising cost of living reduce Edgar's savings. A long stint in a nursing home costs him $30,000. For the last three years of his life, Edgar is obsessed with the fear that his savings will run out and he'll lose his independence, all because he has to survive on the reduced Social Security benefits he chose. He takes to splitting pills in half, which increases his pain. He dies at 84, a lot later than he expected.

Steady Betty sticks to her plan, putting away savings every month. At 66 she begins collecting her full retirement benefit of $2,133 and enjoys a fulfilling new chapter. A fatal aneurysm brings her life to an abrupt end midway through her 74th year, much earlier than she expected.

**REMEMBER**

Things turned out differently than either Eager Edgar or Steady Betty planned. The point is that you can't be sure how long you'll live. When you're deciding when to begin collecting Social Security, keep different possibilities in mind and consider the implications for your standard of living and sense of well-being.

# Considering Your Spouse When You Claim Social Security

Earlier in this chapter, you find out how timing your collection of Social Security affects your *own* bottom line. But the issue of timing is even bigger than that. You and your spouse could face decisions on when to collect benefits that could affect your household for many years. We're talking about benefits that go to a dependent spouse, based on a breadwinner's work record, and benefits that go to a survivor after the breadwinner dies. Women are more vulnerable than men to poverty in old age, so these decisions may be of great consequence to many wives, but the same principle applies to everyone: Choices on when to begin Social Security benefits could have a lasting impact on you and your spouse's financial well-being.

If you're eligible for Social Security as a dependent spouse, you face a real choice about when to begin benefits. You may claim this benefit if you have reached 62 and your partner has begun collecting retirement benefits. But your own spousal benefit is reduced for each month you claim it before you've reached your own full retirement age. At your own full retirement age, your spousal benefit can be 50 percent of the breadwinner's full retirement benefit. But if you don't wait, and you claim it as early as 62, it's reduced significantly.

By the way, if you've established your own earnings record with Social Security, that could change things. In that case, your payment is the greater of the benefit you've earned yourself or the amount you qualify for as a dependent spouse.

For workers with a full retirement age of 67, claiming the spousal benefit early reduces benefits by as much as 17.5 percent for those claiming at 62 to a little over 4 percent for those claiming at 66. Suppose your spouse has begun collecting his or her full retirement benefit of $1,000 per month. If you wait until you reach your full retirement age of 67, you get $500 per month in spousal benefits. If you start as soon as possible, at 62, you get about $325. You can get more details on what the spousal benefit means to you, and how your amount is affected by when you claim it, at www.ssa.gov/oact/quickcalc/spouse.html.

**REMEMBER**

If a dependent spouse starts collecting before reaching his or her full retirement age, the amount is reduced. But unlike some benefits, it doesn't work the opposite way: Social Security provides no "bonus" for waiting past full retirement age. The upper limit of a dependent spouse benefit is 50 percent of the benefit that would go to the breadwinner at full retirement age. (The breadwinner can't push the spousal amount higher by delaying collection of benefits past his or her own full retirement age.) *Note:* A spouse who has reached full retirement age will get 50 percent of the breadwinner's full retirement benefit, *even if the breadwinner begins collecting before full retirement age.*

Table 3-3 shows the monthly reductions that affect spousal benefits taken by a dependent spouse before reaching full retirement age. It also shows that the monthly reductions differ, based on year of birth.

**TABLE 3-3**     ## Primary and Spousal Benefits at Age 62*

| Year of Birth | Normal or Full Retirement Age | Number of Reduction Months | Primary | | Spouse | |
|---|---|---|---|---|---|---|
| | | | Amount | Reduction | Amount | Reduction |
| 1937 or earlier | 65 years | 36 | $800 | 20% | $375 | 25% |
| 1938 | 65 years and 2 months | 38 | $791 | 20.83% | $370 | 25.83% |
| 1939 | 65 years and 4 months | 40 | $783 | 21.67% | $366 | 26.67% |
| 1940 | 65 years and 6 months | 42 | $775 | 22.5% | $362 | 27.5% |
| 1941 | 65 years and 8 months | 44 | $766 | 23.33% | $358 | 28.33% |
| 1942 | 65 years and 10 months | 46 | $758 | 24.17% | $354 | 29.17% |
| 1943–1954 | 66 years | 48 | $750 | 25% | $350 | 30% |
| 1955 | 66 years and 2 months | 50 | $741 | 25.83% | $345 | 30.83% |
| 1956 | 66 years and 4 months | 52 | $733 | 26.67% | $341 | 31.67% |
| 1957 | 66 years and 6 months | 54 | $725 | 27.5% | $337 | 32.5% |
| 1958 | 66 years and 8 months | 56 | $716 | 28.33% | $333 | 33.33% |
| 1959 | 66 years and 10 months | 58 | $708 | 29.17% | $329 | 34.17% |
| 1960 and later | 67 years | 60 | $700 | 30% | $325 | 35% |

* Based on a $1,000 primary insurance amount

Your decision about when to collect benefits also has a major effect on the amount of Social Security you leave behind for a surviving widow or widower. If you die, your spouse (at his or her full retirement age) can get 100 percent of your benefit. That means the bigger a benefit you wait to receive, the more you leave your surviving spouse. You could look at it this way: A retirement benefit you claim at 70 is 76 percent more than what you get if you start at 62. That much larger benefit is what you could leave a surviving spouse, who may rely on it for a long time.

Widows and widowers also face timing decisions. They can collect their survivor benefit as early as 60, but with a substantial reduction. (We're speaking here about aged widows and widowers who are not disabled or raising children — factors that allow for earlier eligibility.) Generally, it will cost the surviving spouse about 30 percent of the benefit to take it at 60, when compared to waiting until full retirement age.

TIP

Social Security offers a lot of material online about survivors' benefits and other categories of benefits. To find out more about survivors' benefits, go to www.ssa. gov/benefits/survivors/.

# Recognizing the Potential Payoff of Working Later in Life

Suppose you're approaching 62, so you're still years away from full retirement age. You're still on the job, and you like it that way. Maybe your employer's health plan is cheaper than any healthcare coverage you could get on your own, because you're still too young for Medicare. Maybe you're making good money. If so, you may be increasing your future Social Security benefit if your current earnings are higher than some of the earlier years on your record.

At 62, you could face a decision on whether to work *and* start to collect retirement benefits. You already know that Social Security pays less each month for early retirement. But there's another consideration: You're likely to smack right into the earnings limit.

The earnings limit is a potential issue for individuals who claim retirement benefits before their full retirement age. What it means is that if you begin Social Security while still earning money and you haven't reached full retirement age, the SSA will withhold part, or even all, of your benefit if you earn above a certain amount per year. At full retirement age, though, you can say goodbye to the earnings limit. The SSA will raise your payment to give back the money it withheld.

For early retirees, the SSA holds back $1 for every $2 earned above a certain amount ($21,240 in 2023). The limit changes for the year in which you reach full retirement age. For individuals in this category, the SSA withholds $1 for every $3 earned above a certain limit ($56,520 in 2023). The withholding stops during the month that you reach full retirement age. The earnings limit rises each year to keep up with rising wages.

**REMEMBER**

The earnings limit, combined with early retirement reductions, creates a potential double whammy: You temporarily get a smaller benefit because of working, and — more important — you *permanently* get a smaller payment because you claimed retirement benefits early. Does that make sense for you? It could. You may need the money. You may be improving your earnings record, which will boost your Social Security benefit. (You can get insight on this point by working with Social Security's online calculators or by calling the SSA.) But think it through. Think about how long you could live. Think about whether you really need the early Social Security benefit. If you make enough money on your own, you may be better off working (even part time) without collecting Social Security. Later, you can enjoy a larger retirement benefit for the rest of your life.

**REMEMBER**

You don't permanently lose the money withheld because of the earnings limit. At your full retirement age, the SSA returns the withheld money in the form of higher benefit payments.

# Putting It All Together: The Right Time to Begin Collecting Benefits

**TIP**

Selecting the right time to begin benefits is a personal matter. Only you know what makes sense for your family. But you should keep in mind some key points when you make this critical choice:

>> **Make sure that you know when you qualify for full benefits, but remember you have broad discretion about when to claim.** Refer to Table 3-1.

>> **Know your benefit.** By using the Social Security retirement calculators (see the earlier section "Estimating how much you'll get each month based on when you retire"), you can quickly get an idea of the benefit you'd receive

before, at, and after your full retirement age. Each year you wait to collect beyond your full retirement age will add 8 percent to your benefit. Each year you begin collecting before your full retirement age will reduce it between 5 percent and 7 percent. In other words, the earlier you retire, the less Social Security you get each month. For many people, that's a powerful argument to hold off claiming benefits.

>> **Be realistic about your life expectancy.** If you don't like to think about how long you'll live, get over it. Your life expectancy, and the possibility that you may exceed it, should be factors when you make plans for Social Security and retirement in general. Of course, no one knows how long you'll live. But there's plenty to consider:

- Do people in your family tend to live long?

- How would you grade your own lifestyle in terms of fitness, exercise, diet, and other personal habits that affect health?

- How healthy are you? Do you suffer from a chronic condition that is likely to shorten your life?

- Do you have a lot of stress? If so, do you have ways of managing that stress that make you feel better?

- Do you lug around a lot of anger and worry? If so, can you do anything about it?

>> **Think about all your sources of income and your expenses.** Consider your savings, including pensions, 401(k)s, IRAs, and any other investments. Make realistic calculations about how much money you need. Look at several months of statements from your checking account and credit cards to review what you spend on and look for waste, while you're at it. Ask yourself: Do you have the option to keep on working? Are you physically up to it?

>> **Think about your spouse.** If you die first, it could determine how much your spouse gets for the rest of his or her life. Consider your spouse's life expectancy and financial resources. Does he or she have a chance of living for many more years? If so, what are the household finances (beyond Social Security) to support a long life? Does the spouse have health issues that could cost a lot of money in the future? Husbands should bear in mind that wives typically outlast them by several years, because wives are typically a few years younger and because women have a longer life expectancy than men. Is that the case in your marriage?

>> **Talk it out if necessary.** Couples should discuss this topic together, even though, in many marriages, one person may be the one who makes most of the financial decisions. You also may want to discuss your finances with a financial planner, especially if you've built up a nest egg and you have questions about how Social Security income will fit in.

>> **Be clear on the trade-offs.** You can choose between a smaller amount sooner or a bigger amount later. It often makes sense to talk with a financial advisor, especially if you have investments to help support your lifestyle in retirement. Your decision about when to start retirement benefits will affect your family income for the rest of your life.

**REMEMBER**

Experts agree that it is often unwise to claim Social Security retirement benefits as soon as possible (age 62). But that is not always the case. Early claims may make sense for individuals who need the income for necessities and lack other financial resources to pay for them or who do not expect to live much longer.

# Chapter **4**

# Financial Matters: Wills, Trusts, and More

I n many families, money is a taboo topic. Talking about bank accounts or wills happens only when a crisis occurs. All too often, when people die, they don't even leave a will to guide the heirs. "Why make a will," some people reason, "when it will be expensive and complicated? My family will know what I want." And predictably, conflict and confusion ensue.

**REMEMBER**

Wills are only one of the legal and financial instruments that should be discussed, created, and periodically reviewed as part of a future care plan. Knowing how to deal with someone's funds is essential for handling home care or assisted-living expenses. This chapter reviews general reasons for the primary legal documents and suggests some points to consider. But, like other chapters in this book, it doesn't substitute for the advice of an experienced attorney or financial advisor (or both).

# Sharing Control of Your Money

Understanding how to manage money is one of the most important skills we can acquire and pass on to our children. Yet it's one of the least-taught skills. Some people never think about money, and some people think about nothing else. But most of us get some basic introduction to financial management that serves well enough in ordinary times. Illness or aging, however, can create special situations that challenge our usual routines. This chapter describes some of those challenges. One is loss of control over one's money (or fear of that happening). For others, it is the daunting responsibility of taking charge of someone's financial affairs when they were shielded from money problems as they grew up.

Giving up control of money matters is often difficult for us, just as it is hard to give up driving. You may view losing any control over your finances as the beginning of the end of your independence. Because financial matters are so vital to aging comfortably and can be so difficult to manage, however, passing part of the control over to a trusted person not only makes sense but is also imperative in certain situations.

TIP

Right now, before a crisis, talk to your children or trusted advisor about the options for managing money should illness or injury occur. Two basic options allow for shared control: a joint bank account or a financial power of attorney. The two options can be combined. The following sections delve into the logistics of each option.

## Opening joint bank accounts

When you are no longer able to control spending or keep track of money coming in and out, it may be in everyone's best interest to have a shared bank account with a trusted family member responsible for managing it. But many people have had their own bank accounts for decades, possibly a joint account shared with a spouse, and giving up some or all control to a child or other relative can be hard. If you're thinking of opening a new joint bank account, there are pros and cons to consider. As with other financial and legal matters, check with a professional.

>> In most joint bank accounts, with a right of survivorship, there is no "my money" and "your money." Two people have access to the account in its entirety, no matter which one earned or deposited the money. One person can withdraw the entire amount for any purpose without notifying the other owner.

>> Most joint accounts are set up so that if one person on the joint account dies, the entire account passes to the second person. But in certain states, this

presumption can be challenged. The joint amount of money in the account is not included in the person's estate to be divided among the heirs. If the amount in the account is substantial, other family members may object. Even if the amount is small, other heirs may see this uneven distribution of assets as unfair. There may be income and inheritance tax implications as well.

» An alternative but little-used option for a bank account is a *multiparty account without a right of survivorship,* sometimes called a *convenience account.* The account is held by a primary person, with a cosigner. In this type of account, the cosigner has the authority to make deposits and withdrawals, but if the primary person dies, the remainder of the account goes into the estate and does not pass to the cosigner. Although banking laws permit these accounts, many banks do not encourage their use, possibly because they require extra training of staff and monitoring. Still, if this seems a good option, talk to a banker about it.

WARNING

Adding another person to a bank account can have implications for future Medicaid eligibility. The account can be considered a transfer of assets at less than fair market value. If this transfer happens within five years of an application to Medicaid, the primary account holder will be penalized according to Medicaid look-back rules. That is, Medicaid looks back five years to determine eligibility.

WARNING

Obviously, setting up a joint bank account should be done only with someone you trust completely. Even so, it may be prudent to keep only the minimum amount necessary to pay bills and avoid bank fees that may apply to a minimum balance. A large amount of cash sitting in a bank account can turn out to be an "attractive nuisance." This term is more commonly used to describe something on a property, like an open pipe, that a child may find both dangerous and appealing. If the joint owner of the account takes out money for personal use, even with all the best intentions of repaying the money, there's always the possibility that they won't be able to fulfill that promise. The annals of elder abuse are filled with stories of relatives, household help, and new "friends" who have taken advantage of a trusting older adult to enrich themselves or to pay themselves for taking care of an older person when that was never part of the agreement. Best not to put temptation into the picture.

REMEMBER

A key concept when someone has access to another's money is *fiduciary duty,* which occurs when one person depends on another to act in their best interest. The responsible person has a duty of loyalty to act only for the other person's benefit, to act with good faith in furthering the other person's interests, and to disclose all relevant information. Anyone taking on the responsibility of a joint bank account should be reminded about these ethical and legal requirements.

## IS CASH SITTING IN AN OLD BANK ACCOUNT?

Some people open a variety of bank accounts and then forget about them. In an earlier era, banks offered toasters and other items to entice new customers, and thrifty people took advantage of the offers. Sometimes a spouse opened an account to keep some money hidden. Make sure you look for any bank accounts that may fit this profile. Check drawers and folders for evidence of these accounts. If the accounts are unused for a period of time, usually three to five years, the bank or financial institution is required to send a letter to the account holder (which probably goes into the pile of junk mail) before the money is turned over to the state. Newspapers periodically publish lists of unclaimed bank accounts. One estimate is that $70 billion in unclaimed funds are in the United States. To search for unclaimed funds, go to www.unclaimed.org.

TIP

Consider drawing up an agreement that states the sources of money to be deposited into the account (such as Social Security, pension, and family contributions), how it will be spent (such as rent or mortgage, household expenses, medical bills, and household help), and what should happen to the balance if one party dies. This document is not legally binding but makes clear to both people (and to the rest of the family) how the joint account is intended to be used. The agreement may need to be changed if circumstances change.

# Granting financial powers of attorney

An alternative to holding a joint bank account is receiving financial power of attorney. Two types of financial power of attorney are available: conventional and durable.

## Conventional financial power of attorney

*Conventional financial power of attorney* is granted by a document, signed by one person, giving another person permission to take care of different kinds of financial affairs, such as signing checks, paying a contractor for home repairs, handling bank accounts, and taking care of other tasks. The power of attorney may be limited to specific tasks, such as paying monthly bills, or it may be general and all-encompassing (allowing everything including selling property and assets like stocks, filing taxes, and managing a retirement account).

Depending on state laws, some powers can't be assigned to another person. Those include the power to make, amend, or revoke a will or change insurance beneficiaries.

The person signing the document is known as the *principal,* and the person who is designated to act in the principal's name is called the *agent* or *attorney-in-fact.* Unless specifically stated, a power of attorney goes into effect right away. But the principal can set it to expire on a certain date, and the principal can revoke the power of attorney at any time. Furthermore, conventional power of attorney ends if the principal becomes legally incapacitated, which means they are unable to understand choices and make decisions.

**TIP**

To avoid personal liability, agents should sign a check or any document, for example, as John Brown (your name), attorney-in-fact for Mary Brown (your mother).

## Durable financial power of attorney

An alternative to a conventional financial power of attorney, which ends when the principal (the person who signed away some powers) becomes legally incompetent, is a *durable financial power of attorney,* which continues even if the person becomes incapacitated. Therefore, durable power of attorney lets the agent remain in control of certain financial and legal matters even if the principal is no longer able to understand the decision to be made or its implications. For example, a person with advanced dementia would be considered incapacitated, as would someone in a coma. All states recognize some form of durable power of attorney, but the specifics vary.

A version of durable power of attorney is called a *springing durable power of attorney.* It sets conditions under which the durable power of attorney "springs," or goes, into effect — for example, when a doctor certifies that the person has become incapacitated. The springing durable power of attorney may be more acceptable to an older person and avoids the lengthy, costly, and emotionally difficult process of guardianship, an alternative discussed later in this chapter. However, the springing durable power of attorney must be very clear about what counts as the springing event so that the principal, agent, and other third parties who need to rely on the power of attorney can easily determine when the principal intended the agent to take over. Without clarity, a court may have to decide. This would negate one of the benefits of having a power of attorney, which is that financial and legal matters can be handled without going to court.

**TIP**

Even if you have a durable power of attorney in a form approved by your state, your bank or other financial institution may require its own form. Even the Social Security Administration requires its own version of a power of attorney. Be sure to ask your financial institutions whether they honor the standard form or require their own.

**REMEMBER**

The fiduciary duty applies to durable power of attorney as it does to joint bank accounts (discussed earlier in this chapter). Agents are required to act in the person's best interests, maintain accurate records, and avoid any conflict of interest. Most people are not well versed in the fiduciary responsibilities that accompany being named an agent in a durable power of attorney. The same temptations that can occur in a joint bank account are present with a durable power of attorney, and here the stakes may be even higher. Therefore, all financial actions taken on behalf of the person who is incapacitated must be transparent, and all family members involved in the care of the older person must be apprised of significant outlays. Disagreements may arise, but better to have them resolved early rather than cascade into serious trouble.

**REMEMBER**

A financial power of attorney does not extend to making healthcare decisions. That requires a separate document, which can be called by different names but is usually termed a *healthcare proxy* or a *durable power of attorney for healthcare*.

# Where There's a Will . . .

If you have any money, property, family heirlooms, or just personal treasures, or if you have children or other dependents who will need a new guardian after your death, you need a will. (In some cases, a trust is an appropriate way to distribute property instead, and that type of document is discussed later in this chapter.) A will ensures, as much as possible, that your wishes are followed.

Many people believe that if you die without a will, your family will automatically divide up your property. Not exactly. A person who dies without a will is legally *intestate* (defined, simply, as not having a will). In that case, state law operating through a probate court determines how the property will be divided, often leading to outcomes that the person would never have wanted. Blood relatives will likely be favored over domestic partners. Children will be treated equally, even if one of them has been estranged from the parent for years. Stepchildren may not be included, even though they are well loved. Such unwanted outcomes can be avoided through the creation of a valid will.

Many people overestimate the monetary value of their possessions but underestimate their sentimental value to family members. An older person may say, "That old painting? Who would want that?" The answer may be, "A lot of your children or grandchildren who remember it hanging on your wall when they came to visit." Or that item may be promised to more than one person. An older person may say, "When I'm gone, that painting is going to be yours. It's worth a lot of money." Whether the painting has financial value or not, promising it to several people is bound to create conflict.

"Who Gets Grandma's Yellow Pie Plate?" is an online resource that has advice about distributing items that are laden with family history and thus have great potential for conflict. For example, a widowed father who remarries should consider his biological children's wishes about their mother's belongings. The website has many cautionary stories. Check it out at extension.umn.edu/later-life-decision-making/who-gets-grandmas-yellow-pie-plate.

Instructions about burial or cremation and funeral or memorial service plans should not be put in a will. A will is generally read several days or weeks after death, when it is too late to honor the person's wishes. Specific directions about those logistics should be put in a separate document and shared openly with close family or, if not, opened at death. It is best to alert family members about this document to avoid conflicts. AARP has helpful guidance on planning funerals at www.aarp.org/home-family/friends-family/info-2020/planning-your-own-funeral.html.

Preparing a will is very important, and it will be a valued document when an older person passes. Look at the following sections to take inventory of your assets, determine what kind of will best suits your situation, choose the executor, consider provisions to include, and finalize the will.

As early as possible, consult an attorney who can guide you through the process of creating a will.

## Taking inventory of your assets

In considering a will (and for estate planning in general), start by making a list of assets to be distributed and indicating whether they are jointly held or have a designated beneficiary, including:

>> Liquid assets (things that can quickly be turned into cash), such as bank accounts (checking and savings), certificates of deposit, savings bonds, and money market funds.

>> Fixed assets, such as a home or other real estate.

>> Certificates of deposit that are payable to a named person on death.

>> Retirement accounts, such as 401(k) plans, IRAs, Keogh accounts, and pensions. These accounts should be included in the inventory whether or not they have a designated beneficiary. If there is no beneficiary, they go into the probate estate. If there is a designated beneficiary, they are not distributed by the will or the probate estate.

>> Stock or investment accounts.

>> Transfer-on-death stock accounts, which are payable to a named beneficiary.

>> Valuable personal items such as jewelry, antiques, and artwork (items with only sentimental value can be kept in a separate list).

**TIP**

Community property is the law in nine states (Arizona, California, Idaho, Louisiana, Nevada, New Mexico, Texas, Washington, and Wisconsin). Alaska recognizes community property if both spouses agree to divide their assets in this way. This means that property acquired during a marriage is shared equally by a married couple regardless of who purchased the property or earned the money. Only the share owned by one person can be distributed in a will. This may call for some Solomonic decisions, but it can be addressed in a will by a spouse giving their half of the community property to the surviving spouse.

## Considering types of wills

According to the American Bar Association, there are several types of wills:

>> For an uncomplicated estate, a *simple will* provides for the outright distribution of assets.

>> A *pour-over will* assigns some assets to a trust that has already been established.

>> A *holographic will* is handwritten but not witnessed. About half the states recognize this kind of will, but it's not a preferred option.

>> An *oral will* is spoken but not written down. Very few states recognize this kind of will, and then only in cases of final illness. It, too, is not a good option.

## Choosing the executor

Choosing the executor — the person responsible for making sure that the instructions in the will are followed — is an important step. Being named as an executor is not an honorary title; it involves a considerable amount of time-consuming work. The executor must create an accurate accounting of assets to be distributed, find all debts that need to be paid, and resolve tax questions. Consultants such as accountants and attorneys may need to be hired. Unhappy relatives may need to be placated. The ideal executor is a person who is adept at understanding finances, detail-oriented, and even-tempered.

If this job description fits someone in the family, then that person would be a good choice. If not, then look outside the family for a trusted friend or professional.

A professional will expect to be paid, and fees may be a flat amount or a percentage of the estate.

TIP

The person named as executor should be willing to take on that job, because if the person declines, a court will name another executor and it may be someone you would not choose. You should name an alternate in the will in case your first choice to be executor cannot serve.

## Taking the final steps

After you've made these decisions about the will, the American Bar Association says there are several more steps to take:

**1.** **Execute the will.**

This step means having witnesses present as you sign the will. All states require at least two witnesses as proof that the will is valid — that is, the person signing the will knew what they were doing. Witnesses' signatures must be notarized. The witnesses should not be the executor or people named in the will to receive any gifts (even of modest value). Usually the witnesses are employees in an attorney's office, who do this every day.

**2.** **Decide where to keep the will.**

You should have only one signed original that you keep in a safe place. The attorney who drafts the will may or may not take the responsibility of storing it for you. Family members who need to know about its contents can be given unsigned copies and told where the original is stored.

WARNING

Putting the original will in a safe deposit box is not a good idea, because upon death, some banks restrict access to safe deposit boxes until there is a court order that it can be opened, which may not happen quickly.

**3.** **Review the will at regular intervals.**

Creating a will is important for all adults. But people who create a will at one stage of their lives (for example, when they have young children) may forget about the will as the children grow up and have children of their own. In that case, almost everything has changed in their lives, but the same will exists. Any major life-changing event — divorce, death of a family member named in the will, remarriage, birth or adoption of a child, sale of a business, moving to a new state, onset of a life-threatening illness — is a reason to review a will and make appropriate changes. In the case of moving to a new state, you need to make sure that the new location will honor your will executed in another state, or you may need to draw up a new will. Your priorities may be the same or they may be different. In either event, the will should be kept up-to-date.

## DO-IT-YOURSELF WILLS: CHEAPER BUT RISKIER

In recent years, many books, software, websites, and services offer templates for writing a will without consulting an attorney. The appeal is obvious: You still have to pay for the basic materials, but the cost is much less than an attorney would charge. However, do-it-yourself wills do not consider the specific circumstances that need to be addressed and may not have as precise wording as a lawyer-written will. Unless someone is watching out for details, the will may not be signed and witnessed in a way that makes it valid in your state. A court may conclude that an invalid will is no will at all and determine how to distribute the estate.

If you decide to take the DIY route, make sure that you have thoroughly considered all the worst-case scenarios so that you can account for them in the will. Also have someone else check the document for proofreading errors ($100.00 when you meant $10,000) or failure to include a person's name where you are asked to [Insert Name Here].

# Settling the Estate with Probate

*Probate* is a word that is often preceded in advice columns by the word *avoiding*. What exactly is probate and why do so many people want you to avoid it?

*Probate* is the process of settling an estate. It is also the name of the state court that handles wills and estates, among other responsibilities. The probate court determines the validity of the will, reviews the executor's inventory of assets and list of creditors, and determines what debts should be paid and what taxes are owed. After all these obligations are taken care of, the remainder of the estate is distributed according to the terms of the will. Failing to write a will is not a good way to avoid probate, because a court will be involved in settling your estate anyway.

REMEMBER

Probate addresses only certain assets in an estate, mainly assets that are not designated to go to a named beneficiary. Probate assets typically include a home, other property owned solely by the person, artwork and other personal items, and bank accounts held only in the person's name. Assets that normally don't pass through probate include joint bank accounts, pay-on-death accounts, life-insurance policies, retirement accounts, and other assets with a named beneficiary. Property held in trusts does not normally pass through probate.

Why are people so eager to avoid probate?

>> **It can be costly.** It involves court fees, attorney fees, and other fees, which can add up. Some costs are set; others may depend on a percentage of the value of the estate.

>> **It can take time.** Heirs eager to have closure or get their share of the estate may be frustrated by the slow but steady process of probate. Time has to be allowed for creditors to be notified and to come forward, ownership of assets to be determined, and all the other details that must be resolved and can complicate settling an estate. It can take 9 to 12 months to close a larger or complicated estate.

Many states have streamlined the probate process, allowing spouses and minor children to get the money they need to live on without waiting for the entire estate to be settled. Other states have a simple probate process for smaller estates that can be closed in weeks at reduced costs.

There are different kinds of probate, depending on state law:

>> **Small-estate:** The simplest form of probate that can be used (but not in every state), for estates ranging in value from $1,000 to $10,000, depending on state law.

>> **Unsupervised or independent:** A reasonably simple and less expensive form of probate used when the estate is more than the value of a "small estate" but doesn't require a lot of court supervision. It can be requested when all the beneficiaries agree (and consent, if the will requires consent).

>> **Supervised:** Typically applied to large estates and wills with complicated provisions, with the court playing a major role in approving every action. Supervised probate is used if the will is contested, someone named in the will requests it, or the court is concerned about the executor's abilities.

**REMEMBER**

If the will involves property in more than one state, the probate court in each state will be involved, adding to the costs.

**REMEMBER**

One of the best ways to avoid the costs and delays of probate is to have a good estate plan in place. If the will is up-to-date and properly prepared, all the provisions are made in clear simple language, and the beneficiaries are advised about what they can expect (and won't be getting), chances are that the will can be probated at minimum cost and with minimum delays. The more money that is involved and the more people who will stand to gain (or lose) from the will, the more likely it is that there will be complications. Even so, planning can reduce some of the potential problems.

# Reviewing the Rules on Estate Taxes

"In this world nothing can be said to be certain, except death and taxes." So said Benjamin Franklin in 1789. And in the administration of estates after a person's death, the two are inextricably linked. To add to the complexity, the Internal Revenue Service itself says, "The laws on Estate and Gift Taxes are considered to be some of the most complicated in the Internal Revenue Code." Among its many publications is a guide to estate taxes, available at www.irs.gov/pub/irs-pdf/p950.pdf.

Part of the executor's responsibilities in overseeing the provisions of the will is to ensure that all taxes have been paid, including income taxes and estate taxes.

In 2017 the basic amount an individual could exclude from estate taxes was $5.25 million, doubled for a married couple. At that level, according to the Tax Policy Center, a nonprofit arm of the Urban Institute and the Brookings Institution, just 3,800 estates were expected to be big enough to owe any federal taxes. All that changed with the Trump administration's tax reform bill, enacted in 2018. The estate tax exclusion doubled so the base for exclusion became $10 million for tax years 2018–2025. Because the exemption is adjusted for inflation, an individual can shelter $12.9 million in assets in 2023. Another federal estate law provision called *portability* lets couples who do proper planning double that exemption. So, a couple can exclude $25.8 million for 2023. But in all likelihood, individuals who have this much money already have tax accountant numbers on their speed dials.

The law is designed to "sunset," or end, in 2025. If Congress does not renew it, the exemption amount will revert to the $5 million base, again adjusted for inflation.

With regard to making gifts to family members or others, the amounts that someone can give to each of these individuals as a gift tax-free each year increased from $14,000 in 2014 to $17,000 in 2023. States have their own estate or inheritance taxes, so be sure to investigate the rules in your state. State taxes are typically lower than federal taxes but still can affect the distribution of assets — and the tax man gets paid before the family.

**REMEMBER**

Consulting a very experienced tax attorney or accountant is recommended. There may be some ways to reduce a tax bill, but unless the estate is worth many millions of dollars, estate taxes may not be an issue for you.

# Establishing a Trust

If, after reviewing information about wills and probate, you realize that the estate will probably qualify for a simplified probate process, will not have a big tax bite taken out after death, and will not involve complicated financial arrangements to distribute your assets, then setting up a trust will probably not get you much but will be costly and cumbersome. Even so, many people are attracted to the idea of a living trust (maybe it's the word *living*, which sounds like it moves planning out of the realm of death).

A *trust* sets aside certain assets or an amount of money for another person. It allows money to be disbursed over time rather than as a lump sum both before and after the grantor's death. A trust is a good option to consider for people with beneficiaries who aren't able to manage money well. These beneficiaries may be minors, have intellectual disabilities or cognitive impairments, or just be unreliable with money. Sometimes trusts are used to transfer property, such as a vacation home, that is not easy to divide evenly among several beneficiaries. If that vacation home is in another state, putting it into a trust avoids having to go through the probate process in a second state. Trusts are also often used by people with very substantial assets because they can help reduce estate taxes. Probably the most common reason people set up trusts is that they want to control the disposition of the property more readily than they can in a will.

You can set up a trust so that the beneficiary receives the proceeds of the trust after your death or upon reaching a certain age. For instance, you can set up a testamentary trust in which you put some assets with conditions on their use, such as for a grandchild's education or when the child reaches the age of 25.

**REMEMBER**

If you choose to prepare a trust, you still need to have a will. The will provides a safety net if for some reason some of the trust property can't be transferred. A will may include specific provisions about the distribution of assets that are not in the trust. A trust can hold money, real estate, stocks and bonds — anything of monetary value. You need to pick which assets you want held in trust and which ones you want to be distributed by your will. The trustee is a person or institution that you select to manage the trust property. The trustee has a fiduciary duty (that term again!) to use the property as the grantor has indicated. The property stays in the same place, but legal ownership is transferred to the trust.

A living trust is often touted both as a way to retain control of assets and to avoid probate. This is how a living trust works: While you are alive and not disabled, you set up a trust that you own and control as both the trustee and the beneficiary. You also name the successor trustee who will manage the trust after your disability or death, and you name successor beneficiaries who will get the assets in the trust after your death. You can name someone else as trustee while you are alive and able, if you choose, and you can revoke that decision later.

Read on for a list of advantages and disadvantages with living trusts and information on other kinds of trusts.

## The pros and cons of living trusts

Living trusts have the following advantages:

>> If you have an accident or illness that makes you unable to manage the trust and you have named someone as a successor trustee, the trust provides a way to manage the assets placed in the trust while you are still living.

>> A trust is a private document and does not become public as does a will. Anyone who wants a copy of a will can request it from the court, so trusts have more privacy protections.

>> A trust is easy to change. A will is easy to change too but may involve costs.

>> Assets in the trust do not go through the probate process.

There are, however, some potential problems:

>> You must transfer legal title to the assets you want to be held by the trust and add new assets as you acquire them.

>> Just like a will, you should remember to update the living trust in case of a life-changing event. For example, the person named as beneficiary may now be an ex-spouse.

>> Having a trust can affect your eligibility for Medicaid or other benefits. Your state may count assets in a trust in determining eligibility.

>> Because the management of a living trust is outside a court's jurisdiction, there is no oversight, which means no probate court costs but also no supervision in case of disagreements. You can go to all the trouble of creating a living trust and still have your estate wind up in litigation.

Be wary of salespeople who pitch kits that promise to include everything you need for a living trust — at a cost of several thousand dollars. They take the money and run, or give you a document that does not fit your circumstances and may not even be valid in your state. The "free lunch" session on how to avoid probate with a living will kit is going to cost you. Several states have filed consumer fraud actions against these con artists. If you're really a good candidate for a living trust, you need competent legal advice from an experienced lawyer in your community.

## Special-needs trusts

There are many kinds of trusts — such as charitable trusts to give money to favorite organizations, generation-skipping trusts, spendthrift trusts, and others — but one additional type deserves attention because it applies to a lot of people. A *special-needs trust* is an instrument that allows a parent or other person to set aside money for the care and needs of a person with disabilities. This money does not count in the determination of the person's eligibility for Medicaid or other government benefits, an important consideration. It can be spent on items and services that improve the person's quality of life. The trustee may be a parent or other relative who manages the trust in the disabled person's best interests.

Special-needs trusts are valuable protections for people with disabilities and help assure that they get appropriate care. The Special Needs Trusts Fairness Act, which allows individuals to set up their own special-needs trusts so they do not have to rely on family or courts, was included in the 21st Century Cures Act, which became law in 2016. For more information, see `https://attorney.elder` `lawanswers.com/snt-fairness-act-becomes-law-15906`.

# Considering Guardianship

While many people see the value of living trusts, online wills, and other financial instruments, guardianship has few advocates because it is a costly and often demeaning process for the person, whose frailty and inabilities to manage have to be presented in court. Court-appointed guardianship (or conservatorship) does have a role in protecting the property and interests of adults who are unable to make decisions themselves and do not have natural advocates such as a trusted family member with authority to make decisions. Generally, guardianship is used as a last resort for people who have failed to plan for their disability and now need the help of someone else to make important decisions about their care and finances. Having a stranger appointed as guardian introduces another element into an already difficult situation. Some court-appointed guardians have failed to follow their fiduciary duties and have made decisions that benefit themselves rather than the person for whom they are legally responsible.

**REMEMBER**

Even if the court-appointed guardian is a family member, the responsibilities of being a guardian are more onerous than simply being a caring child, niece, or nephew. You will be required to report periodically to the court about how you're spending the money and how you're caring for the person. You have a fiduciary duty to properly manage the resources for the benefit of the family member.

Following are the two kinds of guardianship:

>> **Guardianship of the estate:** Having authority to manage money and other assets; this is called *conservatorship* in some states

>> **Guardianship of the person:** Having the responsibility to make healthcare and other decisions that affect the well-being of the person

Guardianship situations usually arise when a person is mentally ill, has an intellectual disability or advanced dementia, or otherwise lacks capacity. Courts determine capacity in different ways, depending on state law, but it generally involves a legal finding that a person cannot make certain kinds of decisions. Capacity is specific to the task or decision. Someone may have capacity to make healthcare decisions but not to manage money.

If there is conflict among siblings, for example, over whether a parent's assets should be used to hire home care workers or to place the parent in a nursing home, one sibling may file a guardianship petition to be able to make the decision. The court may appoint one person or co-guardians.

If no family member or friend seems to be an appropriate guardian or the family situation appears irrevocably torn, the court may appoint a person outside the family to take on this role. It can be a private professional guardian, public guardian, volunteer, or attorney.

**WARNING**

Although the guardian is required to act in the person's best interests or expressed interests, sometimes courts do not fully investigate the background of the guardians they appoint, and their shortcomings are realized only after they have committed fraud or abused or neglected their wards.

**REMEMBER**

Money matters and legal issues are complicated. Don't make any decisions without consulting an experienced attorney or accountant.

# 2

# Getting the Job You Want

# Contents at a Glance

Chapter **1**

# Scoping Out Your Prospects

F inding a job, at any age, takes effort, dedication, and time — whether the job is full time or part time, paid or volunteer. Some older job seekers assume that employers would rather hire younger, less experienced workers for lower wages or outsource jobs to cheaper workers overseas. While that may be true for some companies, current studies show that employers are increasingly willing to consider older candidates for the experience, loyalty, motivation, and analytical, communication, and personal skills they bring to the job.

This chapter helps you shift your attitude about job hunting from one of apprehension to one of hope and possibility and shows you a few simple ways to rev up your job-search mojo to today's new workplace reality for 50-plus job seekers.

## Recognizing the Need for and Value of Experienced Workers

Whether you want to work in an office job, teach yoga, or head up a company, more employers are starting to realize that hiring workers age 50 and older is good for business. More and more employers are discovering the value of experienced workers. Unfortunately for 50-plus job seekers, the fact that demand for experienced workers is on the rise is a well-kept secret. Realizing that employers need you is an important first step in the process of finding and landing the job you want. It gives you the enthusiasm and confidence to set out on what may be a long and arduous journey.

The following sections reveal the reasons the demand for 50-plus workers is rising to invigorate you for the journey ahead and remind you of just how valuable you are to employers who need your skills, talents, and experience.

**REMEMBER**

The job search can be disheartening for anyone, regardless of age. If that's what you're feeling, never show it to a prospective employer. Always highlight the value you have to offer in every job search communiqué you send out. If you need a confidence lift, take some time to review all your previous achievements.

## Seeing experienced workers as an affordable option

The old concerns that hiring someone your age would probably be too pricey are being debunked. Contrary to common perception, workers age 50-plus don't cost significantly more than younger workers. Shifting trends in reward and benefit programs mean that adding more age 50-plus talent to a workforce results in only minimal increases in hard dollar total labor costs. These trends include a broad move by large employers to performance-based versus tenure-based compensation, the decline in traditional benefit pension plans, and the fact that health-care costs are increasing at a slower rate for older workers compared to younger workers.

Meanwhile, in today's global and fast-paced workplace, firms often don't have the time to squander while a younger worker ramps up skills and knowledge. Companies are slowly realizing that to stay competitive, it's smarter to seek out and hire experienced workers. You're on the cutting edge of a sweeping change in the demographics of the workplace.

Surveys show that companies are realizing that it's strategically smart to pay more attention to recruiting and retaining workers age 50 and older. When organizations need someone to step in and do the job right now and solve an existing problem, it's the experienced worker they're eager to hire.

## Capitalizing on lower turnover

Employers find that workers age 50 and older are more loyal and aren't as likely as younger workers to job hop. And that lower staff turnover benefits the bottom line. The costs of high turnover are tangible. Finding, hiring, and training a new employee is a costly venture, and it becomes even more costly when that well-trained employee decides to jump ship and work for a competitor.

Plus, it's hard to put a price on the institutional knowledge that goes out the door with a departing employee. Now, tack on the stress that managers and coworkers must shoulder to make up for the work that falls between the cracks when an employee leaves. And finally, toss in the toll of lost morale that accompanies the departure of a valued team member. Now the employer has a serious problem. And that's clearly a big incentive for hiring a worker over 50. Older workers often anchor a team.

## Harnessing the power of highly engaged workers

Aon Hewitt data show that older workers, in general, *love* their jobs more than younger workers do. Yes, we're more engaged than our younger counterparts. Perhaps we're grateful for the jobs in a way that someone new to the workforce has yet to learn to value and appreciate.

For example, 65 percent of employees ages 55 and up in large companies are "engaged," compared to fewer than 60 percent of employees under age 45. Although this gap may seem small, it represents a statistically significant difference in engagement that can have a noticeable impact on business outcomes.

In addition to being the most highly engaged age group in the labor force, workers age 55 and older are also the most motivated. A whopping 81 percent of workers age 55 and up are "motivated" — meaning they say that they exert extra effort and contribute more than is normally required in their job — compared to 76 percent of their age 25 to 34 peers. Talk about selling points for older workers on the job hunt!

## Reaping additional benefits

In addition to all those wonderful attributes mentioned in the preceding sections, older workers typically have the following:

>> An ability to make quick decisions and solve problems

>> Greater maturity and professionalism

- » Superior communication skills, both written and oral

- » Analytical skills

- » Interpersonal skills

- » Motivation

- » The capacity and willingness to learn new tasks, processes, and technologies

- » The ability to serve as mentors

- » Reliability and dependability

- » More knowledge, wisdom, and overall life experience

**REMEMBER**

Shoulders back. You're valued. Put all this positive juju in your back pocket and never forget how much you have to offer on the job.

# Tallying the Benefits of Staying in the Workforce

To get you even more fired up about your job search, here are five money-wise reasons to stay in the workforce as long as you can:

- » **The more years you contribute to your retirement plans, the better off you'll be down the road.** You'll be able to delay taking Social Security, which will dramatically boost your eventual payout. Start collecting at age 70, and your monthly check will be 32 percent higher than if you begin benefits at 66 and 76 percent more than if you start taking benefits at 62 (when most people do).

- » **The longer you work, the longer you delay tapping retirement funds.** Allowing your investments to continue to grow even two or three more years can make a big difference.

- » **Working longer provides income to pay for health insurance until you're eligible for Medicare at 65.** Fewer employers are offering their retired workers medical benefits, and those who do are ramping up the amount retirees must contribute to the cost of coverage. Even better, you may find a job that offers you access to a health plan.

- » **Money aside, you may want to keep working to maintain a sense of well-being.** For people over 50, being engaged, not just involved, is important, according to a report by The Sloan Center on Aging & Work at Boston College. Similarly, when asked about their life and careers, 75 percent of people in their forties and fifties said they want to make their life more meaningful, while 82 percent said they want to give back more, according to a study commissioned by Life Reimagined, which was created by AARP to help people with midlife transitions. Nearly 30 percent plan to make a career change in the next five years; top reasons include having the opportunity to learn more and giving more back to the community. Work gives you a sense of purpose and of feeling connected and needed. It makes you feel relevant. Pinning a dollar figure to that is difficult, but it's real.

>> **Work sharpens the mind.** Researchers from the RAND Center for the Study of Aging and the University of Michigan published a study showing that cognitive performance levels decline faster in countries that have younger retirement ages. What? Brain cells dying from lack of use? You bet. It's the old "use it or lose it" axiom. Many aging experts say that to stay healthy, older adults have to learn new things, stay active socially, and exercise.

REMEMBER

Bottom line: We're living longer, healthier lives. As a result, we're staying in the workforce longer because we can, because we want to, and often because we need to, in order to have a financially secure retirement.

# Reorienting Yourself to Today's Job-Search Realities

What's new since your last job hunt? If it's been a while, you'll quickly find that technology has made job searching easier in some ways but more complex than ever in others. Although the internet has improved access to openings, it has also increased competition for those same openings. Typically, an average of more than 250 résumés are submitted for every job posting, and the first résumé appears within 200 seconds (just over three minutes) of the posting "going live," according to online job-search expert Susan P. Joyce.

While job-search sites make finding jobs easier, online applications and automated screening technologies pose additional obstacles to getting past the gatekeepers. According to a study by job-match site TheLadders (www.theladders.com), many companies use talent-management software to screen résumés, weeding out up to 50 percent of applications before anyone ever looks at a résumé or cover letter.

REMEMBER

Little wonder then that a CareerXroads survey shows that only 15 percent of positions were filled through online job boards. So visiting job boards and applying for jobs is probably not the best use of your time, even though you feel like you have to. Most jobs are either filled internally or through referrals. Yes, the old-fashioned way. In fact, only about half of the jobs now open in the United States are ever advertised publicly. Employers still prefer to hire people they know either directly or indirectly through a referral. In studies of many different employers going back to 2001, employee referrals are the top source of people hired into a company — not job postings. In fact, employee referrals provided more than 55 percent of the hires in one of the studies.

In other words, employers want to hire someone who has already been vetted in some way, which can save a lot of hassle and cost of the hiring process and of replacing people who don't work out, even if they looked great on paper and interviewed like pros. Employers love it when someone who already works for the organization can vouch for the person. And the employee making the referral often has some skin in the game, so to speak. Many employers pop a bonus reward of up to $1,000 or more for referring someone who's hired and does a good job in the first few months on the job.

Does this mean that applying for a job on job boards isn't worthwhile? Not at all! Scanning the boards gives you a sense of who's hiring, what types of openings are out there, and salary ranges. But it does mean that other approaches, such as networking and marketing yourself, may ultimately forge a better route to landing a job.

# Deciding What (Else) You Want Out of Work

In AARP's *Love Your Job: The New Rules for Career Happiness*, hundreds of workers were interviewed about what made them love their jobs. Interestingly, their paychecks aren't generally what get them juiced about going to work. Most people say they're motivated by the people they work with, the opportunity to keep learning and growing, or the mission or cause of their employer's services or the products it makes. Sometimes they say they love the travel opportunities. So don't get locked into a must-have salary. When searching for jobs and comparing offers, be sure to account for other benefits, including the following:

>> **Flexible workday:** Being able to work from home or having flexible hours or a compressed schedule is a biggie. It comes down to being treated as a responsible adult and weaving work more seamlessly into the fabric of your life. And that may be getting easier to achieve. A Bank of America Merrill Lynch survey of 650 human resources executives found that half of employers are willing to offer flexible arrangements, such as working part-time or job sharing, to their most skilled and experienced workers.

» **A healthy work-life balance:** Three in five people interested in a second career midlife say it's very important that the job leaves free time for things they want to do, such as travel, education, or engagement in other activities they enjoy, according to a report by Encore.org (now CoGenerate), a nonprofit organization that's building a movement to tap the skills and experience of those in midlife and beyond to improve communities. Indeed, many of those interested in encore careers appear eager to mix fewer hours of work per week with more years of work in total. Finding more flexibility may make working a few more years more palatable.

» **Meaningful work:** More than 25 million Americans 50 to 70 years old are eager to share their skills, passions, and expertise in encore careers that address social needs, typically in education, healthcare, human services, and the environment, according to a study by Encore.org (now CoGenerate) and Penn Schoen Berland. Of those 25 million, more than 4.5 million are already working for social impact.

» **Opportunities to interact with others and stay productive:** Human beings are hard-wired to create, produce, and collaborate, and rewarding work provides opportunities to remain active and productive. A Pew Research Center survey found that working for nonfinancial reasons, such as job enjoyment or the desire to be productive, increases with age.

» **Competitive benefits:** An AARP/SHRM survey of workers age 50 and up suggested older workers place significance on having competitive benefits and flexible work arrangements. When these workers consider a job offer, health insurance, retirement savings plans, and paid time off benefits play an important role in their decisions. For example, approximately eight in ten workers age 50 and older consider the availability of benefits such as health insurance (82 percent); a pension, 401(k), or other retirement plan (77 percent); and paid time off (80 percent) to be "very" or "somewhat" important considerations in the decision to accept a job.

» **Learning opportunities:** Workers 50 and up tend to be curious, eager, and adventuresome. They're not geared to be couch potatoes passively absorbing entertainment. As such, they value learning opportunities both on the job and through employer-sponsored continuing education programs.

Employers are increasingly tuning into these incentives. So while they worry that they may not be able to meet your salary expectations, they're discovering that 50-plus workers are attracted to more than pay. So employers are increasingly offering such nonfinancial perks as flexible work schedules, telecommuting options, and training and education opportunities.

# Pursuing Your Passion and Finding Purpose

When it comes to finding a successful and meaningful second act, most people simply don't know what they're passionate about, even when they know that they want to move in another direction. The following sections encourage you to explore other careers and check out some of the fastest growing job markets to find the right fit. And you'll find some tips and cautions to help guide you as you set out to pursue your passion and add purpose to your life.

**REMEMBER**

Pursuing your passion is fine, but you don't want to end up in the poorhouse doing it. Look for ways to align your passion with what's in demand.

## Considering other careers

One way to discover a passion that you can transform into gainful employment is to consider other careers. If you've ever thought to yourself, "I'd like to have their job," you have a head start. Think about those jobs you've always dreamed of having. Maybe you've always wanted to be a writer, a graphic artist, a wedding planner, an interior designer, a private investigator, or a sports announcer. Perhaps you've always dreamed of owning a bed and breakfast, brewing your own beer, making candy, or producing movies.

No, it's not too late to start thinking about pursuing a totally new career, and many your age have done so successfully. Think of it this way: If you live to 100 and look back 50 years or so, will you still think you were too old back then to pursue that dream job?

**TIP**

Start now. Pursuing a new career is likely to require a significant commitment of time, money, and effort. The longer time frame you have to plan, the better. Start working at age 50 on a career you may not get around to until age 60. You can start now to research a career you're interested in, take classes, and perhaps even secure an internship in the field to take the new career for a test drive to gauge your true interest in it before going all in.

Test-driving a career in some form is always a good idea. Career changers may enter a period of mourning after starting their new careers. All of a sudden, they realize how much they miss their old careers and aren't really open to replacing what they once had. Check out Chapter 2 in Book 2 for more on internship opportunities — one way to test-drive different work.

Money is the biggest roadblock for most career changers. When you start over in a new field or move to a nonprofit, chances are you need to take a salary cut at least initially. If you have an emergency fund to buy you time, you can do a more thoughtful job search. If you need to, pare back your discretionary living expenses to reflect a more realistic view of what you'll earn. See the later section "Navigating a career change" for details.

## Checking out fast-growing job markets

One way to pursue your passion while ensuring your marketability is to consider employment in fast-growing markets. Certain industries, such as energy and healthcare, are experiencing more profound talent shortages than others. According to Indeed.com, here are some jobs that U.S. employers are having trouble filling:

>> Home health aide

>> Construction laborer

>> Electrician

>> Financial advisor

>> Registered nurse

>> Physical therapist

>> Medical services manager

>> Application software developer

>> Information security analyst

>> Medical technologist

>> Data scientist

Here are a few sectors that are likely to be hot over the next few years:

>> **Healthcare:** Look for opportunities in healthcare support, such as nursing assistants, physical and occupational therapists and assistants, skincare specialists, physician assistants, genetic counselors, and social workers. Here again, recruitment and retention efforts aimed at the 50 and older workforce can help address this shortage.

According to the Bureau of Labor Statistics (BLS), occupations related to healthcare, healthcare support, construction, and personal care services, such as physical therapists, skincare specialists, and social workers are expected to add a combined 5.3 million jobs in the United States, an increase representing approximately one-third of all employment gains over the coming decade.

» **Leisure and hospitality:** The leisure and hospitality sector is growing. People will be spending money to eat out and go on vacation. Chefs, cooks, waiters, bartenders, and restaurant and hotel managers will be in demand.

» **Engineering:** Hundreds of thousands of engineers in the United States are age 55 and up. As these workers approach (and pass) retirement age, there may not be enough new workforce entrants to replace their loss in key roles. Focused efforts to retain and recruit older workers can mitigate these gaps.

» **Skilled labor:** BLS projections show that considerable job growth is expected in skilled labor professions, including brick masons, block masons, stonemasons, and tile and marble setters (and their helpers), and electricians' helpers. As mentioned earlier, employers are currently having the most trouble filling openings in these and other skilled trades.

» **Translators:** For those who speak foreign languages, labor experts also project that there will be a rising need for interpreters and translators in courtrooms and other settings.

TIP

Look for jobs and opportunities that leverage experience. Check out job websites, including `www.aarp.org/work`, `cogenerate.org/`, `www.job-hunt.org/`, `www.retiredbrains.com`, and `www.Workforce50.com` to get a flavor for what others are doing and what jobs are out there now.

## Taking the first steps in pursuing your passion

TIP

"Pursue your passion" is the kind of advice you might receive from friends or relatives who either never pursued their passion or knew from the day they were born what they wanted to do. It sounds like great advice until you pause to think about it and realize that you have no idea what your passion is or how to take that first step from point A to point B. Here are some suggestions to ease you into figuring this out, with a tip of the hat to career coach Beverly Jones:

» **Find a place to start.** You don't need a precise definition before you get going. Start by making a list of what you want in the next phase of your career. Don't look for a perfect path or ideal starting point.

» **Get things moving by taking small steps.** Get moving in the general direction of where you want to go. One small step may be calling someone who works in a field that appeals to you to discuss possibilities.

>> **Silence your inner critic.** If you have a negative refrain that goes through your head and sabotages your efforts to make a change, such as, "I'm too old to do that," make note of it. Write that thought down in a notebook and reframe it with a positive thought, such as, "I have these specific skills, and I'm going to use them in a new career." You need to get rid of that old blocking message to move forward with your dreams.

>> **Ask the basic questions.** Does your second act fit your lifestyle? Can you afford it? What does your partner think? Ask yourself how a certain career will work with your social life, your spending habits, and your family situation. It will help you to dig deeper and get a clearer picture of what you truly want in your life and your options to get there.

>> **Keep a journal.** Journaling is a great way to map out your new career direction. Make lists: the best times in your life, the things you really like, the experiences you've enjoyed, what you've excelled at, the best moments in your current career. These lists will help you hone in on your passion and visualize yourself harnessing it to pursue something new and exciting.

>> **Get a business card.** Want to be an artist but still working as a lawyer? Get an artist's business card. As soon as you have a card, it makes the career real. You can get your second-act card long before you finish your first act. Printing your new information on a card can be transformative.

>> **Have a mental picture of where you want to go.** Tape a photograph to your office wall of what your new career might look like. Or create a collage. Journal about your goals.

>> **Be practical.** You may need to upgrade your skills and education, but take one class at a time. You can add more classes as your direction and motivation become clear.

>> **Get your life in order.** Get physically and financially fit. Change is stressful. When you're physically fit, you have more energy. Less debt gives you more choices. Debt is a dream killer. With your finances in order, you have more options. You can be more nimble.

**WARNING**

Don't ruin your hobby. Consider the example of one particular woman who loves to garden. When she started thinking about what to do next, she considered being a landscape designer. But she quickly realized that she'd get lonely in the garden all day; she prefers working with people. Gardening is a great hobby and escape from work, but it wouldn't be the right career move for her. Make sure you think hard about how your passion will look and feel as a career.

# Putting Proven Success Strategies into Practice

You're not the first person to be looking for a job later in life, and that's good news for you. Others have led the way from unemployment to rewarding work in their 50s and beyond. And although these trailblazers haven't beaten down a path for you to follow (because there are so many paths to follow), they have revealed some strategies and techniques that have survived the test of time. The following sections introduce you to several of the more effective strategies for securing employment, most of which apply to all job seekers but a couple of which apply specifically to 50-plus job seekers.

## Starting sooner rather than later

The sooner you start looking for a job after losing a job, the more likely you'll find a new job. According to the AARP Public Policy Institute report "The Long Road Back: Struggling to Find Work after Unemployment," by Gary Koenig, Lori Trawinski, and Sara Rix, those who waited three months or longer before beginning their job search were less likely to have become reemployed.

Why wait so long to look for work? The most popular answer was that they needed a break. Other reasons survey respondents cited include that they took time to think about what they wanted to do next (57 percent), had savings or other sources of income (56 percent), and found it hard to get motivated (42 percent). Twenty-five percent of respondents waited to begin their job search because of caregiving responsibilities, about the same number who waited because they didn't know how to get started. Whatever the reason, postponing the search for three months or longer worked against them.

## Giving yourself a full-body makeover

TIP

Being physically fit, well groomed, and properly dressed is better than Botox. Aim to look and dress with an eye toward a vibrant, youthful appearance:

>> **If you aren't physically fit, make that a priority.** Eat healthy, avoiding sugary and starchy foods and sugary drinks. Exercise at least 30 minutes every other day. Quit or cut back on caffeine, nicotine, and alcohol, if you're so inclined to use those substances.

>> **Maintain a well-groomed appearance.** Get a haircut. Try a new 'do to give yourself a fresh look.

>> **Spruce up your wardrobe.** Get the right look for the job that you're seeking. Free personal shoppers are available at many department stores to help. Or you can also ask friends for tips on looking your best. If you wear glasses, consider getting contacts, Lasik surgery, or new glasses with more contemporary frames.

People do judge a book by its cover. Showing up for an interview looking vigorous, well groomed, and sharply dressed demonstrates that you're up for the job and have the requisite stamina, which is often a concern for employers when they consider hiring someone over 50. This advice also applies to any headshots you use for your social media and networking profiles.

# Using the most effective means to get a job

When reemployed workers were asked about the most effective steps they took in finding their current jobs, the overwhelming majority attributed their success to networking, according to the AARP's "The Long Road Back: Struggling to Find Work after Unemployment." Here are the most effective steps:

>> Reaching out to a network of contacts

>> Asking relatives and friends about jobs

>> Contacting employers directly

>> Using a headhunter

>> Consulting professional associations

Based on these findings, consider these points:

>> If you're interested in a particular industry, join an association connected with it and seek out volunteer openings. Go to industry and professional meetings and conferences. You never know who will know someone who is hiring. And many college and university career centers are reaching out to alumni to help, too.

>> Volunteer while you're out of work. By putting your volunteering on your résumé, you won't show a blank period of unemployment. To the extent that you can, be out in the world using your skills.

>> Be aggressive in your job search. Network as much as you can and keep an eye out for openings. The people who are aggressive are more likely to be reemployed.

**REMEMBER**

Networking is not optional! After all, "networking" is just one letter off from "not working." Simply put, you probably have better networks than do younger people. Employers want to hire someone who comes with the blessing of an existing employee or colleague. It makes their job easier. That's a card younger workers, who often have smaller networks, can't play as often as older workers. LinkedIn, for instance, is a great way to pull together your professional network. And you have got to pick up that darn phone. Ask for help and advice. Here are some concrete ways to network:

>> **Contact everybody you ever worked with and every employer you ever worked for.** That's the way to get an interview. If you don't establish a personal connection to the company, submitting an application is probably a waste of time.

>> **Call friends of friends; people in your faith community, athletic club, and volunteer organizations; and parents of your children's friends.** Heck, call your children's friends, too!

>> **Contact trade and professional associations you belong to.** Many have job boards.

>> **Connect with alumni associations and your fraternity or sorority if you belong to one.** College and university placement offices are there to help no matter how long ago you graduated.

>> **Canvas local lawyers, accountants, and bank officers in town and see if they know of any clients who are hiring.** In short, you really have to "kiss a lot of frogs" to find a prince. Leave no stone unturned.

>> **Join LinkedIn and Facebook, find and reconnect with people you know, and let everyone know you're looking for a job.** (See Chapter 3 in Book 2 for details on marketing yourself on LinkedIn.)

**TIP**

For a treasure trove of job search tips and information, head to www.aarp.org/work.

## Broadening your job search

Broadening your job search simply means being open to other possibilities — considering a different profession in a different industry, making trade-offs in terms of salary and flextime, stitching together a full-time position with part-time gigs, and so on. It doesn't mean applying to every job opening you find. You really want to focus your efforts in one area for maximum impact. But you don't want to pass up a golden opportunity just because it doesn't happen to conform to your notion of the ideal job.

**REMEMBER**

One way to broaden your search is to think less in terms of job title and more in terms of skills, knowledge, and experience — all these assets may be transferrable to a different profession, a different line of work. If you're focused on a full-time job, you can broaden your search by considering contract work or a temporary assignment, which may lead to a full-time position or even starting your own business.

## Navigating a career change

**TIP**

More than half of U.S. workers want to change careers, according to one survey. To make a switch, you'll probably have to learn new skills, make new professional contacts, sock away cash, and more. Here are the best moves to make your change a successful one:

- >> Be adaptable and embrace change.

- >> Do your research. Reach out to people doing the work you want to do and ask them all you can about their jobs. How did they get started? What do you need to succeed? And what can you expect to earn, both at first and later on? Because you aren't asking for a job, the discussion should be relaxed. Be inquisitive.

- >> Moonlight or apprentice yourself to someone already in the field.

- >> If you want to work for a nonprofit in a cause meaningful to you — a common goal among career changers — then volunteer; you'll not only see what the day-to-day work entails but also meet people in the organization.

- >> Identify the skills you need. Be prepared to spend the time and money to get the skills, credentials, and contacts you need to get relaunched, but don't assume that you'll need a costly degree. See the next section for details.

- >> Get financial aid. Nearly half of employers offer tuition assistance to employees. You may have to repay the funds, though, if you don't stay with the company for a certain number of years afterward.

- >> Assess your finances. Following your passion is great, but make sure you can afford your dream job.

## Getting the training you need

Once you reach a certain age, you may be branded with stereotypes that make you vulnerable: resistant to change, technologically challenged, complacent. You know this is a misconception, but you may need to demonstrate your tech aptitude to disprove this perception. To increase your market value, obtain the education, training, and certifications required to do the job you're seeking.

**WARNING**

Before taking classes or training for new skills, research the demand for those skills locally. In an AARP Public Policy Institute study of unemployment, of the 31 percent who participated in training or education programs in the past five years, more said doing so "did not help at all" than those who said it "helped a great deal." This could be pointing to a mismatch between the training they received and current job openings. Before enrolling in time-consuming, often expensive courses or classes, do your due diligence:

>> Contact a local community college and ask about skills that local employers are looking for.

>> Talk to graduates and employers to find out whether the educational and training programs are truly valuable.

>> Consider what you can afford and the return on your investment. Look at free options as well as paid ones.

## Seeking help

During your job search, don't hesitate to ask others for help. People are generally glad to assist if you ask politely for what you need. After all, wouldn't you be eager to help friends or relatives revamp their résumé or assist in any other way you could if they were looking for a job? Sometimes, the most generous people are the least likely to ask for help, never realizing that others may want the opportunity to help someone else. Sometimes, you have to be a taker. Here are common areas where older job seekers often need help:

>> Writing or updating a résumé (see Chapter 5 in Book 2)

>> Getting emotional support (someone to listen)

>> Searching for jobs online

>> Navigating LinkedIn, Facebook, X (formerly Twitter), and other social media and networking sites (see Chapter 3 in Book 2)

Here are some resources to consider checking out when you need help:

>> Family and friends

>> Workforce centers/one-stop job centers

>> Online job-search sites

>> Career or job coaches

>> Your local library

>> Educational institutions, including placement services

# Dealing with Ageism

News from the job front isn't all roses. Ageism is real. If you're over 50 and pounding the pavement these days, you face certain challenges. Once becoming unemployed, it typically takes an older worker longer to find a job than it does a younger person, according to the Bureau of Labor Statistics (www.bls.gov/web/empsit/cpseea36.pdf). If you have felt the disappointment of a floundering job hunt at a gut level, you have plenty of company. Many people are frankly furious, discouraged, and dumbfounded by their inability to land a job that suits their experience and desired salary.

The key to overcoming ageism is to understand employers' concerns and address those concerns, as the following sections explain.

## Knowing what employers are so worried about

Some employers figure that your salary demands are out of their ballpark, and that if they hire you for less, you'll resent it and probably jump ship if you get a better offer. They often perceive, true or not, that you're set in your ways or lack the cutting-edge skills or even the energy to do the job.

Then, too, some hiring managers may surmise that you have age-related health problems, or are likely to, and you'll be taking too much sick leave. And, of course, there's the nagging issue that you're not in it for the long haul, even if that's far from the truth. Finally, there's concern about reverse ageism — the employer may think you won't want to take orders from a younger boss who is probably making more than you.

**REMEMBER**

Landing a job can be difficult for anybody, and everyone seems to have a different take on what it takes to break through. It's not automatically your age that's holding you back. Employers want to hire people they know or can trust. In addition, employers want to reduce their exposure to risk, and you may present a risk regardless of your age. For example, if you made more money than the employer has budgeted for the position, you've been out of work for six months, you've held a higher position (and may be unable to accept a drop in status), or you've had three jobs in the past three years, you may be perceived as a risk. Some of those risks come with age, but they're not caused by age.

# Laying their worries to rest

TIP

One way to sell a product is to take away every reason a prospective customer has for saying "No," and that's the strategy for overcoming ageism. If you do everything else right in terms of revamping your résumé, marketing yourself online, networking, and so forth, you've already given employers plenty of reasons to say yes. Now, you just have to take away their reasons for saying no. Here are some suggestions for doing just that:

>> **Look your best.** Be physically fit, well groomed, and properly dressed.

>> **Keep up with the times.** Do everything you can to keep up with technology and changes in your field or research the skills or certifications required for your new venture. Add the essential expertise and degrees before you apply for a new job. If you've recently updated any software certifications, or you are proficient in social media, let the recruiter or hiring manager know, even if that's a side comment in your discussion.

>> **Build and maintain a strong online presence.** Invisibility is a liability, demonstrating that someone is out-of-date and unable to navigate the online world. See Chapter 3 in Book 2 for guidance on building and maintaining a strong positive online presence.

>> **Establish your ability to learn and adapt.** Speak up about your flexibility in terms of management style, your openness to report to a younger boss, your technological aptitude, your energy, and your knack for picking up new skills. For many employers, it's not only about the candidate with the best credentials; it's about who's the best fit overall for the team. You have to make the case that you're the person who is going to both play your position masterfully and help the team.

>> **Downplay the risks.** If you held a higher position or earned more money in the past, or if you've been unemployed for some time or worked several jobs over the course of several years, find ways to downplay yourself as a flight risk. If there's a gap in employment, you may explain, for example, that you were financially solvent and could wait for the job you really wanted, and this is it.

>> **Market your age as a plus.** Think brand management. You're responsible for your own image. Workers 50 and older tend to be self-starters, know how to get the job done, and don't need as much hand-holding as those with less experience. A great benefit to being older is that you have a good deal of knowledge and leadership ability. And whether you realize it or not, you probably have a broad network. You have a lot more resources to draw on than do people in their 20s and 30s. So pitch your age as a plus. You need to be able to articulate your value. Strut your stuff.

» **Practice positivity.** In truth, one of the biggest stumbling blocks to landing a job is negativity. You probably don't need a Botox treatment. What works better is a faith lift. You've got to believe in yourself. When you do, it shows from the inside out. People dwell on the bad news. "I've been unemployed for too long. I'm too old." Have faith in yourself. After you've been out of work for a while, you forget your value. You take for granted your accomplishments and contributions.

» **Stay present.** Don't chatter on in interviews about successes you had ten years ago. Focus on what you've done lately.

TIP

Sometimes it's hard to toot your own horn. Self-promotion can be uncomfortable, especially if you've always thought of yourself as a team player. Ask people who know you well, whose opinions you value and trust, to evaluate you in writing: your best skills and talents, your personality, the roles you've been really good at.

Guess what comes back? All the accomplishments, all the positives that you need to be reminded of to prove to yourself that you're a talented individual who has a contribution to make. Then when you're in the interview, networking, or doing informational conversations, you can say, "Well, people have said about me that blah, blah, blah."

All of a sudden, you have all the words to use, and it's easier to talk about your attributes because you're using someone else's tribute, advises career coach Maggie Mistal.

>> **

# Chapter **2**

# Using Skills to Your Advantage

To fill a specific position, an employer chooses the most trusted candidate who has the best track record of doing the job — the person who comes most highly recommended and has the requisite skills and experience. Skills are an essential component to securing employment, so this chapter focuses on knowing which skills are valued, identifying the skills you have, and developing the skills you need.

## Recognizing the Skills Employers Value

Employers look for skills in two categories: hard skills and soft skills.

>> *Hard skills* (also referred to as *work skills*) are those required to do the job, such as network security, accounting, programming, marketing, data analysis, and graphic design. These skills are typically learned and are quantifiable; for example, you can earn a degree or certification or at least point to a course on a transcript showing that you received training in a particular area. Or you can point to jobs you held in the past that required those same skills.

>> *Soft skills* are more subjective and harder to quantify, such as an ability to communicate clearly, solve problems, manage your own time, and be a team player.

In this section, you discover the hard and soft skills that employers value most and how to dig deeper to find out which skills are most highly valued in a particular field or required for application to a certain position.

## Finding out which hard skills are required

Nearly every position, whether advertised or not, requires certain hard skills. No book can possibly cover them all, because they can be highly specific for certain positions, such as knowing how to program in C++, operate a computer numerical control (CNC) milling machine, or translate Farsi. To find out which hard skills are required, hit the job boards, as explained in Chapter 4 of Book 2, pull up job descriptions you're interested in, and make a list.

REMEMBER

Following are a few broad hard skill sets that employers look for in nearly every field:

>> **Technology skills:** Nowadays, employers expect employees to be comfortable with a range of technological applications. Even if computer work is not a big part of your job, you will do yourself a favor by being somewhat savvy about how to use a computer, tablet, and smartphone and how to navigate your way around the web. See the later section "Getting tech savvy" for details.

>> **(Real) social media skills:** In recent years, social media has been a popular item in the skills section of many job seekers' résumés. But what does it really mean to be skilled at social media? It's more than simply having a LinkedIn or Facebook account. You need to be able to show an interviewer that you're active on these networks and understand the nuances of each one's distinct community. If you don't know the difference between a price tag and a hashtag, you have some work to do.

>> **Data science and analytics:** Three of the fastest-growing occupations are data scientists, statisticians, and information security analysts, according to the Bureau of Labor Statistics (BLS). This means that candidates with a strong background in data science and analytics have a real advantage in the job market. Smart employers are looking for people who understand data and its value to a business.

# Recognizing the soft skills employers value

Soft skills may seem basic, so bear with us. In many ways, these *softer* skills, which include your outlook and attitude, are gauges of how well you'll fit in. Employers want to be sure that you'll work easily and efficiently with your coworkers, your supervisor, and perhaps the organization's customers or clients. They also want to be sure that you can think on your feet and are equipped to make smart decisions.

Here are some softer skills to think about, arranged in alphabetical order. Rate yourself and mark areas where you may need improvement. Then make a plan to bump it up in those areas, if possible.

>> **Analytical thinking:** Employers want people who think logically, can size up situations, seek additional information when necessary, and make fact-based decisions.

>> **Communication (oral and written):** Employers value workers who communicate well both orally and via the written word. When you're a good communicator, you generally interact better with coworkers, supervisors, clients, customers, vendors, and others.

>> **Confidence:** Being confident means you can take initiative without the constant need for permission or approval.

>> **Cooperation (team player):** Success on the job almost always requires an ability and willingness to cooperate and collaborate with others, including coworkers, supervisors, vendors, clients, and customers.

>> **Creativity:** Even in non-creative jobs, you're expected to be able to think creatively to adapt to changing conditions and solve problems.

>> **Decisiveness:** If you're a confident decision maker, you're less apt to waste time mulling over options. This doesn't mean, however, that you make rash decisions. You want to establish a healthy balance between analyzing options and being able to make decisions.

>> **Flexibility:** Employers truly value an employee who can easily shift gears. Everyone is multitasking these days, so you need to be able to seamlessly shift from one project to another without missing a beat. You must be willing to put in the extra hours when necessary and to balance assignments — both independently and as a team member — depending on how quickly a project must be completed and the best method to accomplish it.

>> **Honesty and integrity:** Honesty and integrity are essential in building trust. As an employee, you're a reflection of the organization and its values. The popularity of social media has made employers much more sensitive to the image an organization projects all the way down to its employees.

>> **Leadership qualities:** Leadership doesn't necessarily mean you're prepared to fill in for the CEO. Employers are just trying to get a bead on whether you believe in your own abilities and have an inner confidence that centers you and enables you to focus on the company's needs and not solely your own. They're looking for candidates who are ready and motivated, who want to achieve great things for the firm that reflect back on *all* the team members.

>> **Learner:** Employers know that to beat the competition, they need a team of people eager to keep pushing the envelope, to learn new ways of doing things, and to be fearless about pushing themselves to constantly acquire knowledge and skills.

>> **Listening:** Listening is a big part of effective communication, and it may take the form of active or passive listening. Passive listening is an ability to hear, understand, and follow instructions. Active listening involves asking questions that elicit the information and insight needed to perform a task, solve a problem, or clear up a misunderstanding. Both are valuable.

TIP

Practice listening with a friend. Have your friend tell you a story, work or personal. Then retell the story to make sure you recalled all the key facts correctly.

>> **Literacy (reading and math):** Nearly all jobs require literacy in reading and math. If you have a high-school diploma or a GED, you're covered. If not, work on developing the requisite knowledge and skills. You can find plenty of books and online videos to help you get started.

>> **Organization:** Well-organized people tend to be more efficient and make fewer mistakes. Keeping some sort of day planner on a portable device or in print shows that you can organize your time.

>> **Patience:** Many jobs are stressful, and employers want to see that you can keep your cool when things heat up.

>> **People skills:** Your ability to connect with others and form solid working relationships is exceedingly important for most jobs. Being charismatic is a big plus for sales, management, customer service, public relations, and other jobs that require close contact with others, particularly customers, clients, and the public. Look around at people you like to work with and note what you admire. Try to emulate those attributes.

>> **Planning prowess:** Success in the workplace often comes down to how well you can prioritize your work demands. You've got this one. Just remind yourself of all the times you have had to sift through the piles of to-do lists and urgent delivery dates and have made it all work with a professional attitude and without skimping on quality.

>> **Positive attitude:** This is not a time to be cool and ultra–laid back. Upbeat and energetic people are a plus for most employers, and the truth is, it makes you more engaged in your work, too. It's a win-win.

>> **Problem solving:** If you're a confident decision maker and adept at problem solving, you save your company time and money and regularly keep customers happy, too. Being a good problem solver generally comes down to breaking a problem down into smaller pieces and addressing each piece in turn.

>> **Punctuality:** In some jobs, nothing gets done until everyone shows up. But even if you have a flexible schedule, certain occasions require punctuality. Showing up a little early for an interview helps to demonstrate that you're punctual.

>> **Reliability:** Reliability simply means keeping your promise, and when you agree to work for someone, that's a promise to do your job 100 percent of the time.

>> **Resilience:** The ability to recover from setbacks or failure is essential for success. Employers don't expect you to succeed all the time, but they do expect you to keep doing your job when adversity strikes.

>> **Resourcefulness:** Resourcefulness is measured by how much you do with what you're given. Creative problem solvers figure out ways to succeed with the resources available.

>> **Self-management:** Companies are eager to find employees who are able to keep themselves on track with little or no supervision. Employers value someone who shows up on time, gets the job done professionally, and is easy to work with.

TIP

Check out the later section "Beefing Up Your Skill Set" for tips on how to make any improvements you may need.

# Making the Most of What You Have

Nobody makes it to the age of 50 without developing some marketable skills. If you held a job, raised kids, bought a house, played computer games, surfed the web, balanced your bank accounts, read a few books, or did anything else that required getting off the couch and away from the television screen, you've acquired marketable skills. Now, you just need to identify them and put them to use in finding a job. The following sections show you how.

## Auditing your skills

Job seekers often don't know what they know or what skills they already have until they sit down and write a list. Making your own list will come in handy when preparing your résumé, filling out job applications, and preparing for interviews. Take an inventory of your skills by following these steps:

1. **Write down any formal education you received in high school, college, or trade school that has given you a work skill, such as welding, programming, business management, or public speaking.**

2. **Include any other coursework, seminars, or workshops you attended.**

3. **List any licenses or certifications you currently hold or held in the past.**

4. **Record any proficiencies you have in any subject areas.**

   Perhaps you picked up a foreign language on your own, taught yourself how to build websites or blogs, or developed public speaking skills as a member of a local Toastmasters group.

5. **List all office software you're proficient with.**

   This includes spreadsheet applications, presentation programs, database management software, desktop publishing or graphics programs, and blogging platforms.

6. **Jot down any hobbies that have taught you new skills or helped sharpen existing skills.**

7. **List your soft skills.**

   Maybe you're good at solving problems, planning and overseeing projects, or resolving conflict. See the earlier section "Recognizing the soft skills employers value" for a longer list.

8. **Ask friends, relatives, and former coworkers and supervisors to list your best qualities.**

   You may not realize skills you possess until others call attention to them.

**REMEMBER**

Don't restrict yourself to skills you developed on the job. If you volunteered as treasurer for your local parent-teacher organization, for example, you have experience with financial management and budgeting. If you raised children, you have experience in childcare, scheduling, and training. How you developed your skills is less important than the fact that you have the skills and that you can present those skills in a way that meets an employer's needs.

**TIP**

For additional ideas, search the web for "job skills list" or "jobs skills checklist." The U.S. Department of Labor's CareerOneStop has a Skills Matcher that generates a list of skills in several categories based on the job type and work activities you specify. Check it out at `www.careeronestop.org/Toolkit/Skills/skills-matcher.aspx`.

## Taking note of transferrable skills

Although you may need additional training and skills to pick up a new job or navigate a career change, many skills are *transferrable* — the knowledge and skill required are the same, but you're applying it in a new way or to a different situation. The ability to manage projects, for example, is a transferrable skill. In the publishing business, you may use this skill to coordinate efforts with writers, editors, graphic artists, and producers. In a shipping business, you may use the same skill to coordinate pick-up and delivery schedules. Same skill, different application.

**REMEMBER**

Look at your skill set and past experience as transferrable to diverse fields. If you're switching industries, you're "redeploying" skills you already have in place.

Most soft skills are transferrable. Every job requires good written and oral communication skills, confidence, creative thinking, problem solving, decision making, self-management, and so on. Whether a hard skill is transferrable depends on the skill and the position you're pursuing. For example, if you worked as a restaurant manager and were in charge of scheduling and budgeting, you can transfer those skills to project management in industrial settings, managing a healthcare facility, or even subcontracting. Knowing how to operate and troubleshoot an injection molding press, on the other hand, wouldn't transfer over to those other fields.

**REMEMBER**

Whether you realize it or not, over the course of your life, every class you've ever taken, every book you've ever read, and every job you've ever had has prepared you for this moment. You'll know you've succeeded in finding the right job for you when your preparation meets the right opportunity.

## Reframing your experience and skills

*Reframing* consists of presenting your experience and skills in a way that makes them relevant to the position. For example, suppose you just finished raising your kids and your job experience over the past 15 years consists of volunteer positions you held over the years. You're applying for a job as a director of a temp agency. Instead of merely listing the volunteer positions you held, the years you served, and your responsibilities, you may reframe your experiences and skills to make them relevant to the director position, like so:

**President, Norfolk PTA: 2021–2023**

- Organized and presided over monthly meetings.
- Introduced and implemented new-member outreach program that grew membership 7 percent each year.
- Increased fundraising revenue 20 percent in my first year.
- Led parent-teacher task force to improve student performance by 10 percent over the course of two school years.

Keep in mind that many experts advise against listing dates on résumés. More information on this is in Chapter 5 of Book 2.

# Beefing Up Your Skill Set

If you can show a hiring manager that you're taking classes, participating in a workshop, or working toward a professional certification, it shows that you're not stuck in your ways and are open to learning. Plus, the very activity of learning makes you feel unstuck and more alive. Research shows it reinvigorates your brain and stimulates the growth of new neurons and the development of new communication pathways. Yes, even old dogs can learn new tricks.

Of course, you'll never know all there is to know, especially when information is such a rapidly growing and moving target. But you can keep up with changes in your field, acquire new knowledge and skills to change careers, and improve your mental capacity through continuing education opportunities. The following sections describe several ways to get the education and training you need.

## Asking yourself some strategic questions to get started

Although learning for learning's sake is great, Book 2 is about landing the job you want, so before you set out on your quest for knowledge, ask yourself the following questions:

>> What skills can I add that will expand my job opportunities?

>> Which skills can I get from a life experience, and which ones will I need to hit the books for?

>> Am I willing to make a hard-and-fast promise to myself to make learning and self-development part of my daily activities? How committed am I?

>> Am I willing to invest the time (and perhaps money) in myself?

Taking classes and pursuing certifications consumes evenings and weekends, and most people are leery of adding one more thing to their to-do list. One way to find the time and the will to shake things up is to start with baby steps, one class at a time. Starting your career education doesn't have to cut too deeply into your schedule or your wallet.

TIP

Before enrolling in any program, determine whether it's worth the time, effort, and money:

>> Track down graduates of programs that interest you to get a sense for how valuable it was to them.

>> If it's related directly to learning new job skills, ask people you trust who know the field you're interested in or the job you're pursuing for their opinion.

>> Get a list of employers who have hired graduates from the program.

>> If appropriate, ask your former employer to weigh in.

WARNING

Keep in mind that the shorter the training, the less value it may have. A certificate that you earn in a long weekend probably won't deliver the knowledge and gravitas you would get from one that requires 100 or more hours of class time at a top university.

## Checking out community colleges

Take a class at a community college. Community college courses are usually a few hundred dollars per credit. In recent years, community colleges have reached out to adults interested in practical continuing education. Many U.S. colleges and universities let older students take classes either tuition-free or at rock-bottom prices. Inquire about specific residency, age, and other requirements at schools in your area.

TIP

Try a certificate program. Compared to full-blown degree programs, certificate programs are generally cheaper and more focused on the professional skills you may want to add now.

Online webinars and workshops offered by industry associations are other avenues to consider. For example, the National Association of Realtors offers a number of continuing education courses for its members.

## Enrolling in a Massive Open Online Course (MOOC)

*MOOC* is the acronym for the trendy *massive open online courses*, offered by education providers such as Coursera (www.coursera.org), edX (www.edx.org), and Udacity (www.udacity.com).

Offered by top-tier universities like Stanford and Princeton, MOOCs offer cheap ways to learn from their instructors anytime, anywhere.

TIP

Check out other free course options. You may be able to audit or take free or low-cost courses at your alma mater or via a noncredit personal enrichment program.

## Pursuing a degree or certification online

If spending time on a college campus isn't your thing, you can pursue a degree or certification online. Several online universities offer accredited bachelor's and master's degree programs and certifications in high-demand career fields. Many traditional colleges and universities also offer online courses and degree programs. Search the web for your state followed by "online university."

TIP

Negotiate for an accelerated degree. You may be able to get your tuition lowered by having the college waive some required courses because of your "experiential" credit. You may have a strong case that you've learned through work and life what some of the required courses cover. Don't be bashful about advocating for yourself.

## Acquiring on-the-job training on the cheap

Learning by doing is one of the oldest and best ways to acquire a new skill. Trouble is, you're usually required to have the skill to get the job where you can learn the skill by doing it. Still, there are a few ways to get on-the-job training without the experience required to actually land the job. Perhaps you can even earn a little money by doing it. The following sections offer some guidance in this area.

## Seeking apprenticeships and fellowships

You can build experience in an industry or job that appeals to you in all sorts of ways. If you want to become a chocolatier, for instance, you may be able to volunteer to help out at a local gourmet grocery or restaurant that makes its own confections. If you're interested in learning the ropes of the restaurant industry, you can offer to help out on weekends in some fashion, perhaps sautéing for the chef or filling in as a greeter or even keeping the restaurant's books if that's your forte.

**TIP**

If you're looking for a career with a social purpose, consider applying for an Encore Fellowship at `cogenerate.org/encore-fellowships`. These are paid fellowships, typically in a professional capacity at a nonprofit, to help mature workers re-enter the job market.

## Exploring internship and returnship opportunities

Internships and returnships (see the nearby sidebar) can fill a gap in your résumé, and, from the standpoint of an employer, the programs offer a chance to test prospective employees before committing. If you sense that a hiring manager is interested in hiring you but still waffling because you have been out of work or are making a career shift, consider asking whether they would consider an internship to appraise you based on your work for several weeks.

To get some leads on internship programs for 50-plus workers, visit these sites:

>> iRelaunch (`www.irelaunch.com`) is a company that helps connect individuals who want to return to work after career breaks with employers interested in hiring them. The site features a list of career reentry programs worldwide (`www.irelaunch.com/return-to-work-programs`).

>> OnRamp Fellowship (`www.onrampfellowship.com`) is a program that places experienced attorneys with law firms for a one-year, paid training contract. This experiential learning program gives returning women lawyers — many of whom have opted out of the legal field for a period of time to raise children or manage other family obligations — an opportunity to demonstrate their value in the marketplace while also increasing their experience, skills, and legal contacts.

Older interns are sometimes paid respectable wages.

Several years ago, Intel introduced the Intel Encore Career Fellowship — a program that pays a one-year, $20,000 stipend to help retiring employees transition into post-retirement careers with a nonprofit organization. Hundreds of retiring Intel employees have become Intel Encore Career Fellows.

## WHAT'S A "RETURNSHIP"?

Goldman Sachs launched the first "returnship" program in the fall of 2008 to give individuals who had taken a career break an opportunity to restart their careers after an extended absence (two or more years) from the workforce. The returnship is a paid ten-week program designed to help facilitate the on-ramping process in a variety of Goldman Sachs divisions.

Since then, other companies have followed Goldman Sachs' lead.

Consider looking for organizations in your area that offer similar programs or even suggesting such an arrangement to an organization you want to work for that doesn't have such a program in place.

## Taking on a part-time job in the field of your dreams

To get a feel for what a new career will really be like, take on a part-time job in the field that interests you. (Try moonlighting if you're currently working to see how you like the prospective field.) If you're interested in teaching, you may offer to guest lecture at nearby colleges or universities. You may discover that teaching is your calling or that it's not as great as you had dreamt it would be. Even if you have to do the job for free, it's probably still worth your time so you can make sure this is what you really want. If the dream fits, you can go all in to sharpen your skills and pursue the degree or certifications you need. If the dream fizzles, you haven't lost a huge investment.

Some careers, such as teaching and real estate, may require a new degree or certificate. Others may require a new set of skills that you may not even realize you need until you work in the industry. For example, if you open a bakery or any retail business, you'll need to learn about inventory management, bookkeeping, and marketing to be successful.

## Getting started as a volunteer

Look for possibilities to volunteer for a nonprofit organization that provides opportunities to build the skills you need. In addition to helping with skill-building, volunteering gets you outside of your own head and that swamp of negativity and helps you gain some perspective on others' needs.

Search for prospects at AARP's Giving Back (www.aarp.org/giving-back) or Create the Good (www.createthegood.org), and VolunteerMatch.org (www.volunteermatch.org). If you're good with numbers, look into AARP Foundation Tax-Aide program (www.aarp.org/taxaide), where volunteers help lower-income seniors with their taxes. It's a great way to get some tech skills (taxes are done on computer). AARP trains all volunteers.

Seek out nonprofits that need your particular professional expertise through the Executive Service Corps—United States (www.escus.org) and Taproot Foundation (www.taprootfoundation.org). Idealist (www.idealist.org) has a searchable database of both volunteer and paid positions.

**REMEMBER**

Never sit around feeling sorry for yourself. If you're unemployed, try volunteering or doing pro-bono work that keeps your skills current. These activities allow you to network and potentially get your foot in the door with a future employer. They also plug gaps in your résumé. Moreover, you may meet someone who will lead you to a job opening elsewhere.

### Gaining experience through contract gigs

Consider taking a contract job that can lead to a full-time post or gives you the ability to weave together a patchwork of jobs. All jobs are a work in progress. After you get in the door, you can try to make the job your own and grow the position to fit your talents.

## Getting tech savvy

**REMEMBER**

Employers worry that older workers are behind the times in technology, so if you're not tech savvy, your number-one priority is to get plugged in and up-to-speed on the latest office and consumer technologies. At the very least, learn to communicate through email, to cruise the internet, and to use Microsoft Office applications, particularly Word, Excel, and PowerPoint. Here are some suggestions on how to hone your computer skills:

>> **Check out Senior Planet from AARP** (https://oats.org/senior-planet-from-aarp). Senior Planet programming affords older adults the opportunity to engage with a dynamic mix of offerings to achieve measurable change in one or more areas of their lives: financial security, social engagement, creative expression, health and wellness, and civic participation. In addition to structured, multi-week courses, Senior Planet programming also includes a robust series of lectures, workshops, guest speakers, and special events, high-quality online content, and participant-driven affinity groups.

» **Take classes at your local library or community center.** Many local libraries and community centers offer a range of classes, including computer and technology courses that suit skill levels from beginner to advanced. You can often find introductory classes to Microsoft Excel, QuickBooks, and more. Some courses may be offered online as well.

» **Watch videos.** Although videos don't provide the tactile learning required to become comfortable with technology, videos show you how it's done, so you can try it yourself. You can find helpful videos on YouTube (www.youtube.com) and on educational sites such as the Khan Academy (www.khanacademy.org) and TED (www.ted.com).

» **Read books.** You can find plenty of books on a variety of technology topics, including computer basics, Microsoft Office applications, blogging, building websites, computer graphics, and more. Consider reading such books when you're sitting at the computer and practice the skills being taught.

» **Get help.** Ask a tech-savvy friend or relative to help or contact a local high school or college to see whether a high-school or college student may be interested and available to tutor you.

# Chapter **3**

# Marketing Yourself on LinkedIn

Whether you're job hunting or shaking the bushes for contract work, LinkedIn can offer a useful professional networking place. On LinkedIn, you can reconnect with old colleagues, expand your professional network with friends and relatives, make new contacts, obtain endorsements in your areas of expertise, dig up information on companies and positions you're interested in, find out about the people who'll be reading your cover letter and résumé or interviewing you for the job, get the inside track to certain positions, and much more.

LinkedIn is a place where hiring managers can go to scan the horizon for potential candidates, particularly to fill positions in the management and professional categories.

This chapter shows you how to open a free LinkedIn account, create a professional profile to make you a more attractive candidate, and tap the power of LinkedIn's most useful features. Along the way, you get guidance and tips specifically for job seekers over 50.

LinkedIn is continually changing. When it rolls out new features or formats, it does so progressively to the overall network. So what you're seeing on your screen may not be what someone else is seeing. And because these features change frequently, what you're reading here may differ from what you see when you log in to your LinkedIn account, so remain flexible. You may need to poke around a little or consult the LinkedIn help system to find a certain feature.

# Knowing How LinkedIn Can Help You in Your Job Search

Studies show that employers and recruiters routinely use LinkedIn in their recruitment and hiring efforts. If you're not convinced yet to use it, here are some ways you can use LinkedIn to land your next job:

>> **Create a multi-faceted tech-savvy résumé.** Unlike your one-dimensional print résumé, your LinkedIn profile highlights all your skills and interests in a far richer fashion, even featuring videos, slideshows, work samples, and more.

>> **Build a professional network.** Your LinkedIn profile makes you a member of the largest online professional network in the world, and networking is the number-one way to find a job.

>> **Spread the word.** When you find yourself out of work, your first impulse may be to hide, but the best thing you can do is let everyone know you're looking for a job. LinkedIn helps you do just that.

>> **Catch the eye of recruiters.** Recruiters prowl LinkedIn to find the most qualified candidates. Just being a LinkedIn member increases your chances of being discovered.

>> **Research organizations and people.** When you need to know more about organizations that require your skills or about a person who'll be interviewing you, turn to your connections on LinkedIn. You can also use LinkedIn to reach out to others in your field who may be able to offer valuable advice or assistance with your job hunt.

>> **Help hiring agents perform their due diligence.** Prior to hiring a candidate for a job, a hiring agent must perform due diligence to weed out any candidates who may not be suited for the position. Take away any reason they may have to reject you by putting relevant details in your profile. If they can find the information they need on LinkedIn, they may not dig any deeper.

# Putting Yourself on LinkedIn

Getting a LinkedIn account is a snap. Head to www.linkedin.com, click the Join Now button, follow the on-screen prompts, confirm your email address, and you're on LinkedIn. Your LinkedIn account is free and takes less than two minutes to create.

However, making yourself an attractive target for employers and recruiters requires additional time and effort. The following sections offer guidance on how to create an attractive professional profile that serves as your LinkedIn résumé and raise your profile's impact on LinkedIn to get yourself noticed. You will also find guidance on tweaking your privacy settings to limit access to certain people and, more importantly, avoid annoying your connections with unsolicited notifications from your account.

## Building an irresistible LinkedIn profile

**REMEMBER**

Your profile is your personal representative on LinkedIn, reflecting the person you are and the employee you will be. It's where recruiters and prospective employers go when they want to find out more about you. When a hiring manager looks at it, you want that person to see a clear portrait of your background, skills, and experience and to learn a bit about how you spend your time outside the workplace.

Equally important, a comprehensive online profile subliminally helps ease concerns about your age: It sends the message that you've successfully transitioned to 21st-century culture and technology. A well-crafted LinkedIn profile can give you a substantial advantage when you're on a job hunt, so it's worth taking the time to launch one or give your existing LinkedIn profile a makeover.

The following sections guide you through the process of creating an irresistible profile.

**TIP**

Be very open about the fact that you're looking for new opportunities and very clear about the opportunities you're looking for. Having a definite idea of what you want shows employers that you're not going to waste their time trying to "find yourself" as so many younger candidates are apt to do. In addition, it lets headhunters and employers know that you're not someone they have to persuade to switch jobs or companies.

## Conducting preliminary research

Before you start to flesh out your profile, do some preliminary research to find out more about your industry and the people in it and to get some ideas for how to create an attractive profile:

>> **Check out the competition.** Use the Search box at the top of any LinkedIn page to search for people in your field, and then check out their LinkedIn profiles. Collect key words to include in your summary and note ways to clarify the work you do in a clever, non-jargon way. With a little sleuthing, you can come away with some great models to use as a springboard to help your profile stand out.

>> **Read postings for jobs you may be interested in.** Click Jobs, near the top of any LinkedIn page, and search for jobs you're interested in. Read the job descriptions, and note the knowledge and skills required for those jobs, so you know which skills to highlight in your profile and which skills you need to develop. See the later section "Finding Job Postings on LinkedIn" for details on how to search for jobs.

## Starting with an attractive photo

According to the experts at LinkedIn, a profile that contains a photo is seven times more likely to be viewed by a recruiter or hiring manager than a profile without a photo. And nobody really knows how many job candidates are passed over by a prospective employer simply because the employer can't access a photo of the person.

REMEMBER

Look at it this way: If you leave a networking event with a handful of business cards, intending to follow up on LinkedIn, it's much harder for you to remember who's who without pictures. A missing photo can easily lead to missed connections.

Get a professional head shot. By "professional," we mean one that makes you look professional and looks as if it were taken by a professional photographer. Your profile photo should be of you and you alone, not of you and your significant other. It should have a muted background. Groom yourself, dress the part, strike a pose, and have your photographer snap the photo and send the digital image to you in the form of a JPEG file. Unless you're the Annie Leibovitz of selfies, don't go there.

Log in to your LinkedIn account and pull up the page to edit your profile. Click the spot for the profile photo and use the resulting dialog box to upload your photo.

TIP

To personalize your profile, consider adding an attractive background image. Click the spot for the background photo atop your profile page and use the resulting dialog box to select a photo to upload; you can also choose an image provided by LinkedIn. Don't choose anything that's too busy and might distract from your personal photo.

## Claiming and using your branded URL

A *branded URL* (often called a *vanity URL*) is your portfolio's web address that contains your name instead of a generic entry. On your Edit Profile page, you can see your LinkedIn URL at the top of the right-hand column. If your name appears at the end of that link in the form you want it to appear, you're good to go. If it doesn't match the name you want to use to establish yourself as a brand, then take the following steps to change it.

1. **Click the Edit icon next to the Public Profile & URL heading at the top of the right-hand column.**

   Your Public Profile page appears.

2. **Under the Edit Your Custom URL section on the right, click the Edit icon next to your URL.**

3. **Type your name in the form you want to use for building your personal brand.**

   Your name can be 5 to 30 letters or numbers but can't contain spaces, symbols, or special characters. Stick with letters — no numbers.

**REMEMBER**

   Custom URLs are available on a first-come, first-served basis, so if the name you want to use is already taken, you must use a slightly different version of your name, perhaps by adding a middle initial.

4. **Click Save.**

Make the most of your branded URL by including it in all correspondence, including in the heading of your résumé, below your signature on your cover letter, and near the bottom of all email messages you send.

**TIP**

Consider creating a Quick Response (QR) code that links directly to your profile. A QR code works like a bar code. Anyone with a smartphone and a QR reader (app) can scan your QR code and instantly access your LinkedIn profile. Search online or in your app store for a free service to generate your QR code. Add your LinkedIn QR code to your business cards and résumé.

## Creating a captivating headline

Your *headline* is the text that appears near the top of your profile, just below your name. When employers run a LinkedIn search, the search results display names, photos, and headlines. Your headline can be up to 120 characters long, and you should make the most of those 120 characters.

To edit your headline, mouse over that area of your profile and click the pen icon that appears next to your headline. A pop-up appears, prompting you to enter your professional headline. Click in the box and type a headline that's likely to catch a viewer's interest and that describes exactly what you do or want to do professionally. One example is Expert/Author/Speaker. Make sure your professional headline highlights any key words you want to use to promote yourself.

TIP

If you're job hunting, include some indication that you're actively looking for employment, something along the lines of "Actively pursuing new opportunities X, Y and Z." This signals to recruiters and hiring managers that you're on the market and saves them the time of trying to woo someone away from an existing employer. Another option is to place your desired job title in your headline and then use your summary to mention that you're looking for a particular position. (See the later section "Writing your summary: Your career story" for details.)

## Editing your contact information

The Contact Info section of the LinkedIn profile is perhaps the most overlooked section of all. In this section, you can add links to your other online properties, including your personal website, blog, social media accounts, and portfolio. You can also add your branded email address, an instant messaging (IM) address, and your phone number to make it easy for recruiters and employers to contact you. Fill in as many links as you can to give recruiters a wide range of ways to get in touch with you and to provide a well-rounded look at what type of person you are.

REMEMBER

Having other websites, including LinkedIn, link out to your personal website or blog raises your website or blog's search engine ranking, so when someone uses a search engine to search for you or for someone who does what you do, your site appears higher in the search results.

To edit your contact information, click the Contact Info button at the top of your profile and click the pen icon. Follow the on-screen cues to enter and save your change.

## Writing your summary: Your career story

The About section is where you tell your story in your own voice. It becomes your mini-bio, your sizzle reel. Take this opportunity to hook anyone who pulls up your profile and persuade them to dig deeper to find out more about you. Here are some guidelines to follow when composing your summary:

>> **Write one or two short, snappy paragraphs.** Highlight your key skills and examples of accomplishments. Approach your summary as though you're writing a short cover letter.

>> **Write in the first or third person.** Use the first person — *I, me,* and *my* — to add a personal touch, or describe yourself in the third person — *he, she, him,*

*her, they, or them* — to make your summary sound more objective. Neither option is better or worse, but choose one and stick to it; don't have one paragraph in third person and another in first person.

>> **Focus more on skills and less on experience.** By focusing on experience, you may pigeonhole yourself into certain positions and limit your opportunities. By focusing on skills, you expand your horizons, because skills developed in one area of expertise may transfer to another. This is especially important on LinkedIn, where you can have only one summary; you can't customize it for different positions you're interested in as you can with a résumé and cover letter.

>> **Tell what you're looking for.** Conclude with a sentence that starts with something like, "I am currently looking for new opportunities . . ." followed by a description of the work and situation you're looking for. For example, "I am currently looking for an opportunity to use my skills in writing and analysis in the field of green energy."

TIP

Although you can add a separate section to your profile for volunteer gigs, consider mentioning any volunteer work that you're particularly passionate about. This gives you an opportunity to write about what motivates you, the type of work that excites you (the work you choose to do even when you're not getting paid for it), and the skills you've developed in that capacity. You may conclude your summary with something like, "I am passionate about the work I did with [nonprofit organization], where I [description of skills or accomplishments]."

## Detailing your job experience

When you get to the Experience section of your LinkedIn profile, you may want to pull up or print out a copy of your résumé, which should contain most of the information you need to flesh out this section. Then, go at it. Enter your entire work history. For each position you held, mouse over the Experience section, click the + at the top, enter your information in the resulting form, and click Save. As you enter details about the positions you've held, follow these guidelines:

>> **Include all positions you held for six months or longer.** Don't try to obscure your age by including only the last two or three positions. As a mature employee, your experience and longevity in the workplace is what differentiates you from younger job seekers.

>> **Use your formal job titles.** Don't try to be creative by using a job title such as Money Guru or Sales Slam-Dunker. You may want to tweak your title to make it more descriptive of what you did or want to do; for example, if your previous job title was Investment Specialist, and you want to specialize in mutual funds, you may change your title to "Mutual Funds Specialist."

- » **Keep it punchy.** When describing job responsibilities, skills, and accomplishments in the Description box, lead with verbs and keep them short; for example, "Led strategy," "Developed budget," "Managed . . . ," "Devised . . . ," "Created . . . ," and so on.

- » **Include accomplishments.** In the Description area, mention quantifiable accomplishments; for example, "Completed key project two months ahead of schedule," "Outperformed projections by 40 percent," or "Increased sales by 20 percent."

- » **Rearrange positions strategically.** Arrange your positions in reverse chronological order with your most recent position first, unless you have good reason to do otherwise. For example, if you're looking for a particular position, you may want to list previous positions in which you excelled in skills required by the position you're seeking.

**TIP**

You can get creative in the Description box by creating and formatting your job description in your word processing application and then copying and pasting it into the Description box. You may need to experiment with formatting to see what works best. For example, short bullet list items (that don't wrap) look good, but long bullets don't. Also, bullets tend to look better if you create them manually with tabs and dingbat characters than if you use the word processor's bullet style.

## Including volunteer positions

Scroll down to see whether your profile has a Volunteer section. If it doesn't and you've served as a volunteer, add the Volunteer section and list any volunteer positions you've held. (The option to add sections is just below your profile photo.)

Highlighting your passion and commitment to philanthropic organizations shows employers that you don't spend your time away from the workplace sitting on the couch but rather out doing something and making a difference, giving back. According to LinkedIn, some 40 percent of hiring managers surveyed said they view volunteer experience as equivalent to formal work experience. It can set you apart from other candidates.

## Adding your educational achievements

Letting LinkedIn know the diplomas and degrees you've earned does more than just pad your profile for the benefit of recruiters and employers. It also helps you get connected with people who attended the same schools. Based on the information you enter about the schools you attended, LinkedIn can recommend people you know who may be on LinkedIn and get you connected.

To add a school, scroll down to the Education section, mouse over it, click the + at the top, fill out the resulting form, and click Save.

**TIP**

You may wonder whether 50-plus job seekers should include graduation dates, which are a nod to their age. This is a personal choice. Omitting graduation dates probably won't completely mask your age. Some experts think it offers a point of connection with possible hiring managers who may be peers.

## Listing your skills

LinkedIn allows you to list up to 50 skills or areas of expertise. Your connections on LinkedIn can then choose to endorse you. (See the later section "Giving and getting recommendations and endorsements" for details.) To add skills, scroll down to the Skills section of your profile and click the + at the top. Click in the Skill box, type a skill or area of expertise, and click Save. You can drag and drop skills to arrange them in their order of importance.

**REMEMBER**

Carefully choose words to describe your skills and areas of expertise. Use words that recruiters and employers are likely to enter when searching for someone with your experience and skills. If you're targeting a specific job or job title in your search, you may want to choose words that match those used in job descriptions for positions you'd like to apply for.

## Adding other important sections to your profile

The more details you include in your profile, the bigger the target you become for recruiters and the more reasons you give prospective employers to give you the thumbs up. Just below your profile picture is the Add Profile Section area. Click this link to check out other sections you can add to your profile. Here are a few of the available sections you should consider adding if you have anything relevant to put in these sections:

>> **Causes:** Adding a Causes section shows that you're more than just the work you do. You're sensitive to the needs of others.

>> **Licenses & Certifications:** In certain industries, certifications are essential in demonstrating that you have the knowledge and skills to perform the job. A certification in some cases may be the equivalent to holding a college degree, and more important.

>> **Courses:** Include seminars, classes, workshops, and other educational achievements to show that you're a lifelong learner and dedicated to self-improvement.

>> **Honors & Awards:** Include any honors or awards you've achieved, such as Employee of the Year, competitions you've won, or other notable and relevant achievements.

- » **Languages:** If you have proficiency in any languages other than English, add the Languages section to your profile and indicate the languages you know and your proficiency in each. In the global economy, knowing another language may be key in landing certain jobs.

- » **Organizations:** List organizations you're involved with and leadership and service positions you hold now or have held in the recent past.

- » **Patents:** If you hold or have held patents for innovative products or designs, list them here.

- » **Projects:** Highlight any projects you've been involved with to demonstrate that you have the experience and skills relevant to any positions you're pursuing. This is also a great section for adding side gigs you've had, say, as a consultant, speaker, or home-based business, even one that's a hobby.

- » **Publications:** If you've published anything at all, you're a step ahead of most people on the planet. If you published on a topic related to an industry in which you're trying to find work, that publication shows that you're an expert in some aspect of the industry.

## Adding media samples to your profile

If you're in a creative profession in which employers or clients review work samples as part of their evaluation process, add samples to your profile. You can add documents, presentations, videos, and so on to the Featured section of your profile.

REMEMBER

For best results, use compatible file types or content providers. Visit www.embed. ly/providers to check out a list of compatible content providers.

To add samples to your profile, click the + at the top of the Featured section, choose Add Media, and follow the on-screen cues.

## Knowing what to omit

The more you include in your profile, the more likely you'll be discovered by a recruiter or employer. Likewise, if an employer is considering you for a position, the more the person is able to find out about you on LinkedIn, the more likely they'll choose you over other candidates. Of course, that depends on whether they like what they find. Here are a few suggestions on what to omit from your profile:

- » **Anything you don't have time to do properly:** Spend some time crafting everything you post. Anything that's slapped together in a hurry will look that way. A little high-quality detail is better than a lot of junk.

>> **Mentions of political or religious affiliations:** Unless you're looking for a job with certain political or religious organizations, you probably don't know the affiliations of the person who's going to make the hiring decision, so don't mention which way you lean. Choose other "Causes" with care; choosing "Environment" may seem harmless, for example, but it could get misinterpreted in industries that often come into conflict with environmentalists.

>> **Current position:** If you're currently unemployed, remove the check mark from the I Am Currently Working in This Role box for any position you listed under Experience. Don't be concerned that your job shows an end date. It's okay to be in between jobs.

## Keeping it current

**REMEMBER**

Completing your LinkedIn profile doesn't mean you're done. Whenever you achieve a new milestone — you land a new position, earn a relevant certification, complete a major project, whatever — log back onto LinkedIn and update your profile. Every achievement demonstrates that you're progressing and growing as a person and a professional, that you're not stuck in the past. One of the biggest mistakes people make on LinkedIn is letting their profile stagnate.

## Controlling what you share in your public profile

By default, your entire profile is online for all to share. It's likely to appear in search results whenever someone searches for you by name (or for someone who has a similar name), and unless you specify otherwise, everybody can see everything in your profile. Making your profile accessible to all is what you usually want, particularly if you're actively job hunting. You want recruiters and employers to have full access to your public profile.

If you want to be more selective or simply want to check how much of your profile LinkedIn is set up to share, click the pen beside Public Profile & URL at the top right of your profile page. Doing so displays your profile as it will appear in public along with a bar on the right that contains your public profile settings. Under Edit Visibility, you can choose On or Off for Your Profile's Public Visibility. If you choose to make your profile public, you can then click the box next to any item you want to hide from the public to remove the check mark next to it.

**TIP**

Below your public profile settings is a link called Public Profile Badge. Click the link to get a code you can copy and paste on your website to display a link that visitors to your website can click to access your LinkedIn profile.

# Checking and adjusting your privacy settings

Before you become very active on or invested in LinkedIn, you should check your privacy settings. These settings are important not only for protecting yourself but also for preventing any of your contacts from being inundated with notifications of activities you've engaged in on LinkedIn and becoming annoyed with you because of them.

To check your privacy settings, click the Me heading in the upper-right corner of any LinkedIn page, and click Settings & Privacy. Click on the links below Visibility to find out what your options are and make adjustments. Until you get a feel for LinkedIn, you may want to keep your profile public (as explained in the previous section) but adjust the two following controls to maintain a lower profile on LinkedIn:

>> **Turn on/off your activity broadcasts:** Turn this off if it isn't already until you gain experience on LinkedIn, especially if you're the type of person who likes to experiment with a new technology. You don't want to inundate your connections with notifications of everything you're doing until you know what you're doing and can be more deliberate in what you share and the activities you engage in. You can turn this setting on before updating your profile, so your connections are informed of the change.

>> **Select what others see when you've viewed their profile:** If you want to be able to check out other people's LinkedIn profiles without them knowing it was you, change to one of the anonymous settings under Profile Viewing Options in the Visibility menu.

TIP

If you're currently employed, consider removing the check mark next to the I Am Currently Working in This Role box for your current position under Experience. Otherwise, LinkedIn broadcasts anniversary notices to all your LinkedIn contacts every year on the starting date you entered, which some people find annoying.

# Getting Connected on LinkedIn

The whole point of putting yourself on LinkedIn is to get connected. Networking opens the door to employment opportunities by converting cold calls into warm connections. Ideally, people get to know you *before* you need a job, so you have an inside track when you do need a job. Less ideally, LinkedIn enables you to find the jobs you're interested in and leverage your existing connections with current and former coworkers, people you've gone to school with, friends, and relatives to find that all-important inside track to the job you want.

Getting connected on LinkedIn involves more than simply reaching out to people you know on LinkedIn, although that's a key first step. It also involves giving and getting endorsements, engaging in relevant group discussions, and following the right companies and individuals. The following sections introduce you to the various ways to get connected on LinkedIn.

## Connecting with people you know

The first, easiest, and most effective method to connect with people you know on LinkedIn is to reach out to your current contacts and invite them to connect with you.

**TIP**

When possible, write your own personal notes instead of sending a generic invitation that LinkedIn sends when you click the Connect button. It may sound old-fashioned, but etiquette never goes out of style. Remind the people you reach out to of how you know them, when you met, or someone you know in common, and then say you'd like to connect with them.

Before you can connect with someone on LinkedIn, however, you have to find the person. Fortunately, LinkedIn provides several tools to help you do just that:

**TIP**

» Search for people you know by entering their full name in the search box atop any LinkedIn page and clicking the Search button. If LinkedIn displays any matches, click the match that looks most promising to pull up the person's profile and verify that this is the person you want to connect with.

Flip through business cards you've collected from colleagues and clients and search for them on LinkedIn. Send them an invitation to connect.

» Mouse over My Network near the top of any LinkedIn page, click Add Personal Contacts, and use the resulting options to import your email contacts from Gmail, Outlook, Yahoo! Mail, or other email programs or services. LinkedIn uses your email address book to track down any of your email contacts who happen to be on LinkedIn. You can then choose which ones you'd like to connect with.

» Mouse over My Network near the top of any LinkedIn page and scroll down to see people who attended one of the schools you listed in your Education section whom you may know. Click the person's name or profile photo to access the person's profile, where you can choose to connect with them.

» Engage with others on LinkedIn, as explained later in this section. When you meet someone you'd like to connect with, send the person an invitation to connect.

Do your homework before sending an invitation to people you don't know or barely know. Research the person carefully and invite the person only if you sincerely believe that you can establish a mutually beneficial relationship. The people who can help you most are generally the most successful in their field and hence the busiest. Have a compelling reason the people should accept your invitation before sending it. They know the connection will help you. You need to show them how connecting with you will help them.

## Giving and getting recommendations and endorsements

When you're trying to impress employers, what you say about yourself isn't half as important as what others who've worked alongside you say about you. LinkedIn provides two ways for colleagues, bosses, clients, and others on LinkedIn to vouch for you:

>> **Recommendations:** A recommendation is a written statement by a LinkedIn member vouching for the quality of your work or the services or products you offer. They may come from former or current teachers, mentors, managers, coworkers, or clients. Positive recommendations give recruiters and employers more reason to trust one candidate over another who doesn't come as highly recommended.

>> **Endorsements:** An endorsement is an acknowledgement by a LinkedIn member that you have a skill you claim to have. Your LinkedIn connections can endorse your skills with a click of the mouse, making them much easier to give.

One subtle way to encourage your connections to give recommendations and endorsements is to write positive recommendations for them and endorse their skills. To give a recommendation to one of your LinkedIn connections, click My Network, near the top of any LinkedIn page, click Connections on the left-hand side, click the connection you want to endorse or recommend, scroll down to the Endorsements or Recommendations section, and follow the on-screen cues to endorse a skill or recommend your connection. When you do, your connection is notified and is likely to reciprocate by endorsing your skills or recommending you.

### Requesting a recommendation

To ask for a recommendation, head to your profile page, scroll down to the Recommendations section, click the + at the top, and click Ask for a Recommendation. Follow the on-screen cues to complete your request; you need to specify what you want the person to recommend you for and choose up to three connections to ask.

TIP

When you're ready to request a recommendation, consider the following suggestions:

- » Make it easy for someone to write your recommendation, by giving them some idea of what to write, as in this example:

  - Hi, Maria. Hope all is well with you. I'm writing to ask you to write a brief recommendation for my LinkedIn profile related to the project that we worked on together, perhaps highlighting the time sensitivity of the project and how my project management and problem-solving skills helped to expedite our efforts. I'm currently trying to secure a position that requires strong project management and problem-solving skills and could really use your recommendation in those two areas. Thanks for your consideration. If I can return the favor in any way, please let me know.

- » If you feel comfortable doing so, request that the person write a recommendation that upends older-worker stereotypes that a hiring manager may have by highlighting the fact that you're a source of timely and creative ideas or have up-to-date technical skills.

- » Request recommendations from coworkers or managers in several different age brackets. Having a younger colleague go to bat for you sends a subtle message that you work well with those younger than you.

- » Send requests to your LinkedIn connections who are most likely to write a recommendation that's relevant to the type of employment you're currently seeking. For example, if you worked in sales and marketing in the past and are currently looking for a marketing position, ask the people you worked with in marketing for recommendations.

- » Request recommendations from connections who can offer different perspectives, such as a supervisor, a coworker, and a client.

## Managing endorsements

LinkedIn has no system in place for you to request endorsements, although you're certainly free to contact your LinkedIn connections by sending them a message on LinkedIn or emailing them outside of LinkedIn to request that they visit your profile and endorse your skills. Otherwise, you generally receive endorsements organically as your connections check out your profile and as LinkedIn prompts your connections to endorse your skills (especially if you endorse theirs).

TIP

Rearrange your skills in the Skills section of your profile to list the skills most relevant to the job you're seeking first. You can rearrange skills by clicking the pen at the top of the Skills section, then clicking the three dots at the top of the screen and choosing Reorder. For example, if one of your skills is public speaking, or that's the area you want a recruiter or employer to see first, you can slide that public speaking category within your skills list to the top of the chart. Otherwise, LinkedIn lists your skills in the order in which they're most highly endorsed.

## Getting involved in LinkedIn Groups

A great way to show recruiters and employers what you're interested in, to demonstrate your expertise and ability to communicate in writing, and to expand your LinkedIn network is to join groups and actively engage with other members in those groups. You can find LinkedIn groups related to specific organizations and industries, certain professions, schools you attended, past employers, and a wide range of other interests. You can even create your own group.

To find groups you may be interested in, enter a topic or keyword(s) that describes your interest in the Search box at the top of any LinkedIn page, and click the Search button. LinkedIn displays a list of groups that match your search entry under the Groups heading in the results. Click the group's name to find out more about it and, if you're interested in joining the group, click the Join button. If you choose to join a private group, the group manager needs to approve your request before you can engage with the group; this may take a few minutes to hours or even days.

After you join a group, you can and should engage with others, but before you post anything, try hanging out for a while and read some of the discussions to get a feel for the group's culture.

To check out other discussions, click My Network at the top of any LinkedIn page and click Groups on the left-hand side. You'll see a list of the groups you belong to; you can click a group icon to go directly to that group and explore its offerings.

In addition to helping you grow your LinkedIn network and engage with other professionals in your field, groups offer the following perks:

>> Let you keep up with the latest trends and technologies in your field.

>> Give you an opportunity to establish yourself as an expert in your field.

>> Allow you to connect with professionals in your field in a less formal forum. You never know where that spark of something you have in common may come into play.

>> Demonstrate that you're willing to learn new things.

>> Provide you with another opportunity to post fresh content. According to LinkedIn, if you share once a week, you increase your chances of having your profile viewed by a recruiter tenfold.

## Following companies and individuals

LinkedIn allows you to follow companies and certain high-profile individuals on LinkedIn without necessarily establishing a LinkedIn connection. Following a company offers the following benefits:

>> Keeps you in the loop about anything new that's going on at the company or in the industry. This information can come in handy as you compose a cover letter and résumé or prepare for an interview.

>> Lets you know who you know. When you visit the company's page, a box on the right shows your connections at that company. If you're seeking employment with that company, these connections can be very helpful in getting the inside scoop about a job or what the company is like.

>> Lets you keep an eye on who's being hired and who's departing. If someone's leaving the position you want, this could be the perfect opportunity to get in touch with the company's HR department.

To find a company you want to follow, search for the company by name, or search for a topic or keyword and click Companies to browse a list of companies that LinkedIn deems relevant based on your experience and connections. When you find a company you want to follow, click its Follow button.

You can also follow thought leaders — high-profile individuals who publish popular articles regularly. This feature lets LinkedIn members follow people they want to learn from and may want to connect with in the future without establishing a formal connection, and keeps thought leaders from being inundated with invitations to connect.

# Finding Job Postings on LinkedIn

Any company can pay to post a job on LinkedIn, making it now one of the leading job boards. To check job postings, click Jobs near the top of any LinkedIn page. Scroll down the page to view job postings that LinkedIn recommends based on information you entered in your profile, your LinkedIn connections, and on your search history.

You can also use the Search box atop every LinkedIn page to conduct your job search, and then you can filter the results according to date posted, experience level, and more.

Your job activity is private, so if you have a job right now, you needn't concern yourself about your current employer finding out that you're looking for something else . . . unless, of course, you're using the company computer to conduct your job search or you posted on your (public) profile that you're looking for a new job.

Although you may have a pretty good idea of the basic job you're looking for, begin with a broad search and then gradually narrow your criteria until you get to a reasonable number of results. CBS, for example, may have 400 job listings on LinkedIn, but they're nationwide and in a range of the company's divisions. So whittle down to the type of work you're after and where you want to work.

When you find a job that catches your eye, click it. The job page that appears typically has a button you can click to apply on LinkedIn or go directly to the organization's website to apply. It also shows how many people have applied for the job so far, whether any alumni from your schools work for the company, and whether any of your first-degree LinkedIn connections work there.

It's always a good idea to network yourself into companies through your connections before applying directly. Here's how:

>> If you have any first-degree contacts who work at the company, consider contacting them to find out more about the company and the opening.

>> If you don't have a first-degree contact at the company, you can click the company's link, near the top of the job's page, to open the company's page and check to see whether you have any second-degree contacts who may be able to provide the connections you need.

>> If you find connections who may be able to help you, click their name or profile photo to access their profile and click the Message button to send a message.

>> If the job listing contains a photo of an individual who posted the job, possibly a recruiter, click the photo to find out more about the person. If you're lucky, the person is a first-degree connection, and you can contact them directly. If the person is a second-degree connection, consider asking one of your first-degree connections who's connected to the person for an introduction.

For additional guidance on tapping the power of LinkedIn, check out the latest edition of *LinkedIn For Dummies*, by Joel Elad (Wiley).

# Chapter **4**

# Checking Out Promising Job Markets

When job hunting, you're faced with two challenges: figuring out what you want to do for a living and then finding someone who's willing to pay you to do it. This chapter helps you meet both of those challenges by steering you to the hottest job markets and listings. By knowing what's out there, you can find a job with more of what you want and employers need. In the process, you narrow your focus so that your subsequent job-seeking efforts have greater impact.

**REMEMBER**

As you get rolling with your job hunt, consider a wide range of options and broaden your search to different fields. In the AARP report "The Long Road Back: Struggling to Find Work after Unemployment," many older workers who had been unemployed were able to find work by considering new occupations. In fact, of those who succeeded in finding jobs, more than half had an occupation different from the one they had prior to becoming unemployed.

# Exploring the Possibilities and Gathering Ideas via Job Boards

At the age of 50, it may seem a little late to start thinking about what you want to do when you grow up, but more and more people who are looking at 50 in their rearview mirrors are thinking about what *else* they want to do now that they are grown up. Times have changed, and maybe the employers of today no longer need what you used to do. And maybe you really don't want to do what you used to do anyway. The time has come to explore exciting new opportunities and perhaps consider opportunities you passed up along the way.

One of the best ways to start thinking about work opportunities you're interested in and qualified for is to browse online job boards — websites where employers post job openings or the site itself gathers postings from around the web. Job postings via online jobs boards can be a first-rate source of intelligence about who's hiring for what jobs and where. The following sections lead you on a tour of well-known and lesser-known job boards.

**TIP**

Many of the job sites mentioned in this chapter have corresponding smartphone apps. Networking apps are also very useful for reaching out to people and checking out job listings.

**WARNING**

If you're looking for a new job right now and still holding down a current one, tread carefully. With so much recruitment or job hunting done online these days, getting "found out" by a current employer is a growing risk.

## Checking out the big boards

Start with the big job boards, where you'll find the greatest number and diversity of listings:

>> **AARP** (https://jobs.aarp.org/)

>> **CareerBuilder** (www.careerbuilder.com)

>> **Craigslist** (www.craigslist.org)

**WARNING**

Watch out for scams on job boards. The site organizers police postings for scams, and you can "flag" postings that may be considered inappropriate. To help its visitors, craigslist has a section called "Avoid Scams and Fraud." Protect your privacy if you post your résumé. Those postings are visible to anyone who visits the site, so limit the contact information and details that you include.

**WARNING**

Be especially careful on craigslist, because anyone can post a job opening. Research the employer carefully before sending any sensitive information, and don't go to your initial interview alone. (See the later section "Taking extra precautions with online job postings.")

>> **Glassdoor** (www.glassdoor.com)

>> **Indeed** (www.indeed.com)

>> **Job-Hunt** (www.job-hunt.org/)

>> **LinkUp** (www.linkup.com)

>> **Monster** (www.monster.com)

>> **SimplyHired** (www.simplyhired.com)

**TIP**

Check out Payscale (www.payscale.com) and Salary.com (www.salary.com) to research salary ranges based on position and location. PayScale's database filters search results based on salary, location, education, and flexibility.

**WARNING**

Job boards are great for conducting research, but you should be aware of the following potential drawbacks:

>> Online job postings aren't always removed in a timely fashion, so the job opening may no longer exist by the time you discover it.

>> Recruiters sometimes post jobs to determine whether the description is alluring for job seekers. If too few people respond, they change it and the true posting goes live a few days or even weeks later.

>> Sometimes recruiters put up false posts to gather résumés for future headhunting searches.

>> Employers may post jobs to satisfy the public posting requirement before hiring the in-house applicant who already has been chosen.

>> Scammers collect résumés and other information from job seekers.

## Combing niche job boards

Large job boards, such as CareerBuilder, Indeed.com, Monster.com, and Simply-Hired, are popular for employers and employees alike. They give job seekers access to plenty of openings, but the competition for those openings is stiff. You may find more success by becoming a bigger fish in a smaller pond — by combing through smaller job boards that are more focused on workers with your talents and interests. Whether you're in IT, media, engineering, sales, or another field, look online for niche job boards to help narrow your search.

These smaller, more targeted sites, including those operated by industry and professional associations, usually include openings that don't show up elsewhere. They also sometimes offer contact information for the hiring manager instead of routing you to a generic application, which means your résumé is less likely to disappear into a black hole. And although applicants from niche sites tend to be more qualified — because their skill set more often matches what the employer is looking for — you'll compete with fewer candidates there than you would on well-known sites.

Small businesses in particular tend to opt for niche boards to find candidates because they tend to get applications from higher-quality applicants, which means they have to filter through fewer applications to find the spot-on hire.

## Digging up more niche job boards

TIP

Almost every industry seems to have its own niche job board(s) and sometimes job boards for sub-specialties within the industry. They're not as front and center as the gigantic job websites, so you have to do a little sleuthing to find one that's relevant:

>> Visit the websites of professional organizations in your field, such as the Society for Technical Communication, to see whether the site has a job board or links to other sites that post relevant jobs.

>> Ask people who work in your industry about where they look or have looked for jobs, or ask hiring managers at businesses in your field where they post openings.

>> Search the web for <your city> or <your state> or <your county> followed by "jobs" to find any local job boards. You may have to scroll down through several pages of results to find more specialized job boards, because the top search results are likely to steer you toward the big job boards.

>> Search the web for <your industry> followed by "jobs." Again, you may need to scroll through several pages of search results to find more specialized job boards.

## Exploring job boards for people 50 and older

Now that you're included in the category of workers 50 and older, you can take advantage of the job boards that eliminate some of your competition:

- **AARP job board** (www.aarp.org/work): You can search for jobs by job title, key words, or company name and by location.

- **CoGenerate** (cogenerate.org/): This site can help you find a second career in the nonprofit sector.

- **NEW Solutions** (newsolutions.org/): This organization "is connect professionals age 55+ with part-time and full-time opportunities throughout the country by providing skilled and experienced workers to government agencies."

- **RetiredBrains** (www.retiredbrains.com): This online job board connects to jobs for those over 50.

- **RetirementJobs** (www.retirementjobs.com): This site is geared toward positions for 50-plus job seekers.

- **Seniors4hire** (www.seniors4hire.org): Job seekers can submit a résumé, post a description of their model job, or apply for posted jobs.

- **Workforce50** (www.workforce50.com): Workforce50.com "has jobs and information to help navigate your job search or search for a new direction."

TIP

Check out AARP's Employer Pledge Program (www.aarp.org/work/employer-pledge-companies/), directing job seekers to more than 1,500 employers that value and are hiring experienced workers.

## Looking into government jobs

Government jobs are often available at the federal, state, county, and municipal levels. The largest employer in the United States is the federal government, which employs millions of employees. To find out what's available, do the following:

- Visit USAJobs.gov (www.usajobs.gov) to search for jobs by key word, job title, government agency, and location, or to track down the government agency you want to look for and check its list of openings. Most agencies have their own job boards, and you may see additional positions on those sites that you don't see on the broader site. In most cases, you still have to go through USAJobs to apply, but some positions are exempt from the competitive system and allow for more direct hiring.

- Visit GovernmentJobs.com (www.governmentjobs.com) to search specifically for jobs posted by employers in the public sector. You can search by job title or key word and by location or browse jobs by category or location.

- Search for your state's website, access it, and then poke around to find job-related links. You may find links for jobs in education or a more general

Jobs or Human Resources link that leads to an area where state job opportunities are posted.

>> Search for your county's or city's website, access it, and look for job links. Less populated counties and municipalities are less likely to have their own websites or to post jobs on those sites, but it's worth a try.

Landing a federal job can be quite a challenge. Talk to practically anyone who has tried to secure a job with the federal government, and they'll tell you the hiring process can be painfully slow and bureaucratic. Follow these steps to expedite the process and improve your chances of success:

1. **Find the right fit.**

   Find the job you want and are qualified to do in the agency you want to do it. If you're passionate about the environment, for example, use that as a starting place to figure out which agency will be the most compatible for you. Look for openings at the Environmental Protection Agency (EPA), the U.S. Department of Agriculture (USDA), and other agencies dealing with environmental issues.

TIP

   Find out more about the various agencies by attending events sponsored by government-related associations, such as the American Council for Technology (ACT). You can also tap into government-related websites, such as Go Government (www.gogovernment.org), which can help you research federal agencies and government careers, and Best Places to Work in the Federal Government (www.bestplacestowork.org).

2. **Go directly to the agency's website.**

   After pinpointing the agency you're aiming for, check out its job board directly, which may contain additional job openings that aren't posted on USAJobs.gov. You still need to apply on USAJobs.gov, but these positions may be exempt from requirements for posting jobs there.

3. **Apply.**

   Even if you find and eventually secure the job through your networking efforts, you need to jump through this hoop. Regardless of where the job is posted and how you find out about it, you must apply for openings on USAJobs.gov (www.usajobs.gov).

4. **Network.**

   Although the application process is rigid, it helps to reach out to anyone you know who works for the federal government. You want to get a sense of what it's like from an insider. It's not just about the job but the culture and environment as well. In addition, federal employers are no different from those in the private sector; they want to hire people that they know or that someone they know knows.

**TIP**

Consider starting with a short-term appointment, which involves working on a specific assignment or project for one year or longer. You can find term appointments on USAJobs.com. Check out special programs. For example, the Peace Corps actively recruits retired leaders to be volunteers for short-term shifts. Some positions are paid. The Presidential Innovation Fellows program recruits the best and brightest in the technology field to do a yearlong stint in federal service. Government-sponsored fellowship programs, such as Code for America and Fuse Corps, place leaders from the private sector into government positions for assignments.

**REMEMBER**

When looking for a government position, expect the usual bureaucratic delays and be persistent. Although timing varies from one agency to the next, 80 to 90 days between application and hiring is the norm. You can easily wait four months or longer to get an offer. Prospective job applicants may want to apply to numerous jobs over a series of months and give it time. One applicant applied to 40 jobs over three months. He got four interviews and two offers. The time from first application to starting the position was approximately three months.

## Taking extra precautions with online job postings

**WARNING**

Be careful when responding to online job postings, especially on generic classified sites, such as craigslist, because anyone can post a job listing. Look for the following warning signs:

>> Any posting that requests sensitive personal or financial information, such as your Social Security number or a credit card number. Work-from-home postings are notorious for *phishing* expeditions (gathering personal and financial information to steal your identity or worse), charging to get started, and promising payment that never comes.

>> Requests to email your response to a free email address ending in gmail.com or yahoo.com, for example, instead of to a company email address ending in something like wiley.com or ibm.com.

>> A link that redirects you to somewhere other than the place indicated in the link. You can usually mouse over the link and look in the status bar near the bottom of your web browser or email window to see the actual address of where the link will take you; if it differs from the address in the link itself, don't click the link.

>> A job listing that requires any form of payment to gain access to additional information or to qualify for consideration.

**TIP**

When first responding to a job listing via email, share your name and email address and little else. Indicate your interest in the position and request the organization's name, physical address, and phone number, so you can do your own background check to make sure the organization is legitimate. Explain that when responding to online job postings, you take certain precautions to ensure that the posting is legitimate before sending any detailed information. They'll understand and appreciate your concern. You may include a scaled-down version of your résumé, with your work experience, education, and so on, but exclude sensitive information, such as your birthdate and the names of education institutions and the dates you attended. Scammers could use detailed information to contact places you worked or went to school to find out more about you.

**REMEMBER**

Protecting yourself against scammers is another reason networking is such an effective means for finding and landing a job. Networking eases the concerns not only of prospective employers who want some assurance that you are who you say you are but also of job seekers like you who need to know that job postings are legitimate. Before responding to a job posting, use your connections to find out whether anyone you know works for the organization. If someone you know works there, you can be less concerned about submitting your application or résumé.

# Investigating Opportunities by Category

Another way to discover what's out there is to search for jobs by category in healthy job sectors or categories, including part-time, seasonal, and holiday jobs; work-at-home opportunities; and jobs for animal lovers. The following sections reveal the hottest job sectors and explore additional categories to consider as you figure out what you want to do and find someone to pay you to do it.

**REMEMBER**

Compensation varies depending on the employer, your experience, and where you live. Jobs may be full- or part-time or have flexible hours. Some may require you to return to school for specific training, while others enable you to repurpose skills you already have.

## Focusing on the hottest industries

One way to conduct your search is to focus on the hottest job markets — industries that have reported rising numbers of vacancies or have projected an increasing need for employees. This section covers several sizzling sectors to consider.

**TIP**

Cast a wide net. Seek out openings at small businesses and big corporations.

## Healthcare

The aging population and longer life expectancies are spurring a wide range of healthcare-related jobs. New jobs are cropping up all the time for people in their 50s, 60s, and 70s that cater to people in their 80s and 90s. The jobs can run the gamut from repairing gurneys and wheelchairs at a hospital to transcribing medical records at a physician's office.

Look for jobs at public and private hospitals, nursing and residential care facilities, and individual and family services. Specific jobs to explore in the sector include dietitian and nutritionist, patient advocate, personal and home healthcare aide, massage therapist, physical therapist (and aide/assistant), registered nurse or licensed/practical nurse, nurse practitioner, school nurse, paramedical examiner (screening individuals applying for life or healthcare insurance), senior fitness trainer, skincare specialist, home modification professional, medical equipment maintenance and repair, and medical records administrator.

## Financial

As boomers slide into their retirement years, they're increasingly seeking help with managing their money, whether it's bill paying, estate planning, or choosing the right insurance policy. There's growing awareness that people need to have financial plans in place to help avoid outliving their savings.

Moreover, as traditional employer-provided pensions are being replaced by do-it-yourself IRAs, 401(k)s, and similar plans, demand is on the rise among all age groups for experts who can make sense of retirement investment.

Jobs to explore in the sector include accountant, personal financial advisor and planner, insurance broker, retirement coach, bookkeeper, financial manager, and tax preparer.

## Leisure and hospitality

Given the snowballing number of retiring workers, demand for travel and leisure activities has surged. Jobs to explore in the sector include barber and hairdresser, cosmetologist, casino worker, caterer, chef, cruise line worker, landscaper, pet sitter/walker, recreation worker, resort worker, tour worker, bartender, waiter, and hotel shuttle van driver.

## Retail

Jobs to explore in the sector include cashier, customer service representative, package preparer, e-commerce analyst, direct salesperson, retail salesperson, sales representative, and product demonstrator.

## Professional and business services

Jobs to explore in the professional and business services sector include grant/proposal writer; green-business consultant; human resource specialist; information security analyst; database administrator; management consultant; market research specialist; meeting, convention, and event planner; and translator/interpreter.

Spanish is the most in-demand language, but other languages are increasingly needed, such as Arabic. Specializing in translating in a particular field, such as the judicial system or healthcare, and knowing its special terminology increases your job opportunities.

## Narrowing your focus to the hottest occupations

If looking at the hottest industries didn't spark any ideas, try narrowing your focus to these fastest-growing occupations (according to the BLS *Occupational Outlook Handbook*) listed in Table 4-1.

**TABLE 4-1**

### Fastest-Growing Occupations (2021–2031)

| Occupation | Growth Rate | 2021 Median Pay |
|---|---|---|
| Nurse practitioners | 46% | $120,680 |
| Wind turbine service technicians | 44% | $56,260 |
| Ushers, lobby attendants, and ticket takers | 41% | $24,440 |
| Motion picture projectionists | 40% | $29,350 |
| Cooks, restaurant | 37% | $30,010 |
| Data scientists | 36% | $100,910 |
| Athletes and sports competitors | 36% | $77,300 |
| Information security analysts | 35% | $102,600 |
| Statisticians | 33% | $95,570 |
| Umpires, referees, and other sports officials | 32% | $35,860 |
| Web developers | 30% | $77,030 |
| Animal caretakers | 30% | $28,600 |
| Choreographers | 30% | $42,700 |

| Occupation | Growth Rate | 2021 Median Pay |
|---|---|---|
| Taxi drivers | 28% | $29,310 |
| Medical and health services managers | 28% | $101,340 |
| Logisticians | 28% | $77,030 |
| Physician assistants | 28% | $121,530 |
| Solar photovoltaic installers | 27% | $47,670 |
| Animal trainers | 27% | $31,280 |
| Physical therapist assistants | 26% | $61,180 |

## Considering positions you may have overlooked

The Department of Labor's *Occupational Outlook Handbook* includes many new job-related profiles that you may not have considered before. These include the following:

>> Compensation, benefits, and job analysis specialists

>> Computer network architects

>> Emergency management directors

>> Fundraisers

>> Genetic counselors

>> Information security analysts

>> Nurse anesthetists, nurse midwives, and nurse practitioners

>> Phlebotomists

>> Solar photovoltaic installers

>> Training and development specialists

>> Web developers

>> Wind turbine technicians

**REMEMBER**

Finding a job after 50 is different from when you were younger, as highlighted as in AARP's *Great Jobs for Everyone 50+: Finding Work That Keeps You Happy and Healthy . . . And Pays the Bills* by Kerry Hannon (Wiley). It sets out jobs workshops and a smorgasbord of jobs to consider. More often, the big-ticket items are out of the way — childcare, college tuition, and mortgages — and you have the flexibility to stretch and try new kinds of work that make you happy and give you purpose. Find a job that ramps up your learning curve, maybe even scares you a little. Perhaps you want to aim for one that sweeps you into an entirely new field where you're able to draw on your previous talents and add new skills as you go.

## Contemplating part-time jobs

To streamline their operations and avoid having to pay employee benefits, many employers hire part-time workers. As a result, more and more employees have to take on two or more part-time jobs to make ends meet. This isn't necessarily a bad thing, if you can earn enough from your part-time gigs to pay the bills and cobble together your own benefits package. In addition, working a couple of jobs can be an attractive proposition for people who don't want to work full-time or are easily bored. You can find part-time gigs on the job boards set out in this chapter, or search for part-time job boards.

## Going green with eco-friendly work

If you're eco-conscious, working for an organization involved with climate change awareness, renewable energy, wildlife conservation, or green construction not only provides a paycheck but also a great deal of personal satisfaction. Whatever your specialty, green organizations can use your expertise and your genuine interest in the environment.

TIP

If you're looking for a green career or resources to help you find a green job, check out the Environmental Career Center (www.environmentalcareer.com), a job-posting resource for the eco-friendly sector, and GreenBiz (www.greenbiz.com/).

Here are three green jobs to consider, depending on your skills and interests:

>> **Green building consultant:** Older buildings, in particular, are getting serious facelifts. States, counties, and cities are offering incentives targeted at green building projects. Find out about the Leadership in Energy and Environmental Design (LEED) green building certification program at www.usgbc.org/leed.

>> **Waste consultant or waste reduction coordinator:** If you're a recycling devotee, you'll revel in the chance to help companies and residential communities reduce waste. The National Recycling Coalition (www.nrcrecycles.org) offers information on a range of recycling topics and more. Some states now offer recycling certification programs via local colleges.

>> **Eco-landscaper:** As an eco-landscaper, you'll be designing and building sustainable gardens and landscaping that are cheaper to maintain and environmentally

friendly. The Ecological Landscaping Alliance (www.ecolandscaping.org) is a great place to find out about the training and credentials required. Many community colleges and universities offer certificates and degrees in sustainable landscape design.

**REMEMBER**

Green employers want to hire job candidates who walk the talk. Claiming that you're committed to the environment isn't enough. Employers will know in a heartbeat if you aren't authentic. If you want to pursue a second, green career, get involved in environmental causes in your community, the nation, and the world.

## Taking your job search on the road

To combine work with travel, consider work camping — taking on jobs at campgrounds, national and regional parks, marinas, and resorts. Jobs may include office work, groundskeeping, housekeeping, maintenance, handyman work, coordinating social activities, managing rentals, serving as an interpretive guide, or handling retail sales. Past experience in the type of available work helps. Expect on-the-job training if necessary.

To find out about work-camp opportunities, visit CoolWorks.com (www.coolworks.com) and Workamper News (www.workamper.com/). Popular gigs are as hosts, housekeepers, and maintenance workers at campgrounds and government-owned parks. Many also work at wildlife sanctuaries, Christmas tree lots, and pumpkin patches.

## Working remotely

One of the great American dreams is to work remotely, having a flexible schedule and working as much or as little as desired or needed to make ends meet. Unless you require a lot of social contact primarily obtained through work, you'll probably like working at home as much as or even more than you had imagined. The two big questions you need to answer before you make the leap are: "Is the work safe?" and "What sorts of opportunities are available?" The following sections answer those two questions.

### Is it safe?

Con artists often dangle the home-based job as a carrot to get people to hand over their cash or their personal information, which the con artists use to steal. Still, many work-at-home opportunities are legitimate. Organizations often save money by outsourcing work to home-based workers, avoiding the overhead of maintaining office space and equipment and paying benefits.

Although you may not be able to avoid risks entirely, you can minimize your exposure to risk by taking the following precautions:

>> Work only for employers that have a physical address, a phone number, and a domain name.

>> Never give any personal or financial information, such as your Social Security number, birthdate, or bank account or credit card numbers over the phone or online until you've done your research and confirmed that the organization and the person claiming to represent it are legitimate.

>> Search the web for the organization's name followed by "scam," "rip-off," or "complaints" to tap into any online discussion about the organization that may reveal it's not legitimate. Also, search the organization's name at the Federal Trade Commission's website (www.ftc.gov).

>> Check for complaints with the Better Business Bureau (BBB) in your area and the area in which the company is headquartered, and verify the organization with its local consumer protection agency and state's attorney general.

>> Contact one of the organization's reps and ask what specific tasks you'll have to perform, whether you'll be paid by salary or commission, who will pay you, and when and how frequently you'll be paid. Ask what the total cost to you will be, including supplies and equipment. Get answers to your questions in writing.

>> Be wary of overstated claims of product effectiveness, exaggerated claims of potential earnings, and demands that you pay for something before instructions or products are provided.

>> Be wary of personal testimonials that never identify the person so you can't investigate further.

## What sorts of opportunities are available?

TIP

If you've set your sights on a remote job, go straight to a company you'd like to work for and see whether it hires remote workers. A good place to start is the career section of its website. Sites such as FlexJobs.com (www.flexjobs.com) focus on legitimate work-from-home jobs and prescreen each job and employer to be certain they aren't scams. Here are some great work-from-home jobs to consider:

>> **Translator-interpreter:** Fluency in two languages generally qualifies you for the job, but to work for certain employers, you need to know specialized vocabulary, such as legal or medical terms.

>> **Mediator:** Arbitration and alternative dispute resolution (ADR) have steadily gained converts from those hoping to bypass lawsuits with onerous fees and often a drawn-out legal process. For guidance on how to make it as a mediator, check out *Success as a Mediator For Dummies,* by Victoria Pynchon and Joe Kraynak (Wiley).

>> **Graphic designer:** If you have a talented and well-trained eye and know your way around graphics programs, you can find plenty of assignments designing websites, logos, letterhead, business cards, restaurant menus, marketing brochures, and much more. Local colleges and universities and the American Institute of Graphic Arts (www.aiga.org) are great places to go to find out how to get the training and certification required . . . and to find a job when you have what it takes.

>> **Writer/editor:** If you have a flair for the written word and a clear grasp of spelling, grammar, punctuation, and usage, you can find a wide range of writing and editing jobs. Reach out to local associations and organizations, community newsletters, and other regional publications. Ask if they need an extra hand on an assignment basis for online and print articles, brochures, and press releases.

>> **Grant/proposal writer:** If you have a knack for research, are detail-oriented, and have fundamental writing skills, grant/proposal writing could be in your future. To find out how to succeed as a grant/proposal writer, check out the latest edition of *Grant Writing For Dummies,* by Beverly A. Browning (Wiley). Check online job boards such as the Chronicle of Philanthropy (www.philanthropy.com) for job postings.

>> **Bookkeeper/accountant:** Duties run the gamut from processing payroll checks to handling invoicing, accounts receivable, accounts payable, and other financial reporting. Some firms may ask you to monitor checking and savings accounts and track credit card bills. Although you may find work without being a certified public accountant (CPA), that certification will open a lot of doors. Visit the American Institute of CPAs (www.aicpa.org) to find out how to become a CPA.

>> **Customer service representative:** You'll need an up-to-date computer (usually a PC), a high-speed internet connection, a dedicated landline telephone during business hours, a telephone headset, a quiet place to work, and people and communication skills. Potential employers include airlines and hotel chains. Others use third-party companies who then hire home-based workers.

# Barking up the right tree: Jobs for animal lovers

If you love animals, and you're good with them, you can tap into this market for full-time, part-time, or seasonal work in the following roles:

**TIP**

» **Pet sitter:** As vacationers head off for school breaks and summer frolic, someone's got to tend to those members of the family that can't fit (or fit quietly) in the suitcase. As a pet sitter, you're generally self-employed, so you'll have to drum up business on your own. After you're established locally as reliable, you should have no trouble filling open slots.

Consider joining the National Association of Professional Pet Sitters (www.petsitters.org) or signing up with a national franchise operator such as Fetch! Pet Care (www.fetchpetcare.com) or Pet Sitters International (www.petsit.com).

» **Pet shop owner or operator:** If you have a head for business, a love of animals, and expertise in caring for a wide range of critters from fish and reptiles to cats and dogs, you can tap into the fast-growing pet care industry and blend your work with your passion by running a local pet store.

» **Pet groomer:** Primping a pooch (or cat) runs the gamut from bathing, brushing, and cleaning ears to clipping coats and trimming nails. You've got to be detail-oriented and in good physical condition. You may work out of a kennel, a pet shop, your own home, or even a mobile grooming van. The National Dog Groomers Association of America (www.nationaldoggroomers.com) offers certification as a groomer and can provide a list of state-licensed schools.

» **Dog walker:** Expect to walk in all kinds of weather at least twice a day. The trek can take a degree of fitness and physical strength, depending on the size and demeanor of your charges. Walking more than one dog at a time is not unusual, if you have the strength and dexterity. This word-of-mouth business can be bolstered by good relations with veterinarians, pet shop personnel, and groomers.

» **Veterinary technician:** If you love animals and have an aptitude for science and the willingness to go back to school to ramp up the necessary skills, you've got a great chance of landing a job as a vet tech — especially if you live in a rural area. Veterinary technicians usually have a two-year associate's degree in a veterinary technology program. Visit the American Veterinary Medical Association (www.avma.org) for details.

# Furthering Your Research

Look to these sites to locate jobs that are available in the industry of your choice:

>> **AnnualReports.com** (www.annualreports.com) allows you to search its database for free electronic files of annual reports. This is a great way for you to better understand the firm's mission, key accomplishments, and problem areas over the past year.

>> **CEOExpress.com** (www.ceoexpress.com) offers links to newspapers and periodicals in a range of industries. It's a way to stay abreast of events that impact companies and industries.

>> **LinkedIn.com** (www.linkedin.com) is a powerful tool for researching a company and its employees. Use the company search feature. See Chapter 3 in Book 2 to find out more about LinkedIn.

>> **Vault.com** (www.vault.com) allows job seekers to read employee surveys on companies and read message boards for sharing job-search information for a nominal fee. The mission is to provide the inside scoop on what it's really like to work in an industry, company, or profession.

>> **ZoomInfo** (www.zoominfo.com) is a business information search engine used to quickly find information about industries, companies, people, products, and services.

You can also set up an alert on your search engine for a particular company you're interested in so you can receive links to the latest news.

# Chapter **5**

# Rehabbing Your Résumé and Cover Letter

Nearly every job worth having requires a résumé and a cover letter as part of the application process. These few pages are often your only shot at getting your foot in the door and landing an interview, so making sure these docs are not only good but better than the hundreds or thousands of other résumés and cover letters the organization is likely to receive is key.

Every résumé and cover letter combination is unique, or at least it should be, so we're not about to stifle your creativity by presenting a formula (as if any such thing exists). And, because creating a résumé when you're over 50 brings its own set of challenges, this chapter provides some résumé guidelines to follow, along with a few do's and don'ts, so you can speak to the needs and expectations of the organization you're applying to in whatever creative way you choose.

## Constructing a Winning Résumé

Your résumé is your calling card, often serving as your only opportunity to make a good first impression. It needs to capture the essence of who you are and what you have to offer an employer. The trick is to boil all that down into a clear, sharp, and engaging two-dimensional presentation. Challenging, yes, but doable. It's called editing. Think of your résumé as your highlight reel.

A great résumé is at the heart of any successful job hunt. But the older you are, the trickier it can be to create a résumé that's not only concise but also detailed enough to do your years of experience justice. The following sections show you how it's done.

## Covering the six essential qualities of a promising candidate

When you're job hunting, the first step is to be certain that your résumé clearly trumpets the qualities that most employers view as non-negotiable these days. Of course, each position has its unique requirements, but these six universal qualities are the ones you must showcase.

**TIP**

Show, don't tell. Don't use the terms introduced in the following sections, such as *self-starter* or *tech savvy*, on your résumé or cover letter. Employers see these terms so often that they've become cliché. Instead, demonstrate through concrete examples that you embody these qualities.

### Self-starter

One reason employers value experienced workers is that they don't need a lot of hand-holding and can hit the ground running. You need to demonstrate that you're capable of working independently, able to get along without lots of supervision, and are great at managing your time and keeping a project on track.

**TIP**

When describing your work experience, use words such as *managed, led, executed,* and *delivered* and describe instances when you took the initiative or completed a project with little or no supervision. For example, "Interviewed machine operators and developed multimedia training programs that reduced training time for new hires by 25 percent." Statements like this *show* rather than *tell* that you're a self-starter.

### Techie

One of the biggest concerns employers have about older workers is they aren't up to speed with technology and perhaps are unwilling to learn. Prove them wrong. Here are a few ways to show that you're tech savvy:

>> **Include your email address as part of your contact information at the top of your résumé.** Better yet, use a personal branded email address, such

as jane@janedoe.com, instead of a generic email address, such as janedoe@gmail.com. Yes, many employers discriminate based on the domain name of your email provider, and it could prevent you from landing an interview.

>> **Mention in your résumé any experience with computer hardware and software, especially any hardware and software indicated specifically in the job description for the position you're applying for.** For example, you can mention AutoCAD, QuickBooks, or WordPress.

>> **Maintain an active LinkedIn presence (see Chapter 3 in Book 2) and list your personal LinkedIn URL on your résumé just below your email address.** Prospective employers can then see for themselves how active you are in relevant industry and professional groups.

>> **Showcase your personal blogging or website.** If you have your own blog or website, include its URL on your résumé so prospective employers can check it out. Even if they don't visit, the URL shows that you're tech savvy enough to create an online presence.

## Problem solver

Employers see employees as either problems or problem solvers, and you definitely want to be in that second camp. When describing your professional accomplishments, add at least one that demonstrates your ability to identify and solve a problem. For example, you may describe an instance when you noticed that several customers had the same complaint, and you recommended a change in your company's policies or procedures that improved customer satisfaction. Perhaps you found a way to cut the time required to perform a certain operation or a way to cut costs.

REMEMBER

When you're able to demonstrate that you're a problem solver, you also show prospective employers that you're more about solving problems than trying to find someone to blame.

## Communicator

Regardless of the position you're applying for, employers want people who can communicate effectively. You need to demonstrate an ability to understand and clearly present ideas and information. In terms of your résumé, your ability to communicate is demonstrated mostly through the organization and writing on the résumé itself. Here are a few tips to make sure your résumé reflects your ability to communicate:

>> **Tailor your résumé to the organization and job description to demonstrate your ability to understand the organization's needs based on**

**what you read.** See the later section "Tailoring your résumé to specific openings and circumstances" for details.

» **Organize your résumé to present the information in a way that makes it easy for the reader to capture your work experience quickly.** Aim for sharp, clear job titles, and easy-to-follow lively narratives of your job responsibilities. For example, you managed X project or led the team that introduced a new product.

» **Carefully proofread your résumé to eliminate errors.** Better yet, have a friend or colleague read it for you and suggest corrections and improvements. An error-free résumé demonstrates attention to detail and commitment to quality, along with showing that you can express yourself clearly in writing.

## Innovator

Most employers are looking for candidates who are creative thinkers. You need to be able to develop and pitch new ways of doing things and navigating challenges. When describing your experience or skills, be sure to include at least one instance when you invented a new idea or a way of doing something. Perhaps you read customer posts online that inspired an idea for a new product or service, or maybe you read something about a competitor that opened up new opportunities for your organization. Try to think of any ideas you may have had that either made or saved your organization time or money or improved it in some way.

## Lifelong learner

Having a high-school diploma or a college degree is a definite plus, but if you earned those in the '70s or '80s, that's history. If possible, include more recent education, training, or certifications. Presenting yourself as a lifelong learner demonstrates that you're humble enough to accept instruction, open to new ideas and information, and eager and willing to learn new things and improve yourself.

# Revealing the seven secrets to making your résumé pop

A résumé revamp can help you stand out from other applicants in the screening process. Here are seven ways experienced job seekers can get their résumés noticed.

## Keep it short and simple

Your résumé has about five minutes to convince an employer that you're worthy enough to advance to the next step in the vetting process, according to a Society for Human Resource Management (SHRM) survey. (And according to some studies, a lousy résumé has only about six seconds.) To improve your odds of surviving the first cut, keep your résumé short and simple:

>> **Limit yourself to two pages.** Anything longer will probably go unread. In certain circumstances, you can go as long as three pages, but make your résumé only as long as needed to highlight your qualifications.

>> **Select a traditional font.** Times New Roman, Calibri, and Arial are all good choices. Stick to a 10- to 12-point size and use black type against white paper for the body of the résumé. Consider going larger for your name (up to 15 points) and your contact info (up to 12 points).

>> **Go easy on text enhancements.** Use boldface type, italics, and underlining sparingly and consistently, and avoid using any of them together.

>> **Choose a common file format.** Save your résumé as a Microsoft Word document that can easily be viewed on most computers. Also saving it in PDF form is wise to prevent format corruption when uploading as part of an online application. Most job postings will state what type of format is preferred.

## Include your contact information

Place your name and contact information and the title of the job you're applying for at the top of your résumé. Here's what you should include at the top of your résumé and in what order:

>> **Your full name:** Use your first and last name. Refrain from using a middle initial or middle name unless it's part of your professional identity.

>> **The city and state in which you live:** Recruiters want to know what town you live in so they can estimate your commute time. Omit your street address for privacy reasons.

>> **Your email address:** Consider getting a branded email address.

>> **Your phone number:** Include only one phone number, the number you're most likely to answer.

>> **Your personal LinkedIn URL and blog or website address, if you have one:** Including your LinkedIn URL and blog or website address makes it easy for recruiters and hiring managers to find out more about you online. (See Chapter 3 in Book 2 for details.)

>> **The position for which you're applying:** Below your contact information, add the specific title of the job for which you're applying — for example, type "Objective: [employer's job title]."

## Cull your professional experience

Just because you've been gainfully employed for 30 or 40 years doesn't mean you have to include all those years on your résumé. When listing your work experience, focus on what you've been doing for the past 10 to 15 years.

Although most job seekers use the traditional chronological or reverse-chronological résumé format, there are alternatives. You may, for example, highlight your specific skills first, focusing on those that are most transferable to the job you're looking for.

In a skills-based résumé, you do, of course, include your employment history — but that goes at the bottom of your résumé. This type of approach can be advantageous if there are gaps in your work history of a year or more, or if you're switching careers or industries and your previous job titles don't correspond.

The top three or four key broad skill categories mandatory for the job you're targeting will help you to pick what to include in this Skills Summary section. In your bullets, you expand with precise achievements or experiences. You will mention companies here, but you don't have to be too specific about the specific position.

Following the skills section, you'll have a concise work chronicle section. Include the company name, your job title, employment dates, and the city and state of the organization. Include volunteer positions or internships in this section. Related experience doesn't just have to be paid positions.

Think advertisement, not obituary. No one wants, or needs, to read every one of your employment entries over a three- to four-decade career.

When presenting your professional experience in reverse chronological order, start with your most recent position. Include the following details for each organization you served:

>> Start and end dates (month and year)

>> Organization's name and what the organization does or did

>> Position(s) you held and major accomplishments at each position (see the later section "Tell your story with gusto" for details)

There's no need to distinguish between paid and unpaid work-related skills on your résumé. Include any volunteer work that suggests you have skills. Being in charge of a gala fundraising event, for instance, converts to sales and marketing chops. Holding a board position shows leadership ability. Also, if you work for a family business, you don't need to mention that it's a family business on your résumé.

Package your earlier experiences into one nice, tidy paragraph at the end of your résumé's Experience section. Include only the work history that's relevant to the job you're applying for now and omit dates. Here's an example suggested by Susan Whitcomb, author of *Résumé Magic: Trade Secrets of a Professional Résumé Writer*:

> **Prior Experience (Commercial Development, Business Development and Technology):** During tenure with Ecolabs, promoted through positions in Food Business Development, Industrial Commercial Development; Applied Research and Commercial Development for Performance Materials; and Applied R&D. Initially recruited from UCLA as Research Chemist for Shell Oil.

## Plug the gaps

If your employment history has any gaps, fill them in; otherwise, prospective employers may think you're hiding something. Try plugging any gaps with educational experiences. Maybe you traveled, performed community service, added a degree, or pursued other educational opportunities. Include a one-line explanation, such as "Caregiving" or "Volunteer for Habitat for Humanity" to fill in for any extended periods of unemployment. Otherwise, the gap is a major red flag that something is wrong with you even if that's far from the truth.

TIP

If you were out of the workforce for caregiving duties, you can market that, too. You were skill building. Perhaps you were a "project manager," supervising a team of other caregivers — from nurses to doctors and physical therapists. Maybe you were a "researcher" tracking down the best doctors and medical care. You may have been a "financial manager" in charge of bill paying and insurance claims. Use strong action verbs to describe your caregiving, or other, experience and skills: *directed, facilitated, hired, supervised, controlled, coordinated, executed, organized, planned, implemented, spearheaded, navigated, negotiated, secured,* and *resolved*.

## Tell your story with gusto

As you populate your résumé with job experiences, focus on quantifiable benefits you delivered to your previous employers. You want to say, for instance, that you grew sales by 25 percent or that you completed a project four months ahead of schedule. Résumé-writing pros refer to this as telling your CAR story — *challenge, action,* and *result*.

Talk about a problem you faced, what you did to solve it, and the specific tangible result of your efforts; for example, "Researched market and identified opportunity for a new service, adding a revenue stream that increased profits 15 percent." As much as possible, make your CAR stories relevant to the job you're applying for.

## REAPING THE BENEFITS OF VOLUNTEERING

Extended unemployment, coupled with age discrimination and other barriers, can add to the challenges older workers face in finding a job, as the AARP Public Policy Institute report "The Long Road Back: Struggling to Find Work after Unemployment" found. One excellent way to plug gaps in your résumé, add to your skill set, gain valuable experience, and perhaps even find your way back into the workforce is to volunteer.

Meaningful volunteering can be an excellent way to eventually land a job. You can demonstrate your skills helping out at a nonprofit and then tout your accomplishments when applying for a paid position.

By putting your volunteering on your résumé, you avoid that blank phase of unemployment. To the degree that you can be out in the world applying your skills, volunteering benefits you as well as those you serve.

**TIP**

There is no *I* in résumé. Technically speaking, your résumé is all about you, but what employers really want to know is what you can do for them as reflected in what you've done for past employers. Keep yourself out of your résumé as much as possible, and never use the word *I*. For example, instead of saying, "I managed," just use action verbs in a bullet point: "Managed X project, Oversaw, Created, Designed, Initiated" and so on.

On the other hand, don't be too formal in your writing. Show a little personality and let reviewers hear your voice and the pride you take in your accomplishments. Include relevant metrics and anything that has made you look like a star, including exceeding national or corporate standards and winning awards.

### Highlight additional education and training

If you've had any specialized education and training over the years, include a section for it on your résumé. By adding recent training, education, and certifications, you highlight your commitment to professional development, show that you're current with industry and management trends, and demonstrate an eagerness to learn new things.

Interests, hobbies, activities, and professional memberships can also help you get noticed or even reveal that you're physically and intellectually active. That can be a great way to subtly address any concerns an employer may have that, as an older worker, you don't have the stamina for the job. A shared interest may also create a personal connection with the person reading your résumé.

## Be mindful of automated screening systems

If you're submitting your résumé via an online portal, tweak it to ensure that it makes it past any automated screening system. Here are some tips:

>> **Save your résumé as a .doc or .txt file.** These programs are the most universal and are easy to upload. Use .pdf files when it's listed as preferred or when you want to keep your formatting intact.

>> **List the names of your employers first followed by the dates you worked there.** Some screening systems reject résumés that present the date before the employers.

>> **Add key words and phrases that match those used in the job description of the position you're applying for.** For example, if the job requires knowledge of "Microsoft Office" or "excellent communication skills," make sure those key words and phrases appear in your résumé. If the job requires someone who has "managed" a team, use *managed,* not *directed* or *operated* or any other synonym.

>> **Don't embed charts or images that the screening system can't read.** Keep it simple — text only. But be sure to include hyperlinks or addresses to sites where additional information can be found, such as to your LinkedIn profile or your website, if you have one.

**TIP**

Before submitting your résumé online, check the site to see whether it contains any guidelines, and, if it does, read those guidelines and follow them exactly.

## Avoiding the top seven résumé turnoffs

Knowing what *not* to include in a résumé is almost as important as knowing what *to* include. Remove these résumé red flags right now:

>> **The "Career Objective" section:** Employers don't care about your objectives. They care about theirs. Career objective statements are old-fashioned. Hiring managers say they're immaterial for the initial screening process. It's all about what the company needs, not what you want. You'll have a chance to talk about yourself during the interview.

>> **College or high-school graduation dates:** The fact that you graduated high school or college is important. When you did isn't. Not only are these dates immaterial, but they also age you.

>> **Outdated tech skills:** Being a certified WordPerfect trainer in the 1980s is about as useful now as once knowing how to operate an elevator in the 1950s.

- **Too much personal information:** If you wouldn't want it on the front page of your local newspaper, skip it.

- **"References available upon request":** If you advance in the process, you'll be asked to provide references. For now, this information just takes up valuable space.

- **Quirky job titles:** Although these can be a conversation icebreaker at a networking event, an offbeat title on your résumé can be a turnoff and inappropriate for a more traditional company. A bigger drawback is that the title could eliminate you from a recruiter's search criteria. "Wordsmith," for instance, is unlikely to show up in an Applicant Tracking Systems Search for the specific keyword "editor." "Happiness activist" won't turn up in a search for an experienced "activities director."

- **Misspellings and grammar mistakes:** Proofread, proofread, proofread. Take the time to check your résumé carefully. And then take someone else's time to recheck it. If you wrote it, you're probably too close to it to catch the errors. Read it out loud.

## Airbrushing your résumé

After you've built a solid résumé, take some time to perfect it by highlighting your distinctions and scrubbing it clean of any imperfections. Of course, nobody's perfect, but your résumé should enhance your best features while concealing any blemishes.

### Highlighting distinctions

The old saying "Play to your strengths" applies to résumé writing. Your résumé should place your distinctions front and center and shine the spotlight on them:

- **Use a personal headline instead of a career objective.** Your personal headline describes who you are or who you want to be; for example, Digital Marketing Executive, Senior Financial Analyst, or Information Systems Administrator. Use your current title or the title of the position you're applying for.

- **Play up your experience in the industry.** Employers and recruiters prefer specialists over generalists. They're more likely to choose someone who has deep knowledge and experience in their industry over someone who dabbles in various industries. So if you're experienced in the industry, play it up.

- **Provide links to a portfolio of your expertise.** Hiring managers want to know that you're on top of your game and can deliver the goods. What better way than to show them? Presentations and documents attached and available to download from your LinkedIn profile are a great way to do just that. You can add a line that directs the reader to your portfolio on LinkedIn. (See Chapter 3 in Book 2 for more about using LinkedIn to market yourself.)

## Omitting imperfections

Prospective employers don't expect a résumé that provides full disclosure. They're well aware that the purpose of your résumé is to highlight your qualifications and accomplishments, so feel free to omit less flattering details, including the following:

>> **Jobs that lasted fewer than six months:** These in-and-out jobs make you look like a flight risk at best and a bad bet at worst. If you can't stay with a company for more than a year or two, it might be a sign that you get bored too easily or that you have trouble fitting into the company culture. Take the opportunity to shorten your résumé by omitting these short-lived jobs. Be up front about these jobs, though, if asked about them in an interview.

>> **Gaps in employment:** If the gap is fewer than six months, don't worry about that. However, if you lost a job and decided to take a break to travel, opted out of the job market for a number of years to raise your children, or have been unable to find work for nearly a year, you have some explaining to do. Recruiters and hiring managers want to know what you were up to during that time. See the earlier section "Plug the gaps" for ideas on how to fill in these dead zones.

>> **Unrelated jobs:** If you work in a field unrelated to one you worked in a decade ago, consider excluding the details of that previous work experience. Include only the years and industries in which you worked, but not the specific employers and positions.

>> **Lower-level jobs:** For jobs you held several years ago that are in the same field but don't reflect your current level, keep descriptions brief.

# Tailoring your résumé to specific openings and circumstances

Every résumé you submit should be tailored to the specific organization and position you're applying to. Open your generic résumé and use the Save As feature in your word processor to save the résumé under another name so you can make changes without affecting the original. After you research the organization and read the job description for the position that interests you, create your custom résumé as explained in the following sections.

## Targeting a specific opening

When you're applying for a specific position, pay close attention to the qualifications and responsibilities described in the job ad, and adjust your résumé accordingly. For example, if the employer asks for "strong Excel and report-writing skills," tuck these key expressions somewhere in the narrative of your past work experience. If the firm is looking for a "sales associate" with "a strong customer focus," then include this phrase two or three times. If a firm is hiring a "communications manager" who is "proficient in the use of web technology, social media tools, and metrics" and "understanding of department budgeting," pop these phrases in your story. The aim is to sprinkle the key words into your description of your work experience.

WARNING

Don't go overboard with key words to the point where they sound forced. You may need to perform significant revisions so that the key words and phrases flow naturally.

## Getting found on a job board

When posting your résumé on a job board, use key words and phrases to help potential employers and recruiters find the talent they need. Put yourself in the shoes of prospective employers and recruiters and ask yourself which key words and phrases they're likely to enter when searching for someone with your skills and experience or to fill the type of position you're looking for. Then add these key words and phrases to your résumé. You can work key words into your personal headline, your experience section, or even your education and training section.

## Adjusting for a career change

TIP

When you're looking to change careers, play up your skills, not your positions. Cast a wide net. Look at your skill set and past experience as transferable to many different challenges and fields. Think of this approach as redirecting or redeploying your skills. Although you may need to list past employers, you can tweak your résumé to focus less on positions and more on the skills needed to do the jobs.

Look inside yourself and answer some important questions: What am I best at? Ask friends and colleagues, too. They may notice skills that you take for granted, such as problem solving, conflict resolution, or an ability to work a crowd. What skills have you gathered in your previous positions that would be helpful in another job? You're not reinventing your work; you're redeploying your skills. You *can* transfer skills and experience you've gained from your primary career into a different industry or position. Scan your past for clues to your future. Think about how your skill set may be transferable to other fields, and then show how those skills the employer is looking for are right in your wheelhouse and easily tapped for your new career.

## Returning to the workforce after an extended absence

If you're returning to the workforce after an extended absence, you have no option but to come clean about it and try to explain what exactly you were doing during that time. (See the earlier section "Plug the gaps" for details.)

TIP

Even though life experience and volunteer gigs are valuable, they're not the equivalent of formal training and job experience. When you're returning to the workforce after an extended absence, try to highlight any education and training you pursued during that time. If you didn't receive any specialized education and training, now is the time to start. Head to Chapter 2 in Book 2 for guidance on getting the training and skills you need to remain competitive in the job market.

## Making use of key word searches

Key words are the industry-specific terms necessary to get attention. By placing them in your résumé, you can get more attention. Try these techniques:

>> Sprinkle key words throughout the résumé.

>> Use them when referring to job titles, accomplishments, experience, skills, education, career objectives, and training.

>> Use the exact key words and language that the employer uses in the job posting.

# Knowing where to go for résumé-writing help

If your résumé isn't getting the response you desire, consider hiring a certified résumé writer. You may be highly qualified to perform tasks that few people on this earth can do and simply fall short when it comes to résumé writing or specifically writing your own résumé. You can spend zillions of hours trying to perfect your copy and still can't get noticed by an employer or recruiter.

TIP

You can find certified résumé writers through Career Directors International (www.careerdirectors.com) or the National Résumé Writers Association (thenrwa.org/). You may be able to deduct the cost of preparing your résumé from your federal taxes. If you're a college graduate, check with your college career center to see whether it offers free résumé services. Another option is to seek the assistance of a career counselor, coach, or consultant to help you write your résumé as well as help you hone your job-search skills and strategies. You can also check out www.aarp.org/work for résumé examples and best practices.

# Writing a Killer Cover Letter

The importance of the cover letter varies by organization. Many large organizations, including corporations and universities, forgo the cover letter and use automated systems to process résumés and match candidates to needs within their organizations. For others, the cover letter is a key component of the application and is used as an acid test to determine how well a candidate understands the needs of the organization and can communicate in writing. For these organizations, your cover letter is the key that opens the door for your résumé.

**REMEMBER**

Unless the job posting states otherwise or you're submitting your résumé on a site that includes no option for including a cover letter, always include a cover letter with your résumé. This is your chance to sell yourself! A well-crafted cover letter demonstrates what you bring to the organization and why you're the best candidate for the job. It showcases your skills, experience, and achievements and highlights their relevance to the organization's needs.

**TIP**

Do your homework. Read the job description of the position you're applying for. Research the industry and your prospective employer. Visit the company's website. Visit the websites of the company's top competitors. Visit Glassdoor and ZoomInfo where you can dig up additional information. Find out who your supervisor is likely to be and look up the person on LinkedIn. If you need to get past a hiring manager, try to find out who that person is and look them up on LinkedIn. The more you know about your audience, the better able you are to appeal to that individual on a personal level.

## Drafting your cover letter

Structuring or outlining your cover letter is the first order of business. Having an outline in place ensures that you present your message in an organized way and cover all the essentials. Your cover letter should be no longer than one page and typically organized by using the following three sections:

>> **Introduction:** In the first paragraph, tell the employer what job you're applying for, why you're applying for it, and (if applicable) who referred you. For example, "Your need for a detail-oriented person with years of experience in strategic communication is precisely what I am in a position to offer and is timed perfectly for my decision to pursue my goal of working for [organization name]."

**WARNING**

Avoid boring, overused opening lines, such as "I am writing to submit my résumé for the position of . . . ."

>> **Body:** Briefly describe your skills in a way that matches your talents to the needs of the organization. Use this opportunity to highlight training, education, and skills mentioned in your résumé that are particularly relevant to the position you're applying for and the organization's needs.

TIP

Try writing an *elevator pitch* — a pithy 30-second summary of who you are, what you do, and what you'd like to do professionally. Doing so will make you feel more confident in your job search, and you can use elements of your elevator speech in your cover letter.

>> **Conclusion:** In the last paragraph, tie in your résumé and express your eagerness to meet with the person to discuss your qualifications and the organization's needs in greater detail. For example, you may write something like, "For additional details, please refer to my résumé (attached). I look forward to the opportunity to meet with you in person to discuss the position and my qualifications in greater depth."

TIP

Be specific without going into too much detail. Think of your letter as a carefully planned appetizer that whets the reader's appetite for the main course — served up in your résumé.

## Fine-tuning your cover letter

After drafting your cover letter, print it, read it closely, and revise it to optimize its impact. Here are a few suggestions on how to fine-tune your cover letter:

>> **Address your letter to a specific person, not just a title or department.** You may need to do some research or call the organization to find out the name of the person who's in charge of filling the position or screening applicants.

>> **In the first paragraph, refer to the specific position you're applying for,** including a reference code if the job description provides one.

>> **Include key words and phrases in your cover letter that match those used in your résumé,** just in case the organization uses an automated system for screening cover letters and résumés.

>> **Write short paragraphs or use a bulleted list to present details.** Leaving plenty of white space makes your cover letter more inviting and easier to read.

>> **Be clear, direct, and terse.** For example, instead of writing, "As was mentioned in the job description for this position, your company is in need of a team-oriented individual with a background in marketing and communications. As you can see from the details in my résumé, my qualifications make

me perfectly suited to that position," write something like this, "Your company needs a team player with experience in marketing and communications. I am that person."

>> **Share your cover letter with friends who will give you their frank reactions.** Does your letter feel intriguing? Does it make the reader want to know more about you? If not, revise it in light of the feedback you receive.

>> **Purge your prose of spelling and grammar errors.** Proofread your cover letter several times and have someone else proofread it as well.

## Avoiding common mistakes

Here is a list of common mistakes you should avoid when writing a cover letter:

>> **Don't send out a generic cover letter regardless of position.** Instead, tailor each cover letter (and résumé) to the specific position.

>> **Don't waste space on phrases such as "I am writing to . . . " or "Let me introduce myself."** Get to the point.

>> **Don't merely repeat the contents of your résumé.** Instead, highlight your skills and achievements that address the organization's needs and qualifications for the position.

>> **Don't call attention to your age by citing your 20, 30, or 40 years of experience.** Instead, use words like *extensive* or *significant* to describe your experience.

>> **Don't include your salary requirements unless the organization specifically requests this information.** Save the salary discussion until you're close to being offered the job.

# Lining Up Your References in Advance

A prospective employer is likely to ask for professional references to confirm your previous employment and to get a sense of what kind of employee you are. They may also ask for personal references to get a bead on the kind of person you are outside of work. Some employers may ask for the exact number of years you've known someone and in what capacity — for example, a previous manager or coworker you've known for more than five years.

Prior to applying for any openings, choose four or five people willing to serve as references. Here are some suggestions for picking and contacting references:

>> Create a list of possible references by reviewing those you've worked with and even volunteered alongside. Bosses, coworkers, professors, and former customers and clients are good choices, but be certain they think favorably of you or are at least neutral about your job performance with their organization. Keep in mind that many employers have policies that reference checkers can only focus on verifying facts and managers must refer requests to the HR Department. So what you're asking for may require someone to break from the "official" policy.

>> Contact your references before you hand over their contact information to see if they're willing to vouch for you. You may need to refresh your reference's recall about the job you held while working with them. If your potential reference is on board, then ask what times and what phone number is best for someone to reach them.

>> When listing a previous employer, confirm with human resources that all information in your personnel file is accurate.

>> Give your references some background on the potential employer, why you're interested in the position, and why you think your skills are a good fit. Forward them a copy of your résumé and the job description, so they're prepared.

>> Let your references know every time you share their contact information with a prospective employer.

>> Each time your reference supports you with a new prospective employer, take the time to send a thank-you letter or at the very least an email message. It's good manners and will keep the good juju flowing.

>> If you land the job, call or email your references and thank them again. You might even spring for lunch or a cup of coffee and pass along your new contact information.

TIP

If you know that a reference check will be an electronic one, let your references know and review how they might check those boxes. It's human nature to answer more coldly when responding to an electronic questionnaire. When asked to rate a person's reliability on a scale of one to five, a reference might check four, thinking that's an honest appraisal, but that four can sink your chances of landing the job. Let your references know of the risks so they can take those risks into consideration when entering their responses.

## DO EMPLOYERS ACTUALLY CONTACT REFERENCES?

After hearing stories of con artists with only high-school educations landing jobs as airline pilots or doctors, you may start to wonder whether employers ever really check an applicant's references or credentials. Research shows they do.

According to a Society for Human Resource Management (SHRM) survey, more than eight of ten human resource professionals said that they regularly conduct reference checks for professional (89 percent), executive (85 percent), administrative (84 percent), and technical (81 percent) positions. And here's what most of them want to know:

- Did you really work the dates you said you did?
- Would a former employer hire you back?
- What are your strengths and weaknesses, and how might they apply to the job at hand?

Chapter **6**

# Acing Your Job Interview

You researched the organization and perhaps the people who'll be interviewing you, prepared responses to common questions, practiced answering questions, and put together a few questions of your own. Now, it's show time, your opportunity to deliver the performance of your life and win the hearts and minds of the small audience that's about to decide whether you have a future with the organization.

Before you take the stage, read through this chapter for additional coaching and stage direction. You'll find out how to make a good first impression, answer and ask questions with ease, avoid serious blunders that could very well sink your chances of landing the job or getting a second interview, deliver your best performance in phone and video interviews, and follow up with a thank-you note that's likely to result in a curtain call.

## Making a Positive Impression

Every career coach will tell you the importance of making a positive first impression. Don't wait until the interview formally begins; make a positive impression from the time you show up to several days after you step out the door. You want to dazzle the interviewers with your grace and sophistication throughout the interview while you present yourself as the best candidate for the job in terms of knowledge, skills, and experience. By the time the interview wraps up, your interviewers should be looking forward enthusiastically to your future with the organization.

The following sections offer guidance on making a good first impression and building on that throughout the interview.

## Feeling your best

TIP

A one-hour interview can feel like a marathon, so have something to eat and drink prior to the interview. Here are other recommendations:

>> **Eat a high-protein breakfast.** Avoid sugary or starchy foods, such as doughnuts or even bread, that tend to give you a quick sugar high and then can make you feel exhausted during the interview.

>> **Drink water to stay hydrated but not too much.** You don't want to have to use the bathroom 15 minutes into the interview. Limit caffeine the day of and even the night before the interview. One cup of coffee or tea in the morning is fine.

>> **If you feel better after exercise, perform your normal exercise routine before showering and getting dressed for your interview.** Exercise can help you work out some anxiety and make you feel more vibrant and relaxed at the same time.

## Getting groomed and dressed

Maybe it's been awhile since you've been on a first date, but you no doubt recall the preparation process — the trimming and primping, the showering and shaving, and carefully choosing an outfit to wear, including the right shoes. Although you want to look more professional than alluring as you prepare for a job interview, practice the same attention to detail as you did or do when preparing for a first date. You want to look your very best.

TIP

If it's been awhile since you had to look your best, you may have gotten yourself into a style rut. You don't want to step into an interview as though you just stepped out of a time machine from the '80s or '90s. Make sure you have a fashionable new suit, shoes, hairstyle, and glasses (if you wear them). You don't have to dress like Gen Z, but do dress in style of the times.

Here are a few additional tips:

>> **Lean toward more formal garb.** Even if the office dress code is "business casual" or you're told that everyone wears jeans and sneakers, dress more formally.

>> **Shine your shoes.** If your shoes are scuffed, buy new shoes or pay for a professional's elbow grease. Skip the super-high heels and open-toe shoes. You do want polished footwear, though.

>> **Take the time to really look in the mirror before you head out.** A quick pit stop in the office building's restroom, or the coffee shop next door, before you enter the firm's actual domain is a good idea. Check for rogue dog or cat hairs, missed buttons, undone zippers, and bits of bagel in your teeth.

## Arriving early

Don't be late. Your interview starts long before you shake hands. Arrive 10 to 15 minutes early. It's more than a case of punctuality. When you arrive early, you have a chance to center yourself. It removes one layer of stress. If you're skating in under the bell, it's probably evident in your startled eyes, hurried appearance, and damp handshake.

## Pumping yourself up just prior to the interview

As you're sitting in the lobby waiting to be called in for your interview, take some slow, deep breaths and say to yourself, "I will do the very best I can." Give yourself a pep talk. Run through your selling points and why you're the best candidate for the position. Remind yourself that you're here to team up with the interviewers to find out whether you're a good fit for the organization and it's a good fit for you; it's not just about selling yourself to the organization. Relax. Smile.

TIP

Approach this meeting as you would a conversation with someone you want to know better and whom you want to know more about you. Look forward to the interview, not with a sense of dread, but with enthusiasm. This is an opportunity to meet and get to know a new colleague, someone who shares your goals and is committed, as you are, to the organization's success. You're teaming up with your interviewers to find out whether you and your prospective employer are a good match. You're allies, not adversaries.

# Beginning the interview at the door

Begin your interview at the door. Greet the receptionist with the same respect as the person who will be interviewing you. You're on stage from the instant you state your name at the front desk. Most one-on-one job interviews last between 25 and 30 minutes, so your total on-site performance time is precious. Because it's short and sweet, milk every minute of it, from your time in the waiting room onward.

TIP

Don't spend your time in the on-deck area gabbing on your cell, for example, or responding to emails or checking social media. Focus on why you're there. It's okay to review a list of questions you want to ask. Soak up the office atmosphere. Look around. It will give you clues as to whether this is a place you want to hang your hat.

# Fine-tuning your delivery

If you haven't engaged in a job interview for some time, you may feel awkward, not knowing how to greet your interviewers, what to say, or even how to behave. You don't want to be overly self-conscious and stiff, nor do you want to be too chummy. Here are a few suggestions on how to handle various stages and aspects of the interview process:

>> **Start with a relaxed meet and greet.** Step up with a firm one-handed handshake. Two hands can be a little forthright and maybe even too familiar.

>> **Kick off the first few minutes of your interview as you would a conversation with someone you just met at a reception.** Keep it relaxed and conversational but not too personal. Some standard advice: Commenting on wall décor or a desk accessory is acceptable, but saying you like someone's tie or shoes may be stepping over the line.

TIP

Consider scanning wall and desk photographs to see whether you can find a common bond. For example, a framed image of a child, pet, or landscape may set an instant connection for you. These initial moments are where the chemistry between the interviewer and you can spark. Think speed dating.

>> **Offer a copy of your résumé before you sit down.** Presenting your résumé to an interviewer is akin to bringing a gift to a host. You're passing along something of value in exchange for the invitation to meet and for the person's time. By handing over your résumé in the opening moments of the interview, you make it an interactive asset, a conversation piece. If you want to emphasize or explain certain areas or responsibilities, the interview is your chance to draw attention to them.

People often think if something is on their résumé, the significance is clear to the interviewer, but those bullet points don't always speak for themselves. You may need to call them out and draw the lines that connect your qualifications to the requirements for the position. See Chapter 5 in Book 2 for more information on polishing your résumé.

>> **Follow the leader.** Sync up with the interviewer's rhythm. Don't try too hard or talk too fast. Answer concisely and in a confident, calm manner. Pause before you respond — even repeat the question if need be — to buy yourself some moments to gather a measured response.

>> **Listen and formulate relevant responses.** Keep focused on your interviewers and the reality that you're sitting in that chair to sell solutions to their problems or challenges. Don't be thinking ahead to what you want to say next about yourself. The interview is about them and their needs and how you can help serve those needs. It's not about you. Listen closely to what they're saying.

>> **Keep answers terse and to the point.** Crisp, relevant answers allow interviewers to ask all their questions and gather as much knowledge about you as possible. Aim toward answering each question in two minutes or less.

Keep your message focused on your three key selling points — why you're the best person for the position. Three key points are generally easy to remember and stick to.

## Shaping up with posture and body language

What you say and how you say it are important, but you also need to focus on what your body is doing and saying while your ears are listening and your mouth is talking. Follow these suggestions:

>> **Sit up straight.** No slouching. Breathe in and out slowly and deeply, and relax.

>> **Maintain eye contact.** A clear, direct gaze portrays candor and sincerity, but don't stare, because that can be creepy. Glance up or over every so often as you carefully consider a point, or shift your focus from one eye to the other to the person's mouth and then back to the eyes every five to ten seconds.

>> **Lean forward to show interest.** When the interviewer begins to answer a question you asked, lean slightly forward to show interest.

>> **Keep hand gestures to a minimum in both frequency and amplitude.** If you've got a point you want to play up, a hand gesture is fine. For most of the

interview, though, keep your hands laced together with your thumbs on top, resting calmly in your lap or propped lightly on the arms of the chair or the table in front of you. Pressing your fingertips together in a steeple formation is also a simple sign of self-assurance, but don't overdo it.

>> **Avoid stroking your neck or throat, which can make you look nervous.** A confident, loose (unclenched) fist lightly tucked under your chin is okay in small doses.

>> **Don't cross your arms over your chest.** You may think this makes you look serious, but it can come off as a defensive stance.

>> **Avoid twisting and spinning your pen, hair, rings, necklace, or bracelets.** You may do this unconsciously, so be mindful of what your hands are up to. For an interviewer, it sends off a signal of nerves or even anxiety.

## Interviewing with a younger hiring manager

When interviewing with a younger hiring manager, treat the person as a colleague and not as a mentee:

>> **Focus on the organization's current and future needs.** You may be the deal of the century for the organization based on your past accomplishments, but focus less on those and more on how your experience and skills meet the organization's current and future needs.

>> **Don't cop an attitude.** For example, don't try to tell them why the job description is faulty or unrealistic in some way. If you feel more qualified than the interviewer, hide that fact. Try not to be condescending or professorial.

>> **Let go of any resentment at being in this position.** Having to prove yourself to someone less experienced or skilled than yourself bruises the ego. You can't fix that, and if you try to bury your resentment, it'll bubble up to the surface, so let it go.

>> **Don't be a fuddy-duddy.** Avoid reminiscing about the good old days or complaining about anything, especially the current state of the industry or culture. Don't suggest that something a hiring manager says is like something your children would say; don't chat about details that date you, such as the grandkids' birthdays; and don't start a sentence with "When I was your age. . . ."

>> **Find common ground.** Even if you and your interviewers are literally generations apart, you can find common ground by focusing on the needs of the organization.

TIP

Prep yourself for the interview by including plenty of people in your professional network who are younger than you, so you can tune into the needs, interests, and qualities of the millennials you may be working for. Reverse-mentoring is another useful approach. You'll have more success interviewing with people younger than you if you network with younger people and treat them as your peers on a regular basis.

# Preparing to Answer and Ask Questions

Interviews are extended Q&A sessions, which makes them difficult to prepare for because you never really know what questions will be asked or which direction the interview will turn. By preparing answers to questions in several different categories, however, you place your brain in Q&A mode and dredge up information buried deep in your memory banks that enables you to more nimbly field a wide variety of questions.

The following sections lead you through the Q&A preparation process, so you're prepared to answer some of the most common and uncommon questions and have a few questions of your own.

TIP

Engage in a few mock interviews. Although you can't anticipate every question an interviewer may ask, you can improve your speed and responsiveness. Think of it as playing shortstop in baseball. You never know how fast or at what angle the ball is coming at you, but if you field enough balls, you develop the instinct required to catch anything hit in your direction.

## Answering general questions

The following sections reveal common questions interviewers may ask, and even if they don't, these are good questions to ask yourself and answer prior to the interview.

REMEMBER

Keep your answers short, especially when talking about yourself and your experiences. An interview is all about the company. Interviewers don't want to know your life story, just that you have one and are eager, smart, open to learning, and skilled in ways that will advance the organization.

### What are your hobbies and interests?

This is a great time to show your passion for something you love. Talk enthusiastically about your hobbies, interests, and causes. Passion is appealing and youthful, regardless of your age. When prospective employers notice a twinkle in your eye as you describe your outside interests, they're drawn to you as a candidate and more likely to offer you the job.

TIP

If possible, research your interviewers prior to the interview to find out about their interests, hobbies, and causes. You may even find a common connection or an interest you share that gives you an opportunity to connect with an interviewer on a personal level.

## How do you learn best?

This is your chance to pull back the curtains on what makes you tick, the kind of work scenario that will help you shine and, in turn, help the organization succeed. Identifying your learning style is important, because whether you learn best independently or collaboratively, it helps your future employer determine where you fit best in the organization. A good fit is mutually beneficial.

## How would you solve the following problem . . . ?

You can't possibly anticipate the specific problem the interviewer will describe, so try to think up a few work-related problems you solved in the past. Come up with CAR stories — challenge, action, and result. Think of problems the industry is facing right now and how you would go about solving those problems. When answering the question, you don't actually need to come up with a solution. All you need is a strategy for solving the problem; for example, you may gather information, assemble a team, brainstorm solutions, and so on.

TIP

Pause. Don't make rapid off-the-top-of-your-head answers. This isn't *Jeopardy!*. There's no race to push the buzzer. Rattling off the first answer that pops into your head may come off as flippant. Give yourself a little time to mull it over before giving your answer.

## Identify inefficiencies in a process the company uses

Be careful here. Interviewers want to know that you're not wearing rose-colored glasses and can offer a critical analysis. They aren't paying you yet, so point out operations that could be streamlined without offering a specific solution. Show that you have some ideas but hold them close to your vest. It's okay to be a little coy here.

## Have you ever had to persuade other people who were not your direct reports to do something?

"Absolutely" should be your answer. And then give a quick and to-the-point example. You should have this one prepared ahead of time to illustrate your ability to communicate with people and get results even when someone doesn't have to listen to you. Be prepared to answer these two follow-up questions:

>> How did you do it?

>> What were the consequences?

## How have you managed or worked with difficult personalities in the past?

A good answer to this question is that you've found that it's not so much that people are difficult as it is that situations are challenging. By using certain communication strategies, you can often diffuse tension and turn the focus from anger and blame to collaborating on how to resolve the underlying issues or problems. Point out that sometimes what seems to be a difficult personality in the workplace can be caused by a problem outside the workplace that needs to be resolved. Be prepared to give an example.

**REMEMBER**

Of course, this is only one possible answer to this question, but whatever answer you give, you want to show that you recognize the challenges of group dynamics and the complexities that underlie interpersonal conflict — that you're not prone to making snap judgments.

## Give me a tour of your life

Start at the beginning and narrate your highlight reel. Touch on key events in your life. The challenge here is to keep it short. Be prepared with an elevator pitch.

## Tell me three things about how you define yourself

This is a good opportunity to focus on your skills. Spin your answer to explain how your skills, strengths, experience, and goals relate to the company and the position you're interviewing for.

## When you're not at work, what two things do you do better than anybody else?

Without boasting, explain what you're really good at. Maybe you're the idea person, the efficiency expert, the go-to person when something needs done, or the staffer who calms everyone down when tensions rise.

## What am I not going to like about you in 90 days?

One answer to this question is this: "If I thought there was something you weren't going to like about me in 90 days, I wouldn't waste your time by being here. I really think we're a good match." Other options include humor or pointing out a strength as though it's a weakness; for example, if you're being hired to cut costs, you could say something like "My husband seems to think I'm overly frugal."

## What do you think you're not going to like about me?

Wow!, Talk about a loaded question. Humor can come in handy here with an answer such as "Maybe that you ask too many difficult questions." You could also answer, "If I thought there was something I wouldn't like about you, this interview would be a whole lot shorter. I really think we're a good match." Whatever you do, keep your response positive.

## If this interview were reversed and you were interviewing me, what would you be looking for from me?

This is all you. Think about your ideal supervisor. What qualities in that person would you value most? Perhaps you're looking for a supervisor who values your opinion, doesn't micromanage, and provides you with the resources to do your job properly. Or maybe you prefer a supervisor you can work with in close collaboration to improve the department's strategic success.

# Responding to tough questions for people over 50

As a 50-plus job seeker, expect at least a few questions about your age, even if they don't directly reference your age. While potential employers are concerned about your age and how it may affect your job performance, they probably won't come right out and say it because they fear an age-discrimination lawsuit. Here are a few common, age-related questions interviewers may ask.

## Are you up-to-date with the latest technology?

Your research about the company and the position should reveal the technology you need to know to do the job. Check the job description if you're unsure. Mention your knowledge and experience in terms of those technologies along with any other technologies you know that could be beneficial in that position.

## Aren't you overqualified for the job?

Interviewers ask this question because they're afraid you'll be bored with the job, dissatisfied with the pay, or difficult to manage because you know or think you know more than your supervisors. Develop an answer that allays these fears. You may say something like the following:

> At this point in my career, I'm looking for a position I feel overqualified to do, so I can do the job to the best of my abilities and perhaps bring additional skills to the table that may be of use. I know the risks of hiring overqualified candidates who run roughshod over a department, and I can assure you that's not going to happen with me. I'm very willing to let someone else take the reins and make the big decisions, so I can focus on doing what I'm most passionate about.

## Why have you been out of work for so long?

Be candid when answering this question. Perhaps you took a leave of absence from the workforce to raise your kids or care for an elderly parent and then had a tough time getting back into the workforce. If you worked as a contractor during your absence or you acquired additional training and skills, be sure to mention these.

## What is your greatest strength?

When answering this question, think in the context of the position and job responsibilities. Find a strength, perhaps not your greatest strength, that will best serve the organization's needs. This may be your ability to solve problems, manage a team, or identify areas of inefficiency.

## Would you be comfortable working for a lower salary than you had in your last job? Why?

Nobody wants to work for *less* money, and you can admit this freely, but as an older worker, you have the perfect answer to this question (assuming the answer is relevant to your situation) — at this point in your career, you're looking for more than just a paycheck. You're looking for _____. Fill in the blank. Perhaps you've always wanted to work in the industry, you're looking forward to learning new skills, you love the company and its mission and want to contribute in some way, and so on. Don't say you don't care about the money. Say you care more about something else.

## Have you ever worked for a younger boss? How did you make it work?

Even if you've never been supervised by someone younger than you, you need to have an answer to this one. Scour your past for times when you worked for or alongside younger people. You may point out that everyone has different knowledge and skills that aren't dependent on age. Focus on what young people have taught you or are capable of teaching you. Don't get into how much you can offer younger people, because that's probably what the interviewer fears — you trying to take the leadership role with a younger supervisor.

# Thinking over career and industry questions

Certain questions may focus on the industry in general and on your career goals. This section covers a few common questions to get you thinking about these areas.

## What led you to move from one job to the next?

Have some fun with this question as you spin your own career path tale of how you've been challenged and excited and energized with each move. Focus on how the transitions challenged you intellectually and how with each change you were energized and ramped up your skills, growing and stretching and contributing to your employer's bottom line.

## What are your thoughts on where the industry is heading?

No one can predict the future, but employers want someone who's thinking about it every day. Be prepared to discuss the major players in the industry and the challenges they face. Information is readily available on the internet via general web and Google News searches, which is one reason researching the company and the industry prior to your interview is so important.

TIP

Try to identify challenges and problems in the industry and think of creative approaches that may help solve them. For example, an oil and gas company could hire a certain firm to clean up and digitize its land records to boost revenue.

## Where do you see yourself in ten years?

Employers are looking to hire people who are eager to advance in their careers in some way. They want someone who's motivated and has career goals and a strategy for achieving them. Studies show that if you fall into this category, you'll be more motivated, engaged, and productive. There's really no correct response, but it's not going to do you any good to say, "I haven't given it much thought." Also avoid saying anything about retirement. Think in terms of future career goals or challenges you'd like to take on.

## Answering the salary question

When asked about salary in an interview, the best response is to say that although the position is not precisely the same as your last job, you would need to understand your duties and responsibilities in order to establish a fair salary for the job. If pressed to be more specific, ask what the salary range is and factor that in your response. So if the salary range is $50,000 to $60,000 and you want to make at least $55,000, you're probably best off asking for something between, say, $55,000 and $60,000.

Sometimes, if you're working with a recruiter hired by the company, you can be more frank about salary than if you're dealing directly with the hiring manager. Recruiters know what the market demands and may be able to go back to the employer and say that your salary figure is reasonable.

And finally, think beyond salary. If you're hitting up against a salary deal breaker, take a breath and think creatively. Try asking for salary review in six months, tuition reimbursement, parking allowance, transportation passes, or extra vacation days.

**REMEMBER**

Don't take lower-than-expected pay personally. Employers base a salary on the requirements of the job, the availability of qualified job candidates, and their budget, not on what you were paid in the past. Knowing what you're willing to accept is important; if it's outside the range the employer is willing to pay, then say so and move on.

## Preparing a few questions of your own

Much of what makes a great job interview is intuitive. It's chemistry between you and your interviewer(s). When asked whether you have any questions, you have an opportunity to reveal more about yourself and what you're looking for and to demonstrate that you can ask intelligent, challenging questions.

**TIP**

Be respectful, but ask tough questions. Obvious, safe questions make you seem ho-hum compared to other candidates and reveal that you haven't done your research. Challenging questions indicate that you know what you want, you're committed to finding the right fit (not just any old job), and you're smart. In addition, interviewers will remember you for challenging them when other candidates chose to play it safe.

The following sections offer ten questions to consider asking and several questions you should never ask.

## Eight questions to consider asking

Here are eight questions to consider asking and to spark your own imagination to come up with additional questions.

>> **Why did *you* choose this company?** The answer to this question helps you size up the company from the perspective of someone who works there. Variations of this question include "What challenges make you excited to come to work each day?" and "What do you like the most about working here?" These questions let somebody see that you're genuinely attracted to the job and decide whether the company is a good fit for you.

>> **How would I exceed your expectations on a short-term basis, say in the first 30 to 60 days on the job?** This is a great question, because it conveys your eagerness to start and your commitment to serving the organization's needs while providing you with insight into the tasks and challenges you'll be facing if you get the job.

>> **What qualities do your very best employees have in common?** Again, this question expresses your desire to take the position only if it's in the best interest of the organization, while the answer gives you a clear idea of what you'll need to do to succeed as an employee.

>> **Is there anything about me, my skills, or my background that you would like me to clarify?** This question shows that you want the company to make a well-informed hiring decision, plus it gives you the opportunity to talk about your skills and other qualities you bring to the table that may not have been mentioned yet.

>> **Does the company encourage entrepreneurship?** An increasing number of companies large and small are offering workers the freedom, flexibility, and resources to work as an entrepreneur within the organization. The buzzword for it: *intrapreneurship*. An employer or manager who creates a work environment that encourages and supports entrepreneurial culture and opportunities for work on projects outside your direct responsibility can make a huge difference in your happiness at work.

>> **What types of mentoring programs do you offer?** You may go a step further and add that you enjoy mentoring younger workers, and you've also benefited from pairing up with a younger worker who reverse-mentors you — offering help with technology, social media, and so on. This shows you're hip to the underlying perception of intergenerational tension in the workplace. It also demonstrates your willingness to work with younger

coworkers. And it shows that you're comfortable reporting to a boss who may be younger than you.

>> **What's the salary range for this position?** Preface this question by saying that your interest in the position doesn't revolve around money, but you would be interested in knowing what the range is.

Expect a pause and then a ballpark figure. Try not to show delight or disappointment. This isn't a time to negotiate or even to indicate whether the range is acceptable. Save that for the negotiating table, after you get a formal offer.

If the interviewer deflects or struggles to answer, reply smoothly, without missing a beat, that you're looking forward to learning more details when the interviewer is free to share them in your next discussion.

>> **Is full-time the only option, or would you consider a contract or consulting arrangement?** Ask this question only if you're open to such an arrangement; otherwise, you may be giving a prospective employer a reason not to hire you for a permanent position. A contracting or consulting arrangement enables you to pursue your passion while perhaps avoiding some of the less attractive responsibilities of the position.

## Questions you should never ask

**WARNING**

While you're keenly focused on putting your best foot forward and asking smart and sometimes tough questions, it's oh-so-easy to say something that could knock you out of the running. When an awkward question slips through your lips, even the smoothest of interviews can go south. Here are some examples of questions you should steer clear of in interviews.

>> **Does my age concern you?** When you're interviewing for a job and you're over 50, you're painfully aware that ageism is alive and well in many workplaces, but this question is likely to make your interviewers uncomfortable. Instead, ask if they have any concerns about your skills or experience.

>> **Will I be working for someone younger than me?** This question is a red flag indicating that you may have trouble working with or for someone who's younger than you. The best option is to accept the fact that you'll probably have a younger boss. If that's a deal breaker, then, as you get closer to getting the job offer, ask to meet with your potential boss and the team you'll be working with. This approach enables you to subtly obtain the information you need without making an issue out of it.

>> **Can you tell me about your company's benefits?** Don't put the horse before the cart, at least not during your initial interview. Save this question for when you're negotiating the offer.

>> **What training is provided?** Most employers want to hire people who can hit the ground running, not people they have to train and carefully supervise.

>> **How long will it take to get promoted?** The employer is looking to fill a current need, so focus on getting the position first. If you feel compelled to ask about promotions, talk in terms of career paths within the organization, and keep the focus on meeting the organization's needs.

>> **Can I bring my dog to work?** Sure, there are pet-friendly workplaces, but it's probably not worth bringing up unless you see other pooches roaming the hallways.

# Avoiding the Most Serious Missteps

When you're looking for a job, you have a lot on your mind and may be more prone to making mistakes that undermine your efforts. Here are the top mistakes to avoid:

>> **Showing up late:** Punctuality is a soft job skill that employers rank high on their list of deal killers. Showing up late is a big hurdle to overcome unless you have a great reason.

>> **Failing to prepare:** Unless your prospective employer has actively recruited you, you need to show up having done your research about the company and the industry.

>> **Acting arrogant:** Humility rules the day. Employers want people on their team who work well with others and don't hold themselves above anyone else. You should be confident and have swagger, but never go egotistic. If you believe in yourself, you don't need this haughty crutch.

>> **Dropping names:** It's okay to name names of people you may know in common or those big players in your industry whom you've worked with recently, but, in general, this technique is a turnoff and reeks of insecurity.

>> **Bringing up compensation too early:** Wait for signs that the organization wants you before thinking about how much they're willing to pay to get you. Besides, if you bring up the topic too soon, you may end up low-balling yourself.

>> **Focusing too much on yourself:** Focus not on what your employer can do for you. Focus on what you can do for your employer. After your prospective employer decides that you're the best candidate for the job, you can shift your focus to getting what *you* want.

>> **Not being engaging enough:** Although you don't want to chatter away about yourself for any extended amount of time, being stiff and standoffish is just as bad. This is a two-way street. Take the time to dance.

>> **Giving long-winded answers:** Crisp, relevant answers demonstrate efficiency in thought and language. You want to show a potential employer that you're decisive, organized, and clear-thinking.

>> **Misrepresenting the facts:** You have nothing to gain from embellishing or massaging the truth, whether it pertains to past jobs and responsibilities, graduation dates, experience, or simply your age. Honesty is nothing to play around with. After being caught in a lie, you may not be able to restore your credibility or regain your composure.

>> **Not following up:** This is like not calling after a first date. When employers don't hear back from you, they assume that you're not all that interested. (Find out more about following up later in this chapter.)

>> **Backing out of an accepted offer:** This is unprofessional and can come back to haunt you if another employer gets wind of it. Moreover, it portrays you as someone who's fickle and somewhat dishonest.

# Managing Alternative Interview Formats

The world of interviewing has changed quite a bit probably since you were last out pounding the pavement. For employers, telephone and video interviews can cut the amount of time and travel expenses spent recruiting. But for you, the new ballgame may add tensions to an already nerve-wracking process. Without that in-person connection, communicating your enthusiasm and other less tangible qualities can be quite challenging.

The key to performing well in less traditional interview formats is to know what to expect and to practice, so you're comfortable with these formats. The following sections explain what to anticipate and how to successfully navigate these different interview formats.

**REMEMBER**

Regardless of interview setting, preparation is essential to optimizing your performance. You need to do your homework, prepare questions of your own, and rehearse.

# Acing the telephone interview

To improve your performance on a telephone interview, follow these suggestions:

>> **Pick a quiet location.** Find a comfortable place without distractions from people, pets, music, and street noise. Inform everyone in the household that you're going to be on a very important phone call and are not to be disturbed.

>> **Mute the speakers on your computer.** You don't want anything ringing or dinging in the background.

>> **Lay out a copy of your résumé and the job description.** You may need to refer to details from these documents during the call, but don't read off of them, because reading can sound stiff.

>> **Have paper and pen handy.** Jot down notes during the conversation, if that helps you follow the conversation and keep track of what's been said. But if note-taking interferes with your ability to listen and respond, then keep your note-taking to a minimum. You should still have paper and pen handy, just in case.

>> **Have a drink nearby.** A glass of water is best or a cup of coffee or tea if you're looking for a little caffeine bump. Keeping your whistle wet helps you steer clear of throat clearing, which is awkward and ruins the flow of conversation. And if you haven't said anything in a while, warm up your voice before the phone rings.

>> **Smile.** Interviewers can hear a smile over the phone. You'll sound upbeat and convey a sense that you're happy to have the opportunity to discuss the opening. Smile especially when you answer the phone and greet the caller, when you talk about your work and what you're passionate about, and when you ask questions about the company.

TIP

Put a mirror in front of yourself, so you can make sure you're smiling.

>> **Pay attention to your posture.** Stand or sit up straight during the call. Some people find their voice sounds stronger and more energetic standing up. You may even choose to walk while the interviewer is talking.

>> **Be ready to go ten minutes ahead of time.** You don't want to sound hurried.

>> **Answer professionally.** When the phone rings, smile, and greet the caller with something like, "Hi, this is [name]." If you know who's calling, consider following up with "Is this [name]?" Don't try to pretend that you don't know who's calling, because that can make you sound phony.

>> **Listen carefully before you speak.** Pause before you answer to gather your thoughts. Then talk. Try to answer each question in two minutes or less.

Otherwise, your interviewer may tune out. Because you can't see the person, it's tempting to fill in any pauses in the conversation, but rein it in.

>> **Enunciate your words and don't speak too fast.** Projecting your voice distinctly and enthusiastically is fundamental.

>> **Avoid fillers such as "like," "you know," and "um."** Use precise language to communicate your thoughts. Remind yourself that short pauses are acceptable and much preferred over fillers that can make you sound less sophisticated.

>> **End on an up note.** If you really want the job, finish your conversation by saying, "Thanks for the call. I'm very interested in what we've discussed today and would appreciate the opportunity to meet you in person. What's the next step?" Think of this as your call to action.

# Exceling in video interviews

TIP

More and more interviews are held over videoconferencing technology such as Zoom or Teams. These tips can help you become comfortable with these interview formats and ace your interview:

>> **Check your equipment.** You'll need a dependable and fast internet connection, a camera, and a microphone.

>> **Perform a background check.** Look at what will appear behind you. If it's a clutter-fest with file folders and paper piles, or even personal items such as pictures from your vacation, do a clean sweep. Having a painting, bookcase, or attractive plant in the background is best, but make sure the painting and books are tasteful.

>> **Adjust the lighting.** You want soft light illuminating your face. Think of those klieg lights that shine on television anchors' faces. If your room has a window, face it. You can use a ring light or lamp on the desk in front of you. Avoid backlit scenarios that put you in a shadow and glaring front-lighting that makes you squint.

>> **Experiment with the interview platform.** You may need to download the application software and set up an account (if you don't have one already).

>> **Reboot your computer.** Rebooting ensures that you're not running applications that may interrupt the interview. If you have applications set up to automatically run whenever you start your computer, exit those applications.

>> **Adjust your camera and chair.** Adjust your camera and chair so you're in the middle (horizontally) and the top of your head is near the top of the screen.

You should be looking up slightly at the camera, a position that helps define your chin and subtly conveys a message of strength and confidence.

>> **Do a dry run.** Practice with a friend or family member on the platform you'll be using or something similar. This also helps with figuring out just how loud you need to talk and how to position your webcam.

>> **Dress for an in-person interview.** Solid colors are best. Avoid white. Some makeup can take the shine off your skin.

>> **Have a cheat sheet.** Sticky notes on your screen can remind you of talking points you want to be sure to highlight about your experience and why you're a good fit for the job as well as questions about the firm and the position. Have your résumé and the job description handy, too.

>> **Try your best to look into the camera when talking.** You'll be tempted to look at yourself or the interviewers on the screen instead, but doing so breaks eye contact with the interviewers. Remember, their eyes are the camera.

>> **Smile when appropriate.** Smiling provides a big boost for your video presence and energizes the interview. Try warming up ahead of time by thinking of something funny to make you laugh or grinning at yourself in a mirror to loosen up your facial muscles. Smile, especially during the meet and greet.

>> **Moderate your body language.** Breathe deeply and slowly and relax. Keep your shoulders back and your hands quiet. No hair spinning around your pinky, lip chewing, squinting your eyes, or overblinking.

>> **Raise technical issues, if necessary.** If something goes awry — say, your internet connection blips out, or you're having trouble with your computer's camera or microphone — speak up.

>> **Say thanks.** End your interview by saying, "Thank you for considering me for the job. I look forward to hearing from you." Smile, and continue eyeing the camera until the interview stops.

# Following Up Post Interview

After the interview, follow up with your interviewers. Always send a thank-you note, and if you haven't heard back from the organization within a few days, check in to keep your name in the running and find out whether there's anything you can do to help them make a hiring decision. The following sections cover additional details about following up after the interview.

# Sending a thank-you note

Write a thank-you note to everyone you interviewed with that day and send it within 24 hours of the interview. Some people prefer a handwritten note, but email is acceptable. Even better, send an email message, which arrives immediately, and a handwritten note, which takes a day or two to arrive. When sending email, wait until later in the day to send it; don't send it immediately after the interview. You don't want to seem desperate.

Reiterate your interest in the company, your qualifications for doing the job, and your desire to take things to the next level or, if you're not interested, say something along the lines of "During the interview, I realized that the position is not what I am looking for at this time." Use your correspondence to wrap up and leave a positive impression.

**TIP**

Your thank-you note provides an opportunity to mention anything you may not have been able to work smoothly into the interview. You can also clarify responses to questions you stumbled on or feel as though you answered poorly.

# Checking in when you haven't heard a thing

If you haven't heard back from the organization within a few days, be patient. They may be evaluating other candidates. Wait approximately five business days and then follow up with a note asking whether they've made a decision. If you still haven't heard back, consider sending another follow-up note. Then, stop, at least for the time being. It's up to them to contact you if they're interested.

**REMEMBER**

Interviewers not responding after a job interview, as rude as that is, is fairly common practice these days. If they're not interested, they may feel uncomfortable contacting you to relay the bad news or their response could expose them to legal action, so they go silent, torturing you with uncertainty.

If you really want to work for a particular organization, even after they've given you the cold shoulder, keep your contact at the organization posted on any changes in your résumé, new skills added, consulting assignments, and so forth. Periodically remind them that you're still enthusiastic about one day working for them, are passionate about the organization's mission, and believe you have a lot to offer and then say specifically what you have to offer.

Regardless of how antsy you get to hear back from an organization, never do any of the following:

>> Don't call or contact a hiring manager two or three days in a row.

>> Don't give deadlines or ultimatums. Unless you have good reason, such as a pending job offer or promotion you need to decide on soon, don't tell the organization that you need to hear back by a certain date.

>> Don't contact a hiring manager through a personal email, home address, personal cellphone, or home telephone.

>> Don't disparage the potential employer on social media if you don't get a response to your outreach.

>> Don't write snarky emails asking for a status update on the position.

>> Don't be a pest. They may have somehow received your first phone message or email, but not the subsequent ones.

>> Don't send gifts or humorous notes in hopes of getting noticed.

» **Looking into telecommuting, flextime, job sharing, and compressed schedules**

» **Pushing harder for more when you're a woman**

» **Agreeing on a starting date and making other trade-offs**

# Chapter **7**

# Negotiating for What You Want

F ew people in the United States like to haggle, especially when a potential job opportunity is on the line, but if you're not prepared to negotiate, you could end up being paid less than you're worth and falling short of your employment goals. The resulting bitterness or resentment from accepting less than what you had hoped for can negatively affect your job performance and satisfaction, which is bad for you and your employer. Yet you need to come to peace with the fact that you may not get everything you want.

Your goal should be to achieve a mutually beneficial employer-employee relationship, and you may need to make trade-offs to achieve that goal. Perhaps you accept less pay for fewer hours, a more flexible schedule, or a longer vacation. Maybe you agree to provide your own health insurance for a bump in pay, or you accept less pay for the opportunity to earn bonuses tied to your performance. With a flexible attitude and some creative thinking, you can often negotiate a package that meets your needs as well as those of your employer. This chapter describes your options, so you have the information you need to think more creatively about monetary compensation and other perks.

# Evaluating Monetary Compensation: Salary and Benefits

If you're like many people, working in your 50s and beyond often comes down to having a decent salary that reflects your experience, solid benefits, *and* a flexible work schedule. As part of your research when job hunting, consider what compensation packages are feasible for someone in your field with your level of experience and in the location where you plan to work. Prior to interviewing for a specific position, dig deeper to find out more about employer-specific scenarios and benefits.

In addition to health coverage and vacation time, benefits can include sick time, health insurance, short- and long-term disability insurance, life insurance, survivor income, stock options, retirement plans, contributions to retirement, educational and training opportunities, and parking or public transportation. The following sections focus on the various forms of monetary compensation. The benefits of flexible work arrangements are covered later in this chapter.

**REMEMBER**

Don't focus solely on salary. Consider the entire package, including salary, flexible work options, and time off. Do the math. What's your salary requirement? Are you willing to trade less pay for fewer hours? If you can afford to, consider your ideal work-life balance. What benefits will you need, and which ones can you forgo? If your spouse has health benefits through their employer, for example, you may not need them, and that can be a bargaining chip to trade for something else you want, such as more vacation days.

**REMEMBER**

Every dollar the company pays for health insurance, time off, parking or public transportation, contributions to retirement, and so on, is more than a dollar in your pocket, because you're not getting taxed on those amounts.

## Researching salaries

Many employers specify a salary range for the positions they advertise, which takes some of the guesswork (and anxiety) out of salary negotiations. To get a clearer idea of what's generally accepted for a specific position based on job location and your experience, use the following resources as points of reference:

» Candid's 990 Finder (beta.candid.org/) to find IRS Form 990 tax filings for nonprofit organizations, which show how much their highly compensated employees are paid.

» Glassdoor (www.glassdoor.com) is an expanding database of 6 million company reviews, CEO approval ratings, salary reports, interview reviews and questions, benefits reviews, office photos, and more. This information is entirely shared by the employees.

>> PayScale (www.payscale.com) uses crowdsourcing and big data technologies to compile its database of 40 million individual salary profiles.

>> Salary.com (www.salary.com) provides salary information for more than 4,000 job titles.

The salary info you dig up on these sites should give you at least a ballpark number to enable you to negotiate from a well-informed position.

TIP

When applying for a position, tap into your network to find out about typical pay for the job.

## Paying special attention to starting pay

Starting pay is crucial, because after you're on the payroll, ramping up your salary can be painstakingly slow, and you may never catch up to where you would have been had you negotiated a higher starting salary. For example, imagine two people receive a job offer of $45,000. One negotiates for $5,000 more, and both receive 3 percent raises every year. After 20 years, the difference in their lifetime earnings is a stunning $134,351.87! Consider how much more that would represent if it were invested in an IRA over those 20 years.

REMEMBER

Ignore all the lip service you'll probably hear about raises that will likely come your way after your first glowing performance review. Go for the proverbial bird in the hand over the two or three in the bushes.

TIP

If you're offered a salary lower than what you've targeted and the hiring manager won't budge, consider negotiating for an earlier salary review. Most employers review salaries once a year, so ask for a six-month evaluation. Three months is too soon. Nine months is your fallback suggestion. But don't count on this tactic landing you a big bump or even getting one at all. Just be sure that you're confident your performance will support the reconsideration of your base salary.

## Assessing health insurance coverage

Health insurance is often non-negotiable. Either the employer offers health insurance or it doesn't. Health insurance is more likely to play into your decision and your ability to negotiate in these two scenarios:

>> **When you're choosing between a smaller and a larger employer:** A larger employer is more likely to offer health insurance.

>> **When you're already covered:** If you're covered under a spouse's plan, you may be able to decline the insurance plan at work in exchange for a higher salary or other perk. Hiring managers at small businesses, in particular, may be open to this tactic because the cost of offering insurance to workers can be a big ticket item.

That said, you do want to find out what kind of healthcare benefits are available (HMO, PPO, high-deductible HSA). If having super healthcare benefits (dental, vision, prescription coverage, and so on) is important and the company doesn't have them, that could be a deal breaker for you.

## Comparing retirement plans

Unless you're a top executive, you may not be able to negotiate retirement plans, but if you have two or more job offers on the table, you definitely want to compare plans. The best place to get complete information about retirement plans and other benefits is from the human resources (HR) person. Ask how long before you can contribute to the 401(k) or other retirement plan. Does the company match contributions, and, if it does, what's the cap? When are you fully vested?

## Counting vacation and sick days

Time is money. In fact, as you age and your financial responsibilities shrink while your nest egg grows, time may become more valuable than money and can be a valuable trade-off commodity. Many older workers are happy to exchange more time off for less pay, and employers may have greater leeway exchanging time for money than coming up with more money.

When considering an offer, carefully weigh starting salary and time off in the form of vacation days, sick days, personal days, and holidays. If you've become accustomed to four weeks or more of paid vacation days and the employer is offering only two weeks and only after you've worked for the organization for a year, you have some room for negotiation:

>> **Request more vacation days from the get-go.** For example, request three or four weeks instead of the standard two.

>> **Ask that your allotted vacation days accumulate more rapidly.** For example, instead of receiving one day per month, request a day and a quarter or a day and a half per month.

>> **Ask to be eligible to take vacation time prior to your one-year anniversary.** Waiting an entire year before you can take a vacation may be unrealistic

for an older worker who's accustomed to annual vacations, but if the employer needs you to be there, this may be non-negotiable.

>> **Request a certain amount of unpaid vacation time.** If time really is more valuable to you than money, find out how flexible the organization is when it comes to taking unpaid leave.

# Considering bonuses

Employers may be more willing to negotiate performance-based pay, such as bonuses, than base pay. Ask about the possibility of earning a future bonus for an outstanding performance in a certain time frame, or for reaching a certain target goal, say a certain sales figure. To avoid future disagreement, make sure the bonus is tied to a verifiable goal or milestone and get the details in writing. Granted, salary increases are generally based on current salary, not including bonuses.

## EXPLORING THE SIGNING BONUS UPSIDE FOR EMPLOYERS

Why are employers willing to play ball with a signing bonus? Other than the obvious reason of signing high-demand professionals to a contract, a signing bonus tends to boost productivity and loyalty, according to a survey from *The Accounting Review*. The study looks at the effects of signing bonuses on employer-employee relationships. The study finds that particularly when a market has an excess number of workers, a signing bonus can engender more trust and loyalty between the employer and new employees. This may translate into a new hire feeling more committed and working harder.

But a signing bonus can also lead to higher expectations, which can result in strained employer-employee relations if the new employee doesn't live up to them, the study found. "When there is an excess of supply of labor, employers who offer a signing bonus expect greater effort from their workers than they do when either no signing bonus is offered or when there is an excess demand for labor," said Jungwoon "Willie" Choi, the study's author.

Surveys from global human resources association WorldatWork (www.worldatwork. org) and other human resources organizations found that signing bonuses have made a comeback since the Great Recession as the employment market has improved, but bonuses are still not as commonly offered as they were during the dot-com boom of the late 1990s.

If employers in your industry are having difficulty filling a position you're applying for, consider holding out for a signing bonus. These vary among industries and companies from no signing bonus to very generous offers. The amount of a sign-on bonus can range from 20 to 200 percent of the base salary (more for executive-level positions or positions that are hard to fill, such as nurses or skill-based healthcare jobs). If you negotiate for a signing bonus, you may be required to sign a contract committing to work for the organization for a certain number of years. Breach the contract, and you're required to pay back all or part of the signing bonus.

The timing of the signing bonus can also differ from company to company. Some employers pay the entire bonus up front. Others divvy it up, so you get a portion when you start and the remainder in three to six months.

## Prospecting for other perks

You can find plenty of other financial perks around the edges. Here are a few to consider:

>> **State-of-the art equipment and software:** If it will make you excel at your job, this is a no-brainer. Ask what kind of office equipment is customary, what operating systems the devices run on, what programs are commonly installed, and how that equipment is supported. Availability of certain equipment and software, for instance, can be essential for your mobility, productivity, and future raises.

WARNING

Don't push it. Requesting a company cellphone when you'll be on call is fine, but asking for the most expensive brand with an unlimited data plan is going too far.

>> **Share options:** If you're negotiating with a publicly traded company, particularly if it's an executive-level position, ask about share options. Do some research into what's customary with the particular employer. Also be sure the company is in good financial shape before you go out on the limb. You can do this by setting up a Google Alert, reading information under the About Us link on the corporate website, and using corporate research sites.

>> **Free education and training:** Check to see whether your future employer includes reimbursement for certain tuition expenses. Some employers pay 90 percent of all costs of obtaining a bachelor's degree in any field as well as the same percentage of expenses for earning a master's degree related to the employee's field. Job-related certifications are also covered by the employer.

**TIP**

Some companies require a high GPA to receive the full benefit. Others provide reimbursement on a sliding scale, offering the full benefit only to those with a top grade average. Others require that employees remain employed with that particular company for a certain number of years after completing the course. Five years is a typical restricted period.

>> **Professional development:** Professional development includes courses, conferences, credentialing programs, and other facilitated learning opportunities designed to improve a person's ability to do a job. Showing an interest in this benefit should win you some points, because professional development benefits your employer as well, and it shows a long-term commitment to your profession.

**REMEMBER**

You probably won't be able to convince a company that doesn't offer tuition reimbursement to offer it to you. But it's something to keep in mind when choosing an employer.

# Exploring Flexible Work Options

While a 40-hour-plus workweek remains the norm, many workers, including the over-50 set, are looking for more flexibility, including remote work. You may not be able to negotiate such an arrangement right out of the gate, but your employer may allow you to move in that direction over time if you demonstrate a strong work ethic and self-discipline.

To land a position with an alternative schedule or negotiate a flexible arrangement, you need a clear concept of the type of work and schedule you can manage, as the following sections explain.

**REMEMBER**

Chances are good that you won't surprise a hiring manager by asking for a non-traditional work schedule or workspace — not in an era when work-life balance is in and the need for face time is out. But the likelihood of negotiating a flextime or remote arrangement is still up for debate. Someone at the executive level has a greater chance of receiving this type of benefit because they're not as easy to replace, and their skills are at a premium. Entry-level employees may have a more difficult time negotiating such arrangements.

## Taking a look at remote work

The appeal of working from home or some other remote location, partially or entirely, is easy to understand. It gives you a sense of autonomy and control of your time and can save you gobs of time and money commuting to work. When it comes to what makes people love their jobs, this is a biggie. Remote employees are happier and more loyal, and they have fewer unscheduled absences, according to a survey by outplacement firm Challenger, Gray & Christmas. AARP's book *Love Your Job: The New Rules for Career Happiness,* by Kerry Hannon, clearly show that more flexibility in scheduling day-to-day activities leads to greater happiness on the job. That's especially true as you get older.

Obviously, not all jobs are conducive to remote work. With today's wired world, however, it's becoming more popular in many professions and is simple to execute. All you need are a reliable computer, high-speed internet access, and the self-discipline to do your job essentially unsupervised.

When considering remote work, envision the desired arrangement and account for the following factors in terms of meeting your employer's needs:

>> **Days/hours:** Would you work remotely entirely, only a few days a week, or a few hours a day? Do you need to be onsite to perform certain job duties on certain days?

>> **A workplace:** Do you have a suitable place to work? You need a quiet place with few, if any, distractions, along with enough space to lay out whatever you need to do your job. A spare room with a door is best, so you can separate work from the rest of your life.

>> **Equipment:** Are your computer and internet connection up to snuff? Do you have reliable phone and cellphone service?

TIP

Some companies are opting for *hoteling,* sharing offices and desks. The impetus: Cutting the soaring cost of office space in some cities. You may be able to negotiate an arrangement in which you work part of the time at home and part of the time in a shared office setting, where you have access to additional resources and perhaps colleagues.

>> **Work ethic:** Gut check time. Do you have the self-discipline to perform your job duties essentially unsupervised and without coworkers nearby? As an older worker, you're probably more capable of working unsupervised than younger workers, but you may perform better with others nearby to hold you accountable.

>> **Workplace camaraderie:** One valuable asset that's often lost through remote work is the face-to-face camaraderie that ties colleagues together and gives them the sense that they're working toward a common goal. You may be able to achieve camaraderie through email, video meetings, phone calls, and occasional business lunches, during which you talk shop.

WARNING

If you're a people person, don't underestimate how much you may miss the chit-chat in the hallways, talks at the water-cooler, birthday celebrations, and other forms of human contact. Find a way to connect with coworkers, either by working in the office a few times a month or meeting outside of work.

## PENALIZED FOR WORKING LATER IN THE DAY

Employees who started work earlier in the day were rated by their supervisors as more conscientious and thus received higher performance ratings, according to a study, "Morning Employees Are Perceived as Better Employees," by Kai Chi Yam, Ryan Fehr, and Christopher M. Barnes of the Department of Management and Organization at the Michael G. Foster School of Business, University of Washington, published in the *Journal of Applied Psychology* (June 2014).

Research participants gave higher ratings of conscientiousness and performance to the 7 a.m. to 3 p.m. employees than to the 11 a.m. to 7 p.m. employees. "Compared to people who choose to work earlier in the day, people who choose to work later in the day are implicitly assumed to be less conscientious and less effective in their jobs," the researchers found.

## Seeking more flexible jobs

Some industries and professions are more conducive to flexible work arrangements. Here are a few areas you may want to explore:

» **Government work:** If you're interested in the public sector, the federal government is known for strong employee benefits, including flexible work schedules and telecommuting options. The federal government offers locality pay, so your salary reflects your area's cost of living. Visit USAJobs (www.usajobs.gov) to search and apply for jobs with various federal government agencies. State and local government jobs may be flex-friendly, too. In many school districts, the day ends when school lets out, and many other school districts are transitioning to virtual classrooms where teachers provide instruction remotely via computer.

» **Small companies:** Small-business owners can't always lure top-level talent with sweet benefits such as stock options, 401(k) plans, and generous health insurance, but often they can offer more flexibility than their larger competitors do. Flexible scheduling is a fairly low-cost benefit that enables them to hire and hang on to good workers. One place to start your search is the Great Place to Work Institute (www.greatplacetowork.com), which ranks small- and medium-sized companies according to the level of trust between employees and management and the percentage of employees who say they're happy at their jobs.

>> **High-demand professions:** Look where the jobs are. There's a shortage of workers in both the healthcare and education fields, for instance. Nurses, physical therapists, and elementary and secondary schoolteachers are in demand. These are fields where flexible scheduling is more common than in the 9-to-5 corporate world. You may not need to return to school; within these areas are opportunities for skilled workers who have backgrounds in everything from accounting to marketing and more. Some consulting firms specialize in matching corporations with workers looking for flexible work options.

TIP

Investigate the company culture. Even if you don't line up an alternative schedule right away, you still want to shop for a company where flex arrangements are allowed after you've proven yourself and the employer gets to know you. When interviewing, ask questions about family-friendly policies, if you still have children at home or are caring for an aging relative. If possible, chat informally with a few people who have flexible setups to get a feel for how it's working and any pitfalls to watch out for. Don't assume that a policy is normal practice just because it's on the company website or in the employee handbook.

## Negotiating a flexible arrangement

The key to negotiating an alternate work arrangement when discussing the employee benefits package is to make it clear how this type of perk would benefit the firm, not just you. Coming into work an hour later than the rest of the team, for instance, may save you half an hour on your commute, which is good for you, but it may also enable you to be more productive, which is good for convincing your employer to go along with it.

REMEMBER

Many bosses fear losing control if their employees aren't under their thumb. Your mission is not only to ease that fear but also to show how much better and more efficiently you can do your job if they offer you flexibility.

To improve your chances of convincing your new or future employer of a flexible work arrangement, follow these suggestions:

>> **Get real.** Can you realistically manage working remotely seven or eight hours a day? Are there only certain hours you're able to work each day or each week? Estimate accurately in advance, because if you propose a schedule that you end up being unable to fulfill, you'll lose credibility.

>> **Run it past your supervisor first.** You may not want to propose this initially. Many employers will want you to learn the ropes and company culture before heading out of the office for any period of time. Even if flextime is a company policy, if your manager isn't onboard, the arrangement will never work out.

>> **Put it in writing.** Draft a proposal that plainly describes your work schedule, the total number of hours you would work, how unplanned overtime would be handled, how often you would visit the office, and how often you would talk with your boss. You may agree to work in the office when projects are being launched or problems arise that the company needs to solve.

To seal the deal, ask for a trial period of three to six months so both you and your boss can see how the arrangement works out and fine-tune it if needed.

TIP

>> **Explain what's in it for your company.** This is not about you, really. If the employer doesn't get something out of it, it'll never work. So make a case for what the company has to gain. Maybe it's paying less in salary for an experienced worker willing to work fewer hours, or better productivity, thanks to a telecommuting deal that eliminates wasted rush-hour time. With fewer interruptions by coworkers, maybe you'll get more done in less time. Point out that if you work from home or have a part-time job-sharing deal with a coworker, you'd be saving the company office space and reducing costly overhead.

Improved efficiency should be at the top of your "why you should let me telecommute or give me a flexible work schedule" list. Increased productivity was, in fact, one of the leading reasons for allowing employees to work from home, according to surveys.

TIP

>> **Be willing to compromise.** Stay open to your employer's suggestions, and remember that employers really don't care about *your* cost of commuting. They do care that you perform well and are reliable.

## Avoiding common drawbacks

WARNING

Steering clear of the office and making your own hours sounds like the American Dream come true, but it does have some potential pitfalls, including these:

>> **A bigger workload than expected:** A flexible work schedule — whether it's a work-at-home agreement, a job-sharing setup with a coworker, or a four-day workweek — doesn't always mean a reduced workload. Whatever your schedule, your employer will still expect you to perform at the level you would if you were in the office full-time, under the boss's watchful eye. This means you could find yourself logging more hours than you agreed to — good for your employer but unfair to you.

>> **Flimsy boundaries:** Try to set clear boundaries so that your work doesn't take over your life.

>> **Supervisor distrust:** If your managers sense any sort of work slowdown from your end, they're more likely to assume that you're slacking off than if they were able to observe you hard at work in a traditional work setting.

>> **Coworker envy:** Even when the full chain of command has approved your flexible hours, don't be surprised by underlying envy and resentment from those working a standard, full-time week. Coworker responses can be palpable, making you feel alienated and out of the loop.

>> **Missed opportunities:** It's not quite out of sight, out of mind, but being out of the office means you may miss out on promotions, plum assignments, and certain perks. Without promotions or key opportunities, your salary could stagnate, resulting in lower real income and retirement savings. It's not necessarily a conscious snub, but some bosses and coworkers may interpret your schedule as a sign of low dedication to your job. Do your best to convince them otherwise.

# Looking at Special Considerations for Women

If you're a woman, and you feel as though the job offer is sub-par for your profession and what you're bringing to the table, consider pushing a little outside your comfort zone to get a fair shake. Negotiating can be uncomfortable and risky, especially for a woman. Push too hard and you may just shove yourself out of a good opportunity. Perform your risk-reward analysis, and if you feel that the risk is worth it, hang tough.

Many people in the equal-pay debate argue that second-rate negotiating skills are at the root of the gender pay gap. Teaching women to be better negotiators — or getting them to negotiate at all — would fix the problem. But the causes are more complex than that. Negotiation is a man's game with men's rules.

At the negotiating table, a woman's biggest difficulty isn't that she can't learn to be "more like a man." The real problem is the behaviors that both men and women associate with good negotiators are tied up with ideas of masculinity — such as confidence and assertiveness — rather than more feminine qualities, such as collaboration and consensus.

We don't advise women to "man up," because when they do, they still can lose. Researchers repeatedly have documented that people react more unfavorably to women who ask for more money compared with men who do. A woman who negotiates is often seen as especially demanding and consequently, a less-than-ideal person to have on a team. It isn't fair, but as a woman it is a reality you need to be aware of when considering your options and planning your strategies.

# RECOGNIZING THE GENDER-BASED RETIREMENT GAP

A well-publicized fact is that men generally earn more than women. Those lower earnings hurt a woman's retirement. Factors that contribute to this gender-based retirement gap include the following:

- Many women don't go to bat for themselves when negotiating for starting salaries. They've accepted low-ball offers as far back as their first job, and that has hurt them for decades, because raises are usually based on a percentage of pay. Some women in their 50s or 60s settle for low pay just because they're happy to get hired at their age.

- Men are four times more likely than women to ask for a salary bump, according to economist Linda Babcock of Carnegie Mellon University. A LinkedIn survey of more than 2,000 professionals found men more likely to say they feel confident in career negotiations (from asking for a raise to closing a business deal) than women — 37 percent versus 26 percent.

- Women usually earn less than men. Overall, women working full time and year round are paid 84 cents for every dollar men earn. An analysis by The Institute for Women's Policy Research found that the wage gap is common in almost all occupations. The group's research shows that women have lower median earnings than men in all but one of the 20 most common occupations. The exception: teaching assistants. In this sector, women and men have the same median earnings.

- Women live five and a half years longer than men, on average. This means they need to set aside more money than do men to avoid outliving their income.

- Many more women than men take time off to raise a family or care for an aging relative. That causes them to miss out on raises, slashes the amount they'll receive from Social Security in retirement, and gives them fewer years to finance a retirement plan at work and get their contributions matched by their employers.

- Women are more likely than men to work part-time or for smaller firms and non-profits. This often translates to not having access to an employer-sponsored, tax-deferred retirement plan.

- From the age of 65 to the end of life, nearly half of all women in the United States are single — according to Pew Research, 49% of women 65+ are single: `https://www.pewresearch.org/social-trends/2020/08/20/a-profile-of-single-americans/`. That means they don't have someone to share the cost of daily living expenses or to help with retirement savings. What's more, study after study shows that after losing a partner due to death or divorce, a woman's standard of living generally drops.

The moral of the story is that if you're a woman, it's even more important for you to negotiate a higher starting salary if the compensation package you're offered is less than the industry standard for your profession.

# Settling on a Starting Date

For starters, don't provide a starting date until you have an offer. The starting date is usually a negotiable item, typically two weeks from when you accept a job offer. But depending on the job and your potential employer, it could be as much as a month.

**TIP**

If you're currently working, try to give yourself a breather of around two weeks between jobs, so you're at the starting gate rested and with the energy and enthusiasm a new beginning deserves.

If asked about a starting date, it's okay to give a broad answer. You can say something like, "It depends on when precisely you'd be making me an offer, but in general, I would be available to start three weeks after we've established that." This approach gives you the opportunity to negotiate your exact starting date after you receive a formal offer.

If the employer wants you to start earlier than suits you, be prepared to give a solid justification for why you can't. For example, you can say your current employer requires a specific period of notification or you're committed to finishing a project, or you have a vacation already planned and paid for, or you have a medical procedure scheduled. Most employers will respect your commitment to your current employer, because it demonstrates loyalty and consideration. Be diplomatic. Instead of saying "no" outright, see if you can negotiate a starting date that works for both of you.

Here are a few additional considerations that may impinge on your choice of starting date:

>> If you're currently employed, you may need to smooth your exit by staying through an appropriate time to train your successor or finish a project.

>> If some up-front training is involved for the new job, look for a way to work that into your schedule, so a later starting date is less of an inconvenience for your new employer.

>> If your new employer wants to set an even later starting date, try your best to accommodate this need. Additional time may be needed to run a background check or drug screen or to wrap up a project before the department has time to bring you on board. Perhaps the employee you're replacing gave a longer-than-standard notice, and the firm doesn't have the budget for you both to be on the payroll at the same time. Whatever the reason, try to take it in stride.

# 3

# Getting Started with Downsizing

# Contents at a Glance

» Examining the potential benefits and drawbacks of downsizing

» Gathering your thoughts about your current living situation

» Taking the family's pulse

» Addressing a major issue — whether to sell the family home

# Chapter **1**

# Deciding Whether Downsizing Is Right for You

Thinking about downsizing? The first question is whether it's right for you. It may be, but then again it may not be. You may be better off with the status quo. You may even be better off *upsizing.*

The point is, in the process of making this life-changing decision, you have many factors to consider, including whether you're satisfied with your current living arrangements, how you want to live the next stage of your life, whether downsizing will be worth the time and effort, and whether you want to get your affairs in order for yourself and for your family, should something happen to you.

No one can make the decision for you, but in this chapter, you'll find reasons that people commonly have for downsizing, along with important considerations to inform your decision. In this way, you can start your downsizing journey with your eyes wide open and end it with no regrets.

# Recognizing Common Reasons People Downsize

Downsizing isn't solely scaling back your material possessions; it's more of a lifestyle decision. How do you want to live the next 10–20 years of your life? How do you envision your future?

Your values may have changed over the years. Perhaps you begin to realize that you really can't take it with you — when you die, you'll leave behind all the material possessions you accumulated over the course of your life. What's most valuable is internal: your health, character, memories, accomplishments, and experiences.

The challenge you face now is figuring out how to use your resources most effectively to optimize what you value most. For example, if what you value most is the time you spend with your children and grandchildren, you may want to upsize to a living arrangement that's attractive to them and conducive to visits. On the other hand, if your bucket list is full of trips to exotic lands, selling your home and shedding most of your possessions so you can travel light and have more money for traveling in comfort may be the best choice.

REMEMBER

When deciding whether downsizing is right for you, looking at common reasons other people downsize can often help you discover your own reasons. Here are some reasons to consider:

>> You can no longer afford the life you've been living. For example, you're on a fixed income, but the cost of insurance, property taxes, groceries, gas, and more has continued to rise.

>> You have too much stuff. Clutter can trigger depression and anxiety and make finding what you really need difficult.

>> Your current lifestyle is preventing you from pursuing your dreams, so you want to steer your resources in a different direction.

>> You have more belongings than you're able or willing to maintain.

>> You want to relocate to your dream location and simply want to make the move a little easier.

>> You want to free up some money to invest for a more comfortable retirement.

>> You want to travel more and spend little (or no) time at home, so you want to lighten your load.

>> You have health issues and need to transition to a place where you can get more assistance — not necessarily moving to an assisted living facility or a nursing home, but maybe moving in with a friend or family member.

>> You don't want to leave your loved ones with a huge, complicated mess to sort out after you die.

# Weighing the Pros and Cons of Downsizing

Most decisions involve trade-offs, and downsizing definitely has advantages and disadvantages — some obvious and others you're not likely to discover until you do it. Downsizing is a very personal journey that can take months to fully execute, or even longer if you decide to build a new home. Before you hop on board, carefully consider the pros and cons.

**REMEMBER**

When facing the decision of whether to downsize, consider the pros and cons of downsizing and the pros and cons of *not* downsizing. If you choose not to downsize, what are the likely consequences of that choice? Who will suffer those consequences — you, your children, the state?

## The potential benefits of downsizing

Downsizing offers a long list of potential benefits — too many to cover in a short section of one chapter — but here are the highlights:

>> Less home to clean, maintain, heat, cool, and insure

>> Lower utility bills

>> Less rent or smaller house payments

>> Less debt and more money in your pocket

>> Fewer possessions to organize and maintain, making it easier to find things and less likely you'll misplace them

>> More freedom and more money to do what you want

>> Less anxiety-inducing clutter, resulting in clarity of mind and better sleep

>> A fresh start

>> A chance to escape from any unpleasant neighbors

Think twice before moving just to get away from nasty neighbors; you may end up with *worse* ones!

>> More time to spend with friends and family

>> Improved family dynamic — downsizing to fewer rooms can often force family members to spend more time together in communal areas (which can have a positive or negative effect on the family dynamic)

>> A more manageable life, especially if you're downsizing to a living situation in which you can get the help you need (assuming you need help)

## Potential downsizing drawbacks

You can't shed belongings and move without experiencing some pain. Here are some of the possible downsides of downsizing:

>> **Difficult choices:** You'll need to make some challenging decisions about what to keep and what to let go.

>> **Loss of convenience:** For example, if you have a workout room, downsizing may mean you'll need to hit the local gym instead. You may also need to trim your collection of power tools, kitchen appliances, and personal spa equipment. *What?! No paraffin wax machine?! No bubbling foot spa?!*

>> **Less room for storage:** You never really appreciate how valuable storage space is until you have less of it.

>> **Cost:** Moving can be expensive. Even if you're downsizing your living space, you may have expenses related to buying and selling a home, moving, and furnishing the new place.

>> **Less room for entertaining:** You may need to cut down on your dinner parties, scale them back, or eat out more . . . *yes!*

>> **Cramped living space:** You and your partner may feel as though you're always on top of each other — and not in a good way.

>> **Loss of the familiar:** You'll be taking on something new and unfamiliar. It's like starting over for some people, which can feel as though you're closing a chapter of your life and leaving memories behind.

>> **Loss of friends:** If you have close relationships with neighbors, moving can make you feel as though you're breaking off close friendships.

>> **Change in routine:** You'll need to establish a new routine in a new place. If you're downsizing to an assisted living arrangement, you may also be looking at a loss of independence and freedom.

>> **Disappointment:** You may feel disappointed if the reality of downsizing doesn't quite live up to the ideal you romanticized.

**REMEMBER**

If your first attempt at downsizing doesn't work out and leaves you feeling disappointed, it's not the end of the world. You can always try something different. But moving can be costly, and if you own, agent commissions and closing costs can add up.

# Analyzing Your Situation and Mindset

When you're deciding whether to downsize, you need to do a *gut check* — honestly evaluate your situation and your mindset. Your situation may be that all your children have moved out and you have far more home than you need; or your expenses are rising and you need to budget for the long term; or you are bored and want to finally pursue your dream of joining Cirque du Soleil. You need to evaluate where you are and where you want to be when you're deciding whether to downsize.

Likewise, you need to look inside yourself to get a sense of what you really think and feel about downsizing. What's your vision for the next 10–20 years of your life? What will you be giving up? What do you expect to get in return? Are you looking forward with confidence and excitement or fear and trepidation? If you don't have a solid plan that you're fairly certain will make you happier, you run the risk of being disappointed and getting discouraged, so take some time to analyze both your situation and your mindset.

## Examining your situation

The first section of this chapter presents a list of common reasons people downsize, but what's most important is *your* reason. To discover your *why* (or *why not*) for downsizing, examine your current situation by answering the following questions:

>> **Is your situation such that you have no choice but to downsize?** For some people, downsizing isn't a choice. Financial strain, health conditions, or pressure from family members may compel you to downsize, regardless of whether you want to.

TIP

Even if you're being compelled to downsize by forces outside your control, taking the initiative and being proactive can give you more control over the outcome. Don't just throw up your hands in despair; be an active participant as much as you're able.

>> **Are you lonely?** You may be able to improve your social life by downsizing and moving to a community where you're more likely to meet compatible individuals — for example, an over-55 community with lots of social activities.

>> **Is your home too much for you to clean and maintain?** If you're done with vacuuming floors and climbing the ladder to clean out the gutters, or you're tired of shoveling snow and moving the lawn, it may be time to consider downsizing.

>> **Are you burning through your savings?** Whether you want to die without a penny in savings because you've enjoyed every minute of your life, or you want to leave a legacy for the next generation, examine your finances carefully to make sure you're not burning through your savings too quickly. If you are, downsizing may be the solution.

>> **Do you have more house than you need?** If you have rooms that you never use, you may be a good candidate for downsizing. Or you can rent those rooms to generate additional income. Or invite family or friends to live with you.

>> **Do you need to unlock the equity in your home to finance your dreams?** If you have significant *equity* in your home (you can sell it for much more than you owe on it), you may want to sell your home to use the proceeds to support the lifestyle you envision for yourself. Of course, other options are available for unlocking the equity in your home, such as refinancing or opening a home equity line of credit (HELOC).

>> **If you were to die today, would you leave everything for your loved ones to deal with?** Many people downsize to ease the burden on their loved ones, in which case shedding possessions, organizing documents, and moving to a smaller space become top priorities. If you've already done a fantastic job of organizing everything and living simply, though, downsizing may be unnecessary.

>> **Do you need assistance with medical or personal care?** If your health is declining or you simply need a little more help than in the past, downsizing can be an opportunity to move into housing where you can get the help you need.

>> **Are you and your partner on the same page?** If yes, make a plan together. If no, it's time for conversations and collaboration to decide your next steps. (See the later section "Making sure you're on the same page as your partner" for details.)

**REMEMBER**

Knowing your *why* for downsizing is important not only for deciding whether it's right for you but also for motivating you as you move forward and guiding subsequent decisions, such as these:

>> Your choice of lifestyle

>> Your dream location

>> Your timeline

>> The resources you'll need to execute your plan

Keeping your reason for downsizing in mind and taking an honest look at the full scope of your situation will help you devise an effective and efficient plan.

## Taking stock of your thoughts and feelings

Downsizing can be physically, mentally, and emotionally draining, so you want to go into it with the right mindset. If you're feeling forced to do it or filled with fear or dread, those negative feelings will sap your motivation and energy and can result in a less desirable outcome.

To take stock of your thoughts and feelings, answer the following questions:

>> **What do you dread most about downsizing?** Most people dread the time and effort it will take, while others are more put off by the idea of having to give up things they're emotionally attached to. By knowing what you dread most, you can start thinking about how to make it less dreadful — for example, by getting others to help or by keeping only the things you're most emotionally attached to.

>> **What's the biggest perk you're expecting from downsizing?** For example, you may be able to retire earlier, have more time to pursue your interests and have fun, or move to a place you've always wanted to live.

**TIP**

To maximize your motivation and energy, keep your eyes on the prize — the freedom, independence, and peace of mind you'll gain when you have fewer possessions to worry about.

>> **Are you downsizing because you want to or because you're being "forced" to?** Downsizing because you want to can boost your motivation and energy. Feeling forced to downsize can have an equally negative effect. Focusing on the potential benefits, especially if you're feeling compelled to downsize, can help you establish a more positive attitude.

>> **Are you afraid you'll get rid of something you'll want or need later?**
Chances are good that if you haven't used or looked at something in 5 years, you probably won't in the next 10–20 years.

>> **Are you worried that others will think less of you if you own less?**
Downsizing is about what *you* think and the life *you* want. Don't concern yourself with society's norms or what others think or expect from you. You have one life, and you need to live it fully.

>> **What does "enough" look like to you?** Advertising ensures that we never feel as though we have enough. We're constantly being enticed to want what we don't have. Take a different approach. Think about the least you need in order to live the life you envision for yourself and think less in terms of possessions and more in terms of adventures, experiences, personal fulfillment, and people.

**REMEMBER**

If you are married or have a life partner, you'll have to be on the same page every step of the way. Downsizing is stressful, so work toward developing a positive mindset and a common goal. If either of you feels overwhelmed, encourage each other.

# Considering Your Loved Ones

The bigger your family, the more complicated the decision about whether to downsize can become, because more people will be impacted by your decision. You certainly want to involve your partner (if you have one) in the decision-making process, but you may want to consult your children, grandchildren, and close friends as well.

The following sections present the option of involving other people in your decision to downsize and guide you through the process.

## Making sure you're on the same page as your partner

If you're in long-term relationship, you're well aware of the importance of communication, especially when you're making a life-changing decision that's likely to affect someone else. If you're thinking about downsizing, you definitely need to involve your partner in the decision.

The bottom line: Everyone who will be involved in the downsizing decision and activities needs to be on the same page. Downsizing is stressful, and any dissension will make it even more so.

REMEMBER

When communicating with loved ones, be open and honest. Commit to full transparency, so everyone has all the information and insight they need to form honest opinions and make well-considered decisions. Here are a few suggestions for communicating effectively with your spouse and other loved ones involved in the process:

>> **Share both your thoughts and your feelings.** Are you reluctant? Eager? Angry? However you feel about downsizing, get it out there so your emotions can be addressed. If you don't, you're at an increased risk of feeling regret, bitterness, and resentment later. Encourage everyone to express their thoughts and feelings.

>> **Hold meetings specifically to discuss downsizing.** Scheduled meetings will keep the discussion focused on downsizing and reduce distractions. Limit each meeting to no longer than one hour.

>> **Come to meetings prepared with notes and take notes during the meeting.** Coming prepared with notes or a list of topics you want to discuss and share helps keep the meeting on track and ensure that all your concerns are addressed. Encourage others to come prepared as well. The more prepared everyone is, the more productive your discussions will be.

>> **Focus your first meeting on the big picture — whether everyone thinks downsizing is a good idea and your visions for the future.** In later meetings, you can go into more detail about how you'll downsize, who's going to be involved in the process, and who gets what.

## Listening to your kids' opinions

When you're thinking about downsizing, consider bringing your children into the loop. We say *consider* because you may have good reasons not to involve them in your downsizing decisions. If they want to participate and you want them to, then we encourage you to involve your kids in the festivities. Just as parents are affected by their children's decisions, children can be affected by what their parents decide. And in some cases, downsizing involves a role reversal, with children caring for their parents and making decisions for them. In certain situations, grandchildren may be calling the shots.

Whoever's affected by or involved in the downsizing should be included from the get-go, such as when your children live with you. Start by involving them in the decision about whether to downsize. Present them with a list of pros and cons, instructing them to hold off on expressing their opinions until they've had time to think about it. Then, schedule a meeting to be held several days or a couple weeks later to get everyone's input. Delaying the discussion elicits more thoughtful feedback and deeper insights.

Every person is different, so no one can tell you specifically how to communicate with each of your children most effectively, but here are some insights into what you can expect from them in different situations — for example, children who are still living with you versus those who've moved out, and adult children versus younger children. The following sections address those differences.

TIP

Whether you're a parent, child, or grandchild, be honest, open, and assertive. Don't just roll over and do what other people tell you to do. Be open to negotiating, and don't let your concerns and interests be ignored or discounted.

## Holding firm with adult children who still live with you

If you have adult children still living with you, you're in a challenging scenario because your downsizing could disrupt their lives. If they haven't been contributing to the household, they may feel threatened by the lack of financial support. And they may wonder where they'll live, and where they'll put their stuff.

The conversation can be difficult, but stay firm in your decision and work together to find a solution that works for all of you.

## Considering younger children who live with you

If you have younger children who live with you, you may want to postpone any decision to downsize until after they have graduated high school. And if a child plans to attend college and stay closer to home (or even continue living at home and commute to college), you may want to delay your decision even longer.

Of course, your children may be all in on downsizing and even moving. Maybe they're struggling to fit in at school, or they share your dream of managing a coconut plantation in the Philippines. The only way you'll know is to start discussing your dreams and preferences as a family.

## Involving adult children who don't live with you

If you're close with your adult children, including them in your discussions and decisions is likely to come naturally. If they're distant physically or you rarely communicate, they probably won't be involved, regardless of whether you want them to be. Here are a few guidelines for gauging your adult children's level of involvement:

>> If your adult children live near you and spend time with you, you may want to get them involved and stay in close contact throughout the process, sharing your thoughts and listening to their opinions.

>> If they live far away or you rarely see them for other reasons, consider whether trying to get them involved is worth the time and effort.

>> Share financial information, such as your budget — water, gas, electricity, taxes, maintenance — to the degree you feel comfortable and believe your adult children are responsible enough to know.

>> Set parameters on acceptable involvement and feedback. For example, you may want your children to accompany you as you check out properties and express their opinions, but make clear that you are making the decisions.

## Letting close friends and neighbors in on it

If you have close friends and neighbors who will be impacted by your downsizing decision, and who will be supportive whatever you choose, consider drawing them into your discussion circle. They may have unique insights to share or feelings about you that you weren't aware of, especially if they've gone through the process themselves.

You may realize, through your discussions, that you don't want to live without them nearby, or maybe they'll decide to downsize and join you on your adventure! Perhaps you'll decide to move in together, buy a duplex, or arrange for side-by-side condos.

# Settling a Major Dilemma: To Sell or Not to Sell Your Home

If you own your home, one of the big decisions that comes with downsizing is whether to sell it. In some cases, the decision is a no-brainer: You need to cash out the equity in the home to finance your new life, or you simply want to get rid of it, and nobody else in the family wants it. In other cases, if it's the family home, you may feel pressured by relatives to keep the property in the family.

**REMEMBER**

As you mull over this important decision, keep the following considerations and options in mind:

>> You can cash out equity in the property in ways other than selling it. For example, you can mortgage it, take out a HELOC, or arrange a reverse mortgage. Check the terms closely, and read the fine print.

>> You may be able to lease the property to full-time or part-time residents, something that has become increasingly easy through services like Airbnb and Vrbo. You can even use these services to lease a portion of your home while you still live there.

>> You can sell interests in the property to other family members so that you share ownership of it. You can even arrange it so you're acting as the bank, collecting monthly payments.

>> If maintenance is the reason you want to sell, you can hire a property management company to maintain the home and arrange for regular cleanings.

>> If you want to move because of your declining health, home healthcare may be a viable alternative to selling your home and moving to an assisted care facility. Crunch the numbers to see what the costs would be for both.

» Deciding where to live during the next stage of your life

» Digging up details about potential destinations

» Sampling a place or lifestyle before making the leap

# Chapter **2**

# Envisioning Your Future: Lifestyle and Location

D ownsizing isn't necessarily limited to getting rid of a bunch of belongings and moving to a smaller place to make your life more manageable. It can be an exciting opportunity to reinvent yourself, move to a new location, and adopt an entirely different lifestyle.

These days, maybe you have more freedom to explore life in a new way, and a life of less (as in fewer material goods) may be the perfect solution to free you up for other adventures. This is your chance to determine what the rest of your life will look like and what your priorities will be.

This chapter provides the encouragement, inspiration, and guidance to dream big in the context of downsizing.

REMEMBER

Consider all the factors that go into making one of the biggest decisions of your life, so you'll get it right the first time. A major mistake some people make when downsizing is to invest significant resources into a choice that in the end doesn't work out the way they had hoped. By following the guidance in this chapter and taking the time to think about what you really want, you'll have a much better chance of avoiding that trap. But if your first choice doesn't work out, just use this book again to move ahead.

# Building Your Vision

A fortunate few have a clear vision for their future. They can close their eyes and imagine, engaging all their senses, the life they desire — the location where they want to end up, their living quarters, the people around them, the activities they're involved in, the food and beverages they're consuming, and more. Most people, however, struggle to answer one of life's simplest, yet most challenging, questions: *What do you want?* Even after mulling over that question for months or years, they may still have only a fuzzy idea, at best.

Before you downsize, honestly answer some important questions: *What do you want? How do you want to live the rest of your life? How do you want to live the next 10–20 years of your life?*

The following sections present a few different approaches to building your vision of your future life.

## Complete a lifestyle questionnaire

Here's a lifestyle questionnaire to start you thinking about what's important to you and engaging your imagination in the process. These may seem like heavy questions to start with, but they are the key themes to keep in your mind when deciding what the next phase of life will look like and focus on. Simply write or type your answers; you might want to keep a separate notebook or computer file:

>> When are you happiest?

>> Are you holding onto any emotional baggage — regrets, disappointments, bitterness, resentment? List them all. Can you let all that go and replace it with gratitude?

>> What will people say about you at your funeral? Now is the time to start living the stories you want them to tell about you.

>> What would you do if you had only six months to live?

>> What's your reason or purpose for living? What motivates you — or what would motivate you — to wake up in the morning eager to face the day?

>> What's holding you back? Who or what is standing in the way of the life you want or need to transition to?

>> What do you hope to accomplish? What legacy do you want to leave behind?

>> Who will play a key role in your future life? Think in terms of friends, family members, colleagues, and so on. If you don't have anyone in mind, that's okay.

>> Are you envisioning permanent housing or a more nomadic lifestyle that involves lots of travel and adventure?

>> Will you be working? If so, is it paid or volunteer work? Full-time or part-time? Permanent or temporary? Describe the type of work you want to do. Are you running your own business or working for someone else? Do you need to live near your place of employment, or can you work remotely?

>> What do you envision yourself doing in your free time? List activities you'd like to participate in, such as specific hobbies, swimming, biking, walking, working out, fishing, playing golf or tennis, learning or playing a musical instrument, attending concerts, dancing, visiting museums, boating, traveling, learning a foreign language.

>> What are you thinking in terms of location and climate? Hot and dry? Temperate? Seasonal? Inland or coastal? Mountains, plains, or forest? Domestic or foreign? Will you migrate, living in a cooler area over the summer and wintering in a warmer area?

>> Will you need assistance? If yes, what level of assistance? For example, do you need a healthcare worker 24/7, a daily check-in, a few hours a week, or only on-demand care? Maybe all you need are cleaning services, help with preparing meals, and transportation.

>> What types of services do you need or desire nearby? Medical facilities? Shopping? Restaurants? A gym? A library? Museums? Theaters? Golf courses? Cultural events? A church, synagogue, or mosque? Or are you envisioning living in a remote location, perhaps off the grid?

**REMEMBER**

Living for others is okay if it gives your life purpose and meaning, but if you don't focus on your own personal happiness and wellbeing, you may become resentful doing too much for other people. You'll be doing everyone the most good if you're taking good care of yourself.

## List your must-haves, nice-to-haves, and please-no's

One way to figure out what you want in life is to create three lists: one for must-haves, another for nice-to-haves, and a third for what you want to avoid. This approach is especially helpful if you have to negotiate with a partner or additional family members to address everyone's interests and concerns. Here are the three lists:

>> **Must-haves:** List everything you can't or won't live without. Your list may include location, house size (style, square footage, types and number of

rooms), furnishings, access to shopping and entertainment venues, ease of movement through the home, assistance, proximity to family, and so on. It's likely to be a long list, but include only those things you won't compromise on.

>> **Nice-to-haves:** List everything you'd like to have but you're willing to negotiate. For example, maybe you'd like to have a gym in the building, but it's not a deal-breaker if there's one nearby.

>> **Please-no's:** Make a list of everything you consider unacceptable. Perhaps you plan to rent out your home a few months every year so you can travel, so you'd refuse to live in a community that has covenants restricting renting your unit. You may have certain locations that you'd never consider.

TIP

If you're downsizing with a partner or other family members, work together as a group to create three master lists instead of having each person create three lists of their own. You can negotiate as you create your master lists.

## Build a vision board

A *vision board* is a collage of pictures, motivational phrases, and other items that reflect a person's dreams, ambitions, and anything else that truly matters. You can cut pictures and text out of magazines and mailers, use your own photos, or copy and print ideas and images you find online. What you choose to include on your vision board is entirely up to you, but here's a list to spark your imagination:

>> Photos depicting the location you want to live in

>> A photo of your dream home or a blueprint of its floor plan

>> Pictures of rooms that inspire you to downsize

>> Pictures of people you'd like to have in your life

>> Inspirational quotations or phrases, such as "Less is more" and "Make life fantastic!"

>> Pictures or phrases that represent your personal, professional, or financial goals

>> Lists of your downsizing priorities, such as your list of must-haves from the previous section

>> Photos of people engaged in activities in which you want to participate

>> Photos of places you'd like to travel to

TIP

If you're downsizing with other family members, hang your vision board in a central location to remind everyone of your shared vision and to encourage everyone to contribute to the board. Your vision board can be as neat and tidy or as cluttered as you all agree to.

TIP

There's no right or wrong way to create a vision board. You may prefer the old-school approach using a poster board, glue, and magazine clippings, but many people go digital, using social media platforms such as Pinterest or Instagram to create online vision boards. You can even copy and paste images into a Word or Google doc or use a graphics program such as Photoshop.

## Gather more details in vision folders

TIP

A vision board is a big-picture document; it's not suitable for collecting and storing details. So supplement it with *vision folders*. You can create a vision folder for each aspect of your downsizing project, such as the following:

>> Location

>> Housing

>> Healthcare

>> Transportation

>> Budget/expenses

>> Employment/business opportunities

>> Activities/entertainment

>> Amenities

>> Shopping and restaurants

>> Belongings to keep

>> Belongings to hand down

>> Belongings to get rid of

After labeling your folders, you can start to stuff them with documents, brochures, photos, lists, advertisements, and other relevant items. You can then consult specific folders over the course of your downsizing, depending on the stage of the process. For example, when you're ready to start sorting your many possessions, you can consult your Belongings folders to determine their fate.

# Choosing a Location: Factors to Consider

Where will you live? On its surface, that question may appear easy to answer, until you start digging into all the factors you need to consider to formulate a thoughtful response: climate, terrain, cost of living, proximity to loved ones, and so on. You may even contemplate a nomadic lifestyle — wandering from place to place instead of settling down. (Find more on this in Book 4.) The following sections present some of the key factors to consider when choosing a location or opting for a nomadic lifestyle.

## Settled or nomadic

Traditionally, people settle in one location that acts as their home base, even if they travel frequently. Some have two properties — a primary residence and a vacation home, or a winter and a summer residence. Another option is to live a nomadic existence, traveling from place to place.

If you're thinking about becoming a nomad, consider the pros and cons.

### Pros

Living a nomadic existence, you can look forward to the following potential benefits:

>> Freedom

>> Low cost of living

>> Flexible working conditions

>> Frequent travel

>> Unlimited opportunities to meet new people

### Cons

**WARNING**

While the nomadic lifestyle has lots of benefits for people suited to it, you may experience the following drawbacks:

>> Little to no support network

>> Reduced privacy and security

>> Uncertainty and the anxiety that can accompany it

>> Loneliness if you start missing friends and family

>> Exhaustion, because living on the road can be draining

# Foreign or domestic

One of the big questions you may face if your downsizing plan involves a move is whether to relocate abroad or within your home country. Either way, you may be able to reduce your cost of living to create a more affordable lifestyle. The following sections present the potential advantages and disadvantages of each option.

## Foreign

More and more people in the United States are choosing to relocate to foreign countries to stretch their incomes or experience a life filled with more play and adventure and less work. Foreign destinations may have a lower cost of living overall due to lower taxes, lower housing prices, reduced healthcare and pharmaceutical costs, and lower food prices.

When choosing a foreign destination, consider the following key factors:

>> Climate

>> Affordability

>> Quality healthcare

>> Languages spoken

>> Safety and security (crime rates)

>> Rules and regulations for relocating there (countries often require proof of income, assets, and health insurance to ensure that you won't be a financial burden)

TIP

For a list of top retirement destinations, do a web search. Here are five top places to retire in 2022 from the World Economic Forum at www.weforum.org/ agenda/2022/02/best-places-to-retire-list:

>> Panama

>> Costa Rica

>> Mexico

>> Portugal

>> Colombia

## Domestic

Even if you choose to remain in your home country, certain areas may have a lower cost of living than others. For example, in the United States, some states, counties, towns, and cities are more affordable than others based primarily on their popularity and tax rates. Property tax rates can vary considerably, and some states don't levy a state income tax.

If you're relocating domestically in the United States as part of your downsizing plan, check out *U.S. News & World Report*'s top 10 retirement destinations at money.usnews.com/money/retirement/articles/the-best-places-to-retire.

TIP

If you're looking to move to a state with no state income tax, check out AARP's "9 States With No Income Tax" at www.aarp.org/money/taxes/info-2020/states-without-an-income-tax.html.

## Terrain

*Terrain* refers to the surface features of an area of land, such as desert, mountain, valley, oceanfront, riverside, forest, and so on. Each has its pros and cons.

The prime consideration is affordability. Waterfront property is probably the most expensive, comparatively speaking, but even some desert areas, such as Phoenix, Arizona, can be very expensive. You can also expect to pay a premium for living anywhere with awesome views, such as some mountain locations.

## Climate

Climate determines not only what your heating and cooling bills will look like but also how comfortable you'll be and how much you'll be able to enjoy the outdoors.

Most people prefer a comfortable temperature year-round without excessive precipitation, which is why, in the United States, the southwest and southeast coastal areas are so popular (except during hurricane season). Some people consider San Diego, California, ideal: 12 inches of rain, no snow, sunny about 266 days of the year, 7 comfortable months when the average high is in the range of 70–85 degrees Fahrenheit, only about 3 days when the average high is over 90 degrees, and only a few months where the nighttime low drops to 45–50 degrees.

Phoenix, Arizona, has both desert and mountain terrains, so residents can head up into the mountains in midsummer for relief. You can be in the arid desert one day and the cool mountains the next, and even get caught in a blizzard in a few hours' drive.

If you're generally happy at your current location, you can skip this section completely and stay as close to your current home as possible.

## Size/population

You can downsize your home while upsizing from a small town to a big city. Or maybe you prefer vice versa. When deciding where you're going to live, you basically have the following three options with respect to size and population density:

>> **Urban:** In urban areas, you can expect high population density, lots of traffic, homes close together, more cultural diversity, more to do, a greater selection of stores and restaurants, better public transportation, more job opportunities, more public services, more opportunities for social interaction, and potentially more crime and pollution.

>> **Suburban:** In the suburbs, you have many of the benefits of city living (due to proximity to a city) without some of the drawbacks. Schools are generally better (see the later section "School system"), crime and pollution are less of a problem, traffic may be less congested (though if you commute into the city, that probably won't apply), and homes are usually spaced a little farther apart. But you usually pay a premium in terms of housing prices and property taxes.

>> **Rural:** Rural areas are in the country, closer to nature, and have lower population densities. As a result, benefits include a more relaxed lifestyle, greater privacy, cleaner air, less crime, more peace and quiet, less traffic and congestion, greater affordability, and good schools. Drawbacks of rural living are mostly related to a lack of convenient access to everything urban areas offer: stores, restaurants, sports and entertainment venues, public transportation, public services, cultural offerings, and so on.

## Affordability

Affordability is a key consideration, especially if you are retiring and will have a fixed income. In fact, affordability is one of the primary factors that drives people to downsize. To determine how affordable any given option is, you need to crunch the numbers. Examine your current income and savings in light of estimated expenses, which are likely to include the following:

>> Mortgage or rent

>> Homeowner's or renter's insurance

>> Property taxes

- State and local income and sales taxes
- Utilities (gas, electricity, water, sewer, trash disposal, phone, television, and internet service)
- Homeowner association fees
- Transportation, which may include public transportation, car payments, auto insurance, fuel costs, and maintenance and repair fees
- Health insurance
- Life insurance
- Groceries, toiletries, and other necessities
- Memberships
- Entertainment
- Dining

**WARNING**

Don't get sucked into trying to keep up with the Joneses. Create a life that's affordable for *you*. One of the biggest financial mistakes people make is overextending themselves which can, in the extreme, result in bankruptcy and foreclosure. By living within your means, you can avoid financial setbacks while reducing your anxiety overall.

## Employment opportunities

Employment may or may not be a consideration for you. If you're retiring for good and plan to live off your savings, pension, and Social Security benefits, employment is a nonissue. Likewise, if you can work remotely, your place of employment won't factor into your decision. But if you need or want to work, and you need to be on-site, consider the employment opportunities in and near the areas on your relocation list.

## Healthcare

Regardless of whether you're downsizing, healthcare can weigh heavily on nearly every major life decision, especially if you or your partner or children have existing health issues. Here are a few tips for dealing with concerns about health insurance and treatment:

- If you're retiring and relocating, consider moving close to healthcare providers or to transportation that can get you to them or a nearby hospital.

>> If you're moving a long distance (such as to a different state), ask your physician for a referral and schedule an initial consultation with your new doctor, to prevent any disruption to any medications you're taking or treatments you're undergoing.

>> If you're turning 65, at which point you become eligible for Medicare, contact your insurance agent to discuss your options or check out AARP's *Medicare For Dummies* by Patricia Barry (Wiley).

REMEMBER

>> Before choosing a place to live, ask your insurance agent to advise you on how the move will impact your premiums. Health insurance premiums are based, in part, on your age and zip code. Moving to a different zip code can impact not only the rates your doctors charge but also your health insurance premiums.

>> If you plan to live in or travel to a foreign country, contact your insurance agent to obtain a suitable traveler's health insurance policy.

## Proximity to friends and family

Don't overlook the importance of friends and relatives in any decision to relocate. It's especially critical if you're relying on others, or they're relying on you, because moving away can leave you (and them) feeling isolated and scrambling to find help.

## Activities, entertainment, and restaurants

If you're planning a relocation, consider moving closer to what you enjoy, such as the following:

>> Walking trails or bike paths

>> Parks

>> Restaurants, coffee shops, and bars

>> Shopping

>> A library

>> A farmers' market or fresh produce stand

>> A college or university

>> Theater and concert venues

>> Museums

>> A racetrack or sports stadium where your favorite team plays

# Getting around

Do you like to walk? Do you enjoy exploring the place you live? Do you like to engage in a variety of activities outside your home and beyond the confines of your neighborhood? Then walkability and transportation may be two key considerations, especially if you don't drive or don't like to drive.

## Walkability

TIP

Walkability is a measure of how walker-friendly an area is. It's gauged by the presence or absence of quality sidewalks (or footpaths) and pedestrian crossings, traffic and road conditions, safety, accessibility to businesses and services, and so on. To get a feel for an area's walkability, visit the area in the morning, the middle of the day, and the evening, and walk around.

Also, consider *where* you like to walk. Do you prefer walking in the country with little or no foot traffic, in the woods, or in an urban setting? Do you like fresh air and nature or walking through the business district, where you can stop at a diner for a cup of coffee or a bite to eat? Where you like to walk can have a big influence over where you want to live — a more rural or urban area.

## Transportation

Transportation can be any combination of riding a bicycle, driving a car, taking a train or bus, calling a taxi, or using ride-sharing services such as Lyft or Uber. Some communities also have vans or shuttles that students and seniors can ride for free or at a reduced cost. In larger metropolitan areas, you can even rent an electric car, bike, or scooter to get around.

When you're considering where you want to settle, give some thought to how you're going to get around and access the businesses, services, events, and other offerings you'll need and want.

# Crime rates

TIP

Before moving to any area, check out its crime rates, which you can do online at sites such as www.city-data.com and www.crimemapping.com. You can also call the local police station or sheriff's office (call the nonemergency number, not 911) and ask to speak with the community resource officer. Or visit the area, introduce yourself to some of the residents, and ask them to weigh in on how safe the neighborhood is.

# Public amenities and cultural centers

Some residential communities offer a broad array of amenities that most individuals or couples couldn't afford on their own, such as a clubhouse, pool, hot tub, gym, golf course, tennis courts, and fishing ponds. They may also organize a variety of events and activities, such as concerts, dances, pickleball tournaments, yoga, and crafts. In some communities, these amenities are available only to residents and their guests, typically for a monthly amenities fee. In others, outsiders can join but are usually required to pay a much higher monthly or annual fee.

REMEMBER

You may pay more for a property in a residential community that offers amenities, but they can make your life more enjoyable and even save you money on things you would otherwise pay for separately, such as green fees and gym memberships.

Towns and cities are often too large and diverse to offer anything like what you can get in a residential community, but you can find other amenities spread across the town or city, such as the following:

>> Libraries

>> Community centers

>> Museums

>> Theaters

>> Concert venues

>> Sports venues

>> Churches, synagogues, mosques, and other religious organizations

# School system

When you're buying a property, consider areas with a quality school system, even if you are an empty nester or have no children. The quality of the school system has a significant impact on resale value.

WARNING

Senior living communities may be located in lower-ranking school districts. Land is cheaper in lower-ranking school districts, which is a key reason senior living centers tend to be built in these areas.

# Existing property or new construction

If you're downsizing to a smaller home, one of the big decisions you need to make is whether to buy an existing home or have one built. The following sections help you weigh the pros and cons.

**TIP**

If you're looking to buy a newly constructed home in a subdivision, get in as early as possible. Builders often offer lower prices to kick-start the development, enabling you to get your foot in the door at the lowest price.

## Pros

Benefits of new construction include the following:

>> Floor plans are generally more open with bigger, brighter rooms, and you may have the option to customize the floor plan.

>> If you buy before the home is finished, you may have the option to choose colors, window dressings, light fixtures, and other custom features.

>> Newly constructed homes tend to be more energy-efficient.

>> Newly constructed homes are more likely to have smart-home features built in, such as a programmable thermostat.

>> Newly constructed homes may be healthier if construction materials have low or zero volatile organic compounds.

>> Maintenance costs are likely to be lower because everything's new.

**WARNING**

## Cons

Here are some of the potential drawbacks of new construction to consider:

>> New construction typically costs more.

>> You'll probably be waiting six months to more than a year for your home to be built.

>> New housing additions typically sprout up in remote locations, resulting in longer commutes. In urban areas, new construction is generally limited to high-rise condos or smaller homes on smaller lots, providing less outdoor space.

>> In new housing additions, mature trees are generally scarce, so don't expect much shade — at least for a few years.

# Researching Locations

Before you move anywhere, do your homework to find out whether the place you're considering checks all your boxes. Here are some valuable sources for gathering information about specific locations:

>> Go to AARP's livable communities (aarp.org/livable), where you'll find information on what to look for in communities and a Livable Communities map locator for age-friendly communities.

>> Visit City-Data (www.city-data.com) to research U.S. cities. Select a state and city to view a large collection of data, including population and income data, median house/condo value, crime rates, climate info, lists of schools in the area, and points of interest.

>> Use the Cost of Living Calculator at BestPlaces.net (www.bestplaces.net/cost-of-living) to compare the overall price of goods and services between different locations in the United States. For an international cost of living comparison, visit www.expatistan.com/cost-of-living.

>> Use social media, such as Facebook and Instagram, to connect with people who live in locations you're considering and pump them for information. (But do be cautious about sharing personal information with people you don't know.) Ask about housing, healthcare, shopping, cost of living, what they do for fun, their favorite restaurants, the quality of area schools, crime, which neighborhoods are popular and which to avoid, and so on.

>> Consult a real estate agent in the area and provide a list of what you're looking for. Ask for information about the area. In the United States, you can find qualified real estate agents on Realtor.com (www.realtor.com/realestateagents).

TIP

Contact a top real estate agent — not necessarily one who sells high-end real estate, but an agent who moves the most homes in the area. Production is a good gauge of how motivated an agent is to help clients.

>> If you're considering relocating to a different country, search the web for "relocate to" or "retire in" followed by the location you're interested in — for example, "relocate to Costa Rica." The search results are likely to include links to relocation services that specialize in that area, along with other informative websites and blogs.

# Test-Driving a Location or Lifestyle

Before you make an offer on a house or sign a lease for an apartment in the location you think you want to live, it's a good idea to try before you buy. Arrange for a short-term rental (at least a couple weeks to a few months) and move to the area on a trial basis. Short-term rentals are more easily accessible than ever through services such as Airbnb (www.airbnb.com) and Vrbo (www.vrbo.com). Of course, if you have friends or relatives in the area, you may be able to stay for free or swap homes for a couple weeks or months.

REMEMBER

For the full experience, you really need to live in a place for at least a year. Winter can differ distinctly from summer. Some areas have alternating dry and rainy seasons. In some locations, a town can seem alive and vibrant over the course of two weeks and then return to being Sleepy Town the rest of the year. You don't have to test-drive a location for an entire year, but during the limited time you're there, talk to the locals to find out what life is like the rest of the year.

TIP

Consider approaching your research as a two-step process: First, visit the top three to top five areas you're considering and test them out. Then, do a deeper dive to dig up details about cost of living, housing, jobs, and more. Or, perhaps best of all, do your research while you're test-driving the area. Use the opportunity of being on location to scope out neighborhoods and communities.

# Chapter **3**

# Laying the Groundwork

The success of downsizing relies on careful planning. While it's not as extreme as executing an ocean voyage, imagine you're planning an Alaskan cruise for 2,500 passengers. You need to prepare the itinerary; line up a ship; hire a captain and crew; stock the ship with food, beverages, and other supplies; schedule activities and entertainment; and more. And even with the most careful planning, you're likely to encounter some unexpected surprises. You might run out of lobster or bump into an iceberg or two.

This chapter guides you through the process of laying the groundwork for downsizing, so you'll be better prepared to embark on your journey.

## Developing a Positive Mindset

If you're excited about downsizing, this isn't the section for you. You already have the positive mindset needed to overcome the emotional challenges of downsizing. If, on the other hand, you're down on downsizing, you need to get your head in the game.

Maybe you feel like you're being forced to downsize by circumstances beyond your control — perhaps you need to cut your expenses, or you or your partner require more care and needs assisted living. If that's the case, you have three choices:

>> Fight to the death to stay put.

>> Fight a losing battle and be miserable.

>> Embrace downsizing as an opportunity and look forward to the potential benefits and opportunities.

You see where this is going — even if you don't want to downsize, try to go into it with a positive attitude, *especially* if it's inevitable.

**REMEMBER**

Let's face it: Who likes to be forced to do *anything*? But the more you're actively and enthusiastically engaged in the process, the more freedom and control you have — and the better the outcome.

Here are a few ways to nurture a more positive mindset about downsizing:

>> **Research downsizing.** The more you know, the less you'll "no." Chances are, if you're reluctant to downsize, you don't know enough about it. Fear of the unknown can be driving your thoughts. Reading this book is a good start, but you also can talk to other people who've downsized and research your downsizing options. Talk to your friends, relatives, coworkers, people at your house of worship, and so on about their experiences.

>> **Sample your new life.** One way to become more acclimated to the idea of downsizing is to visit your destination location and check it out. You may enjoy it more than you expect. Even if you don't, the visit will equip you with more knowledge on which to base your downsizing and relocation decisions.

>> **Hang out with positive people.** Positive thinking is contagious, so consult people who are enthusiastic about *life* and about downsizing. Negative thinking is also contagious, so avoid the Debbie and Danny Downers of the world, who can fill your head with all sorts of negative thoughts and catastrophic scenarios.

>> **Center yourself.** Practice yoga, qigong, or tai chi; meditate or pray. All of these disciplines center your mind on the present, which is especially helpful if you're prone to worrying about the future — what hasn't happened yet and therefore isn't part of your reality.

>> **Just do it.** Downsizing is like a fitness program — getting fit can be overwhelming, but walking a mile a day isn't too hard, and once you get started, progress flows naturally. You just need to overcome the inertia of getting started. Downsize one drawer or closet or room of your home to start building momentum.

Be careful around well-intentioned friends and family members who unintentionally cause you to question or doubt your decisions. They may say something like, "Why would you move from this house? It's so beautiful!" They're not living your life. *You* are.

# Consulting with Family Members (or Not)

Downsizing, especially when it involves a major relocation, is a family decision, but it need not involve *everyone* in the family. The decision is primarily up to the people doing the downsizing — the individual or couple or their caregivers. You may want to involve other family members in the decision or just keep them in the loop — letting them know what you're doing without asking for their advice. But you may not. Some family members may not be helpful, and their attempts to "help" can even be counterproductive.

The following sections guide you through the process of teaming up with your partner (if you have one), figuring out how much family involvement you want or need, and getting everyone moving in the same direction.

## Teaming up with your partner

If you're in a long-term relationship and downsizing together, you're aware of the importance of having a shared vision. As Abraham Lincoln famously warned, "A house divided against itself cannot stand." If your idea of downsizing involves relocating to a cabin on a lake in Minnesota, and your partner dreams of moving to an apartment near downtown Austin, Texas, to enjoy the nightlife, you probably won't be downsizing anytime soon . . . maybe not until *after* the breakup.

Before you involve anyone else in your downsizing decisions, you and your partner need to get on the same page. Here are a few suggestions that may help:

>> **Commit to full transparency.** Communicate openly about your needs and desires. Use the word "know" instead of "no," as in the statement "You don't know enough to say no." Don't say no without giving the other person's position ample consideration; you likely don't know enough about it. In other words, instead of rejecting an idea outright, ask your partner to tell you more about it, so you'll understand what's being proposed.

>> **Leave the past behind.** If you're having to downsize as a result of a financial setback in the past, you can't do anything about that. It's over. You can, however, build a better future. Play the hand you've been dealt instead of stewing over it.

CHAPTER 3 **Laying the Groundwork** 215

>> **Solve — don't blame.** Most disagreements are over problems that need to be solved. Brainstorm a list of solutions, discuss each solution's pros and cons, and choose the most promising one.

>> **Listen twice as much as you speak.** Hear your partner out and ask questions until you fully understand before formulating your opinion.

>> **Research your options together.** If you want to look at different housing options and living arrangements but your partner doesn't, you have a serious problem. You must do it together. It's mentally draining, but you both need to examine your options and decide together what's best.

REMEMBER If you're the one dragging your feet while your partner is doing all the work, take a deep breath and acknowledge that fact. Use this trumpet blast as your wake-up call to play an equal part in your future together. Downsizing requires unity and teamwork.

## Deciding how much input you want and from whom

Assuming that you and your partner are of one mind on downsizing, or if you're on your own, you may not need to include anyone else in your decision or even keep anyone else in the loop, but doing so may be to your benefit, especially if your decision is going to impact others in some way.

For example, if your daughter relies on you to watch her children (your grandchildren) and you're moving 600 miles away, you may want to give her a heads-up. Likewise, if your downsizing plans involve living close to loved ones who provide the help *you* need, including them in planning would be prudent. You can't always rely on other people, especially if you exclude them from the decision-making process.

Here are some guidelines to help you decide which people to include in your downsizing plans, which ones to exclude, and the level of involvement you want them to have:

>> Loop in anyone who's likely to be significantly impacted by your downsizing decisions, unless you think they'll throw a wrench in the works.

>> Engage others in your decision-making process if they will play a significant role in your future — helping you move, visiting you, driving you to appointments, providing in-home care of any kind.

>> Seek advice from anyone you know who's been there, done that — people who have downsized successfully and seem happy in their current situation.

>> Think twice about consulting anyone who's opinionated or bossy — anyone who's likely to nitpick your decisions or cause you to doubt your own judgment. If you're just seeking advice on what color to paint a wall, that's fine, but if someone is questioning (or worse, criticizing) your decision to downsize, that's not helpful.

>> Be prepared for additional complexity depending on your family dynamic. Some people have two or three families from previous marriages, and adult children from different families may try or need to be involved in the downsizing process. Some family members can be helpful, whereas others may try to insert themselves uninvited to protect interests they have or think they have.

**WARNING**

When you buy or sell real estate, all your friends and family members may suddenly become real estate experts. The same is true when you have a baby — everyone knows best how to care for and raise that baby, and it's usually at odds with what you think is best. Some of the information may be very helpful; some, not so much. You have to sort it out for yourself and decide what to accept and what to ignore.

## Getting everyone else on the same page

Major life decisions can rattle families and stir up all sorts of conflict and chaos over what's best or what's right, especially when siblings are making decisions that impact the fate of parents with failing health. Getting everyone moving in the same direction is crucial, but it can be very challenging. Many of the suggestions presented in the previous two sections can help — open, honest communication and mutual respect are keys to success. Here are a few additional suggestions for reaching consensus:

>> Gather everyone together at the same time to discuss what you're all thinking and feeling. You can use a video communications app, such as FaceTime or Zoom, to include anyone who can't be physically present. Make it fun. Schedule a meeting followed by a family dinner.

>> Focus the discussion on the issues at hand. Don't let the conversation wander off into exchanging anecdotes about the past or, worse, dredging up past incidents that caused bad feelings among family members.

>> Parents, consider keeping your children informed about your finances, downsizing plans, and any estate planning you're engaged in. Engaging in ongoing discussions can be less disruptive than having a big discussion in the middle of a crisis or leaving it up to your children when you're unable to help or make decisions.

If possible, avoid excluding any of your adult children from the conversation. Consider how you would feel if you were left out of family meetings, conversations, and decisions.

>> Look for win-win solutions. With compromise, someone always feels that they're the loser, having to give up something. Thinking about solutions more creatively can often benefit everyone.

Be careful about handling sensitive issues via text. If it works for you and your family, great. But texting often leads to misunderstandings that quickly spiral out of control. Phone and in-person communications are less prone to escalation.

# Tabulating Your Net Worth and Monthly Income

Planning for any major life change requires knowing what you have to work with in terms of financial resources. Examine your net worth and monthly income by doing the following calculations:

>> **Net worth:** To calculate your net worth, add the value of everything you own and subtract the total of what you owe, such as mortgage loan balances and credit card debt. Knowing your net worth is important whenever you're applying for a loan. It serves as a good indicator of how much house you can afford and how much money you'll qualify to borrow. (Your Beanie Babies and Longaberger baskets don't count!)

>> **Monthly income:** Total the amount of money you plan to receive and draw each month to cover your expenses. Depending on how, when, and why you're downsizing, you may receive income from the following sources:

- Employment or business income

- Savings

- Social Security income

- Pension income

- Personal retirement savings, such as individual retirement accounts (IRAs) and 401(k)s

- Rents (from property you own and lease)

- Royalties

- Other investment income

**TIP**

If you haven't done so already, create a My Social Security account at www.ssa.gov/myaccount. You can then log in to obtain valuable information, such as your estimated monthly Social Security payments when you decide to start claiming your benefits.

**REMEMBER**

Your net worth can help you gauge your overall financial health. During your working years, your net worth should be rising. After you retire, it may start to decline, which is okay, as long as you don't outlive your savings. Monitor your net worth, checking it at least once a year to ensure you're meeting your financial goals and not heading toward insolvency.

**REMEMBER**

If you struggle with personal finances, consult a financial advisor or a trusted family member skilled in money management for advice on handling the financial aspects of downsizing and retiring or preparing for retirement. Some people are too embarrassed about their financial situation to share it with others, but being honest and open about it with someone who knows how to manage finances is the best way to get some control over your future.

# Distinguishing between Essentials and Extras

Face it, you don't need much to live. For most individuals or couples, a bedroom, bathroom, and kitchen would do the trick. An efficiency apartment. A tiny home. A camper. So, distinguishing between wants and needs usually comes down to prioritizing within a fixed budget.

You know your net worth and monthly income (discussed in the previous section). You're now ready to examine what you need and what you want in light of what you can afford. Here's what to do:

1. **Make two lists — one for essentials and the other for extras.**

   Consider labeling one "What I/We *Need*" and the other "What I/We *Want*."

2. **List everything you need on your essentials list.**

   This list includes all the nonnegotiables, such as housing (mortgage/rent), electricity, gas, water, sewer, taxes, food, clothing, healthcare, transportation, internet, phone, household maintenance, taxes, and so on.

3. **List everything you want (but don't need) on your extras list.**

   This list includes dining out, entertainment, hobbies, gifts, and travel.

4. **Put the items on your extras list in order of priority.**

5. **Assign a dollar value to each item on each list.** You'll probably make this a monthly dollar amount. If you have only annual amounts, divide by 12.

6. **Adjust items on your lists so that their total cost is within your means.**

   If you spend more than your income, consider adjustments such as spending less on eating out, reprioritizing items, and removing low-priority items from your extras list.

The goal of this exercise is to start you thinking about what you really need to live and the lifestyle you can afford. In the next section, you're encouraged to draft a budget that provides a more detailed accounting.

# Drawing Up Preliminary Plans

Planning for downsizing is like planning a vacation. You come up with your big idea — your vision — and then you break it down into tasks that bring your vision to fruition.

In the case of a vacation, your vision is usually a vacation type or destination. You want to go hiking in the mountains or relax on a beach. You then create plans around that vision. Your plan must cover how you're going to get to your destination, what you'll do once you're there, what you need to pack, and how you're going to pay for it all.

With downsizing, your vision usually includes location, housing, and lifestyle (see Chapter 2 in Book 3). To bring your vision to fruition, you need to draw up a budget and a to-do list, create a packing list, schedule activities, and delegate tasks. The following sections lead you through that process.

## Drafting a budget

Unless you're independently wealthy, successful downsizing relies a great deal on your ability to manage a budget. Think of downsizing as a business. You have start-up costs and operational costs, so create a budget for each to identify costs and pinpoint where you'll get the money to cover those costs. The following section takes a big-picture look at budgeting.

## Start-up costs

Start-up costs are those that apply to making the transition, such as the following:

>> If you own your existing home and plan to sell it, the cost of preparing it for sale

>> If you're going to purchase a new home, the cost of the down payment and closing

>> Packing and moving costs

>> Cost of new furniture and furnishings

To cover these start-up costs, you'll probably rely mostly on savings and the sale of existing assets, not on monthly income. For example, the down payment will come from savings or from the sale of your existing residence. You'll have to come up with a chunk of change from your savings or a separate short-term loan to cover the cost of preparing your home for sale and moving and storing (if necessary) your belongings. As for the cost of furniture and furnishings for your new place, you may be able to pay for those out of the proceeds from the sale of your home or from savings.

**REMEMBER**

During your transition, you may have double the expenses for a time — two mortgage or rent payments, for example, while you're waiting to close the sale of your existing residence. Be sure that you have enough cash or credit (such as a home equity line of credit) to cover the additional costs.

## Operational costs

Operational costs are monthly expenses, which include the following:

>> Mortgage/rent

>> Home repairs/maintenance

>> Homeowner's insurance

>> Utilities (electricity, gas, water, sewer, trash)

>> Phone and internet service

>> Auto and auto insurance

>> Health insurance and out-of-pocket medical and dental expenses

>> Groceries

>> Clothing

>> Toiletries

>> Pet care

>> Dining out

>> Entertainment (movies, concerts, plays)

>> Travel

>> Gifts

**WARNING**

Regardless of whether you're downsizing to retire or merely to scale back, don't create a budget that has you living from paycheck to paycheck. Factor in a buffer to cover unexpected expenses and situations. Some couples draft a budget that enables them to live on one income, so that if anything happens to one of them, the other can carry them through at least for a few months.

People have devised all sorts of clever methods for budgeting. One of the simplest is to calculate your fixed expenses — the cost of all essentials — and then pay yourself a monthly allowance you can use to buy anything you want — dinner out, theater tickets, mani-pedis, whatever. If you're a couple, you may want to divide your monthly allowance between the two of you.

**REMEMBER**

Software, including smartphone apps, is readily available to help with creating and managing budgets. You can use a basic spreadsheet program such as Excel, a personal finance program such as Quicken, or a personal finance app such as Mint. Try using a personal finance program or app, because it can automatically track and categorize your spending to help you stay on budget.

## Creating a packing list

Regardless of whether you're moving from one home to another or taking your show on the road as a nomad, you need to figure out what you're taking with you. Chapter 4 gets into the nitty-gritty of sorting belongings, but start thinking now about what you'll be keeping and what you'll be getting rid of.

**TIP**

Create a separate inventory list for each room in the house and divide each list in two — one side for items you plan to keep, and the other for items you know you're going to get rid of. Focus on large items, such as furniture, kitchen appliances, cars, and large power tools. You can deal with the smaller items as you sort your belongings.

# Making a to-do list

Perhaps the most important step to laying the groundwork for downsizing is creating a *to-do list* — a comprehensive list of everything that needs to be done to move you from point A to point B, from your current living situation to your new life.

Everyone's downsizing to-do list is unique. Lists vary based on the person's or couple's current situation, downsizing goals, and what has already been done. For example, someone who's downsizing from a large home to a small condo will have a very different to-do list from someone who's getting rid of nearly all their personal possessions, buying a camper, and hitting the road. Here's a sample to inspire you to start creating your own to-do list:

1. Choose a location and lifestyle.
2. Have a meeting of the minds with loved ones to ensure that everyone is in agreement.
3. Get prequalified for a mortgage loan.
4. Connect with a qualified real estate agent.
5. Research existing homes or new construction.
6. Downsize belongings by half.
7. Place existing home on the market.
8. Make an offer on an existing home or new construction.
9. Pack.
10. Move.

After you have a general list, you can break down the process even further by creating separate lists for each step. For example, you can break down Step 3 into researching lenders and loan rates, choosing a lender, and providing the required paperwork. You can break down Step 7 into lining up contractors to address any repairs and maintenance issues, and meeting with your real estate agent. For Step 9, you can break it down room by room.

TIP

As you create your list, envision the day you'll be transitioning to your new downsized life. Then, list all the steps you must take to reach that point.

## Scheduling activities

With your to-do list (from the previous section) in hand, start scheduling activities. For some items on your list, you can simply choose a deadline — a date by which the task will be completed. For other items on the list, you may schedule a date and time. What's important is that every item on the list has a point in time when it will be completed. As the old saying goes, "A goal without a deadline is merely a wish." And wishes often go unfulfilled when they're neglected. Without goals, you'd never score in soccer, football, hockey, or lacrosse.

**REMEMBER**

With new construction, schedule time to visit the building site frequently to monitor progress, ask questions, and communicate any concerns you have. Builders don't catch everything. And regardless of whether you're buying an existing home or building a new home, schedule time to meet the five neighbors on each side of you and the ten across the street. In real estate, this is known as the *5, 5, 10 rule*. If you're really interested in what's going on in the area, knock on some doors to find out.

**TIP**

If you're buying furniture, appliances, or flooring, schedule time to visit the design center in each store and speak with the professionals on staff to get advice. You can usually walk around on your own to check out what's available and even measure items to see how they'll fit, but you may want to get professional advice when you're picking out styles and colors.

## Delegating duties

With a to-do list and a schedule, you know *what* needs to be done and *when*. Now, you just need to know *who* is in charge of each task — who's accountable for completing each task or ensuring it's completed by the scheduled date and time?

If you're taking care of everything on your own, delegating the work and responsibilities isn't an issue, but if you're relying on others to contribute, assign each task to one or more individuals. Provide each person (professional or not) with a personalized to-do list along with deadlines and let them work out the details. Keep in touch to monitor their progress and ask whether they need help or guidance, but let them handle the details. Don't try to micromanage the process — micromanaging hurts morale.

» Recognizing a key first step — stop cluttering

» Making a monumental task more manageable

» Dividing your belongings into six stacks

# Chapter **4**

# Sorting Your Belongings

A major part of downsizing — perhaps the biggest challenge of all — involves eliminating a good chunk of the possessions you accumulated over the years and organizing the rest. Consider this example: One woman downsized from a 3,000-square-foot home to one half that size. For the first two weeks after she moved, she couldn't pull her car into the garage because it was packed with furniture and other belongings that wouldn't fit inside the new house. Her first order of business — having a garage sale to get rid of it all. Had she decluttered before moving, she would've avoided moving all that stuff. And she moved it twice — from the home she sold to a storage unit and from there to her new home. Moral of the story: Declutter *first* and have the garage sale *first.*

One of the goals of downsizing is to lighten your load — to unshackle yourself from the ball and chain restricting your freedom and your ability to live a richer, fuller life with less worry. No, we're not talking about your spouse; we're referring to that other ball and chain: the home that's larger than you need packed with two or three times the belongings you'll ever use. Yes, it's high time you declutter, and the first step is to sort your belongings. (For more on the art of decluttering, check out *Decluttering For Dummies* by Jane Stoller, published by Wiley, and AARP's *Keep the Memories, Lose the Stuff,* by Matt Paxton.)

This chapter delivers the guidance and motivation you need to begin decluttering your life. It starts by covering decluttering basics and then leads you room by room through the process with the ultimate goal of creating six easy-to-manage stacks:

>> Keep

>> Store

>> Sell

>> Donate

>> Give away

>> Toss

With six convenient stacks, you'll be well on your way to meeting your downsizing goal, addressing each stack in turn.

# Mastering Decluttering Basics

Let's be honest: Decluttering is difficult. We're attached to our belongings. As a result, people can end up moving or storing much of what they don't need, which defeats the very purpose of downsizing.

To avoid this common mistake, master the following downsizing basics:

TIP

>> **Start with the end in mind.** Before packing anything to move to your new place, be sure you know where you're going to put it.

Think about downsizing in terms of a percentage or fraction. If you're moving to a place that's a third the size of your current home, set a goal of getting rid of at least two-thirds of your belongings.

>> **Take inventory of what you have.** One of the first things a moving company does is a walk-through of your home to estimate the number of trucks and movers needed. Start with the big items — furniture and large appliances — and measure carefully for fit. Decide whether to keep what you have or buy new. After furniture and appliances, move on to smaller items. An accurate inventory helps you determine how many moving boxes you need and starts you thinking about what you'll keep and what you'll get rid of.

>> **Set a reasonable deadline.** Downsizing takes time, but set a deadline to motivate yourself.

>> **Divide and conquer.** After setting a reasonable deadline, set even more reasonable milestones. For example, you can set a separate deadline for each room or set interim deadlines — 25, 50, and 75 percent completion dates. You can also divide and conquer by delegating some of the work among friends and family members who have volunteered to help.

>> **Take out the trash.** Eliminating trash is a no-brainer — an easy way to declutter without having to spend much time and effort deciding what to get rid of. For example, go through your spice cabinet and clear out spices that you *never* use and *will never* use.

>> **Start with small, easy downsizing projects.** Ease into downsizing by starting with a cabinet, closet, or small room. Getting started is often the biggest obstacle. By tackling small projects, you build momentum, motivation, and confidence to tackle bigger jobs.

>> **Eliminate duplicates.** If you have two or three or four of the same item, get rid of all but one. You're not downsizing to Noah's Ark, where you need two of every animal.

>> **Digitize photo prints and paper documents.** Eliminate as much of the paper you store as possible by shredding what you no longer want or need and digitizing the rest.

>> **Don't rely on storage.** Strive to get rid of as much as possible without having to rent a storage unit for the overflow. You're downsizing to reduce your expenses and free yourself from the burden of having too many possessions.

Storage can be a crutch to avoid making difficult decisions.

**REMEMBER**

# Stopping Yourself from Cluttering

One of the keys to decluttering is to stop cluttering. Now that you're downsizing, the time has come to stop doing that. Put a moratorium on buying anything new until you're living in your newly downsized home. And after you transition to your downsized existence, reconsider every purchase.

To determine whether you really need something, ask yourself the following questions:

>> **Do I really need this? Can I live without it? How often will I use it in the future?** If you're not going to use it often, is it something you can borrow?

>> **Do I already have one of these?** Are you thinking of buying an item simply because you've misplaced the one you have?

>> **How much value will this add to my life?** Is the cost, care, and storage you'll invest in the item more than the utility or joy it will bring into your life?

**REMEMBER**

As the old saying goes, "When you find yourself in a hole, stop digging." If you're thinking of downsizing, stop buying stuff. In the process of downsizing, you may discover that you already own it.

# Decluttering One Room at a Time

According to a Chinese proverb, "A journey of a thousand miles begins with a single step." Likewise, the long process of decluttering starts with a single room — and usually with a single drawer of a single cabinet in that room.

Decluttering a large home can be an overwhelming task, especially if you or others in your household have lived there for years or even decades. Approach this task room by room to make it more manageable. The following sections offer guidance on a room-by-room basis.

## Bedrooms

Assuming that your bedrooms contain only typical bedroom items, decluttering is fairly straightforward: You're dealing mostly with clothing and bedding. However, if your bedrooms are packed with books, a TV, plants, and other items, each bedroom can be like a microcosm of your entire home (without the kitchen and bathroom, of course). Start with the nightstands, dressers, and closet.

### Nightstands

Nightstands are clutter magnets, especially when they have not only a top but one or more shelves or drawers. You have your bare essentials: lamp, alarm clock, book, headphones, charger, paper and pen, glass of water, coaster, reading glasses, CPAP machine. And then you have all the extras: sleep mask, candles, hand cream, body lotion, knickknacks . . . the list goes on and on.

Sort all the little stuff (not the lamp or alarm clock, for example) into two piles — what to keep and what to get rid of — pack everything you want to keep into the smallest box possible, and label it "Nightstand."

**REMEMBER**

The more clutter you have on surfaces, the more time you spend cleaning. Every item and every horizontal surface collects dust. You must dust every item, move it to clean the surface, and then move it back. As you downsize, strive to keep all horizontal surfaces (tabletops, counters, and shelves) as barren as possible. Trim your knickknack collection down to a point at which your favorites will fit in a small box and get rid of the rest.

### Dressers

Dressers are notorious for becoming cluttered over time — the top and all the drawers. Decluttering the top is like decluttering a nightstand. The drawers pose another challenge. If the drawers are so packed that you need to push clothes down to open or close them, you have a problem. If they're stuffed with clothes you haven't worn in six months, there's hope.

Drawer by drawer, remove everything and sort it into two stacks: what to keep and what to get rid of. Fold everything you're keeping so items can be stored vertically instead of stacked on top of one another. Then, place them back in their designated drawer — for example, sock drawer, underwear drawer, T-shirt drawer, and so on.

**REMEMBER**

The good news about dressers is, you can pretty much move them as is to your downsized abode, assuming you're going to keep them.

**TIP**

Start thinking about how you can declutter in terms of the container shapes and sizes you'll need when you're ready to sort all your belongings.

### Closet

Closets are sort of like mini storage units for rooms. The best approach for decluttering any closet is to empty it first. Lay out everything so you know what you're dealing with. Then create two stacks: one for keepers and one for everything you're going to get rid of — mostly anything you haven't used over the past year or so. Sort everything you're going to keep and then pack it (if you're moving soon) or return it to the closet.

**TIP**

All sorts of new closet cabinets and organizers are now available to maximize storage space while keeping everything in convenient reach. Explore your options before returning items to your closet. When your closet is empty is the perfect time to install new shelving, rods, and organizers.

## Bathrooms

Bathrooms start their lives as simple spaces — toilet, tub/shower, sink, medicine cabinet, and some sort of storage below the sink. Then, you need somewhere to hang your towels, so you install hangers or hooks for towels in use and shelves for clean towels. Maybe you even install hooks on the bathroom door. As your needs grow, you bring in another cabinet or install more shelving and hooks. Soon, you can barely move without bumping into something or knocking something over.

Here are a few suggestions for decluttering your bathroom:

>> **Review your towel collection.** Get rid of any towels and washrags you don't use. Animal shelters are a great place to donate towels and linens.

>> **Properly dispose of old medications and any meds you're not going to use.** Check the expiration dates and contact a local pharmacy to find out where to take your old medications for disposal.

>> **Thin the herd of shampoos, conditioners, creams, lotions, and medicinal ointments.** Combine partially used products when possible and dump anything you haven't used for more than a year and don't plan to use in the foreseeable future.

>> **Clean out all drawers.** Empty the drawers onto a large table, sort everything by kind (hair care, dental hygiene, makeup, and so on), install drawer organizers, and return to the drawers all items you decide to keep while maintaining the groupings you created when you sorted.

## Kitchen

A good sign that your kitchen needs decluttering is that you're using more than two-thirds of your cabinet or counter space. A good goal to work toward is to clear about 90 percent of your counter space and organize your cabinets so that you don't have to dig through everything to find what you're looking for. Here are a few recommendations:

>> **Reduce your collection of pots and pan.** Unless you're a master chef, you can usually get by with a small, medium, and large pot and a large frying pan.

>> **Reduce your storage container collection.** Ten to 15 medium-large stackable storage containers should do the trick. Pitch or recycle the rest, including any containers that don't have a matching lid.

>> **Lessen your amount of cups, glasses, and dishware.** If you're like most people, you have a collection that greatly exceeds the needs of three to four households.

>> **Clear your countertops.** Having nothing more than a coffeemaker and maybe a toaster on your countertops is ideal. Clear off anything you don't use at least once a week. If you have a dishwasher, you can do without having a dish drainer on your counter, or you can buy a dish drainer that fits inside one of your sinks. Evict any non-kitchen items — mail, pens, paper, keys, and so forth.

>> **Use drawer dividers to organize utensils, knives, and small gadgets.** Don't just dump items back into a drawer.

>> **Dump any food or spices that are over six months old.** When you return items to your pantry, group them by type — cereals, pastas, canned foods, condiments, baking supplies, and so on.

>> **Minimize your cookbook collection.** Store your favorite recipes on your computer or smartphone and simply look up recipes online when you want to cook something new. If you're old school, keep a few of your favorite cookbooks!

## Living room

Technology has done much of the heavy lifting in decluttering living rooms. An entertainment system now consists basically of a flat-screen smart TV with a soundbar, and you no longer need storage for DVDs or videotapes — you can stream whatever you want to watch. However, living rooms can still become cluttered with books, magazines, knickknacks, remote controls, game controllers, and other items. Here are a few suggestions for reducing the clutter:

>> Donate books you'll never touch to the local library and toss old magazines into the recycle bin.

>> Keep a few of your favorite belongings on display and hide everything else that's sitting on shelves, tables, and other surfaces, including photos, knickknacks, and candles.

>> Store remote controls, video game controllers, device chargers, and other electronics in a separate box or basket in a drawer or under an end table.

**TIP**

If you're in the market for a new coffee table or ottoman, look for one that includes storage. While you don't want to enable any pack rat tendencies you may have by providing yourself more storage space, small furniture with built-in storage can replace the storage you're losing by downsizing to a smaller space.

## Office

Whether you have a bona fide office or just a desk and a filing cabinet set up somewhere in your home, here are a few suggestions for downsizing and organizing your files and office supplies:

>> **Eliminate anything that's not office-y.** Anything that belongs in a kitchen, closet, gym, playroom, or knickknack cabinet needs to go. Your office should be all business, free from distractions.

» **Clear the bookshelves.** Start by removing anything that's not a book — office supplies, photographs, medications, nutritional supplements, old tech (hardware and software), and CDs and DVDs. You can combine some items with similar items from other areas of your home or place them in clear or labeled storage boxes for easy as-needed access. And, of course, you can dispose of anything you haven't touched in a year.

» **Dump old files and folders.** Consider using the following three-pile system:

- **Shred:** Junk mail, receipts (except those you need for warranties, proof of purchase, or taxes), last year's monthly bank and investment statements, last year's pay stubs, maintenance and repair records for cars or homes you no longer own, documents for organizations you no longer belong to, expired service contracts, expired warranties, your deceased pet's vet records

- **Scan:** Tax returns older than three years (or longer, in some instances; check with the IRS); receipts and credit card statements needed for warranties, proof of purchase, and noncash charitable donations; annual bank and brokerage statements; pension documents; social security statements

- **Store:** Birth certificates; passports; marriage certificates; divorce certificates; death certificates; Social Security cards; titles and deeds to cars and real estate assets; estate documents (wills, trusts, life insurance policies, powers of attorney, advance medical directives, and end-of-life documents); loan and mortgage documents (including paid-in-full statements for every loan you've ever had); military service records; medical records; your three most recent tax returns

  Store difficult-to-replace documents, such as your birth certificate, passport, titles, deeds, and Social Security cards in a lockbox or a home safe that's rated for temperatures above 450 degrees for 60 minutes.

**REMEMBER**

» **Get organized.** After getting rid of as much excess as possible, organize the rest. Buy drawer dividers to organize everything in your desk and use boxes or a filing cabinet to organize all the folders, documents, and office supplies you decide to keep. Your goal is to make sure everything is easy to move and find, and fits in a designated space in your new destination.

Consider using clear boxes to store folders and supplies, so you can quickly and easily see what each box contains.

**TIP**

# Laundry room

Laundry rooms are often much larger than they need to be and end up being used as auxiliary closet space. Downsizing your laundry room possessions depends on what you have stored in it. Here are a few general suggestions:

>> Tighten the caps on all laundry and cleaning products and place them in a plastic box or in a plastic bag inside a cardboard box in case they leak in transit. You're better off moving these items yourself instead of placing them inside the moving truck. (Take this opportunity to combine products, such as two half bottles of the same stain remover.)

>> If your laundry room doubles as a linen closet, sort your towels and bedding and get rid of anything you haven't used in the past six months and have no plans of using in the next six months.

If you're moving soon, you can use the towels and bedding to wrap fragile items or pack them in boxes or trash bags for your move.

>> Throw away any hangers you no longer use (you know the ones), and sort the remaining hangers by size and type.

>> If you store anything else in your laundry room, use this opportunity to find a more logical place for it.

All you really need is room for a washer and dryer, a folding table, a drying rack, possibly an ironing board, and a little space for supplies.

# Garage or shed

Decluttering a garage or shed can be a monumental task. You may have some heavy-duty equipment and tools, such as a riding mower, push mower, power washer, log splitter, and shop vac along with a collection of smaller tools, gardening equipment and supplies, sports gear, and more.

Start by emptying your garage or shed completely so you can see everything you have, sort the contents more easily, and clean the space when it's empty. Having a clean, empty space will gently discourage you from putting anything back into it that you don't absolutely need. Choose a weekend that won't be too hot, too cold, or wet, starting on a Saturday, so you can spill over to Sunday, if necessary.

TIP

Before placing anything back into your garage or shed, designate various zones for storage — for example, designate one area for gardening tools and supplies, another for sports gear, and another for power tools. Visit your local hardware store to check out products for organizing garages and sheds, such as toolboxes, shelves and racks, cabinets, workbenches, and wall organizers. Take the opportunity to not only downsize but also get organized.

# Sorting Your Stuff into Six Categories

Every downsizing expert has a system for sorting items. Some recommend a four-box system: keep, trash, donate, and sell. Others narrow it down to two: keep and get rid of. We recommend that you sort items into the following six categories:

>> Keep

>> Store

>> Sell

>> Give away

>> Donate

>> Toss

**REMEMBER**

Use any system that works best for you. If having six stacks of items seems too complicated, feel free to opt for a simpler method. The method here provides a separate category for items you can offer to family and friends first. It also provides an option for people who have excess stuff they want to put in storage instead of getting rid of entirely.

**TIP**

You may want to add one more category to the list: overnight essentials or personal necessities. If you're planning to stay at a motel or somewhere else between the time you move out of your old place and move into your new place, pack a bag with the clothes, toiletries, medications, and other items you'll need when you're between homes.

## Keep

The keep category is for everything you plan to move with you and put to good use, such as the following:

>> Your bed and dressers

>> Living room furniture

>> Your main TV

>> Cookware and dinnerware you'll use regularly

>> Clothing you'll wear at least once a year

**REMEMBER**

The guideline for getting rid of clothing is this: If it doesn't fit or you haven't worn it in the past year, get rid of it.

>> Bedding (one or two sets per bed at most)

>> Framed photos and other keepsakes

>> Essential documents

>> Jewelry

**REMEMBER**

Keeping may involve rearranging. You may not be able to display everything the way you did in your old house. Some items that were previously on display may now need to be in cabinets.

## Store

Reserve storage for items that you'll probably use once or twice a year. If you can't imagine using something or even looking at it for several years, you should probably get rid of it, regardless of how attached you are to it emotionally. Store items in the basement, attic, garage, or shed of your new home. Avoid renting a storage unit, which defeats the purpose of downsizing!

**WARNING**

Don't store items merely because you're struggling to make the tough call to get rid of them. If it can't pay rent, then you're providing free housing to something that's not offering you anything of value in return.

## Sell

The only way some people will get rid of anything is if they can sell it for what they think it's worth. Unfortunately, most people won't buy anything you own for what *you* think it's worth. Whether they're shopping online or at a garage sale or an estate sale, they're looking for deep discounts, which is one reason that some people never sell anything.

**REMEMBER**

Often what stands in the way of people getting rid of stuff is that they can't bear the idea of losing money on it. Selling a $350 juicer for $20 hardly seems worth the trouble, so you pack it up and move it to your new house, and there it sits gathering dust. Try to get past the idea of what you paid for something and think about what you *will* pay for it in terms of moving it, storing it, and thinking about it in the future. Cut your losses and sell it for whatever you can get for it, or just give it away.

## Give away

One of the easiest ways to get rid of anything, especially large, bulky items, is to offer it free for the taking. All you need to do is take photos and post them to your social media accounts or send a group email or text to all your friends, family members, and colleagues letting them know what you're getting rid of. Even if nobody you know wants it, someone may know someone who does.

Don't coerce your children into taking things they really don't want just because you lack the courage to make the tough call to get rid of them. You don't want to saddle your adult children with a burden you no longer want to carry yourself.

## Donate

One of the easiest ways to get rid of household items is to donate them to a charitable organization: Goodwill, The Salvation Army, a veterans organization, a local house of worship, a local shelter, or some other philanthropic organization that accepts clothes and household items. With some organizations, you can get rid of everything you want to donate simply by boxing it up and making a single phone call!

You can donate just about anything, including the following items:

>> Clothing, including shoes and accessories

>> Jewelry

>> Cookware, dinnerware, glassware

>> Books, DVDs, CDs, videotapes

>> Stereos, radios, small electronics

>> Bicycles

>> Tools

## Toss

You're down to the last category, which contains all the stuff that didn't make the cut in any of the other categories. These are the items that belong in the dumpster, such as the following:

>> Old food storage containers

>> Anything that's broken and not worth fixing

>> Clothing that is stained and ripped

>> Personal items that nobody wants

>> Food items and spices past their expiration date

» Deciding whether to buy, rent, or build

» Calculating your target living space

» Making your new place more livable, ergonomically

» Scoping out different housing designs

» Considering the costs of various living arrangements

# Chapter **5**

# Gimme Shelter: Choosing a Home

Unless you're opting for a nomadic lifestyle (see Book 4), you're going to need a place to live when you downsize — a home, condo, apartment, or some other shelter. The good news is, you have more options than ever before. The bad news is, you have more options than ever before. Which option is best for you depends on multiple factors, including your desired location, afford-ability, your health and fitness, how close you want to be to loved ones, and more.

This chapter introduces you to a broad range of options to increase your aware-ness of the possibilities and start you thinking about the pros and cons of each option. By the end of this chapter, you should hopefully have a pretty clear idea of where you want to live and the type of living quarters that are the best fit for your desired lifestyle.

# Finding Your Place in the World: Location, Location, Location

Location means something different to everyone, but when you look at property values, you realize that most people value nearly all the same things in a neighborhood:

>> Healthy environment (clean air and water)

>> Affordable cost of living

>> Attractive surroundings (landscape and development)

>> Low crime rates

>> Considerate neighbors

>> Good schools

>> Convenient access to services, shopping, restaurants, and things to do

>> Proximity to family members and friends

Answer the following questions to guide your search and narrow your options:

>> What's the climate like? If you don't want to be trudging through snow in the middle of winter, you can instantly rule out a variety of locations.

>> Are there family members or friends I want or need to live near?

>> Which locations would be most conducive to the lifestyle I envision? (See Chapter 2 in Book 3 for lifestyle considerations.)

>> Of the locations I would consider, which are most affordable? Compare costs of living, taxes, travel costs, and other budget considerations.

>> Is the location easy to get around? Think in terms of traffic, availability of public transportation, airports, trains, and the ability to walk or ride a bike to get where you want to be.

>> Does the location facilitate my health and fitness? For example, if you have terrible seasonal allergies, you may want to move somewhere you can breathe more easily.

>> Will I feel safe there?

>> Where will I go for essentials (doctors, dentist, groceries), and how will I get there?

**REMEMBER**

When you're buying into or building in an area, consider the value of the home not only now but in the future. Approach your home as an investment, not just a place to live.

# Deciding Whether to Buy or Rent

When you're in need of a place to live, you always have the option of buying or renting. The following questions can guide you through the process of making the right choice:

>> **Can you afford to buy?** If you can afford to pay cash for a home or you have the income and creditworthiness to qualify for a mortgage loan, along with the financial resources to cover insurance, property taxes, homeowner association fees, and maintenance, buying may be the better option, but that depends on your answer to the next question.

>> **Does buying or renting offer greater value?** Basically, if you can rent something comparable for less than a monthly mortgage payment plus the cost of insurance, property taxes, homeowner association fees, and maintenance, renting may be an attractive option, especially if you don't expect property values to increase very much over the time you plan to own the property. In most cases, if you can pay cash or you have good credit, owning isn't much more expensive than renting (it may even cost less), *and* you have something to sell later for a profit.

>> **Do you want to take care of the house or hire people who will?** When you buy a home, you're on the hook for maintenance and repairs. When you rent a place, you may never have to worry about mowing the lawn; shoveling sidewalks; replacing the roof, furnace, or hot water tank; fixing a leaky toilet; recarpeting; or painting.

**REMEMBER**

Buying is a long-term commitment; renting isn't. If you've just lost your spouse or experienced some other traumatic event that's prompting you to move, consider a temporary living arrangement, such as renting or moving in with a relative, until you're through the grieving process and in a better position to develop a long-term plan. Don't make any major decisions about your future for a year or so — that will give you the time you need to grieve and get back to a position to make rational decisions, not emotional ones.

Don't even think about buying until you've met all the following criteria:

>> You're debt-free or you have a manageable level of debt.

>> You have decent credit (generally a credit score of 680 or higher).

>> You have enough cash reserves to cover a down payment.

>> You have an emergency fund to cover at least three months of expenses.

>> You plan to stay put for several years.

# Deciding Whether to Build or Buy

If you're going to buy something instead of rent, you have the choice of buying an existing property or building from scratch. Buying an existing property offers the following advantages:

>> **Convenience:** If you have cash or preapproval for a mortgage loan, you simply find the home you want, make an offer, and then close on the sale.

>> **Speed:** You can buy a home and move into it in a matter of weeks.

>> **Simplified financing:** When you buy an existing property, you have one loan that's typically at a fixed rate.

>> **Lower cost (maybe):** Assuming you can find the perfect place and it's in good condition, an existing home typically costs less than a new build. If the existing home needs substantial repairs and renovations to suit your needs, though, building may be the less costly option.

>> **More predictable cost:** When you buy a home, you know up front what the cost will be. When you're building, costs may change over the course of the project, and they usually go up, not down.

By contrast, building a home from scratch comes with the following advantages:

>> **Customization:** You can build the home you want instead of settling for what's available.

>> **Modernization:** A new home meets all the latest codes and standards for heating, cooling, ventilation, insulation, electricity, and plumbing, along with health and safety standards for building materials. Newly constructed homes are typically *greener* — more efficient in terms of energy and water use — which can also save you money.

>> **No maintenance or repair costs:** Since everything's new, and usually under warranty, you can look forward to at least a few years with little to no maintenance or repair costs.

>> **Possibly better resale value:** Most buyers prefer newer homes over older ones, so if you decide to sell your home later, you'll likely profit more from a home you built.

Unfortunately, while having a shiny new custom-built home to move into is an attractive proposition, new construction has several disadvantages, including the following:

>> You have to find a suitable lot on which to build the home, which can be quite a challenge.

>> You must find a reputable builder who's committed to quality construction.

>> Financing is complicated. You'll have a separate loan for the lot, a series of construction loans, and then a final mortgage loan at the end to consolidate the other loans.

**TIP**

Work with a lender that specializes in new construction loans to help simplify the process.

>> Your interest rate is less predictable. When interest rates are on the rise, you may be looking at having a much higher interest rate by the time your new home is finished than at the time construction began. Think about what your interest rate will be a year from when you break ground. (Of course, any decline in interest rates works in your favor.)

>> The cost may be less predictable. When you buy an existing home, you know the cost up front. However, when you're building, costs may change depending on the price of construction materials and labor.

**REMEMBER**

When negotiating a building contract, if possible, opt for a lump-sum contract over a cost-plus contract. With a *lump-sum contract,* you pay the price you've been quoted. With a *cost-plus contract,* the price covers the builder's expenses plus a certain amount or percentage over that amount.

>> You need to communicate and collaborate closely with your builder to ensure you're getting what you want and the project stays on schedule.

**WARNING**

If you're building a new home, nail down all the details about what you want *before* construction begins. Every change you make during the process can cost you more money.

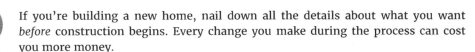

# Estimating the Living Space You'll Need

When you decide to downsize, you need to estimate the living space you'll want or need to support your new lifestyle. According to some sources, the average person needs 100–400 square feet of space to feel comfortable in their living quarters, but that's a wide range and an arbitrary number. Some people may feel more comfortable with 1,000–2,000 square feet.

You can take various approaches to estimating your desired living space, such as the following:

>> **Subtract rooms.** Suppose your current residence has three bedrooms, two of which you never use, and two full bathrooms, one of which you never use. You can probably easily downsize to a unit with two bedrooms and one bathroom, one bedroom and a bathroom, or even an efficiency apartment. Can you live without a basement or garage?

>> **Envision where you're going to put everything.** Think about where you're going to put everything you're taking with you — your bed, dressers, living room furniture, dining room table and chairs, kitchenware and appliances, office furniture, and so on. Draw a floor plan showing where everything will go and estimate how much space you'll need for everything to fit.

>> **Visit homes of various sizes.** Check out different-sized homes to see how they feel to you. If you feel cramped, you may have found your lower limit.

REMEMBER

Keep in mind that a home's floor plan can make it feel more or less spacious. You may feel more comfortable in less space depending on how the rooms are arranged.

The following sections look more closely at what you should consider when determining the amount of living space you'll need.

## Total square footage

Downsizing doesn't necessarily require you to live the rest of your life in cramped quarters. By shedding belongings and making more efficient use of existing space, you may feel *less* cramped in *less* space, especially if you move to an area and adopt a lifestyle that has you spending more time outside your home.

REMEMBER

Having a *great room*, which combines your kitchen, living room, and dining room into one large area, can make each of those areas feel larger while placing everything within convenient reach.

## Rooms and room sizes

One way to look at living space is to break it down by room and estimate the square footage for each:

>> Kitchen: _____ square feet

>> Living room: _____ square feet

>> Dining room: _____ square feet

>> Main bedroom: _____ square feet

>> Second bedroom: _____ square feet

>> Main bathroom: _____ square feet

>> Second bathroom or half bath: _____ square feet

>> Office: _____ square feet

**REMEMBER**

Consider your current and future needs. You may need only one bedroom and one bathroom, but what if you have guests? Will you need a second bedroom for family members or friends who visit from out of town? Do you think you may need a bedroom for a live-in caregiver in the foreseeable future? Will you need a separate office, or can you carve out an area of your living room for office space?

## Living room and dining room or office/den?

Most people who downsize move to a place without a formal dining room. They eat at the counter or at a table in the kitchen or great room, but if you're buying an existing home, it may come with a dining room. You don't necessarily need to use it as a dining room, however. You can use it as an office or den, or knock out a wall or two to expand your kitchen or living room.

**WARNING**

Be careful about removing walls. In some homes, certain walls support the upper floors or the roof or may have plumbing or electrical wires embedded in them. Before removing any wall, consult an expert — an architect or a builder.

## Entertainment areas

By *entertainment areas,* we mean spaces used specifically for games, such as billiards, poker, or table tennis; a home theater; or a bar. Chances are, if you're downsizing, entertainment areas will be the first to go, but everyone's different — if you entertain frequently and need a wide-open space for your guests to hang out and have fun, your game room may be the biggest room in your house.

**REMEMBER**

Entertainment areas don't need to be part of your traditional living space. They can be your garage, extra space above a garage, or a basement. You may also consider your living room or great room your entertainment area.

## Office space

With computers shrinking in size and books and paperwork going digital, office space can be anything from a converted den or bedroom, to a desk in the living room or kitchen, to a cubbyhole under a stairwell. Your "office" doesn't even need to be a permanent physical location — it can be a laptop or tablet computer that you can take anywhere with you.

**REMEMBER**

When you're downsizing, look for opportunities to consolidate and create multi-purpose spaces; for example, a single room that serves as an office can double as a guest bedroom. Your living room can double as your game room. You can consolidate your kitchen and dining room.

## Outdoor living areas

Outdoor living areas like porches, decks, and balconies are great, assuming you use them and they're easy to maintain. Otherwise, you can usually do without them or adjust to smaller versions.

**REMEMBER**

Outdoor living areas aren't essential, but they can significantly enhance your quality of life. Some people will spend entire days working on their porch or reading, while others will barely peek out a window. Some like to go outside but would rather sit at a coffee shop, visit a park, or walk around the neighborhood. Envision how you'll be spending your time and plan your living space accordingly. If you love spending autumn evenings conversing with friends around a fire, a deck or patio may feel like a necessity to you, but if you rarely step outside, allocate your space and resources to other living areas.

## Pool or hot tub (or both)

Downsizing and maintaining a pool or hot tub may seem to be at cross-purposes, but we're talking about reinventing your life in the process of downsizing, so these luxuries are something to consider. Just keep in mind that both options require additional space and come with additional upkeep and expenses. People who downsize typically transition *away* from pools and hot tubs to shed the burden and save money.

# Basement (or not)

Assuming the place you're downsizing to isn't on a floodplain, a finished basement is always a plus. It serves as storage space, provides easy access to mechanicals (heating, cooling, and ventilation system, hot water heater, water softener, and electrical panel), and may even be converted into an extra bedroom, a bathroom, or a game room, provided there are doors or windows.

If your basement has its own entrance and windows that let in a lot of natural light, all the better. You have a perfect place for some extra living space. You may even be able to rent out the space for additional income.

REMEMBER

If you do live on a floodplain, be careful about buying a place with a basement. Make sure it has a reliable sump pump with backup power, and be sure to purchase flood insurance.

# Garage/parking

If you own a vehicle, don't overlook the importance of having a parking space for it, preferably an attached garage. Second best is a detached garage. Third best is having your own driveway. If you have to park on the street, visit the area in the evening when everyone is home from work to see what the parking situation is. If you can't find a place to park, think twice about buying into the area.

WARNING

In some housing additions, parking overnight on the street is illegal. Your vehicle may be ticketed or towed. If you visit a neighborhood at night and nobody's parking on the street, they're following either a written or an unwritten rule.

# Storage space

Even if you do an incredible job of reducing your possessions to the bare minimum, you'll need some storage space. You'll probably have at least several boxes of items you rarely use (or even look at) that you can't bring yourself to get rid of. Whether you're renting, buying, or building, think about where you're going to store those items. Does the place you're planning to rent, buy, or build have storage space built in — maybe a basement, attic, or closet under the stairs?

REMEMBER

Storage space isn't all the same. Some storage space is organized, and some isn't. The best storage exhibits the following qualities:

>> **Efficiency:** You can store more in less space with efficient storage.

>> **Convenience:** Shelves and drawers that are designed to enable you to see everything and easily access it are better than storage in which items are buried or pushed to the back.

>> **Protection:** Quality storage protects your belongings from dust, moisture, and pests.

# Considering Mobility and Accessibility

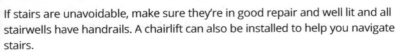

As you shop for a place to call home, give some thought to *mobility* and *accessibility* factors — how you're going to come and go, move around inside the place, and reach everything you need. You want your home accessible to babies in strollers, teens on crutches with sports injuries, grandparents with walkers. Consider, too, whether you and your partner will want to walk up and down steps 10 or 20 years from now.

Consider the following accommodations as you look to rent, buy, or build as well as to place in your home once you've moved in.

### Throughout the home

>> At least one entryway without stairs or with a ramp

>> Wider doorways and hallways to accommodate wheelchair and walker access

>> Doors that are easy to open with lever door handles instead of traditional round ones (automatic, motorized door openers may also be available)

>> Stair-free design (everything on one level)

REMEMBER

If stairs are unavoidable, make sure they're in good repair and well lit and all stairwells have handrails. A chairlift can also be installed to help you navigate stairs.

>> Smooth flooring and thresholds to facilitate movement within rooms and from room to room

WARNING

Avoid high pile carpeting, area rugs, and any textured floor that may pose a trip hazard.

>> Nonskid mats or nonslip strips on any slick or slippery surfaces

>> Soft floors (no ceramic tile, for example) to prevent falls, reduce injuries from falls, and prevent glass and ceramic items from shattering

>> Closets with low, easy-to-reach shelves and rods

TIP

Consider adding reinforcement between studs to ensure that all handrails have something solid to mount to.

### Lighting

>> Adequate lighting during the day (use the brightest bulbs approved for each fixture) and night-lights at night

>> Convenient, easy-to-operate light switches or automatic switches

>> Glow-in-the-dark switches

>> Convenient locations for flashlights throughout the home

>> Blackout shades in bedrooms to enhance sleep

### Bathrooms

>> Grab bars in the tub or shower and near the toilet

>> Walk-in shower or bathtub with a nonslip floor

>> Shower seat

>> Elevated toilet seat

>> Conveniently accessible cabinet, sink, and countertop

### Kitchen

>> Conveniently accessible cabinets and drawers

>> Lower countertops and sinks

In the kitchen, be sure to opt for lightweight pots, pans, and kitchenware. You may also want to look for a stove with controls on the front (instead of top) and a side-by-side refrigerator/freezer or one with a bottom freezer.

REMEMBER

Keep mobility and accessibility in mind when arranging furniture, such as coffee tables, and locating cables and cords to allow for unimpaired movement within and between rooms and eliminate any trip hazards.

# Exploring Your Housing Options

Housing comes in a variety of sizes and styles — from efficiency apartments and tiny homes to mansions. When you're in the market for a place to live, consider your options carefully.

## Traditional house

Traditional houses, often referred to as single-family homes, typically have a front and rear entrance, a garage, and a front and back yard. They come in a variety of styles. Here are a few styles that are more conducive to downsizing:

>> **Ranch:** These single-story houses are great for mobility because they have no stairs to climb. They also tend to be easier and more efficient to heat and cool.

>> **Cabin or cottage:** These small, compact, affordable homes are often perfect for downsizers. They cost less than the typical home to heat and cool, maintain, furnish, decorate, and insure. They may feel cramped to some or cozy to others. You may pay extra for the location and views, but you'll probably save money on the house itself.

>> **Bungalow:** These homes are typically compact and single-story with a low-pitched roof. Sometimes a second story is built into the attic space. They commonly have a front or wraparound porch.

>> **Townhouse:** A townhouse is typically a two- or three-story home that shares a wall with one or more other townhouses. They may cost less than single-family homes in the same area, but because of their proximity to the neighbors, they generally come with less privacy.

>> **Duplex/triplex:** A duplex or triplex is a single building with two or three separate units, which can be the perfect solution if you're downsizing and want supplemental rental income or need room for family members or a caregiver to live right next door.

## Apartment

An *apartment* is a room or suite of rooms generally located in a building occupied by more than one household. Apartments are usually rental units, but in some cases, you can buy them. If you're in the market for an apartment, think about the type you want.

>> **One or more bedrooms:** Conventional apartments have one or more bedrooms, at least one full bathroom, a separate kitchen, a living room, and sometimes a dining room and office.

>> **Studio:** A studio apartment has an open floor plan that combines the kitchen, bedroom, and living room, plus a full bathroom.

>> **Loft:** A loft is like a studio apartment but generally has high ceilings, usually large windows, and exposed brick and support beams. Lofts are often located in commercial buildings that have been converted into residential units.

>> **Efficiency:** An efficiency is a small apartment with a combined bedroom and living area, a bathroom, and a tiny kitchen or kitchenette.

Some apartment complexes may offer valuable amenities, such as a community pool, clubhouse, gym, and laundry facilities.

TIP

Renting an apartment may be the best option if you're between homes or you want to spend a trial period in a new location before buying a home there.

TIP

You may be able to trim your heating bill by renting a unit on one of the upper floors or trim your cooling bill by renting a unit on one of the lower floors.

# Condo

A *condominium* (*condo* for short) is a building or complex in which individuals own their residential units and jointly own the grounds and the overall building or complex. In some ways, a condo provides the best of both worlds: home owner-ship and apartment living. You own your unit but have less upkeep and monthly maintenance. Typically, you're responsible only for repairs and maintenance of anything inside your unit.

Condo living isn't for everyone. Carefully weigh the pros and cons.

**Pros**

>> Less maintenance than your own home

>> Better security in some cases

>> Amenities (a condo may have a pool, fitness center, clubhouse, pond, community activities, and other perks)

>> Affordability (a condo typically costs less than a traditional home, although condo association fees can make condo living more expensive)

**Cons**

- ❯❯ Condo association fees, which can be substantial and increase considerably over time

- ❯❯ Potential for mismanaged condo association funds

- ❯❯ Potential for other residents not paying their condo association fees

- ❯❯ Less privacy than a detached home

- ❯❯ More rules and restrictions

WARNING

Before buying a condo, do your research. Read the condo association's covenants and restrictions, so you fully understand what you're getting yourself into. Also find out how much the fees are, what they're used for, how and when they're collected, and how much and under what conditions they can be increased. Request a copy of the association's financial statements.

## Granny pod (also known as an accessory dwelling unit)

If you want to live with your adult children and your grandchildren but want the privacy and independence of your own living quarters, consider building an accessory dwelling unit (ADU). This is a modern version of the old mother-in-law cottage. It typically includes a kitchenette, bathroom, and combined bedroom and living room. You can equip it with a monitoring system and other safety, security, and accessibility features built in.

TIP

If you're not ready to sell your property, consider placing a granny pod or small home or cottage on your land, move into it, and rent out the big house.

## Mobile home

A *mobile home* is a prefabricated structure that's built in a factory on a permanently attached chassis before being transported to a site. It may be placed on a foundation on a lot of its own or in a trailer park, where it serves as a permanent dwelling, like a traditional home.

Some mobile homes, called *park models,* are no larger than tiny homes, maxing out at about 400 square feet. They're often parked in permanent or semipermanent locations in trailer parks, campgrounds, or RV parks. Like RVs, in many jurisdictions, park models aren't permitted as residential living units on private lots.

## 55-and-older community

If you're 55 or older and you're looking for a safe, quiet, and well-established community of peers along with a host of amenities, check out some *55-and-older communities*, which typically offer the following advantages:

>> A safe, stable neighborhood

>> Community and camaraderie

>> A rich social life with plenty of events and activities

>> Desirable amenities, such as a pool, hot tub, clubhouse, and fitness center

>> Transportation, such as a shuttle service

**WARNING**

Beware of the potential drawbacks of some 55-and-older communities, such as the following:

>> One-time buy-in fee, which may be substantial and may have refund restrictions

>> Homeowner association fees or other fees

>> Lack of diversity

>> A culture that clashes with your desire for independence and privacy

>> Separation from friends and family

>> Excessive rules and restrictions

>> Financial risk related to whether you own your unit and whether the organization that manages the community is financially sound

**REMEMBER**

Perform your due diligence before buying into a 55-and-older community. Talk to residents to find out what they like and dislike about living there. If you know anyone who lived there and moved out, find out why. Read the community's rules and regulations. View ratings and reviews online.

## Assisted living community

If you or your partner needs help, an *assisted living community* may be a good option. These communities are created for people who need various levels of care. Services provided typically include the following, some for an extra fee:

>> Meals

>> Medication monitoring

>> Personal care, including help with personal hygiene and getting dressed

>> Housekeeping

>> Laundry

>> Social and recreational activities

>> Transportation

>> Limited medical services

**REMEMBER**

Different facilities deliver different levels of care, so determine the level and types of care needed along with how often help is needed before choosing a facility and care plan. If all you need is someone to check in on you and do some housecleaning and meal prep, you may be able to get by with some level of in-home care instead of transitioning to an assisted living community.

# Accounting for Additional Costs

When you're comparing housing options, don't focus solely on the purchase price. One property may have a lower purchase price but additional costs that can make it a more expensive option over time. The following sections cover costs that many homeowners often overlook.

## Utilities

Regardless of where you live, you'll need to pay for utilities and basic services — gas, electricity, water, sewer/septic, and trash removal. However, when you're downsizing, one goal is to reduce these expenses substantially, typically by moving to an area where they're more affordable and living in a smaller space.

**REMEMBER**

Before renting or buying a place, find out how much the previous owner or renter paid in monthly utility bills. Request copies of the bills or a spreadsheet showing you what they paid. If they won't provide documentation, ask the utility companies.

## Maintenance and repairs

Maintenance, repairs, and updates can be costly, so when you're comparing housing options, consider the cost of any work required to bring a property up to the market standard. Get the home inspected by a reputable and knowledgeable individual, someone in construction, to reduce the likelihood of getting blindsided by a big repair bill shortly after moving in — such as a bill for replacing the roof, furnace, or air conditioning unit or for mold remediation.

TIP

Here are a couple other ways to avoid large, unexpected repair and maintenance bills:

>> Buy a condo, so the condo association will at least be responsible for exterior repairs and maintenance, although condo fees can be steep and some condos apply assessments for large expenses.

>> When you buy a home, purchase a home warranty to cover major repairs, such as replacing the furnace or air conditioner. A home warranty is always a good idea for the first year you own a home until you have more knowledge of the mechanicals in your home.

## Homeowner or condo association fees

If you buy a condo or a home that's part of a homeowner association (HOA), you'll be subject to annual or monthly fees. In both cases (HOA or condo association), fees cover maintenance and repairs of common areas, such as a clubhouse, community pool, park, and sometimes roads. In the case of a condominium, the fees also commonly cover the costs of external repairs and renovations to residential buildings, such as the cost of replacing the roof or siding.

Association fees can vary considerably — from a few hundred to thousands of dollars annually — and they tend to increase over time to keep pace with inflation. What the fees cover may also vary. Some associations merely cut the grass and clear snow from roads, walkways, and driveways. Others handle retention pond maintenance, pool maintenance, clubhouse repairs, all exterior building repairs and maintenance, and more. You usually get what you pay for.

REMEMBER

If you're opting for a nomadic lifestyle, living in an RV or on a boat, you may avoid association fees, but you're likely to be subject to similar expenses in the form of RV park fees or dock fees. Some RV parks have associations that allow you to buy a space and contribute time, money, or both to maintaining the grounds.

## Property taxes

Whether you buy a home or a condo, one expense is a sure thing: property taxes. Unfortunately, the amount you'll be charged can present you with an unpleasant surprise in areas where property values are soaring. When you close on the property, you file a *transfer affidavit* notifying the county that the property is being transferred to you. This notification also contains the purchase price, which can trigger a reassessment of the property's value and a significant increase in property tax.

To avoid an unpleasant surprise, whenever you're buying a home, check with the county assessor's office to find out what the property tax rate is for your area and how it's calculated. You may even want to tell your county assessor what you're thinking of buying and ask for a ballpark estimate of what the property tax will be.

TIP

To simplify your monthly budget, consider setting up an escrow account through your lender for paying homeowner's insurance and property taxes. With an escrow account, you have a larger monthly payment, but what you pay in excess of your mortgage and interest payment is deposited into your escrow account. When your homeowner's insurance or property taxes are due, your lender pays those bills out of your escrow account, so you don't get hit with large, unexpected bills.

> » **Scheduling transportation and a crew for moving day**

> » **Making sure your gas, electricity, and water are turned on**

> » **Unpacking without cluttering your new home**

# Chapter **6**

# Executing a Successful Move

I f you're like most people, you dread moving — and for good reason. Although moving can be exciting, it's often overwhelming. You have so much to do and so little time, and you'd better be ready when the moving truck shows up, or you'll be in for a chaotic and aggravating experience.

Imagine showing up at the truck rental site at 8:00 Saturday morning to find out that they have no record of your reservation after you scheduled a crew to meet you at your house at 9:00 a.m. Imagine the movers showing up at 10:00 a.m. when you're only halfway through your packing. Imagine showing up at your new place on Friday and discovering that everything has been turned off — you have no water, gas, or electricity. These aren't just imaginary scenarios; they've happened, probably more often than anyone likes to admit.

Avoiding these and other moving fiascos requires careful planning, coordination, and communication. You need to schedule everything in advance and then check and double-check that everyone's in sync leading up to moving day. This chapter explains how to prepare in advance to execute a smooth and successful move and prevent any unpleasant surprises.

# Changing Your Mailing Address

At least two weeks before your scheduled moving date, submit a change of address notification to the postal service to have your mail forwarded to your new home and then start letting everyone know that you're moving. The post office will forward your mail for 12 months for standard mail, 60 days for magazines and newspapers, so you need to give all your personal contacts your new address and change it on all your accounts, such as your bank accounts, health insurance accounts, credit card accounts, and so on.

The following sections lead you through the process of changing your mailing address to prevent or mitigate any interruption in mail service.

## Notifying the postal service of your change in address

You can submit a change of address notification to the U.S. Postal Service (USPS) to have your mail forwarded from your old address to your new one. In the United States, you can pick up a change of address form at your local post office, complete it, and mail it in (or return it to the post office) for free. Or you can file your notification online at USPS.com for a small identity verification fee.

Having your mail forwarded for 12 months is free. You can pay more to have it forwarded for an extended period.

Whether you're filling out a paper form or submitting your notification online, you'll need to enter the following information:

>> Your current mailing address

>> Your new mailing address

>> Whether the change in address is just for you or for everyone at your current address

>> Your contact info (name, email address, and phone number)

>> Whether you plan to return to your current address within six months (whether the change of address is temporary or permanent)

>> The date on which mail forwarding is to begin

**WARNING**

If you're the only one in your household who's moving and the rest of your family is staying, be sure to choose Individual instead of Family when you fill out the form, or the postal service will forward all your family members' mail to your new address and they'll need to file forms to reverse the process.

And don't submit a change of address request if you're only going to be gone for a couple weeks. Instead, submit a mail hold request. The postal service will hold your mail for up to 30 days and then deliver it when you return, or you can pick it up at your local post office.

## Changing your address on your accounts

As soon as you move into your new place, start changing your address on all your accounts, including the following:

>> Bank accounts (savings and checking)

>> Credit card accounts

>> Lenders (mortgage and car loans)

>> Investment accounts

>> Cellphone service

>> Magazine and other subscription services

>> Insurance providers (healthcare, car, homeowners)

>> Social Security Administration (www.ssa.gov)

>> Online shopping sites

**TIP**

Once you've moved, whenever you receive a piece of mail, check whether it was sent to your old address; if so, notify the sender of your new mailing address. Do this for about a month, and you'll have notified most of your providers of your change of address.

## Sending change of address notifications

The USPS used to provide free change of address postcards (though you had to pay the postage when you mailed them). You'd simply send these postcards to everyone you knew, and they'd change your address in their address books. Well, things have changed since the 1970s. Now, you can notify people of your change of address by blasting a single text to everyone on your cellphone's contact list or sending a message to all your email contacts.

If you want to go old school and send change of address cards to all your contacts, you can order custom cards through online services such as Zazzle, VistaPrint, Etsy, and even Amazon.

# Making the Move: Transportation, Movers, and More

If you're hiring a moving company to pack and move everything, you don't need to arrange transportation — the moving company takes care of that for you. On the other hand, if you're moving yourself, you need to reserve one or more trucks or have moving containers delivered to your home so you can load your belongings into them. Then, you need to recruit or hire some helping hands to assist you in loading your stuff. The following sections guide you through making the actual move to your new place.

## Deciding on trucks or portable containers

First things first: truck or portable containers? While a moving truck is generally the lower-cost option, moving containers offer the following advantages:

>> You load the containers at your leisure as opposed to having a limited time to load a truck or pay for additional days.

>> Portable containers feature ground-level loading as opposed to having to lift items into a truck, although some trucks come with lifts or ramps or have low decks for easy loading.

>> Moving containers double as storage units, which comes in handy if you need to store your belongings between moves.

>> The container service does all the driving.

Whether you're reserving a truck or portable containers, call the provider several weeks before you're planning to move to ensure availability. When making your reservation, you need to have some idea of the size and number of trucks or containers you'll need. Professional movers are experts at making these assessments, but most people underestimate the space they'll need, often because they can't pack a truck as tightly as skilled movers can.

Details in Table 6-1 can help you estimate the truck size you'll need. If a large truck doesn't have the capacity you need, you'll have to make more than one trip or hire a moving company with one or more semis. However, most people who are doing any serious downsizing won't need a semi — a 26-foot truck or smaller is usually sufficient.

**TABLE 6-1**     ## Estimating Moving Truck Size

| Truck Size | Cubic Feet | Recommended For | Number of Medium-Size Boxes | Number of Furniture Items | Maximum Weight in Pounds |
|---|---|---|---|---|---|
| Cargo van | 357 | Efficiency or studio apartment | 40 | 1–2 | 3,400 |
| 12 feet | 380 | Studio apartment up to a 1- or 2-bedroom apartment | 120 | 1–5 | 3,610 |
| 16 feet | 658 | 3–4 rooms or a 1-bedroom house | 250 | 1–10 | 4,460 |
| 26 feet | 1,698 | 5–8 rooms or a 2- or 3-bedroom house | 500 | 1–15 | 10,000 |

**WARNING**

If you have a king-size bed, you'll need at least a 16-foot truck. The mattress and/or box spring won't fit in a cargo van or a 12-foot truck.

**TIP**

When renting a truck or portable containers, you'll have the option of renting furniture pads or blankets, hand trucks, and an appliance dolly (for moving heavy appliances such as a refrigerator/freezer). Be sure to rent plenty of furniture pads/blankets, and if you have a refrigerator or freezer, pay the extra $20 or so to rent the appliance dolly. It's well worth it. A hand truck is also useful for moving heavier items and stacks of boxes instead of having to carry one or two at a time.

## Scheduling movers

If you're reserving a truck or portable containers, you'll need your own moving crew. You have two choices: friends and relatives or hired hands. Sometimes you can use both, but if you're hiring helpers, they usually expect you to stay out of their way. They may be required, for safety reasons, to not let you help, they may not want your free help cutting into their hours, or both.

Friends and relatives are the most affordable option, assuming they're physically fit, they show up, and they're careful not to damage your property. If you have reliable help, using volunteers isn't a bad choice. However, if someone gets injured, they or you will be paying the price, and you'll probably feel bad about it. It's a gamble, but one that many people feel is worth it.

The higher-cost option is to hire helpers, and the easiest approach is to go through the moving truck or container rental company. Most companies that lease moving trucks and portable containers have an option on their website or app for hiring helpers. You choose whether you want loading help, unloading help, or both, and specify the loading and unloading dates and addresses, and the service provides a list of third-party helpers along with rates, ratings, and reviews. You then have the option of booking available crews online.

Assuming all goes as planned, you pick up the truck (or the container is delivered), and your moving crew arrives at your home to load it. They load the truck (or container), and then you drive it to your new place (or the container is picked up by the rental company).

Moving crews vary in their level of expertise. Ideally, the team leader is highly skilled in packing a truck or container and overseeing the other members of the crew doing the loading. In some cases, though, you can end up with a crew that's careless and does a poor job of loading the truck, which may result in damage to your home and your belongings and the need for additional trips when the crew is unable to fit everything on the truck.

TIP

Choose a moving crew that asks lots of questions and provides an on-site or virtual estimate. An experienced crew can take a quick look at everything that needs to be moved and give a very accurate estimate of the size and number of containers/trucks you'll need and the number of helpers to meet your goals.

REMEMBER

Hire only helpers who are insured. If they're not insured and get injured on the job and decide to file a lawsuit, you may be on the hook for expensive bills depending on what your homeowner's insurance covers. Spending extra for experienced helpers who carry their own insurance is a wise investment.

## Being available on moving day

When moving day arrives, your job is to answer questions and direct traffic. Regardless of whether your crew is volunteers or hired hands, try to avoid any temptation to help with the lifting, carrying, or loading unless you absolutely have to. You will be more useful answering questions and directing traffic, especially when the time comes to unload everything and carry it into your new place.

**WARNING**

If you're busy packing, carrying, and loading, you'll either be getting in the way and slowing others down, or you'll have a lot of people standing around not doing anything because they don't know what to do.

If your crew is composed of hired help, a team leader will usually supervise. If you have any questions or concerns, address them to the team leader. Otherwise, just stand back and let the crew do its job. Don't try to micromanage the process.

On the other hand, if you have a crew of volunteers, you'll be required to provide more direction — which items and rooms you want loaded first and next, and which areas you want specific people to work on. For example, you may have a couple friends who are built more for moving heavy, bulky items and others who are more suited to carrying boxes and transporting fragile items such as lamps and TVs in their vehicles. In these cases, you should be telling people what to do.

**TIP**

When unloading the truck, consider stationing yourself at the entrance where items will be moved in and directing traffic from there. In some cases, you'll need to decide on the fly where a specific item needs to go, especially if rooms at your old place don't match up with rooms at your new place. For example, if your old place had a den but the new place doesn't, something that was in the den at the old place may need to be moved to the living room or office at the new place.

# Switching Your Utilities

Some utility companies (gas, electric, water, sewer, and trash) are very responsive in providing uninterrupted service to their customers. Others are not. If you treat utilities as an afterthought, you'll almost certainly experience a service interruption, especially if you move on or close to a weekend, so you need to be proactive. Take the following steps:

1. **Make a list of services you'll need at the new place, such as the following:**

   - Gas
   - Electricity
   - Water
   - Sewer
   - Trash
   - Cable TV
   - Internet

If you're moving into a community that has a homeowner association, check with the association to determine whether any services, such as water, sewer, and trash pickup, are covered.

2. **Research your destination location to obtain contact information for providers of each service.**

   You may want to ask the previous homeowner, one of your future neighbors, or the agent who showed you the property for recommendations. In some cases, such as water and sewer, you have only one choice.

3. **Contact your utility providers 2–3 weeks in advance to let them know when you're moving in.**

   If you need equipment installed, you may need to call up to a month in advance.

   Consider having utilities turned on in your name a day before you're scheduled to move in and having them switched from your name (at your previous residence) on the day, or day after, you close on the sale. The best approach usually involves the buyer and seller calling the utility companies together right after the closing to have services switched over.

4. **Contact the water and sewer service providers to be certain you'll have these essential services the day you move in.**

   You usually get water and sewer through the town or city, and the offices are generally closed on weekends.

When you're moving out, notify the utility companies that were providing service to your old home to remove your name from those utilities or, better yet, transfer service to the names of the new owners. Let the utility companies know the date you're moving out, so they won't charge you for services you didn't receive. And check any bills you receive in the future to make sure they didn't charge you.

When you're stopping a service, consider telling the utility company rep something like, "I'm going to be moving in on such and such date, and so-and-so is going to be moving in on this date, and they'll be calling to give you their information." Most utility companies are flexible and will try to work with buyers and sellers to prevent any interruption in service. Communication is key.

In some areas, you may have a choice of trash and recycle services, but the community as a whole may have a preference for using one particular service. Large trucks put a lot of wear and tear on roads, so having one company service the entire area can help reduce the need for costly road maintenance. In addition, everyone can put their trash out on the same day, and the neighborhood won't have that eyesore several times a week. Some trash services offer a neighborhood discount as well. Check with your neighbors before choosing trash and recycle services.

# Unpacking: Decluttering, Round 2

Unpacking goes more smoothly and you end up with a more organized home when you have a system in place. The following sections provide guidance on unpacking that can save you time and energy while preventing clutter. For direction on decluttering before the move, see Book 3 Chapter 4.

**TIP**

Here are a few overall suggestions before you go through the process room by room:

>> Unpack your essentials first — the boxes or bags containing your changes of clothes, towels, toiletries, medications, phone chargers, and so on.

>> Prep rooms before unpacking. If a closet needs an organizer, install it before unloading anything you're planning to put in the closet. If cabinets or drawers need liners or organizers, do it now.

>> Focus on unpacking the kitchen and the main bedroom first. You can then take your time with the other rooms.

>> In every room that contains furniture, arrange the furniture before unpacking any boxes.

>> Start with a plan for each room. For example, in your main bedroom, you may want to unpack your bedding and pillows first and make the bed before unpacking anything else. If you have a photo or inventory of each box's contents, refer to those documents to determine the best sequence for unpacking the boxes. Otherwise, open all the boxes before you start unpacking them.

## Kitchen

You don't have to put everything away in the kitchen all at once, but you probably want to at least start with the following high-priority items:

>> Make sure the refrigerator and freezer are empty, clean, plugged in, and set to the desired temperature.

>> If you have any items in a cooler, unload those first and place them in the refrigerator.

>> Line the cabinets and drawers if they aren't lined already and you want them to be. Lining cabinets and drawers is always a good idea to prevent scratches and water damage.

>> Place any small appliances you want out on the counters close to electrical outlets, such as your coffeemaker and toaster.

>> Put away your pots and pans.

>> Put away your dishes, cups, glasses, utensils, knives, and silverware.

>> Put away your pantry items.

>> Unload and put away everything else that belongs in the kitchen, including all those refrigerator magnets you can't live without.

# Bedrooms

After the kitchen, arrange and unpack the main bedroom so you have a place to sleep. You can then arrange and unpack any other bedrooms at your leisure or the day before your first guests arrive. Take the following steps:

1. **Assemble and make the bed.**

   Be sure it's in the spot where you want it and oriented in the direction that feels right for you — feng shui, anyone?

2. **Place the dressers and other furniture where you want them and put the drawers back in, if necessary.**

3. **Install closet organizers and put away your clothes, shoes, and extra bedding.**

# Bathrooms

You'll need at least one bathroom the night you move in. Focus on the main bathroom first.

**REMEMBER**

Check the plumbing is working properly before putting away anything in your bathroom. Flush the toilet, run the sink faucets and shower, and check for leaks under the sink. Call a plumber to address any issues before you put anything away.

When you're ready to unpack, take the following steps:

1. **Place the toilet paper near the toilet.**

2. **Hang the bath towels and hand towels you're going to use.**

3. **Place soap, shampoo, conditioner, and other items you use in the shower or bath area.**

4. **Put away your medicine cabinet items.**

5. **Lay out the items you'll keep on the countertop and around the sink —
   hand soap, toothbrushes, combs, swabs, and so on.**

6. **Unload and put away all the items you store under the sink or in the
   bathroom closet.**

## Living room

The big challenge related to the living room is figuring out how to arrange the
furniture and where to put the TV/entertainment center. If you already have
that worked out, then it's simply a matter of reassembling furniture, connecting
all the electronics, putting away any books, setting out your knickknacks, and
hanging pictures.

**REMEMBER**

Don't do anything in the living room until you have a clear idea of how you
want the large items arranged — the sofa, recliners or armchairs, and
TV/entertainment center. Otherwise, you're going to subject yourself to a lot
of unnecessary rearranging. Even before moving in, Draw a plan on a piece of
paper first if you need to.

## Dining room

People usually downsize their way out of a formal dining room, so chances are
good that you don't have to deal with a dining room. However, if you do, moving
into it is usually simply a matter of reassembling the table and placing your dining
room chairs around it. If you have a dining room cabinet, you'll have some dishes
and silverware to put away as well.

## Garage/basement

Most people use their garage and basement for storage, but for many people these
are important work areas for crafts and hobbies. Before unpacking anything in
your garage or basement, organize the area. You can find shelving, cabinets, toolboxes, and garage organizers at your local hardware store to make maximum use
of your available space while placing everything within easy reach.

**REMEMBER**

One of the key goals of downsizing is to reduce clutter. You don't want to be digging through a pile of stuff in your garage, basement, or closets to find what you
need or, worse, buying items you already have because you can't find them. Follow the adage "A place for everything and everything in its place."

# 4
# Living the Nomad Life

# Contents at a Glance

Chapter **1**

# Getting a Taste of the Nomad Lifestyle

The idea of being a *nomad* — someone who can live and work from anywhere — resonates with many people for a reason. It's the ultimate form of personal freedom, a way to blend where you want to live, the types of experiences you want to have, and even what you do for work. Affordable travel and portable technology make it possible in ways never before available. You can be a nomad for a few weeks or longer, domestically or abroad, with family or on your own; the possibilities are endless.

Anyone can become a nomad, but breaking free from the status quo can be hard. Before taking the leap from a traditional lifestyle to a nomadic one, it helps to know what to expect.

This chapter helps you consider whether being a nomad is right for you and, if so, gets you started in the nomad lifestyle. You get familiar with the many paths to becoming a nomad, as well as the pros, cons, and costs. This chapter also debunks common misconceptions and explains how nomads can make money.

If the idea of becoming a nomad seems like a pipe dream to you, this chapter shows that nomads are just like everyone else. And you can be one too.

# Defining Nomads

Nomads are hard to define because the nomad lifestyle can mean different things to different people. At a basic level, a nomad is someone who can live from anywhere. Some work, while others live on income from pensions, investments, and other recurring revenue streams.

Digital technology has all but erased borders for communication and business. Your home can be wherever you are.

Nomads can work from anywhere with an internet connection, and often do. Whether you want to work from an Airbnb or an RV, technology makes it possible. You're only limited by your imagination, and perhaps cellular data networks.

Nomads have all types of different jobs. They can work for themselves or someone else. They can work part time, full time, or on a contract basis. They can even *stop* working if they develop ways to live off automated or passive income streams.

REMEMBER

Nomads can include the following:

>> Home-based remote workers who can technically live anywhere but choose to remain in one city or country.

>> Partially nomadic people who keep a home base and travel part time.

>> Fully nomadic people who don't have a fixed address. They may have sold everything they own or keep a storage unit and travel year-round or without an end date.

>> Temporary nomads who are fully or partially nomadic sometimes and static sometimes. Some folks also live like nomads for a few months or years before returning to a traditional lifestyle.

Table 1-1 goes into detail about the different types of nomads.

REMEMBER

Remoteness is a sliding scale. Just as there are hybrid organizations, there are also hybrid nomads. You can combine different types of jobs and income streams to create a lifestyle that suits you.

**TABLE 1-1**    Types of Nomads

| Type of Nomad | Description |
|---|---|
| Remote employees | People who work remotely on a salary for a company or organization |
| Online freelancers | Self-employed, independent contractors who offer services on an hourly, per-project, or other basis |
| Online business owners | Entrepreneurs, startup founders, and anyone who runs a virtual business of any size |
| Influencers and content creators | People who earn a living through social media, publishing online content, and leveraging their personal brand |
| Retirees | People who are retired and living off of investments, retirement accounts, pensions, and Social Security |
| Passive income entrepreneurs and investors | People who have achieved financial freedom through investment income or automated income streams |

# Seeing Who's Adopting the Nomad Lifestyle

The following sections dig deeper into nomad demographics. You find out where digital nomads are from, what they do for work, how old they are, and how much they earn.

## Multiple generations

You may think that a nomad lifestyle is more suited to younger generations or to retired people, but research shows that people of all ages dabble in nomadism. MBO Partners found that in 2023, 17.3 million American workers (or 11 percent of the U.S. workforce) described themselves as digital nomads. The number of U.S. nomads increased by some 130 percent since 2019, as the pandemic world adopted remote work on a mass scale. Fifty-eight percent of digital workers are Gen Z and Millennials, 42 percent Gen Xers and Baby Boomers.

## People of various means

Fiverr's Anywhere Workers Study found that more than half of "anywhere workers" were freelancers in 2018, although the ratio of salaried to self-employed nomads is evening out. MBO's research suggests that the number of salaried nomads tripled between 2019 and 2021, with many remote employees being "high earners." FlexJobs reports that 18 percent of nomads make six figures or more, with 22 percent making between $50,000–100,000.

Remote working women tend to earn less than men, though, with Fiverr's study finding that "the gender pay gap has no borders."

Either way, there's no limit on how much money you can make in the nomad lifestyle, especially when you combine multiple income streams. You can also save a lot, too. Many remote workers engage in what's been called geo-arbitrage, making your income go farther by living in rural areas or developing countries with a low cost of living.

Fortunately, freedom doesn't have to cost a lot. One in four nomads earns less than $25,000 a year, per MBO Partners. But regardless of how much money digital nomads make, 81 percent are highly satisfied and 9 percent are satisfied with their lifestyle and work. It just goes to show that money doesn't necessarily buy happiness — so long as it buys the ability to travel!

## Why roam?

A better question might be "Why not?" Being a nomad gives you ultimate freedom and flexibility. You decide where you live and what you do for work (if you work at all), and you also control how you spend your time.

**REMEMBER**

Being a nomad gives you options. You can change your mind at any moment about where to travel, when to settle down, and which country to pledge your citizenship to. There are few restrictions on the nomad lifestyle other than how you want to live and what you can afford.

### THE HISTORY OF TELECOMMUTING AND REMOTE WORK

Humans have been working from home or in nomadic tribes since the beginning of recorded history. Over time, the workplace shifted from homes to farms to marketplaces and international trade. The Industrial Age was a turning point, however. The number of cities jumped from fewer than 1,000 in 1800 to more than 34,000 by 1950, attracting job seekers by the masses.

The Technological Age of the 1970s brought a shift from factory work to knowledge work, paving the way for the nomads of the future.

1760–1840: 1st Industrial Revolution (coal)

1870–1914: 2nd Industrial Revolution (gas)

1969–1999: 3rd Industrial Revolution (electronics and nuclear energy)

2000–today: 4th Industrial Revolution (internet and renewable energy)

In 1976, a NASA engineer named Jack Nilles released a book called *The Telecommunications-Transportation Tradeoff*, suggesting telecommuting as a new way of life. But despite the logical arguments for remote work, employers were resistant to change. Organizations such as HP and IBM tested flexible work policies in the 1980s and 1990s, only to retract them in the early 2000s.

Of course, the internet era changed everything. In 1997, *Digital Nomad* by Tsugio Makimoto and David Manners came out, predicting the return to a nomadic lifestyle. In 2007, Tim Ferriss's *The Four-Hour Work Week* became a nomad "bible." And In 2020, the COVID-19 pandemic finally tipped the global scales toward remote work.

The World Economic Forum attributes remote work as one of the biggest drivers in the workplace.

Although working from anywhere has been possible since the 1970s, it's finally become the new normal. The nomad revolution may be a bit late to its own party. But either way, it's arrived.

# Understanding Truths about the Nomad Life

If you've always pictured nomads as 20-something-year-old tech workers, think again. There are plenty of stereotypes about nomads, but that doesn't mean they're true. The following sections bust a few of them!

## Nomads aren't always traveling

*Is a nomad who stops traveling still a nomad?*

Although nomads are defined by their ability to roam into perpetuity, that doesn't mean you have to always be traveling.

As a nomad, you can choose when you want to travel, where, and for how long. You can also decide when to *stop.* So long as you can support yourself, you can remain location independent forever. Eventually, nomads will probably just be considered regular people, because living and even working from anywhere will be part of the status quo.

In that sense, identifying as a nomad is a mindset. There's no generally agreed-upon definition on how far, often, or wide nomads must travel each year to maintain their "status."

You don't have to leave your home country to become a nomad. According to MBO, 53 percent of nomads plan to stay domestic rather than travel overseas.

## Traveling is more affordable than you think

At first glance, the nomad lifestyle may appear expensive. After all, going on vacation certainly gets pricey. But many people end up saving money when they go remote by lowering their average cost of living, buying less stuff, and potentially decreasing their tax burden. Find out how to calculate your nomad budget and cost of living in Chapter 3 of Book 4.

# Deciding Whether the Nomad Lifestyle Is Right for You

Becoming a nomad doesn't need to be an extreme decision where you quit your job, sell your stuff, and book a ticket to Bali the same day. *Your* version of location independence can follow one of the examples in this book, or it can be something you design.

But for now, the following sections note some of the pros and cons to help you decide whether the nomad life is for you.

## Exploring the potential benefits

Becoming a nomad could be the best thing since sliced bread. These are some of the benefits:

>> **Community:** Imagine if your friendship circle included thousands of people from every country in the world — that's possible when you live the nomad life.

>> **Cost savings:** Nomads can save money in many ways, such as lowering their cost of living and increasing their savings rate through geo-arbitrage (earning in a strong economy while living in a lower cost of living location), buying fewer material things, and changing their tax base.

>> **Creativity and innovation:** Immersing yourself in new cultures and places is a good way to gain inspiration in your work. Researchers have found a correlation between travel and increased innovation.

>> **Earning potential:** Many nomads use their newfound freedom, flexibility, and time to build multiple income streams. Many salaried nomads are high earners, while freelancers could earn more working for themselves than for an employer.

>> **Family:** When you're a nomad, you don't have to wait until the holidays to see your loved ones. You can visit them anytime! Nomad parents with young children can spend more time together while homeschooling or remote learning.

>> **Freedom:** As mentioned, freedom of all shapes and sizes is the top reason people want to become nomads. You have micro freedoms, such as how to spend every minute of the day. And you have macro freedoms, such as changing your country of residence, taxation, or citizenship.

>> **Fulfillment:** Nomads are happy campers! According to MBO, 90 percent of nomads report being satisfied or highly satisfied in their lifestyles.

>> **Fun:** Being a nomad can be really fun. Whatever you like to do, you can do more of it when you live a nomad lifestyle.

>> **Health and wellness:** With more time and control over your schedule and environment, you can make healthier choices as a nomad. Eliminating your commute can also reduce stress and increase well-being.

>> **Productivity and focus:** Researchers have found that remote workers suffer from fewer distractions compared to working in an office.

>> **Time:** Nomads can save hundreds if not thousands of hours per year that were previously spent on commuting, office distractions, and household chores.

>> **Travel:** Undoubtedly, one of the biggest draws of the nomad lifestyle is being able to travel. Imagine being able to work with a view of the Eiffel Tower. That's possible when you can work from anywhere!

# Recognizing the potential drawbacks

**WARNING**

Every decision in life has pros and cons (even eating cupcakes). For all the benefits of a location-independent lifestyle, there are some downsides:

>> **Being unsettled:** Not having a fixed home can wear on you over time. If you're planning to be a temporary nomad, this isn't much of a concern. But many long-term nomads eventually find somewhere to settle so they have more stability and community.

>> **Burnout:** Although the majority of nomads are happy and satisfied with their lifestyles, remote work and travel burnout is still a thing.

>> **Dating and relationships:** Living nomadically can complicate relationships, whether you're single and dating or living with your significant other. Friendships and partnerships at home may suffer the longer you're away. If you're considering traveling with a loved one, be sure you're compatible 24/7! And, although you may meet lots of people while traveling, you may not see them again.

>> **Loneliness:** Everyone can experience loneliness sometimes, whether you're a nomad or not. But solo nomads can feel lonely at times. And if you're in a place where people don't speak your language, you could feel isolated. In a Fiverr study, 30 percent of respondents said lack of community and human connection was their biggest struggle.

>> **Productivity and motivation:** Many nomads are self-motivated, with only 7 percent of "anywhere workers" citing motivation as a challenge. It's still a factor, though, especially when combined with occasional loneliness and isolation.

>> **Risk of failure:** Failing at work in a foreign place can be a scary prospect, especially if you don't know the culture well or lack a local support system. It's important to keep a stash of emergency savings in case you end up between jobs or need to cut your adventure short and fly home.

>> **Uncertainty:** Uncertainty is the flip side of the excitement and adventure of a nomadic lifestyle. There's a fine line between living outside of your comfort zone and living in anxiety. Manage uncertainty by being as prepared and organized as possible.

# Chapter **2**

# Seeing Yourself as a Nomad

Your journey to becoming a nomad is uniquely yours. But taking the first step is often the hardest part. This chapter can help you start designing your life as a nomad. You uncover your why, blast through any blocks that could be holding you back, and begin to see that this lifestyle can be a reality for you.

## Defining Your Passion and Purpose: Establishing Your Why

A nomad lifestyle includes many benefits, which you can read about in Chapter 1 of Book 4. But *your* reasons for becoming a nomad are unique to you. This section can help you figure out what's motivating you. The reasons may be different than you think!

Whatever your goals are in life, your *why* informs your *how. Why do you want to become a nomad?* Do you want to see the world? Meet new people? Work remotely and have more freedom and control over your time? Enjoy a dish of authentic pad thai?

Answering this question helps you clarify your next steps and stay on track toward your goal. Think about the following questions to help define your why:

1. Why is becoming a nomad important to you?

_____

2. What about [your answer for #1] is important to you?

_____

3. What about [your answer for #2] is important to you?

_____

4. What about [your answer for #3] is important to you?

_____

5. What about [your answer for #4] is important to you?

_____

6. What about [your answer for #5] is important to you?

_____

7. What about [your answer for #6] is important to you?

_____

Compare your seventh answer with your first answer. How are they different?

**REMEMBER** Things are not always what they seem. This exercise is designed to help you peel back the layers of why you *think* you want to become a nomad and reveal a deeper motivation. A desire for more freedom, for example, could mean you want to spend more quality time with your family. Wanting to learn a new language may reveal how important it is for you to connect with people from different cultures.

Take this exercise one step further:

What are some of the ways your life would change for the better if you had the freedom to live, work, and travel anywhere?

_____

_____

_____

_____

What could happen if you *don't* take action? What regrets might you have 10 or 20 years from now?

_____

_____

_____

_____

# Envisioning Your Future as a Nomad

The brain loves a plan, and few things are more enjoyable than designing a fulfilling and rewarding life for yourself.

The following sections explain the differences between the types of nomadic lifestyles. This is your opportunity to brainstorm what *your* nomad life would be like. As you read through, make a note of which type of nomad resonates with you.

## Full-time nomads

Full-time nomads are people without a permanent home base. Some are always on the move, changing locations every day, week, or month. Others are slower travelers who stay in one place for a few months at a time. What they all have in common is that their home is wherever they are. Some people become full-time nomads forever, while others want to experience a nomadic lifestyle temporarily. MBO Partners found that 69 percent of nomads want to stay nomadic for at least two to three years, while only 10 percent plan to discontinue the lifestyle. Among those who decide to take a pause from the peripatetic life, many want to go nomadic again in the future.

The benefit of being a full-time nomad is that you can travel for as long as you want. If you're traveling overseas, you can keep going as long as your passport allows. And when you travel as a tourist, there's less paperwork than if you were moving. If you're just passing through, you don't have to worry about applying for residency permits or changing your tax base.

**WARNING**

Being all-in as a nomad has its downsides, however. Traveling takes time, money, and energy. The more resources you invest in travel, the less you have for work, hobbies, and your personal life. And the more often you change locations, the harder it is to adapt to the local culture, form long-term relationships, and, if you're working, stay productive. Traveling full time can also get expensive and feel lonely after a while.

## Part-time nomads

Being a part-time nomad is a hybrid option where you travel but keep a home base. Part-time nomads may work at home for a while, take time off to travel, and repeat. Others may elect to bring their work with them wherever they go. Some part-time nomads *could* travel full time but choose not to. What they have in common is that they can't or don't want to be *completely* nomadic, *all* the time. Perhaps they have family obligations at home, they prefer having a home base, or their job doesn't allow it.

An upside to being a part-time nomad is stability. You don't have to sell your house, get rid of your stuff, and start living out of a backpack (or an oversized suitcase or RV). You get many of the benefits of being a full-time nomad while having a home, routine, friendships, and your favorite bunny slippers to come back to.

**WARNING**

The downside to being a part-time nomad is that it's expensive to pay a mortgage or rent plus monthly bills at home while you're out traveling. It's possible to offset these expenses by renting out your house or car when you're away.

## Expats and settlers

Nomadic settlers are people who move to another city or country and stay there. Not all settlers are expats, however. And not all expats are nomads.

The exact definition of an *expat* (or *expatriate*) is subjective, but typically refers to someone who voluntarily relocates to another country. Some expats are nomads, but many are full-time employees with traditional, location-based jobs. Others may be military service members, study abroad students, retirees, and volunteers. They live abroad, but they aren't nomadic.

Some nomads decide to settle down or become expats when they find a place that they really like.

The benefits of being a long-term settler come from having more stability. When you settle in one place, it's easier to lower your cost of living and adapt to daily life in a different culture. It also frees up your time and energy for other pursuits, such as studying a new language, making friends, learning new skills, or working on your side hustle. You don't have to worry about where you're sleeping tomorrow or how you'll get there. It can also be easier to lead a healthy lifestyle and be productive when you have consistency and routine.

**WARNING**

The downside of being a settler is that it can be a bit less exciting and adventurous compared than globetrotting. If you move outside of your home country, you'll eventually have to apply for residency or citizenship status and potentially pay taxes there, which you can read more about in Chapter 4 of Book 4.

As a settler, you also stay in places long enough for the "honeymoon phase" of the cultural adaptation process to wear off, which has its good and bad sides.

## Your type of nomad

Which type of nomad are you? If you're not sure, you can create your own category of nomad.

What does your ideal version of being a nomad look like? Would you want to travel the world on a one-way ticket, find a place to settle, or try a hybrid model where you travel a few months per year?

Would you like to be a sailing nomad or live in a van or RV?

Do you see yourself backpacking on a budget or investing in real estate abroad? Would you like to live on the beach, on a farm, or in a city skyscraper? Take a few minutes to dream up your ideal lifestyle:

_____

_____

_____

_____

_____

_____

_____

There are no wrong answers. Your priorities may change during different phases of your life. Adjust your nomadic identity accordingly.

# Traveling with a Group

Once you know what type of nomad you'd like to be, whether you're traveling alone or with your partner or family, there are pros and cons to joining a bigger group.

Both types of travel — solo and group — offer valuable life experiences.

» **Going solo:** When traveling without a larger group, you may feel free, adventurous, and independent. You may also like the agility and spontaneity of being able to do what you want, when you want. British Airways found in its Global Solo Travel Study that people's biggest motivation for traveling alone was the freedom and independence to do as they pleased.

Traveling by yourself has its downsides. Although you may meet more people this way, it can get lonely sometimes. There's also no one to share the planning logistics or watch your luggage at the airport when you go to the bathroom. Safety, too, is a factor.

Solo travel can be an exhilarating experience and a crash course in living outside of your comfort zone (if that's what you're after). It's not for everyone, however.

» **Going as a group:** Group travel has always existed in some form or another. After all, humans are tribal creatures. There's no shortage of modern-day group travel opportunities, either. You can join a tour group for a quick vacay or go on a "workcation" with fellow remote workers.

A benefit of group travel is having a built-in community of friends from the first day you arrive in a new destination. You also have someone to turn to if you have questions or need help. And your itinerary and arrangements are made for you. If traveling with other people is your thing, Chapter 6 in Book 4 has plenty of info on co-living and group travel opportunities.

Group travel has its disadvantages. For one, you may be more likely to stick with your larger group, so you'll miss authentic connections and adventures in the new locale. It can also be hard to get time alone. You may feel that the itinerary is either too structured or too disorganized. And some people will feel like the group is traveling too fast while others want to speed up the pace. Group dynamics can also be tricky to navigate. Personality clashes can be an issue, or you may flat out dislike some of the folks you're with. Group travel can also be more expensive than traveling on your own, or you could join a trip that doesn't meet your expectations.

**TIP**

Always read reviews and research group travel and co-living providers before booking.

Regardless of whether you're an introvert or an extrovert, it's worth trying both types of travel to figure out what you prefer. If you need independence, the freedom to go and come as you please, and some quiet time, travel without a large group is your bet. If you're feeling sociable, give group travel a try.

**REMEMBER**

If you can't find anyone to travel with, don't let that stop you! You'll meet people in your travels either way.

# Discussing Your Vision with Family, Friends, and Colleagues

Once you've made your decision to become a nomad, you may feel the urge to spread the good news.

Becoming a nomad is an exciting prospect, but it can also give your friends and family a shock. They may have questions (lots of questions) about your plans, your safety, and what your decision means for them.

How you approach this conversation differs depending on whether you're talking with friends, family members, or colleagues.

The following sections offer a few different strategies for when and how to tell people that you're making a life change.

## Breaking the news that you're pursuing your wanderlust

Timing when to disclose your dreams and ideas to others is an art. Sometimes you're too early in the process and you don't feel comfortable sharing your plans just yet. That's okay. Announcing a big change like quitting your job, starting a business, or moving to another country (or all) can illicit an avalanche of "buts" from well-meaning friends and family.

TIP

At every turn, someone may try to talk you out of becoming a nomad, especially when overseas travel is involved. Before broaching the conversation, here are some tips to keep in mind:

>> **Don't make assumptions.** You may expect resistance to your plans, only to find that everyone supports and encourages you.

>> **Use empathy.** Think about the other person's point of view. Contemplate how you can ease any possible concerns.

>> **Listen to their side.** Even if you don't agree with their perspective, show respect by hearing them out.

>> **Be assertive.** Are you telling people what you're going to do or asking their permission? If they sense any uncertainty, they may try to change your mind.

>> **Sooner isn't always better.** Consider waiting until your plan is solid or in progress before telling people.

>> **Prepare to compromise.** If your kids rely on you for childcare, your parents are ill and need your support, or your company's lack of a remote work policy is an issue, suggest a hybrid model that would work for both of you. Perhaps you settle for being a nomad a few months a year.

>> **Agree to disagree.** Sometimes you won't see eye to eye. It's perfectly okay to live life the way you want, regardless of how anyone else feels about it. You may never get others' approval, but you don't need their permission, either.

WARNING

If you want to continue working with your current employer, you'll of course want to talk with your supervisor and human resources department prior to finalizing your plans. Some companies have restrictions on where you can work remotely.

## Addressing common concerns

Your friends and family members probably want what's best for you, but they may still worry. These are some of the most common questions you'll face:

>> What if you get hurt? Explain that you have an international travel and health insurance policy.

>> What if you run out of money? Assure them that you've budgeted accordingly and saved money for emergencies.

>> What if you fail? You won't know until you try. It's a risk you're willing to take because reaching this goal is important to you.

>> Isn't it dangerous? Unless you're traveling to a war zone, most countries are generally safe. You'll check the Department of State travel advisories.

>> When will we see you again? Include a trip home in your travel plans. A benefit of living a remote lifestyle is that you can visit anytime (not just on holidays).

**REMEMBER**

>> What about them? Pressure is a big reason why people don't move. It can be hard to have friends, family members, and other people you care about tell you you're making a mistake or a wrong decision. But if the nomadic lifestyle is truly what you want to do, go for it.

People are uncomfortable with change for a number of reasons — some selfish, and some less so. When you take action to follow your dreams, it might remind them that they crave a change, too. At the end of the day, you only live once, and you'll never know what you're capable of until you try.

On the work front, your employer, colleagues, or clients will want assurances that your plans won't adversely affect them. Prepare to answer questions about your time zone, availability, internet security, the stability of your Wi-Fi connection, and how you'll handle deadlines and emergencies.

**REMEMBER**

You may never get the green light to travel from others. In that case, you may have to make some hard decisions that involve proceeding without their blessing or changing companies or careers to make it happen.

Chapter **3**

# Setting a Realistic Budget

Although going on vacation gets expensive, long-term travel doesn't have to break the bank. In fact, many nomads end up saving money when they go remote, compared to their average cost of living at home. Some people become nomads specifically to save money, retire sooner, or lower their cost of living.

In this chapter, you get an overview of the expenses that nomads incur. You also find out how to estimate your cost of living in a country you've never been to and calculate how much income and savings you need to become a nomad.

## Considering Expenses and Income Needs When You're a Nomad

Calculating your income and expenses as a nomad isn't much different from how you'd manage your household budget.

Before you get the details in the rest of this chapter, however, these are the main categories of income and expenses to take into consideration:

>> **Monthly income:** How much you earn from your pension, remote job, freelancing clients, or online business.

>> **Miscellaneous income:** One-time windfall earned from selling your car, house, or stuff.

>> **Nest egg:** How much money you have saved for your travel lifestyle.

>> **Startup costs:** Initial costs related to moving, buying equipment, and other miscellaneous one-time expenses.

>> **Travel and transportation costs:** Ongoing travel costs when moving or traveling throughout the year.

>> **Target cost of living:** Your average monthly living budget after arriving in your destination.

>> **Health and insurance costs:** The cost of monthly healthcare, including insurance and out-of-pocket medical expenses.

>> **Business expenses:** Remote salaried employees and retirees may not have any monthly business expenses, but freelancers and online business owners should account for these.

REMEMBER

Costs of transportation and switching locations add up every time you change locations — even weird things you wouldn't think of, such as buying bottles of olive oil and spices, if you don't take them with you. The longer you stay in one place, the lower you can get your expenses. The farther and wider you travel, the higher your travel-related expenses will be.

# Calculating Your Cost of Living

Beyond projecting your nomad income and expenses, how do you figure out which destinations you can afford to live in?

Certainly some regions of the world are more affordable than others. For example, living in Copenhagen costs more than Colombia. Living in Southeast Asia is much more affordable than living in Scandinavia. You can live anywhere on a budget, but your quality of life will be different depending on the country you choose.

Even if you move to an expensive country, such as Switzerland or Australia, you can maintain a low to moderate cost of living. The cost of living within a country varies by city. As a rule, towns are more affordable to live in than cities and capitals.

Your exact cost of living depends on your budget, location, and lifestyle. Living on a sustainable farm and growing and bartering your food is going to cost way less than living in the city and renting an apartment overlooking the Eiffel Tower and having café au lait every morning at the local boulangerie.

**REMEMBER**

You have some control over what you want your cost of living to be, regardless of where you live in the world.

The following tools help you research the cost of living in thousands of cities so you know what to expect. And note that the more you "live like a local," the lower your expenses can be:

>> **Expatistan** (www.expatistan.com/cost-of-living): Compare the cost of living among more than 2,000 cities; data is crowdsourced.

>> **Nomad List** (nomadlist.com): Explore the top nomad destinations by cost of living. There's a different estimate for living like a local, expat, nomad, or tourist.

>> **Numbeo** (www.numbeo.com/cost-of-living): Use this crowdsourced cost-of-living database to compare prices in 10,000+ cities.

>> **Teleport** (teleport.org): Compare cities by their quality of life, cost of living, and more.

Once you have an idea of the cost of living in some of the destinations you're interested in, see how they compare with your current budget. Table 3-1 can help you compare budgets.

**TABLE 3-1**  **Compare Costs of Living**

|  | Cost of Living at Home | Destination #1 | Destination #2 | Destination #3 |
|---|---|---|---|---|
| Monthly Income |  |  |  |  |
| Average Cost of Living |  |  |  |  |
| Balance |  |  |  |  |

**TIP**

A good way to estimate your cost of living in a new place is to follow local or expat bloggers and YouTubers who live there. Many content creators share exact breakdowns of their income and expenses.

**REMEMBER**

Price isn't the *only* factor in choosing where to live, of course. For some nomads, culture, convenience, climate, community, and quality of life are higher priorities.

# Analyzing the Cost of Switching Sites

One thing to keep in mind is that you incur *switching costs* every time you change locations or homes as a nomad. What are switching costs?

Each trip involves a number of logistics — including packing, booking flights or planning your route, and finding accommodations. When you arrive, you get settled, unpacking, purchasing necessary items, and orienting yourself to your new situation. All those logistics combined make up your switching cost. That's why traveling slowly is the most sustainable way for nomads to live long term. Slow travel is subjective. It's traveling at a pace that feels reasonable to *you*.

A lot of little things add up every time you change locations. But the following sections help you know what to expect and reduce some of the associated costs.

**WARNING**

Traveling isn't as fun if you're broke and tired all the time.

## Time-related costs

One type of switching cost is time. Each time you change destinations, you spend a certain amount of time deciding where to go, where to stay, and making your travel arrangements. Most of this time is spent *before* you leave your current destination.

Time-related costs include

>> Thinking about and researching where to go

>> Planning and booking travel

>> Traveling to and from your destination, including unforeseeable travel delays

>> Checking in and out of your accommodations

>> Packing and unpacking

>> Recovering from jet lag

>> Getting acclimated with your new surroundings

>> Finding Wi-Fi

>> Planning what you will do and sightseeing

>> Meeting new people

>> Navigating local transportation options

After the planning process comes the actual traveling part, where you move by car, plane, train, bus, or boat.

Finally, you arrive in your destination. That's when the adjustment phase starts. Spoiler alert: It can take weeks or even months to adjust to a new culture.

To cut and streamline some of the time-related costs of travel, you can

» Structure your nomadic life so you travel less often.

» Hire someone to plan your travel for you.

» Try a home exchange or housing subscription plan for nomads, such as the Blueground Pass (www.theblueground.com/blueground-pass), Home Exchange (homeexchange.com), or Landing (www.hellolanding.com). You can find a service by searching "home exchange." Be sure to verify that the service you're considering is legitimate before using it.

But as a nomad, switching costs can never *completely* be avoided.

## Money-related costs

Besides time, traveling costs *money*. At a minimum, you need to pay for transportation, housing, travel documents, and insurance. Miscellaneous expenses also arise when traveling, such as excess baggage fees, tips, and pricey airport food.

Financial switching costs include

» Additional security deposits for housing

» Cost of transportation, such as airfare, gas and tolls, or train tickets and transportation between your home base and point of departure, such as taxis or ride shares

» Eating out

» Luggage fees

» Accommodations, including short-term accommodations between home bases

» Amenities and staples such as cooking oils, spices, linens, toilet paper, and office equipment or furniture.

In addition to time- and money-related costs, excessive travel — think of it as travel that is wearing you out — can adversely affect your sleep and health.

REMEMBER

Slow travel helps you save money in every aspect of the nomad lifestyle. The longer you stay in one place, the lower your switching costs.

If you move 4 times per year instead of 12, for instance, you'll be paying 8 fewer switching costs. Few nomads account for these costs in their initial planning, but they add up fast.

When in doubt, travel slowly — whatever that means to you!

# Creating a Nomad Budget

Budgeting is a critical step on the path to becoming a nomad. Organizing your finances helps you plan ahead, save money, and choose destinations that are the right fit for you.

Consider creating two budgets — one for your pre-departure income and expenses, and one for your monthly cost of living as a nomad.

In making your calculations, keep in mind that you'll be reaping savings because you are reducing your normal living expenses:

>> Selling your home or giving up your rental property

>> Getting rid of your car and car insurance, maintenance, gas, and parking fees

>> Cancelling your TV, landline, and internet plan

>> Stopping utilities

>> Ending monthly gym subscriptions

## Pre-departure budget

REMEMBER

Calculate your expenses and income streams *before* you leave home:

Income

>> **Emergency fund:** A savings cushion of 3–6 months of living expenses

>> **Initial startup costs:** Anything related to getting to your first destination, including plane tickets, baggage fees, moving costs, monthly storage, shipping costs, passport and visa applications (if you're traveling internationally rather

than domestically), new tech equipment and other gadgets, pets, vaccines, and medical tests

>> **Other miscellaneous income:** One-time windfall from selling your car, house, and personal items; investments; tax refund; employee severance package; and security deposit refund

>> **Pre-departure income and expenses:** Your normal, pre-nomad living expenses

## Monthly cost-of-living budget

Your average monthly cost-of-living budget is how much you expect to earn and spend as a nomad. It includes your remote salary or income less your cost of housing, food, insurance, communication, taxes, healthcare, and other living expenses.

REMEMBER

Examples of nomad living expenses look very much like your normal living expenses:

>> ATM, bank, and foreign exchange fees (although you'll want to find debit and credit cards that don't charge foreign transaction fees)

>> Car and bike rental

>> Childcare

>> Cellphone and plan

>> Entertainment and eating out

>> Groceries

>> Healthcare

>> Housing: Rent and utilities (Find out the cost of digital nomad housing in Chapter 6 of Book 4.)

>> Internet plans and devices

>> Subscription services for music and entertainment

>> Online courses and education

>> Personal expenses: Clothing, fitness, laundry, toiletries

>> Pets and vet bills

>> Transportation locally

>> Taxes

Sample travel and relocation costs :

>> Airfare and airport transportation

>> Cultural adjustment training

>> Customs and import fees

>> Excess baggage fees

>> Foreign exchange fees

>> Furniture

>> Private schooling

>> Relocation services

>> Real estate and rental commissions

>> Remote office equipment

>> Short-term housing or hotels

>> Supplemental insurance

>> Tipping

>> Transportation and tours

Sample online business expenses, if you're a freelancer or business owner:

>> Accounting and bookkeeping

>> Cloud storage and file sharing

>> Credit card processing fees

>> Invoicing software

>> Marketing and customer management software

>> Project management software

>> Remote contractors and virtual assistants

>> Web hosting and maintenance

TIP

A travel budgeting app can help you stay on top of your finances while on the move. Check out Trabee Pocket (trabeepocket.com), TravelSpend (travel-spend.com), and Tripcoin.

# Chapter **4**

# Choosing a Destination

When preparing to become a nomad, one question you might have in mind is "Where should I go first?" And with so many amazing places to visit in the world, how do you decide? This chapter guides you in choosing your first (or next) destination and deciding when to travel there.

## Dreaming of the Ideal Destination

Before researching where to go, know that there are no right or wrong answers when it comes to where you decide to travel or move and why. Maybe you want to travel around the United States visiting family or seeing new sights. Perhaps you've always pictured yourself in Paris. Or eating homemade pasta in Italy. Maybe your dream is to buy a house in Portugal, sail the islands of the South Pacific, or read on the beach in Costa Rica.

Whatever your motivation for traveling as a nomad is, there's no such thing as a bad destination (although some places may cost more, have faster Wi-Fi than others, or speak a language you don't). People crossed borders, immigrated to different countries, and traveled, lived, or worked overseas long before there were any nomad hotspots. Every country has pros and cons. If you end up somewhere that doesn't resonate with you, that's okay. Wherever you decide to go, you'll have a memorable and life-changing experience either way. Plus, you'll gain valuable insights to help you choose your next destination.

An ideal nomad destination is one that

>> You want to go to

>> Fits your lifestyle

>> You can afford

>> You can travel to with a passport, visa, or other entry permit (if you choose to travel internationally rather than domestically)

>> Has attributes you're looking for, such as a certain community, climate, internet speed, or things to do

To answer the question of *where* to go, first consider *why* you want to travel. (See Chapter 2 in Book 4 for how to define your passion, purpose, and reason for pursuing the nomad lifestyle.) What are you looking for in a nomad destination? Jot down your ideas here.

>> _____

_____

_____

>> _____

_____

_____

>> _____

_____

_____

Next, write a list of up to ten cities or countries you'd like to visit or that you see yourself living in someday, whether in your home country or abroad:

1. _____

2. _____

3. _____

4. _____

5. _____

6. _____

7. _____

8. _____

9. _____

10. _____

Now circle or highlight the top three that appeal to you the most. Keep them in mind while reading this chapter to help you narrow down where to go first.

# Considering Key Factors

You should consider eight elements when choosing a nomad destination. Each one represents a *fixed* factor (something out of your control) or a *flexible* factor (something you can control):

The four fixed factors in choosing a destination are

>> **Climate:** The type of weather or temperature you would like to experience

>> **Cost of living:** How well your monthly budget aligns with the average cost of living in a destination

>> **Safety and security:** Always important to consider, especially if traveling alone

>> **Border control:** How long you can stay in the country and the requirements you need to get in

The four flexible factors in choosing a destination include

>> **Bucket list:** Things you want to see, do, or experience

>> **Community:** Opportunities to meet people (or lack thereof) or proximity to friends and family members

>> **Lifestyle:** What you'd like your daily life to be like

>> **Work environment:** Time zones, internet speeds, infrastructure, and the like

As a digital nomad, you have the freedom to choose the lifestyle and experiences you want to have, as well as the type of environment you want to be in. But you may be limited by your budget, visa options, or travel restrictions.

After comparing the places you want to go to with the fixed and flexible factors, you should have a good idea of which destinations will best fit your budget and needs at the moment.

## Climate and seasonality

*When* you go to a destination is almost as important as *where* you go. Use seasonality to your advantage. Planning your move based on seasonal differences can save you money and enhance your overall experience.

Seasonality doesn't just refer to the actual season in a year, such as spring, summer, fall, and winter. It also relates to the ebb and flow of tourism throughout the year. Some destinations have very distinct high and low seasons for tourism. For example, summer is peak season in Ibiza, Spain, or on Italy's Amalfi Coast, so traveling there will cost more, while winter is low season. On the flip side, winter is high season in Whistler, Canada, while summer is the low season.

**REMEMBER**

Keep in mind that seasons are reversed in the northern and southern hemispheres. Ski season in the United States and Canada is from November through April, whereas in Chile and Argentina, it runs from July to September. Traveling to a destination is more expensive in the high season, which may be summer or winter, depending on where you go.

**TIP**

You can often find deals on flights and accommodations — and fewer tourists — during the *shoulder season* (between the high and low seasons). Shoulder season in Europe is April through June and September through October, for example.

Seasonality is important for nomads to think about because the time of year that you arrive in a new place could reduce your housing options and increase your cost of living. A villa in Mexico that rents for $1,500/month in low season could cost $1,500/week in high season or $1,000/night during holidays such as Christmas and Easter.

Likewise, you may want to avoid traveling to the Caribbean during hurricane season (June–November) or to the Philippines during typhoon season (August–October).

The time of year that you travel can also dictate which activities you can do. If you love hiking and want to check out Norway, summer would be a great time to go, when the days are long and the weather is mild.

**WARNING**

Don't underestimate the effect of weather on your life and mood. Moving to a place that's cold and dark can trigger *seasonal affective disorder,* a type of seasonal depression associated with a lack of sunlight. A winter night in Tallinn, Estonia, can last up to 18 hours, whereas the longest day in summer is nearly 19 hours!

## Cost of living

Cost of living is a big concern for budget-conscious nomads looking to save money by traveling or relocating to a new place. See Chapter 3 in Book 4 for how to calculate your budget.

**TIP**

If the average cost of living is higher than you anticipated, don't despair. It's possible to live in an expensive city or country on a budget. You can save money by living in suburbs or small towns, renting long-term or shared housing, and eating meals at home more than going out.

For instance, if you want to move to Canada and keep your expenses low, consider a border town such as Sarnia, Windsor, or Niagara rather than Toronto, Vancouver, or Montreal. You could also move to a rural area in Alberta or Nova Scotia. According to the website Numbeo, rent prices in Windsor are 48 percent lower than Vancouver. Grocery prices are 26 percent lower.

Likewise, if you're from Spain and work remotely from Madrid, you could move to nearby Valencia, shaving hundred of dollars per month off your cost of living.

## Safety and security

**REMEMBER**

Safety is always a concern while traveling. Check the U.S. Department of State travel advisories at `https://travel.state.gov/traveladvisories` for up-to-date information. Also check the Global Peace Index from the Institute for Economics & Peace (`www.visionofhumanity.org/maps/#/`), which lists the most and least peaceful countries in the world.

## Border control

If you're considering traveling internationally, before deciding which country to travel to, it helps to know if you'll need more than just a passport. To determine whether you need a visa for travel and how long you can stay, check with the immigration department in your destination or with your home country's embassy, consulate, or travel authority. You can also use a tool such as Passport Index (`www.passportindex.org/`), VisaHQ (`www.visahq.com/`), or Where Can I Live (`www.wherecani.live`). Chapter 5 in Book 4 explains more about visas and long-stay permits.

TIP

To find out about current travel restrictions and health entry requirements, look up destinations you're interested in at the U.S. Department of State (https://travel.state.gov), SafetyWing Borderless website (borderless.safetywing.com/), or IATA Travel Map (www.iatatravelcentre.com/world.php).

## Bucket list

A fun way to choose a destination is based on the experiences you want to have. What's on your bucket list? Do you want to tour Patagonia, swim in Iceland's Blue Lagoon, or experience life on the Las Vegas strip?

List three things at the top of your bucket list:

» _____

_____

» _____

_____

» _____

_____

Try to check off at least one item in the first place you go.

## Community

Part of choosing a destination is considering the activities and opportunities you'll have to meet people there. You could choose a destination based on the size of its population or the language they speak there. If you want to be around other nomads or expats, find people by searching for nomad or expat Facebook groups in your favorite destinations. Likewise, you may want to move somewhere with a strong business network in your industry. Or perhaps you want to be near family and friends.

TIP

If you're still working and want to find others who are, too, check out the travel calendars of Hacker Paradise (www.hackerparadise.org), Wifi Tribe (wifitribe.co), and Remote Year (www.remoteyear.com) to see upcoming destinations.

# Lifestyle

Quality of life is another factor to consider in choosing a destination. Which aspects of daily life are most important to you? Examples include restaurants and coffee shops; art galleries and museums; theater and concerts; beautiful nature and parks for hiking; clean air quality; public transportation; LBGTQIA-friendly; nearby and affordable healthcare; and accessible public transportation. Your dream may be to live in the countryside or at the beach, while someone else craves a fast-paced city. Your idea of quality of life can be as simple as being walking distance from the grocery store and a good coffee shop. Or having access to public transportation and not needing a car to get around.

List three quality-of-life aspects that are important to you:

» _____

_____

» _____

_____

» _____

_____

Then, look up a city or country you want to go to on a tool such as AARP's Livability Index (aarp.org/livability) or NomadList.com (nomadlist.com) to see how it ranks on the quality-of-life metrics that you value the most.

# Work environment

If you're still working, you'll want to find a location compatible with your job role. For example, it might become an issue if you can't make conference calls with your colleagues because you're trekking the Himalayas without internet service! Consider these questions:

» What time zone is your ideal destination located in? Will that work for your schedule? Compare time zones on TimeZoneConverter.com.

» How fast is the internet? Check global internet speeds on Speedtest.net.

» Where will you work? Are there any co-working spaces in the area or does your company have an office or headquarters nearby? Check with your company or do a web search by typing "your location + coworking space."

# Deciding Where to Go and When

After you've evaluated different destinations against your criteria, lifestyle, and budget, choose where you'd like to go first and what time of year you would arrive.

My ideal first digital nomad destination:

_____

_____

Other places I would like to visit soon:

» _____

_____

» _____

_____

» _____

_____

**REMEMBER**

This is just a starting point. You can always change your mind later.

Chapter **5**

# Creating Your Relocation Plan

This chapter helps you create a plan for your relocation and get your affairs in order before you leave home. It introduces the idea of slow travel and includes handy info you need to know about arranging essential services, such as banking and credit cards, and how you can access your money from different countries (if you choose to travel internationally). You also find out about updating your identity documents, address, and phone plan; organizing and shedding your stuff; and thinking ahead about tax considerations.

At the end of this chapter, you find out about the options for visas and permits for short-term and long-term travel and how to know where you can travel with your passport.

## Finding Your Travel Flow

Even if you stay close to home, traveling more often can be a life-changing experience.

One of the biggest adjustments for new nomads is reframing how you think about travel. For most of human history, travel for leisure was a luxury. But today, it's more accessible than ever. And as a nomad, you don't have to wait for your annual vacation to hit the road.

How often you travel depends on your goals. If you're feeling energetic, you may want to see the world as fast as possible. If you're focused on learning more about a culture, you may want to take it slower. Your nomad goals may also have less to do with full-time travel and more to do with relocating to a new place or achieving a different lifestyle.

When creating your nomad relocation plan, consider how often you will change destinations and why. This section introduces the concept of batching your travel and how far to plan in advance.

## Batching your travel

As mentioned in Chapter 3 of Book 4, you incur unavoidable switching costs every time you travel to a new place. The only way to minimize or avoid such costs is through slow travel or batching your travel.

Slow travel is traveling at a pace that feels sustainable for you. Batching your travel is a way of tying your personal or work goals to a particular location. It's also a way to travel more efficiently.

If you're retired, or working part time, for example, your travel plan could involve settling or hanging out in places with a vibrant international community and plenty of things to do.

Working a full-time schedule while traveling at a fast pace can lead to burnout. But assigning a project to a location and rewarding yourself with time off when you finish can help motivate you.

For example, if you're writing a book or coding a complex project, you can choose to spend a few months in a place where there won't be many distractions. (Iceland is a good option.) Then, you can reward yourself with a month of relaxation on the beach in Mexico.

Likewise, if you have a lot on your travel to-do list, you can arrange your itinerary in a way that saves you time and money. For example, if you have multiple conferences and events to attend, you can schedule them back to back in your calendar. Take a few weeks off for networking, learning, and fun, and then get back to your regular work schedule.

Another way to batch your travel is to plan time to visit family members. You can visit your newborn niece and help out her parents, then visit multiple family members in a row from Texas to New York to London (or wherever your loved ones may be).

REMEMBER

How much and how often you travel is a personal choice. Just keep in mind that batching your travel can help you conserve time, energy, money, and resources without compromising your well-being or work.

## Planning your travel in advance

There are trade-offs to how far in advance to plan your travel. If you plan very far out, you'll have peace of mind over where you'll be and when, and prices may be lower. But if you plan *too* far, your plans can be too rigid and making changes can become difficult and expensive.

If you prefer spontaneity over structure, you can book your travel on a whim. You'll have more flexibility, but you'll likely end up paying more for last-minute transportation and accommodations.

Plan as far in advance as feels comfortable for you. If you *know* you want to be in family in Utah for Christmas or celebrate your birthday in Bangkok, book it! But if you aren't sure which hemisphere you'll want to be in, let alone which country, wait until you have more clarity.

TIP

You can outsource your travel planning to a travel agent, virtual assistant, or remote travel or work group to save time. See Chapter 6 in Book 4 for more about travel retreats and co-living operators.

## THREE TRAVEL STRATEGIES: 6/6, 6/3/3, AND 3/3/3/3

Check out three different slow travel strategies. You can employ these strategies in different countries or in different cities within your home country.

With the 6/6 strategy, you spend six months per year in one place and six months in another. You might spend half the year in Florida and half the year in New York. Or six months in Mexico and six months in Europe. Or six months in Sydney, Australia, and six months in Perth.

*(continued)*

*(continued)*

With the 6/3/3 strategy, you spend six months in one place and three months each in two other destinations of your choice. This strategy works with just a passport and tourist visa if you choose one destination where you can stay for up to 180 days and two destinations where you can stay for 90 days each.

With the 3/3/3/3 strategy, you change destinations every three months. This strategy works well if you want to visit four destinations where you can stay for 90 days at a time with a passport. It's also great if you want to experience the four seasons in four different places (or avoid winter and travel to four summer destinations in a row).

The ability to spend three, six, or nine months in a destination allows you to adapt better to each place, form a daily routine, and, if you are working, stay productive without affecting your work-life balance too much.

Some nomads prefer to move every week or month, but that may be too fast for you to stay happy. How fast and far you travel is up to you!

# Getting Your Finances in Order

Finances can be an intimidating topic when you're thinking of cutting ties to your hometown or home country. But it's not as complicated as you may think! The following sections explain the basics of how to access your money anywhere in the world and where to get help with international tax planning.

## Updating your banking services

**REMEMBER**

It's always a good idea to keep a bank account in your home country. Check that your current bank can serve your needs if you travel abroad. Small, private banks and local credit unions can sometimes be complicated to deal with from overseas. To find out, contact your bank's customer service department. Share your travel plans and try to anticipate any challenges before they occur. Ask if you should change your account type, fill out any paperwork, or authorize another user on your account. Many banks adjusted during the pandemic to offer remote access to services.

The same goes for investment accounts. Check with your financial advisor to ensure that you will be able to access and manage your investments from abroad.

If you are currently banking with a small, local institution and need additional banking features and services, consider opening a second account with a larger or remote online bank, which may be better able to provide the services you need.

Before you move, ensure that

>> You can use your debit card abroad.

>> Your card has no or low ATM withdrawal fees and no foreign transaction fees.

>> Your card can be easily replaced if lost or stolen.

>> You can change the phone number associated with receiving text messages and receive text messages to an international number.

>> You can access your banking system from anywhere.

>> You can send and receive international transfers.

>> Your bank has accessible and helpful customer service.

TIP

If your debit or credit card will expire while you're away, renew it early to avoid disruptions to service or shipping costs. Also consider ordering a duplicate card to leave with a trusted person or in a safe deposit box.

## Accessing your money with money transfer apps

One of the most revolutionary developments that has made nomad life easier is the invention of money transfer apps and services, such as Apple Pay, Cash App, OFX, PayPal/Xoom, Remitly, Revolut, Venmo, Wise, and Zelle. When choosing an app, check the fees for the services you'll want to use. A benefit to using money transfer apps is that it can be cheaper and faster to send, receive, and withdraw money internationally compared to a traditional bank. For example, with a traditional bank, a wire transfer could cost $20–$50 and take multiple days to credit an account, whereas with money transfer apps, you can send peer-to-peer almost instantly.

Money transfer apps may have lower ATM fees compared to traditional banks, and low or no international transaction or monthly account management fees. Compare your bank's fees with those of apps you may use, such as for withdrawal to use an out-of-network ATM and international transaction fees for withdrawals in a foreign currency.

You can link your regular debit card or bank account with a money transfer app to fund your account, withdraw money, or send funds to other people in multiple currencies. In that sense, money transfer services act as an intermediary between your traditional bank account and an ATM or a recipient.

**REMEMBER**

It's a good idea to open an account with one or more banks or money transfer platforms before you leave home, so you have time to receive your debit card in the mail.

## Applying for travel rewards cards

Once your banking is sorted, consider applying for a credit card that offers points or perks for travel. Many hotels, airlines, and travel providers offer a branded credit card. Large banks often also offer their own travel rewards cards.

One benefit of having a travel credit card — as with any credit card with rewards — is that you can earn points or cash back on money you would be spending anyway. If you do all your spending on a debit card, you won't earn much (or anything) in return. Check annual and other fees and read the fine print before applying.

Travel credit cards, like some other credit cards, may also provide extra travel or car rental insurance and be a source of emergency funds through a cash advance. Credit cards can also be cancelled and replaced easily. Most credit card companies will send you a replacement card anywhere in the world via FedEx or UPS, but call your card provider to verify.

The best travel credit card for *you* is the one that meets your needs the most and that aligns with your spending habits:

>> **Airline:** Best for frequent fliers on that particular airline. (Almost all global airlines offer a branded credit card.)

>> **General travel:** Good if you travel often and use different travel providers. Points are worth more when exchanged for travel compared to other purchases.

>> **Hotel:** Best if you stay at the specific hotel chain often. Examples include IHG, Marriott Bonvoy, and Starwood.

>> **Platinum or VIP:** Best for luxury travelers. Be warned that platinum and VIP cards can come with high annual fees of $500 or more.

**TIP**

If you're traveling on a tight budget, consider a fee-free or low-fee card that you can earn points on through living expenses such as groceries, gas, business, and miscellaneous purchases.

Reward credit cards won't save you money if you rack up debt. Pay off your credit card balance every month to avoid accruing interest and fees.

# Accounting for Taxes at Home and Abroad

Taxes! A complex but important topic.

The two biggest questions people typically have about taxes are these:

>> Do you have to pay taxes in your home country if you move abroad?

>> Do you have to pay taxes in new countries that you travel through or move to?

The answers to those questions are complicated and depend on many factors, from where you're from to where you live to your type of employment or business structure. Some information is included below, but check with your tax advisor before making important decisions:

>> The United States has citizenship-based taxation. That means citizens are subject to taxes on worldwide income and must file an annual tax return (unless you renounce your citizenship).

>> If you're from outside the United States, you may be from a country with a residence-based tax system that allows you to change your tax domicile if you stop living there. A typical requirement for changing your tax base is to spend more than 180–183 days out of your home country. However, the specifics depend on your country's tax laws and the tax categories in your destination. Your business classification and earning structure may also affect tax rates and filing/reporting requirements. A tax expert can advise you.

The tax situation can get quite murky and complex for nomads, especially if you're traveling the world on a tourist visa versus applying for a work permit, residency, or other official status. Most tax systems weren't designed with remote workers in mind. But some authorities are cracking down on nomads who don't pay taxes anywhere, who pay taxes in one country but live in another, or who work on a tourist visa.

The good news is that becoming location independent could help you save on taxes. If you're from a U.S. state with high state income tax, such as New York or California, you could establish residency in a state with no state income tax, such as Nevada or Florida. Some nomads from countries with high taxes, such as the Netherlands, Denmark, and Sweden, have established residency in a country such as Bulgaria, which has a 10 percent income tax rate.

U.S. citizens who are physically present in foreign countries for at least 330 days per year and earn money there could qualify for the Foreign Earned Income Exclusion. Read more about it at IRS.gov.

Before traveling internationally or moving abroad, research the tax laws and tax treaties in your home and destination countries. Contact your tax advisor or the tax authorities if you have any questions.

When hiring accountants or tax professionals, ask whether they specialize in working with nomads.

# Deciding What to Do with Your Stuff

Throughout life, everyone accumulates stuff, which can quickly turn into junk or extra baggage that's weighing you down. The longer you've lived in one place, the more stuff you probably have.

Transitioning to a lifestyle of location independence is the perfect opportunity to clean house — in this case, literally.

This process is easier said than done, though. You may find out that you have *a lot of stuff*. But don't worry; it's completely normal!

It might take you a few weeks or months to organize and downsize your belongings. Plan accordingly. See Chapter 4 in Book 3 for general guidance on sorting your belongings.

If you plan to be a part-time or temporary nomad, storing your stuff in your house or a storage unit could be a better option than getting rid of it.

How will you decide what to do with your stuff? For each item, big or small, you can do one of four things with it: trash or recycle it, sell it, give it away, or keep it.

When trying to decide what to do with an item, ask yourself:

>> Have I used this in the last year?

>> Will I need this where I'm going?

>> Does this item benefit me?

If the answer to these questions is "no," it's probably time to part with that item. Repeat the process and do as many rounds as needed until you're happy with what you have left.

## What can you trash or recycle?

You can throw away or recycle anything that doesn't have sentimental or monetary value. Examples include old papers and files you no longer need (shred anything with sensitive information), expired food products, ripped old clothing and worn-out shoes, and open toiletries. Contact your local waste management for how to properly dispose of items.

**REMEMBER**

Throwing things away is the easiest thing to do, but it's also wasteful. Keep the planet in mind. Try to donate or "upcycle" items you don't need before adding them to a landfill.

## What can you sell?

You can try to sell anything that has value but that you don't currently need or use, or if it's something you can easily replace abroad. For example, you can sell designer vintage clothing, art supplies, furniture, appliances, cars, electronics, and other big-ticket items. You can also typically sell anything that hasn't been opened or used.

## What should you do with your house?

Selling your home is a big decision. You can also keep, rent, or sublet your house if you plan on coming back and don't need the money. Another option is to downsize to a small apartment or studio (that can double as a storage unit for your valuables and keepsakes). You can also list your house on a home swap or house-sitting website. See Book 3 for full details on downsizing.

**TIP**

Renting your home through online booking sites, such as Airbnb, FlipKey, or Vrbo, can be an extra source of monthly income to fund your travels if there's demand in your neighborhood and your homeowners or renters association allows it. Airbnb has a step-by-step guide for how to prepare your property to rent and become a host.

## What should you do with your car?

Depending on whether you lease or own a car and what the value is, there are many options for what to do with it. The most common solution is to sell it to a private party or car dealership, locally or online.

If you lease a car, you can get out of your lease by listing it on sites such as LeaseTrader or Swapalease. You can also rent your car to a private party or with apps such as Turo or HyreCar. Or donate it!

WARNING

Storing your car long term can cause it to deteriorate and lose value quickly.

## What can you give away or donate?

You can give away or donate anything that can be used by other people. Perhaps a friend or someone in your family wants some of your belongings. Houses of worship, homeless shelters, and women's shelters often accept donations such as food, clothing, hygiene products, and electronics. Check online for donating to organizations such as Goodwill (goodwill.org), Habitat for Humanity (habitatforhumanity.org), and the Salvation Army (salvationarmyusa.org); contact them to determine what items they accept and whether they pick up.

## What should you keep?

Consider keeping a few family heirlooms or other items with sentimental value, such as certain photographs, books, and jewelry. To lighten your load, take photos and record stories of items you're not going to keep. You may also want to keep items that you expect to use regularly in the future when not traveling, such as winter clothing if you are moving temporarily to a warm destination.

You can store valuables with trusted friends or family members or in a local storage unit. Find a local storage unit near you and choose one that is the appropriate size for your needs (with or without climate control).

# Getting Your Affairs in Order

When preparing to go nomadic, there are many details to think about. The following sections address a few miscellaneous but important things you should do before leaving your home base.

## Checking your health

Schedule a checkup with your doctor at least one to two months before you leave home to discuss your personal healthcare needs, stock up on prescription medications, and plan for care and medications while you're gone. Search online or check with healthcare providers overseas to find out whether any medicines you need are available over the counter. Also verify with the customs or health authorities in your destination whether there are any restrictions on your prescription or over-the-counter medications.

REMEMBER

Make sure you're up to date with any routine and recommended vaccinations. Ask your doctor about any screenings you're due for and whether others will become due while you're away. To find information about vaccinations you'll need at your destination, check with the health department or Department of Foreign Affairs in your home and destination countries. The Centers for Disease Control (CDC) and the Department of Health and Human Services provide resources for U.S. travelers. You can also ask your doctor. The World Health Organization also provides guidelines on international travel, disease outbreaks, and vaccines (www.who.int/health-topics/travel-and-health#tab=tab_1). If you're traveling to more than one destination, the International Society of Travel Medicine provides a list of travel clinics around the world (www.istm.org/AF_CstmClinic Directory.asp).

REMEMBER

Depending on where you're going, being fully vaccinated against COVID-19 may also be an entry requirement.

## Getting insured

To be safe, consider purchasing an emergency travel/medical insurance plan and general health insurance that covers you at home and internationally.

You can book trip insurance with your airline (be sure to read the policy first) or find providers on insuremytrip.com, squaremouth.com, or travel insurance.com.

TIP

Check with your coverage provider to see whether electronics and other valuables are covered under your plan. For example, the Professional Photographers Association of America provides insurance for technology equipment and data loss.

Travel-branded credit cards and platinum cards also may have provisions that cover travel-related incidents, rental cars, or trip cancellation, but each card is different. Check your card's terms and conditions or call the number on the back of your card to ask about extra coverage.

Although many credit card companies offer trip insurance, coverage may be limited and there can be a lot of exclusions in the fine print.

## Managing your mail

For physical mail that can't be received electronically, consider enrolling in a mail-scanning service or virtual mailbox. Such services provide a real street address to retain in your home country and let you open and manage your mail anytime, anywhere.

Anytime Mailbox (www.anytimemailbox.com), Earth Class Mail (www.earth classmail.com), Sasquatch Mail (www.sasquatchmail.com), and Traveling Mailbox (travelingmailbox.com) are popular options among nomads. Prices start at $5–25 per month but vary by how much mail you receive and whether you forward any physical mail to an international address.

If you are in the United States and plan to be a short-term nomad, the U.S. post office may be able to hold or forward your mail temporarily. Ask at your local post office or go to usps.com for more details.

## Choosing a phone plan

If you plan to go international, you have a few options for your domestic phone plan:

» Keep your current number and provider, paying for it monthly.

» Upgrade to an international plan or switch providers to ensure you have good coverage abroad.

» Put your plan on pause or hold, paying a nominal fee per month until you come back (if you plan on returning and want to keep the same number).

» Cancel your phone plan and domestic number altogether.

Contact your phone provider about your plans for travel abroad. Change providers and/or plans before leaving home. Also ensure your phone is unlocked so you can use SIM cards from anywhere in the world.

For U.S.-based nomads, check with your current plan. It may offer short- and longer-term international plans. Ask about pricing, international roaming, unlimited data, and internet speed.

You can also try a free app, without the need for a new SIM card. WhatsApp is a popular option for making calls, texting, and engaging in group chats worldwide. You just have to be on Wi-Fi. Other apps include Messenger, Viber, and WeChat.

TIP

Consider traveling with two phones: one with your home country SIM card and an international plan and another unlocked phone that you can use with SIM cards in different countries. But many Android phones already have dual SIMs.

You can also use internet calling plans to stay in touch almost anywhere. But if you ditch your long-term phone number, you may need a way for people to reach you without updating your number every week or month. In that case, consider getting a Google Voice, NumberBarn, Skype-In number or What'sApp, which run via internet. These services may offer call forwarding and international text messaging.

## Bringing your internet with you

In addition to your unlocked phone, you could also travel with a Wi-Fi hotspot device. You can buy an unlocked device that works with local pre-paid SIM cards and some international SIMs. You can purchase these from many places, such as Amazon, Best Buy, or Target.

A second option is to sign up for an international data plan. Check with your current provider, or search "best international data plans."

# Applying for Travel Documents, Visas, and Permits

Knowing where you can travel and work as a nomad and for how long is an important part of the relocation planning process.

The following sections explain how to find out where you can travel on a passport and the different types of travel and long-term visas you can apply for.

## Obtaining your passport

A passport is a document with your name, birthday, gender, and photo that verifies your identity and country of citizenship. To travel internationally as a nomad, you'll need a passport and, in some countries, an entry visa. Whether you need a visa depends on where you're from, where you're going, and how long you plan to stay. (Find out more about visas later in this chapter.)

Regardless of where you're traveling, your passport should have at least 6 to 12 months left before the expiration date — for *each country* you're traveling to.

If you plan to be gone for more than a year, you may want to have some extra runway (pun intended) on your passport's expiration date. If you don't, you may need to renew your passport from a foreign country, which involves visiting your consulate abroad.

To apply for or renew a passport, visit your country's State Department or Department of Foreign Affairs website. In the United States, it's Travel.State.Gov.

**REMEMBER**

Although many travel authorizations are electronic, it's a good idea to have extra blank pages for passport stamps and paper visas.

When you're looking to apply for a passport or renew your existing passport, follow these tips:

>> Select the correct form to apply for a new passport or renew an existing one. You may also have to fill out a different form if you're applying from overseas.

>> Start the process long before you need your passport. It can take weeks or months to receive a new passport. Give yourself sufficient time for the office to process your application and ship your travel document. If your arrival date is close, you can pay extra to have it expedited.

>> If you expect to travel overseas often, order a passport with extra pages. It costs a bit more, but it's a small investment when you consider that your passport is valid for ten years. Every country is different, but in the United States you have the option of ordering a passport with 28 or 52 pages.

**WARNING**

Avoid getting your passport wet and make sure it's valid for six months beyond your travel date. Some nomads have been deported or barred from boarding a flight because their passports were too close to expiring or in a compromised condition. Renew your passport within one year of its expiration date to be safe.

**TIP**

A passport cover helps you protect your passport and keep it dry. It also makes a nice souvenir or gift! Or just keep it in a zipped sandwich bag.

# Knowing whether you need a visa for travel

A visa gives you permission to travel to (or through) a foreign country. There's an array of different visa categories you can apply for, but some of the most common short-stay visas are for business, tourism, family, or leisure purposes.

For many years, nomads have worked remotely while traveling primarily on tourist visas. It's a controversial practice, however, because working on a tourist visa is illegal in certain countries.

The problem is, there weren't any visas created specifically for remote workers until 2020. Most visas were designed with tourists or other short-term visitors in mind. But with the nomad movement gaining in popularity over the years, authorities have been taking more notice and cracking down on the practice of working remotely while traveling on a tourist visa and deporting people on occasion.

This is a bit of a gray area because most nomads travel for leisure and tourism to begin with — they just happen to be funding their travels with income earned online or accessed remotely. But that doesn't mean it's always legal.

**REMEMBER**

Just know that a tourist visa does *not* give you permission to work in-person or remotely in a foreign country.

The next section describes a few categories under which you can legally reside or work in a different country long term. But this section focuses on ways to get authorization to enter a country as a visitor or travel there short term on a tourist visa.

Some visas are single-entry, where you can enter once per visa application. Some are multiple entry, allowing you to travel in and out without applying for a new visa (such as the Australia ETA visitor visa). Some visas renew each time you re-enter (including the Costa Rica, Panama, and Mexico tourist visas), while others have limits such as 90 days per 180 days (a visa for Schengen, most EU countries except Bulgaria, Cyprus, Ireland, and Romania).

Whether you need to apply for a visa for travel and tourism depends on your desired length of stay, your purpose for travel, the entry requirements of the country you're going to, and the strength of your country's passport.

How to determine the "strength" of your passport? It depends on your country. Countries with a *strong passport* allow you to travel visa-free or get a visa on arrival to many countries, meaning you may not need to apply for a visa to enter a country for tourism purposes.

Singapore and Japan are at the top of the list as the two strongest passports of 2023, according to the Henley Passport Index ranking of 199 countries. The United States, Canada, Australia, New Zealand, and most countries in Europe also rank highly. Citizens of Singapore and Japan can travel to 193 and 192 countries visa-free, respectively, while South African citizens can travel to 107 countries, Armenian citizens can travel to 67 countries, and Iraqi citizens can visit 30 countries without applying for a visa.

In countries where you can travel visa-free or with a visa on-arrival, you can receive a stamp in your passport at border control instead of applying for a visa in advance. In some cases, you may need to fill out an immigration form on the plane or at the airport, but you can also do that sometimes when you check in for your flight online or through your airline's app.

Some countries require a travel permit or electronic authorization for entry. The United States has an online application called ESTA for citizens and nationals of countries in its Visa Waiver Program. Australia has a similar ETA visitor visa that you can apply for through the Australian ETA app.

REMEMBER

You are responsible for knowing whether you need a visa and collecting the correct documents for travel. Your airline will ask for your travel documents at check-in (online or in person) and again before boarding.

You may also come across *transit* visas, which give you permission to pass through a country on a layover or stopover en-route to your final destination. And some countries have *exit visas*, which grant permission to leave a country. An exit visa usually comes in the form of a fee or departure tax you pay at the airport or the border. In the Dominican Republic, for example, it's $20.

You can find out about entry, exit, and visa requirements for your destination through one of following resources:

>> Your home country's government website or Department of Foreign Affairs: In the United States, it's the State Department. In the United Kingdom, it's the Foreign, Commonwealth & Development Office.

>> Your home country's consulate or embassy in your destination: For example, if you're a Finnish citizen traveling to the United States, look up the Embassy of Finland there.

>> Your destination country's immigration website or its embassy/consulate in your home country.

>> Third-party services that provide visa information and application support, such as CIBTvisas (cibtvisas.com), Passport Index (www.passportindex.org/visa.php), or Visa Hq (www.visahq.com/visas.php).

To find the right resource online, you can also search for "travel advice [your country] citizens."

If you overstay your visa, you could be liable for fines or deported and banned from re-entering (in some cases, for years). Tread with caution!

## Applying for visas

Typical visa requirements include filling out an application online, submitting a recent passport photo (and sometimes the passport itself), and paying processing and shipping fees.

Authorities may also ask for a copy of your itinerary, health data, and proof of income (such as bank statements) to ensure that you can afford to support yourself when you're there. In some cases, you may also need to present a letter or invitation from a local company, resident, or sponsor and appear in person at a consulate for an interview.

The processing time for a visa may be weeks or months. Some visas and permits can be obtained while you are already abroad, but many require that you apply *before* you travel.

Again, you can apply for a visa on your own through your destination country's government portal, embassy, or consulate. Or you can hire a service to help you. Some countries, such as Thailand, allow a one-time tourist visa extension. You can extend a Thai tourist visa for 30 days with a 1,900 Baht (USD $55) fee. Other countries require you to exit the country for a period of time before you can re-enter as a tourist. Non-EU citizens visiting countries in the European Schengen Area for business or tourism can get a short-stay visa (permission to stay for up to 90 days in a 180-day period). Tourists from approved countries traveling to the United Kingdom can stay for up to 180 days in a one-year period.

As you're planning your itinerary, keep in mind:

>> Even if you have a valid passport and visa, entry to a country is not *guaranteed*. The immigration or border control agent who stamps your passport can deny you from entering for any reason (or no reason) at all.

>> A travel or tourist visa does *not* necessarily give you permission to work or live in a country. You may need a work permit, residency permit, or digital nomad visa for that.

>> Always check the entry and exit requirements *before* booking travel to any country.

# Extending your stay

If you want to stay in a country for longer than your short-stay or tourist visa allows, you may need to apply for a for a long-stay visa, immigrant visa, or other permit such as work or study. Although many countries now offer visas specifically for digital nomads, you may qualify for other types of visas as well.

The specifics between the application requirements, costs, and details of different visa types vary by country. But the following is a list of long-term visas, work permit, and residency categories you can choose from in some countries:

- >> **Business:** For people starting a small business in another country. Citizens from countries that are part of the Dutch American Friendship Treaty can apply for the two-year DAFT permit in the Netherlands with a minimum investment of €4,500.
- >> **Freelancer:** For people who provide services as an independent contractor. Germany offers a three-month "Freiberufler" (freelancer) visa.
- >> **Investor:** For people who invest in a business, financial products, real estate, or other investment. Also known as golden visas, which you can read about in the next section.
- >> **Marriage:** For people who get married to a citizen from a different country. Many countries also have a civil partnership visa.
- >> **Medical:** For people getting surgeries or other procedures. Colombia has a Special Temporary Visa for Medical Treatment for stays of 6–12 months with an application cost of $175.
- >> **Fixed income:** For people who earn money from a stable or fixed income. Examples include the Portugal D7 visa, the Spain Non-Lucrative visa, and the Costa Rica Rentista visa.
- >> **Retirement:** Specifically for retirees living on pensions. You can apply for the Panama and Costa Rica "Pensionado" visas if you have a retirement income of at least $1,000 per month.
- >> **Student:** For students looking to study abroad. Can also be used for learning a foreign language in many countries, including Hungary and Thailand. Thailand also has a Self-Defense Education visa valid for learning Muay Thai, while Japan has a Cultural Activities Visa for learning skills such as Japanese drumming (Taiko), flower arranging (Ikebana), or hosting a tea ceremony.
- >> **Work:** For people looking to work for a local company. The Taiwan Gold Card is a multi-use work permit and resident visa, popular among digital nomads, that allows cardholders to live and work in Taiwan for one to three years.
- >> **Working Holiday:** For people aged 18–30 who want to work while on holiday in countries such as Australia, Ireland, New Zealand, and South Korea.

**REMEMBER**

Many of these visas offer a path to temporary or permanent residency, which can lead to citizenship. Most countries require that you apply for a visa before arrival.

A strategy that many nomads on tourist visas employ is to go on a "visa run" to extend their stay. This is accomplished by leaving a country and re-entering — even sometimes the same day. In some countries, the act of re-entering is enough to extend your stay. Costa Rica is one country well known for allowing foreigners to renew their tourist visas by leaving and re-entering. Keep in mind that re-entry is not guaranteed, and immigration authorities have been clamping down on perpetual tourism.

Other countries have restrictions on how soon you can re-enter as a tourist after your visa expires. Tourists can stay in the EU Schengen area for up to 90 days per 180-day period . If you stay for 90 days in a row, you must leave for 90 days before re-entering. You can also spread the days out over six months. However, it's difficult to get an extension on a Schengen tourist visa. (Of course, EU nationals have "free movement" to live and work in another EU country without a time limit.) You can find apps that calculate your days in the Schengen Zone in your phone's app store.

**REMEMBER**

One common misconception about becoming a nomad is that you must give up your citizenship or apply for permanent residency to travel abroad long term or relocate to another country. But that's not the case. Although you need permission to reside in another country, it doesn't affect your citizenship status in your home country.

## Understanding golden visas

There's a lot of buzz online about golden visas. It's not Willy Wonka's "Golden Ticket," but it's close. With a *golden visa,* you make an investment, which gets you a passport or residency permit. It's called "golden" because it's expensive— typically six to seven figures. Although most countries offer such a program, the amount of the investment varies dramatically between nations.

A golden visa provides you with long-term residency or citizenship status, depending on the type of visa you buy. A residency-based golden visa, such as the Greece Golden Visa, allows you to live, work, and study in the country for five years. Many countries offer the option to renew your visa or apply for citizenship after five years. Meanwhile, a citizenship golden visa, such as the Turkey Citizenship by Investment Program, makes you a citizen of that country, complete with a passport and local ID number.

The cost of a golden visa depends on how much demand there is to live in a country. Safe countries with low taxes, mild climates, developed economies, and a high quality of life are the highest in demand.

Sample costs of a golden visa include the following:

» **Costa Rica:** $200,000 investment

» **Greece:** €250,000 investment

» **Ireland:** €500,000 investment

» **Malta:** €900,000 investment

» **Monaco:** Varies, but "sufficient financial resources" include at least €500K in a local bank account.

» **Panama Investor Visa:** $300,000 investment

» **St. Kitts and Nevis:** $250,000 investment

» **Thai Elite Visa:** THB 5,000,000 investment for 20-year residency

» **Turkey:** $400,000 investment

» **United Kingdom:** £2,000,000 investment

The main benefit of getting a golden visa is that it's a relatively fast and straight-forward path to long-term residency or citizenship in a country. Having a second passport gives you more freedom and flexibility.

Some countries require that you stay there for a certain number of days per year to be able to keep your residency status, although this isn't the case if you become a citizen.

You can apply for a golden visa through an immigration authority or with the help of a local attorney. Private, third-party companies also offer golden visa services.

REMEMBER

You don't need a golden visa or residency permit to make a country your tax domicile. You can pay taxes in a foreign country without residency or citizenship status. Check with your tax advisor.

# Tying Up Loose Ends

**REMEMBER**

Before officially hitting the road, you'll want to make sure your affairs are in order. Set up a will and/or a trust. Add beneficiaries to all your accounts, assets, and life insurance policies. Store important documents and copies of your ID and passport with a close confidante such as a close friend or relative or your accountant or attorney, or in a safe deposit box, and let trusted individuals know where they are. Photograph or scan and save or make copies of any important documents to bring with you. Also consider leaving a power of attorney for someone to act in your absence. Cancel all services you no longer need, such as utilities and subscriptions. Renew your driver's license, debit and credit cards, and passport (if less than one year from expiration) in time to receive them before you leave.

Consider applying for an International Driver's Permit. In some countries, small rental car agencies require it. If you live in the United States, you can get an International Driver's Permit through AAA at a cost of $30. The permit is valid for one year.

# Chapter **6**

# Finding Housing

inding your new home away from home can be one of the most exciting (and daunting) parts of becoming a nomad. When you're a nomad, your home is wherever you are. You may even have more than one home base. So, it's important to find places where you'll feel comfortable, safe, and, if you're working, productive.

This chapter tells you about the many housing options you'll have as a nomad, from RVs to chalets to sailboats. Plus, you discover how to make the best choice every time you move. You find out where you can find both short- and long-term housing and untraditional ways of living nomadically.

This chapter also provides tips on negotiating prices, avoiding scams, and paying your rent across borders.

## Checking Out Different Housing Types

Imagine living in an ocean view villa in Costa Rica, garden studio in Amsterdam, a cabin on a cruise ships, and homestay in Japan.

Intrigued? In the following sections, prepare to explore a plethora of exciting housing options that await you as a nomad, both domestically and abroad.

# Short term: Just a few weeks or months

Think of short-term housing as anything six months or less in duration.

This category includes nightly and weekly rentals such as hotels, vacation rentals, and any type of dwelling that's offered month-to-month.

A benefit of renting short term is that you have more flexibility with less commitment compared to renting something long term. Short-term rental properties are almost always fully furnished, often with linens, cutlery, and appliances included. If you're lucky, your host or landlord will even include toiletries and kitchen staples such as coffee, tea, cooking oil, and condiments. Some short-term rentals are minimally furnished or lacking the same quantity and quality of pots, pans, pillows, and comforts you have at home.

TIP

Look closely at property photos and listing details to see what's included. If something is unclear, you can ask the owner for a copy of the property inventory.

Short-term rentals are easy to book through well-known international booking sites such as Airbnb and Vrbo, as well as through local vacation rental agencies. Although short-term properties rarely require a signed rental agreement, it's a good idea to ask for one for rentals longer than a month or so to expectations are clear.

WARNING

Short-term rentals may be illegal in some locations. Homeowners association rules may prohibit short-term rentals in some buildings and complexes. Conduct an online search or ask the host to verify before booking. Barcelona and Thailand have cracked down on Airbnb bookings in recent years, while the minimum lease term in Costa Rica is technically three years.

WARNING

A short-term rental may end up costing more than a longer lease term. You may also have to pay your entire stay up front. Watch, too, for cleaning and other one-time fees. A general rule is, the shorter the rental period, the higher the price per night.

You can often book short-term rentals online with a credit card. Vacation rental sites may also offer extra security and support in the case of a dispute.

Utilities, such as water, electricity, and internet, are usually included in the price of a nightly or weekly rental. But the longer the rental period, the more likely it is for utilities (especially electricity) to be additional.

# Long term: Settling in for a few months or longer

Any rental that's 6 to 12 months or more is considered a long-term rental. As with short-term rentals, owners can decide how long of a lease term to offer their properties for and what to include in the rent. Long-term rentals can come furnished, unfurnished, or semi-furnished.

The benefit of renting long term is that it provides you with some stability as a nomadic traveler. You'll also have a physical mailing address that you can use to establish proof of residency should you need it for your job or a long-stay work permit or visa. Long-term rentals may also be the most affordable type of rental properties. The longer your lease, the cheaper your rent tends to be.

**WARNING**

Renting long term does have downsides, though. Long-term rentals can have hidden costs. Utilities are almost always additional and depending on the country, you may need to pay an agency fee to a property representative or realtor. This is usually a commission or "finder's fee" equal to half a month or one month's rent.

**REMEMBER**

Booking a long-term rental could also lock you into a long-term contract, so make sure you like the property and location before committing!

While you can book short-term rentals based on photos or videos without much of a risk, you should always visit a long-term rental property in person *before* signing a lease or wiring funds. Or send a trusted person to view it on your behalf.

**WARNING**

If you sign a long-term rental contract but vacate the property early, you may forfeit your security deposit and pre-paid rent. You may also have to pay a penalty. Always have a local attorney review a rental contract before you sign. Ask questions about the housing law and your rights as a tenant if you're unsure.

**WARNING**

Some long-term rental search sources, such as classifieds websites, can be full of scams and fake properties that don't exist. Get more tips on avoiding scams later in this chapter.

# Private: Having the place all to yourself

When searching for properties online, you can choose between private or shared rentals.

Private rentals are just that — private to you. This is the way to go if you want your own space or are traveling with kids. You also have less noise and distractions compared to living with other people. And you don't have to argue over who takes out the trash.

The downside to private rental properties is that they're usually more expensive than shared rentals. You're paying a premium to have the entire place to yourself. You could also feel lonely or less safe compared to living with others.

Private housing includes the following:

>> Long-term furnished and unfurnished rentals

>> Monthly furnished rentals

>> Weekly furnished rentals

>> Private sublets

>> Nightly hotels and vacation rentals

To sort for private rental properties, check the box for "private" in the search filters of any website.

## Joining a work-travel tribe

Work-travel groups are a form of what's known as co-living. Your home-away-from-home may end up being a group of *people* rather than a specific *place*. Plenty of mobile travel tribes roam the planet at any given time. You can join weekly, monthly, or yearly work-travel groups, depending on what you're looking for.

Examples of co-living operators include

>> Hacker Paradise (hackerparadise.org)

>> Noma Collective (www.noma-collective.com)

>> Remote Year (www.remoteyear.com)

>> Unsettled (beunsettled.co)

>> WiFi Tribe (wifitribe.co)

Joining a work-travel tribe is a great option if you're solo traveling or just want to meet people. Imagine that it's your first time in a foreign country and you already have a built-in group of friends waiting for you when you arrive!

It's also nice to have your housing expenses and logistics simplified. Rent, utilities, some transportation, internet, and co-working expenses are wrapped together when you live with a co-living group. Meals and excursions are sometimes available as well.

When traveling with such a group, you also have access to a chaperone, host, or organizer to go to if you have any questions about the local area.

**WARNING**

A downside to living with a co-living tribe is that it's usually much more expensive than renting on your own. You could pay $2,000–3,000 per week or month to live with a nomadic retreat group in a country where the monthly (total) cost of living is only $1,000.

On the other hand, more conveniences may be included. Remote Year boasts "comfortable accommodation," 24/7 access to a workspace, health and safety support, curated local experiences, ground and air transportation, and a local team leader.

Some providers also include airport pick-up and throw in a SIM card for your phone upon arrival.

## Alternative housing: Boats, treehouses, and beyond

Whether you rent long term or short term, private or shared, nomads have a range of unique accommodation options to choose from.

Have you ever thought about living in a sailboat, houseboat, treehouse, or tiny house? You can find all these options plus shipping containers, caves, domes, and more online. Here are some examples:

>> In 2022, Airbnb released a feature called categories, where you can search properties by much more than their size, price, and location. Why not stay in a castle?

>> Fancy dabbling in #VanLife? Browse vans and RVs for rent on sites such as EscapeCampervans.com, IndieCampers.com, and Roadsurfer.com. Look for flexible plans that include vehicle insurance, service, preparation, and van delivery included. You may also want to test drive a van before renting it.

>> You can rent a tent and campsite on GlampingHub (glampinghub.com), Hipcamp.com, or Tentrr (www.tentrr.com).

>> Experience life on a farm by booking a stay through Farmstay (farmstayus.com/) or, if you prefer an organic farm, Wwoof.net.

# Planning Your Housing Search

Before jumping into your housing search, take some time to envision what you're looking for. Consider the following:

» **Your priorities and goals:** What's most important to you in a rental property? Is it the price? Being walking distance to stores and restaurants? Living with people? Having a balcony or view? High-speed internet? A pet-friendly or accessible property?

  Write down three non-negotiable things you are looking for in a rental property:

  - _____

  - _____

  - _____

» **Your rental budget:**

  - If you have a tight budget, you may have more time than money to spend. If that's the case, your search strategy may include scouring classifieds sites and Facebook groups to find the best deals or planning your travel around pet- and house-sitting opportunities.

  - If you have a flexible budget, you have more options. You can start your search through online booking portals or contact rental agencies or estate agents to find properties for you.

» **Your lease term:** Are you looking for a short-, mid-, or long-term rental?

» **Your destination:** Some websites, such as Airbnb, Booking.com, Craigslist, and Vrbo, are available almost anywhere in the world. Others are specific to different cities and countries. For example, Kijiji is based in Canada while Malta Park is exclusive to properties in Malta.

» **Your timeline until arrival:** When should you start looking for housing? That's up to you, but many people book up 6–9 months in advance. For more flexibility, book 1–3 months ahead.

**WARNING**

The longer you wait to book a rental property, you may encounter less and higher prices.

# Knowing what to look for in a rental property

Before starting your property search, keep the following in mind:

>> **Money, money, money:** Is the property in your budget? Is a security deposit required? Is the price negotiable? Are there added cleaning, resort, and other hidden fees? Chapter 3 in Book 4 helps you calculate your nomad budget.

>> **Location, location, location:** Besides the country or city location, consider a property's safety, walkability, and proximity to stores, restaurants, public transportation, and amenities. (See the next section for how to evaluate a location.)

TIP If you're sensitive to noise, ask if the property is on a busy street or next to a school, nightclub, or construction site.

>> **Safety and security:** Safety is dependent on the country as well as neighborhood. In more high-risk destinations, you may want to ensure that you stay in a secure building or a gated community. In other locations, you may be perfectly safe in a regular house.

More things to look for include the following:

- A concierge or security guard
- A gate to enter the property
- Security bars or reinforced windows
- A safe to store valuables
- Method of entry, such as key, key card, lockbox, or code

>> **Remote work friendliness:** If you'll be working from home, is there a comfortable table or dedicated workspace you can use?

TIP Some properties have only a bar with barstools to sit at, or a coffee table without dining room chairs. Make sure there's a comfortable place for you to sit. If there's nowhere to work within the property, continue your search or find nearby co-working spaces on Coworker.com.

>> **Wi-Fi status:** What's the internet speed? Beware of the term "high-speed internet." To find out what that means, look for the exact upload/download speed in the description or ask the landlord to send you a screenshot of the speed test.

>> **Comfort and amenities:** Scan the description and photos for any other must-haves, such as an elevator; king-sized bed; flat screen TV; feather pillows; coffee maker; or washer, dryer, and dishwasher.

**REMEMBER**

A property rarely has 100 percent of the features you're looking for. Be flexible but also watch out for any deal-breakers. Make a list of non-negotiables and read reviews to avoid any unpleasant surprises, but take caution with the accuracy of some reviews.

**TIP**

If you're short on time and can afford help, consider hiring a virtual assistant to help with your search. You can find one through freelancing sites such as ChatterBoss, Fiverr, Onlinejobs.ph, TaskRabbit, and Upwork.

## Finding out about a location

To decide where you want to rent within a city or town, it helps to familiarize yourself with the different neighborhoods in the area. Doing this can help you narrow your search before you start.

Find a destination in your favorite maps app. Look for neighborhood names, and then research those neighborhoods online. Or, simply search for "the best neighborhoods in *your destination*." The more you zoom on a section of the map, different neighborhoods will appear.

**TIP**

Look up a location on `Walkscore.com` to help you get an idea of how walkable a community is. A "walk score" of 100 is perfect, where daily errands do not require a vehicle. A walk score of 70 means that the city is somewhat walkable or bikeable, but some errands require a car, taxi, rideshare, or public transportation. A walk score of 20 means that having a car is almost a necessity.

You can also search for neighborhoods using AARP Livability Index (`livability index.aarp.org`), which rates communities based on factors such as transportation, accessibility to services, affordability, security, and clean air and water.

# Searching for Housing

Your next step is to start your housing search. Simply read the description of each search method, choose the one that's best for your needs, and happy house hunting!

# Short-term vacation rental websites

You can find short-term rentals on almost any property website, from nightly booking sites such as Booking.com or Hotels.com to sites that specialize more in weekly and monthly accommodations, such as Airbnb and Vrbo.

Here are just some of the short-term vacation-rental portals that nomads can use:

- » **9Flats**
- » **Airbnb**
- » Booking.com
- » Craigslist.com
- » **Flatio**
- » **FlipKey**
- » **HomeAway**
- » **HomeToGo**
- » Hotels.com
- » **Housing Anywhere**
- » **Nestpick**
- » **Plum Guide**
- » Sublet.com
- » **TripAdvisor**
- » Tripping.com
- » **Trivago**
- » **Vrbo**

Be sure to verify any company you use and property you consider. Whenever possible, pay with a credit card, where you can dispute charges.

Housing subscription services are another way to find short-term housing. Take a look at Blueground Pass (www.theblueground.com/blueground-pass), Home Exchange (homeexchange.com), or Landing (www.hellolanding.com). You can find a service by searching "home exchange." Again, be sure to verify the service you're considering is legitimate before using it.

## Finding long-term housing

For lease terms of six months or more, classified sites are a good way to find the best deals and to book directly with owners. The upcoming section explains how you can use classified sites to your advantage.

**WARNING**

You could pay a premium if you book long-term rentals on vacation rental sites.

Reaching out to property developers and condo administrators to inquire about long-term rates is another strategy. Just make sure to specify that you're looking for *furnished* properties.

Real estate offices also frequently have long-term rentals. Read more about finding properties through real estate offices in the upcoming section, "Real estate offices."

Many nomads find long-term housing by searching the Facebook Marketplace or in Facebook groups, which you can read about next.

## Facebook groups and forums

Searching Facebook groups can be a time-consuming but rewarding strategy for finding all types of housing: short-term, long-term, shared, and sublets. You can browse listings passively or post what you're looking for and see who responds.

Tips for finding properties on Facebook include the following:

>> Filter your search for "groups" rather than "all results" that include people, pages, and posts.

>> Check a group's activity before joining to make sure it's been active in the last few days.

>> "Take Over My Lease" Facebook groups can lead you to sublet opportunities.

>> General groups for expats, foreigners, and nomads in a specific city or country can be a good resource for finding rentals.

## Local classifieds listings

Besides international classifieds sites such as Craigslist, local classifieds pages offer plenty of housing options. You can find properties to rent or buy this way, often at local prices.

To find a local classifieds site in your destination, search online for "classifieds [the city you're looking for]." Translate "classifieds" into the local language for better search results. For example, search for "clasificados Playa del Carmen."

**TIP**

There is usually a way to switch the language and search results of a classifieds site to English. If you use Google Chrome web browser, it might translate automatically for you, though that feature can be buggy and fail to work. In that case, try Apple Translate, Google Translate, or Microsoft Translator.

**TIP**

If prices appear in the local currency, use a search engine or website like XE.com to convert into your home currency.

**TIP**

Before inquiring, check the listing details to see when a property was published. Some properties may be months or years old. You can also sort by most recent. If you find an old rental listing where the property has been vacant for a long time, you may be able to negotiate a better rate. But check the details carefully because there might be a reason it hasn't been rented.

It's best to pay with a credit card, where you can dispute the charge if the rental doesn't work out.

## Search engine strategies

You can use a search engine to uncover small or privately owned websites offering housing in different cities.

To find websites not listed in this book, search different combinations of keywords, such as "furnished rentals [the city/country you're looking for]."

If you were to search "furnished rentals St. Lucia," you would find hundreds of thousands of results, including a local agency that may or may not have listings on Airbnb or Booking.com. You would also get results for specific buildings with apartments for rent.

Get creative and see what you find!

**TIP**

If you have a bigger budget, try searching for "executive housing" or "corporate housing" that is geared toward business travelers. It's sometimes more expensive than renting leisure properties, but executive rentals are usually fully equipped with everything a remote worker would need — especially high-speed internet!

## Property management companies

Property management companies represent a large inventory of properties. They may not have the lowest prices you'll find online, but using them as a resource is a quick way to find a property almost anywhere in the world.

You can find property managers through online searches, Facebook groups, and by contacting local real estate offices.

## Real estate offices

Many real estate agencies offer properties to rent as well as to buy. If you get stuck and can't find a property you like online, contact a few real estate offices to see whether they have any short- or long-term listings in their inventory. Sometimes they can also refer you to a local rental agent or agency with additional properties.

TIP

You can find real estate agents on a country's Multiple Listing Service (MLS) website.

## In-person searching

If you have extra time to invest in finding the perfect property, book a hotel or short-term rental so you have somewhere to stay while you look for a long-term rental. Looking in person could mean walking, driving, or biking around, checking out signs for rentals.

Another strategy that pays off in nomad hubs such as Thailand is contacting building administrators or managers to ask about vacancies.

These strategies are labor-intensive but can result in finding some hidden gems. They also give you the opportunity to negotiate rates with people in person rather than paying the listing price online.

# Reserving and Booking Your Housing

Once you find a property you like, it's time to book it! This section gives you tips on negotiating and paying for your housing, as well as recovering your security deposit.

Make sure you aren't renting a property for longer than you're able to stay in the country.

## Negotiating the best price

Your negotiating power depends on the time of year you're renting in (peak, shoulder, or low season) and the current market conditions there at the moment. You'll have more negotiating power in the off season than the high season.

For example, if you're going to Barcelona for a week in the middle of summer, prices will be much higher than if you're going for a month during winter. See Chapter 4 in Book 4 for more about how seasonality impacts travel.

You'll usually also have more wiggle room if you're renting long term versus short term.

If you're renting a short-term rental and decide you want to stay longer, ask the owner if there's a long-term rate. If you're renting a long-term rental for a shorter period of time, be prepared to pay more.

Tips for saving money on rentals include the following:

>> Travel slowly and off-season.

>> Ask about long-term rates that may not be advertised.

>> Offer to pay up front for a discount (if you're sure you want to stay there).

>> Know when to walk away. If you're not getting what you're requesting, it may be better to move on to the next property.

## Paying for housing

How you pay your rent depends on where or who you rent the property from. Here are some possibilities:

>> If you rent online, you should be able to pay by credit card through the site you used to book.

>> If you rent through a private party or agency, you may need to transfer funds to a domestic or foreign bank account.

>> If your landlord has a bank account in the same country, you can probably send a check, domestic wire, or local transfer.

>> If your landlord has a bank account in a different country, you can send a bank wire or use an online money transfer service such as Apple Pay, Cash App, OFX, PayPal/Xoom, Remitly, Revolut, Venmo, Wise, and Zelle.

**WARNING**

Never pay for housing without some form of a written agreement, and try to have a lawyer review the agreement.

**REMEMBER**

Always read the terms of your rental agreement before paying. Inquire about the penalties for terminating a lease early and the options for extending it, should you want to stay longer. Consider hiring a legal professional to review your agreement.

## Avoiding scams

Renting through reputable agencies and booking sites is the best way to avoid scams. If a property on a classifieds site or in a Facebook group looks too good to be true, it probably is.

To reduce the risk of getting ripped off, avoid any properties where the reps say they will "mail the key" to you. Check any photos by doing a photo search; criminals can download photos or buildings and interiors and post them as their own.

Before sending money to someone you don't know, request a video tour or view the property in person. You can also send a local rental agent or someone you know there to view a property for you.

**TIP**

Use a credit card or payment method with vendor's insurance, such as PayPal or Venmo, which allows you to dispute a fraudulent charge.

**WARNING**

Never send money by cash, check, bank transfer, or Western Union to someone you don't know.

Always ask for a receipt or proof of payment.

**REMEMBER**

## Getting your security deposit refunded

A security deposit is usually equal to one month's rent for long-term rentals and varies for short-term rentals, from a few hundred dollars to nothing at all. If you're booking through a short-term rental site, the property description should indicate what the amount and terms of the security deposit are.

**REMEMBER**

When it comes to getting your security deposit back, prevention is the best remedy. Always review the terms of *when* and *how* your security deposit will be returned *before* paying it. Photograph any flaws when you enter and send the photos to the owner to verify you weren't at fault.

# IDEAS FOR FINDING YOUR PERFECT HOUSING

Here are a few examples of different housing strategies nomads have used in the past. Feel free to borrow one or more of them to kick off your property search.

**Exhibit A:** You want to see the world as fast as possible. Housing options for you could include the following:

- Renting a property on a vacation rental site
- Signing up for organized travel retreat groups
- Backpacking around and booking hotels and hostels on the fly

**Exhibit B:** You want to travel slowly, go with the flow, and see where you end up. Housing sources for you include the following:

- Renting a one-month rental on a short-term rental website
- Moving into a short-term rental and getting to know the local area, keeping an eye out for "for rent" signs on properties that appeal to you
- Searching Facebook groups for long-term housing
- Inquiring about rentals with local real estate and rental agencies
- Searching classifieds websites for sublets and local deals

**Exhibit C:** You don't care where you go or how long you stay, as long as you're with cool people. Try the following:

- Starting your nomad journey in a popular nomad hub or at a conference or event where you can meet people quickly
- Signing up for organized travel retreat groups
- Staying in hostels

**Exhibit D:** You're focused on immersing yourself in the culture of one place, your business, and being productive. Check out the following:

- Local classifieds websites for housing
- Local realtors and rental agencies
- A monthly or long-term co-living arrangement
- A homestay
- Long-term house-sitting options.

# 5

# Eating Healthy

# Contents at a Glance

# Chapter **1**

# Starting the Day Right with Breakfast

Everybody knows that eating a good breakfast is the best way to start the day. But do you know why? In this chapter, we take a look at the reasons that eating a healthy and balanced breakfast meal is so important. Then to help you start your day off right, we include six recipes that are easy, delicious, and satisfying.

## Understanding the Importance of Breakfast

During the day, how long can you go without getting hungry? Many people eat meals about six hours apart. So just think about how much your body needs breakfast after eight hours of sleep!

Breakfast provides the fuel for the rest of your day. Studies show that people who eat breakfast perform better at all tasks, have more energy throughout the day, and tend to weigh less than those who skip this important meal. Eating first thing in the morning also lowers your liver's production of bad LDL cholesterol.

And while intermittent fasting is all the rage, people 50 and older generally need adequate protein — 20 to 25 grams at a time — spaced throughout the day to maintain muscle mass and prevent weight gain.

One of the neatest things about being a grown-up is that you get to decide what you want to eat. If you don't like traditional breakfast foods like eggs or cereal, don't eat them. Instead, eat what you like! A pasta salad can make an excellent breakfast, especially if you make it with whole-wheat pasta, high-protein chicken or fish, a yogurt-based dressing, and delicious fruit. You can also prepare a breakfast pizza using homemade whole-wheat crust, scrambled eggs or tofu, sautéed veggies, and good artisan cheese. (You'll find recipes that are vegetarian, vegan, lactose-free, and gluten-free, or substitute items to suit your preferences.)

Whatever you decide to have for breakfast, keep the following guidelines in mind to get the most out of the meal:

>> **Eat enough protein at every meal.** Studies show that people 50-plus who consume 25 to 30 grams of protein per meal could slow the descent into muscle loss and weight gain. If your main dish falls short, add a cup of milk or Greek yogurt, a half cup of cottage cheese, or a slice of leftover chicken or fish.

>> **Eat lots of rainbow-colored fruits and veggies.** Choose whole fruits over fruit juices. If your family has a history of obesity or diabetes, avoiding fruit juices is even more important. If you like to drink your breakfast, make a smoothie with whole fruits. And throw in some greens!

>> **Notch up your favorite breakfast's nutrition.** For example, if you love frosted crisp cereal, try the Baked Oatmeal recipe instead.

# Whipping Up Some Tasty Breakfast Recipes

When you make the recipes in this chapter, follow the directions, but don't be afraid to substitute some of your favorite ingredients for others. For instance, you can add a couple of jalapeño chilies to the Avocado Toast with Scrambled Eggs. Whenever you make a change in the recipe, write it down. Forgetting the little changes you make here and there is easy to do, and you don't want to lose your delicious, new creations!

# Cantaloupe Banana Smoothies

| PREP TIME: 10 MIN | COOK TIME: N/A | YIELD: 4 SERVINGS |
|---|---|---|

**INGREDIENTS**

2 cups peeled, cubed cantaloupe

1 banana, peeled, cut into chunks, and frozen

½ cup orange juice

1 tablespoon lemon juice

1 cup yogurt

1 tablespoon flaxseed

1 teaspoon vanilla extract

**DIRECTIONS**

1 Combine the cantaloupe, banana, orange juice, and lemon juice in a blender or food processor. Cover and blend on high until the fruits are well mixed.

2 Add the yogurt, flaxseed, and vanilla. Cover and blend on high until the mixture is smooth. Divide the smoothie evenly into four glasses and serve immediately.

**PER SERVING:** *Calories 121 (From Fat 28); Fat 3g (Saturated 1g); Cholesterol 8mg; Sodium 36mg; Carbohydrate 21g (Dietary Fiber 2g); Protein 4g.*

**VARY IT!** You can switch up this simple recipe in many ways. For example, use honeydew melon in place of the cantaloupe or add a peeled, sliced peach or pear to the mix. Or add a handful of frozen spinach or kale for even more nutrients.

# Baked Oatmeal

| PREP TIME: 15 MIN | COOK TIME: 40–50 MIN | YIELD: 8 SERVINGS |
| --- | --- | --- |

### INGREDIENTS

2 cups old-fashioned rolled oats

½ teaspoon baking powder

¼ teaspoon cinnamon

⅛ teaspoon cardamom

1 cup cooked farro or barley

1⅔ cups plain almond milk

2 eggs

¼ cup maple syrup

2 tablespoons melted butter

2 teaspoons vanilla extract

### DIRECTIONS

1 Preheat oven to 350 degrees. Grease a 9-inch square baking dish with butter.

2 In a large bowl, combine the oats, baking powder, cinnamon, and cardamom, and mix well. Set aside.

3 In a medium bowl, combine the cooked farro or barley, almond milk, eggs, maple syrup, butter, and vanilla, and mix until combined. Stir into the oat mixture and transfer to the prepared baking dish.

4 Bake for 40 to 50 minutes or until a food thermometer registers 160 degrees.

**PER SERVING:** *Calories 162 (From Fat 44); Fat 5g (Saturated 2g); Cholesterol 8mg; Sodium 47mg; Carbohydrate 26g (Dietary Fiber 3g); Protein 4g.*

**TIP:** To get 1 cup of cooked barley, combine ⅓ cup barley and ¾ cup water in a saucepan. Simmer for 40 to 50 minutes or until tender, then drain if necessary. For the farro, combine ½ cup farro with 1 cup water; simmer for 30 to 35 minutes or until tender.

# Avocado Toast with Scrambled Eggs

| PREP TIME: 15 MIN | COOK TIME: 15 MIN | YIELD: 4 SERVINGS |
|---|---|---|

**INGREDIENTS**

2 avocados

2 tablespoons lemon juice

5 eggs

2 tablespoons plain almond milk

1 tablespoon butter

⅛ teaspoon salt

⅛ teaspoon pepper

4 slices whole-grain bread

1 cup cherry tomatoes, chopped

2 tablespoons minced fresh parsley

⅓ cup crumbled goat cheese

**DIRECTIONS**

1 Peel the avocados, remove the pits, and place in a medium bowl. Add the lemon juice and mash with a fork until the avocado is slightly chunky. Set aside.

2 In another medium bowl, beat the eggs with the almond milk.

3 In a small skillet, melt the butter.

4 Add the eggs to the skillet and sprinkle with the salt and pepper. Cook over medium-low heat until the eggs are set but still moist.

5 While the eggs are cooking, toast the bread slices until light golden brown; set aside.

6 Then, in a small bowl, combine the cherry tomatoes, parsley, and goat cheese and mix gently.

7 Spread the avocado mixture on the toast and top with the egg. Top with the tomato mixture and serve immediately.

**PER SERVING:** *Calories 328 (From Fat 200); Fat 22g (Saturated 7g); Cholesterol 17mg; Sodium 307mg; Carbohydrate 23g (Dietary Fiber 9g); Protein 13g.*

Starting the Day Right with Breakfast

# Whole-Grain Waffles

| PREP TIME: 15 MIN | COOK TIME: ABOUT 15–20 MIN | YIELD: 8 SERVINGS |
|---|---|---|

## INGREDIENTS

1 cup rolled oats

2 cups whole-wheat flour

⅓ cup oat bran

2 teaspoons baking powder

1 teaspoon baking soda

½ teaspoon sea salt

1 cup cottage cheese

½ cup soy or almond milk

2 tablespoons orange juice

2 eggs

3 egg whites

2 tablespoons honey

2 tablespoons olive oil

## DIRECTIONS

1 Place the oats in a food processor or blender. Cover and blend until the oats are finely ground. Place them in a large mixing bowl.

2 Stir in the whole-wheat flour, oat bran, baking powder, baking soda, and sea salt. Mix the dry ingredients with a wire whisk to blend.

3 In a medium bowl, combine the cottage cheese, soy milk, orange juice, eggs, egg whites, honey, and olive oil; mix until smooth.

4 Add the wet ingredients to the dry ingredients and mix just until combined; the batter will be lumpy.

5 Preheat a waffle iron according to the manufacturer's instructions. Brush the iron lightly with olive oil.

6 Add ½ cup of batter to the waffle iron, close the iron, and cook until the steaming stops. The amount of time depends on your waffle iron. Open the iron and remove the waffle. Repeat this step with the rest of the batter. Serve each waffle with fresh fruit, maple syrup, or honey.

**PER SERVING:** *Calories 252 (From Fat 68); Fat 8g (Saturated 2g); Cholesterol 57mg; Sodium 537mg; Carbohydrate 37g (Dietary Fiber 6g); Protein 13g.*

# Toasted Oat and Barley Hot Cereal

| PREP TIME: 15 MIN, PLUS STANDING TIME | COOK TIME: ABOUT 5 HR | YIELD: 12 SERVINGS |
| --- | --- | --- |

**INGREDIENTS**

1 cup steel-cut oats

1 cup uncooked pearl barley, rinsed

1 apple, peeled and chopped

½ cup chopped dates

⅓ cup dried cranberries

1 teaspoon ground cinnamon

¼ teaspoon ground cardamom

1 tablespoon pure maple syrup

6 cups water

**DIRECTIONS**

1 Place the oats in a medium saucepan over medium heat. Toast the oats, stirring frequently, until the oats are fragrant and start to turn a light golden brown. Remove the saucepan from heat.

2 In a 3-quart slow cooker, combine the toasted oats, barley, apple, dates, and cranberries. Sprinkle the mixture with the cinnamon and cardamom and drizzle the maple syrup over everything.

3 Add the water to the mixture and stir gently. Set the slow cooker to hold for 2 hours. Then set it to cook on low for 5 hours.

4 Stir the mixture and serve warm with more maple syrup or honey to drizzle on top (if desired). Each serving consists of 1 cup of cereal.

**PER SERVING:** *Calories 150 (From Fat 11); Fat 1g (Saturated 0g); Cholesterol 0mg; Sodium 2mg; Carbohydrate 33g (Dietary Fiber 5g); Protein 4g.*

**NOTE:** Oatmeal and barley are whole grains that provide lots of fiber, B vitamins, and protein. Steel-cut oats are less processed than rolled oats and can stand up to slow-cooker cooking.

# Chicken Pear Sausages

| PREP TIME: 15 MIN, PLUS FREEZING TIME | COOK TIME: 30 MIN | YIELD: 20 SERVINGS |
|---|---|---|

## INGREDIENTS

1 pound boneless, skinless chicken breast

½ pound boneless, skinless chicken thighs

2 ice cubes

1 large onion, minced

2 cloves garlic, minced

1 tablespoon plus 2 tablespoons olive oil

2 Bosc pears, peeled and diced

1 tablespoon lemon juice

2 tablespoons fresh thyme leaves, minced

½ teaspoon sea salt

¼ teaspoon white pepper

1 tablespoon butter

## DIRECTIONS

1 Cube the chicken and place it in the freezer for 15 minutes.

2 Remove the chicken from the freezer and place it in a food processor; add the ice cubes. Cover and pulse until the chicken is medium grind (chunky but not finely minced). Cover and refrigerate.

3 In a large skillet, cook the onion and garlic with 1 tablespoon of olive oil over medium heat until the onion and garlic are tender, about 6 to 7 minutes. Stir frequently. Add the pears and lemon juice; cook for 1 minute longer. Place the mixture in a large bowl to cool.

4 Add the ground chicken, thyme, sea salt, and white pepper to the onion mixture. Mix gently with your hands until the mixture is combined well. Form the mixture into 20 patties that are about ½ inch thick.

5 Heat the butter and 2 tablespoons of olive oil in a large skillet and add half of the sausage patties. Cook, turning once, until a meat thermometer registers 165 degrees, about 8 to 11 minutes. Move the patties to a covered dish to keep warm. Cook the remaining sausage patties. Serve immediately.

**PER SERVING:** *Calories 38 (From Fat 15); Fat 2g (Saturated 0g); Cholesterol 11mg; Sodium 68mg; Carbohydrate 2g (Dietary Fiber 0g); Protein 4g.*

**TIP:** You can freeze the uncooked sausage patties in a tightly wrapped container for up to four months. When you're ready to cook them, let the patties thaw overnight in the refrigerator. Sauté them in a little olive oil for 6 to 8 minutes on each side, turning once, until the temperature registers 165 degrees.

# Chapter **2**

# Fueling Up for Lunch

A h, lunch. Remember the three-martini lunch made famous by the movie *Wall Street*? Not surprisingly, that particular "meal" isn't healthy. Lunch is a time to take a break from the workday and refuel your body, so put the martini back on the shelf and grab a sandwich (or pita or soup . . . you get the idea).

Lunch is an important meal. It fuels your body for the afternoon and keeps everything running after breakfast. This chapter looks at what makes a healthy and delicious lunch and walks you through some quick and easy lunch recipes. Find more recipes in the Salads and Sides chapter.

## Making Smart Lunch Choices

When you're eating healthy, packing your lunch is an easy way to make sure you get in all the nutrients and energy you need to get through the rest of the day. Packing your own lunch not only saves you money but also helps you feel secure that you're getting the nutrients you need. Having a healthy meal packed and ready to eat can also help you avoid the temptation of the vending machine or local fast-food joint.

**TIP**

To get the most out of your lunches, be sure to do the following:

>> **Make time to eat lunch — even in the middle of a busy workday.** Your body and brain need fuel to function well. You can eat at your desk, but try to take 15 or 20 minutes to get outside for a change of scenery.

>> **Enjoy your food.** Try not to gulp down your meal. Chew each bite thoroughly and concentrate on the flavors and textures of the food.

>> **Get enough protein, fruit, and veggies.** Again, aim for 20 to 25 grams of protein, and keep the rainbow in mind when it comes to produce!

# Healthy Lunch Recipes

The best part about the lunch recipes included here is that you can change them up to include your favorite foods. So, for example, if you're not a big kale fan, use romaine lettuce or Napa cabbage in instead in the Chicken Kale Wraps with Vietnamese Dipping Sauce.

# Slow Cooker Thai Chicken Soup

| PREP TIME: 15 MIN | COOK TIME: 7 HR | YIELD: 6 SERVINGS |
|---|---|---|

## INGREDIENTS

1 onion, chopped

3 cloves garlic, minced

2 large carrots, sliced

2 lemongrass stalks, cleaned and bent in half

2 tablespoons peeled, minced fresh ginger root

1 jalapeño pepper, minced

4 cups low-sodium chicken broth

2 pounds boneless, skinless chicken thighs

1 tablespoon curry powder

1 teaspoon turmeric

One 14-ounce can coconut milk

2 tablespoons lime juice

1 teaspoon miso paste

⅓ cup chopped fresh cilantro

2 tablespoons minced fresh basil leaves

## DIRECTIONS

1 In a 4- to 5-quart slow cooker, combine the onion, garlic, carrots, lemongrass, ginger root, and jalapeño pepper. Add the chicken broth and stir.

2 Place the chicken thighs on the vegetables. Sprinkle with curry powder and turmeric.

3 Cover the slow cooker and cook on low for 7 to 8 hours or until the chicken registers 165 degrees and is fully cooked. Remove the chicken from the slow cooker and let stand for 10 minutes, then shred. Return the chicken to the slow cooker. Remove the lemongrass from the slow cooker and discard.

4 In a medium bowl, combine the coconut milk, lime juice, and miso paste and stir with a wire whisk until blended. Stir into the slow cooker.

5 Cover and cook on low for another 20 to 30 minutes or until the soup is hot. Garnish with the cilantro and basil and serve.

**PER SERVING:** *Calories 226 (From Fat 160); Fat 18g (Saturated 15g); Cholesterol 11mg; Sodium 126mg; Carbohydrate 12g (Dietary Fiber 1g); Protein 8g.*

# Three-Bean Pasta

**INGREDIENTS**

1 pound wide gluten-free noodles

One uncooked 15-ounce can kidney beans, rinsed and drained

One 15-ounce can chickpeas (garbanzo beans), rinsed and drained

1 cup fresh green beans, trimmed and rinsed

½ cup chopped red onion

½ cup chopped red bell pepper

3 tablespoons Dijon mustard

2 tablespoons olive oil

3 tablespoons red wine vinegar

3 tablespoons chopped fresh parsley

1 tablespoon chopped fresh basil

**DIRECTIONS**

**1** Cook the pasta according to the package directions, making sure it's *al dente* (slightly firm). Drain and rinse it under cold water.

**2** In a large serving bowl, stir together the pasta, kidney beans, chickpeas, green beans, onion, red bell pepper, mustard, oil, vinegar, parsley, and basil. Toss the pasta to mix the ingredients.

**PER SERVING:** *Calories 428 (From Fat 55); Fat 6g (Saturated 1g); Cholesterol 0mg; Sodium 336mg; Carbohydrate 76g (Dietary Fiber 7g); Protein 11g.*

**NOTE:** If you can't find wide gluten-free pastas, break a lasagna noodle into ½-inch pieces. Each noodle should be as long as the width of the lasagna noodle.

# Chicken Kale Wraps with Vietnamese Dipping Sauce

| PREP TIME: 15 MIN | COOK TIME: 2 HR | YIELD: 4 SERVINGS |
| --- | --- | --- |

## INGREDIENTS

2 jalapeño peppers, seeds removed if desired, minced

1 clove garlic, minced

2 tablespoons honey

½ cup chicken broth

2 tablespoons lime juice

1 teaspoon miso paste

2 tablespoons olive oil

5 boneless, skinless chicken thighs, chopped

1 onion, finely chopped

2 cloves garlic, minced

1 tablespoon minced fresh ginger root

½ cup shredded carrots

1 tablespoon rice wine vinegar

2 tablespoons chopped fresh cilantro

10 kale leaves, thick stems cut out

## DIRECTIONS

**1** For dipping sauce, in a small bowl, combine the jalapeño peppers, garlic, 1 tablespoon of honey, chicken broth, lime juice, and miso paste. Blend well using a wire whisk; set aside.

**2** In a large skillet, heat the olive oil over medium heat for 2 minutes. Add the chicken, onion, garlic, and ginger root; cook and stir for 4 to 6 minutes or until the chicken is thoroughly cooked. Remove from the heat.

**3** Stir in the carrots, rice wine vinegar, the remaining 1 tablespoon of honey, and cilantro; cover and place in the refrigerator while you prepare the kale.

**4** Rinse the kale leaves well. Place each leaf on the work surface and cut out the thick stem in a V shape. Discard the stem.

**5** Bring a large pot of water to a boil, and prepare a large bowl with ice water. Drop the kale leaves into the boiling water and cook for 2 to 3 minutes or until the kale is just tender. Immediately put the kale into the bowl of ice water. Let stand for 1 minute; then remove the kale and dry it on kitchen towels.

**6** To serve, roll up the cooled chicken mixture in the kale leaves and serve with the dipping sauce.

**PER SERVING:** *Calories 260 (From Fat 97); Fat 11 (Saturated 2g); Cholesterol 72mg; Sodium 255mg; Carbohydrate 22g (Dietary Fiber 2g); Protein 20g.*

# Roasted Veggie Hummus Pitas

| PREP TIME: 20 MIN | COOK TIME: 10–12 MIN | YIELD: 6 SERVINGS |
| --- | --- | --- |

## INGREDIENTS

2 yellow summer squash, cut into 1½-inch pieces

2 cups button mushrooms, cut in half

1 red bell pepper, sliced

1 green bell pepper, sliced

1 large onion, chopped

1 tablespoon olive oil

1 tablespoon plus 3 tablespoons lemon juice

⅛ teaspoon black pepper

½ teaspoon plus ¼ teaspoon sea salt

1 cup canned chickpeas, rinsed and drained

2 cloves garlic, minced

⅓ cup lowfat Greek or regular yogurt

¼ cup sesame seeds

1 teaspoon ground cumin

⅛ teaspoon red pepper flakes

6 whole-wheat pita breads, split

6 leaves romaine lettuce

## DIRECTIONS

1 Preheat the oven to 400 degrees.

2 Arrange the squash, mushrooms, bell peppers, and onion on a cookie sheet. Drizzle the veggies with the olive oil and 1 tablespoon of the lemon juice and sprinkle with the black pepper and ½ teaspoon of the sea salt. Roast, uncovered, until the veggies are tender, about 10 to 12 minutes, stirring once during roasting.

3 Combine the chickpeas, garlic, yogurt, sesame seeds, the remaining 3 tablespoons of lemon juice, cumin, the remaining ¼ teaspoon of sea salt, and red pepper flakes in a blender or food processor. Blend until smooth.

4 Combine the roasted vegetables with the chickpea mixture. Line each pita bread with a lettuce leaf, add ⅙ of the vegetable mixture, and serve immediately.

**PER SERVING:** *Calories 314 (From Fat 69); Fat 8g (Saturated 1g); Cholesterol 1mg; Sodium 668mg; Carbohydrate 54g (Dietary Fiber 10g); Protein 13g.*

**TIP:** To make ahead and avoid soggy sandwiches, pack the vegetable mixture, the lettuce, and the pita bread separately. Assemble the sandwich just before eating.

# Bok Choy Seafood Soup

| PREP TIME: 15 MIN | COOK TIME: 2 HR | YIELD: 4 SERVINGS |
|---|---|---|

**INGREDIENTS**

One 8-ounce package brown rice noodles, broken in half

2 tablespoons olive oil

2 shallots, peeled and minced

1 tablespoon minced fresh ginger root

One 8-ounce package shiitake or button mushrooms, sliced

4 cups coarsely chopped baby bok choy

One 32-ounce box vegetable broth

2 cups water

One 6-ounce wild salmon filet, cut into cubes

1 yellow summer squash, chopped

½ pound Oregon pink shrimp or Pacific spot prawns

1 tablespoon lime juice

**DIRECTIONS**

**1** Place the noodles in a large bowl and pour warm water over them; let stand for 10 to 15 minutes or soften them according to the package directions.

**2** In a large saucepan, heat the olive oil over medium heat. Add the shallots, ginger root, and mushrooms and sauté for 3 to 4 minutes or until fragrant. Stir in the bok choy and simmer for another 2 minutes.

**3** Add the vegetable broth and water and bring to a simmer. Stir in the salmon filet and simmer for 2 minutes.

**4** Add the squash and shrimp and simmer for 3 to 5 minutes or until the shrimp curl and turn pink. Drain the rice noodles and add to the soup along with the lime juice. Simmer for 1 minute and serve immediately. If not serving immediately, add the noodles and lime juice at the last minute.

**PER SERVING:** *Calories 342 (From Fat 104); Fat 12g (Saturated 2g); Cholesterol 110mg; Sodium 687mg; Carbohydrate 36g (Dietary Fiber 3g); Protein 25g.*

**TIP:** You can substitute wild shrimp from the United States or Argentina in place of the Oregon pink shrimp or Pacific spot prawns.

# Salmon Salad Sandwich with Peach Salsa

| PREP TIME: 25 MIN, PLUS REFRIGERATING TIME | COOK TIME: 5–8 MIN | YIELD: 6 SERVINGS |
|---|---|---|

## INGREDIENTS

3 large fresh peaches, peeled, pits removed, and chopped

1 small red onion, diced

3 green onions, sliced

1 jalapeño chile, minced (optional)

1 clove garlic, grated

1 tablespoon lemon juice

1 tablespoon chopped fresh mint

½ teaspoon plus ¼ teaspoon sea salt

⅛ teaspoon cayenne pepper

Three 8-ounce salmon fillets

1 cup cold water

½ cup lowfat Greek or regular yogurt

¼ cup silken tofu

2 tablespoons orange juice

⅛ teaspoon white pepper

1 cup blueberries

2 stalks celery, sliced

12 slices whole-grain bread

6 leaves romaine lettuce

## DIRECTIONS

1 For the salsa, in a medium bowl, combine the peaches, red onion, green onions, jalapeño chile (if desired), garlic, lemon juice, mint, ½ teaspoon of the sea salt, and cayenne pepper. Stir gently to mix; then cover and refrigerate.

2 Place the salmon fillets in a large shallow saucepan. Add 1 cup of cold water and bring to a boil over medium heat. Reduce heat to low, cover the pan, and simmer for 5 to 8 minutes or until the salmon flakes when tested with a fork. Remove the salmon from the pan and let it cool for 30 minutes.

3 In a large bowl, combine the yogurt, tofu, orange juice, ¼ teaspoon of the sea salt, and white pepper; blend well.

4 Flake the salmon, removing the skin. Add the salmon, blueberries, and celery to the yogurt mixture and blend well. Cover and refrigerate for 2 to 3 hours to blend flavors.

5 When you're ready to eat, place the bread on your work surface. Top 6 slices of the bread with 1 leaf of lettuce and ⅔ cup of the salmon mixture. Top each sandwich with some of the peach salsa you made in Step 1 and a second bread slice and serve.

PER SERVING: *Calories 356 (From Fat 67); Fat 8g (Saturated 2g); Cholesterol 66mg; Sodium 651mg; Carbohydrate 40g (Dietary Fiber 7g); Protein 34g.*

# New England Clam Chowder

| PREP TIME: 30 MIN | COOK TIME: 45 MIN | YIELD: 8 SERVINGS |
|---|---|---|

### INGREDIENTS

3 cups fish stock

1 cup dry white wine

½ teaspoon dried thyme

1 bay leaf

½ teaspoon dried parsley

8 pounds fresh, cleaned clams (still in the shell)

¼ pound sliced bacon, cut in 1-inch pieces

2 medium onions, chopped

1½ pounds red potatoes, peeled and diced

2 cups heavy cream

Pepper to taste

### DIRECTIONS

1   In a large pot, simmer the stock and the wine over medium heat. Add the thyme, bay leaf, and parsley. Add the clams, cover the soup, and cook it until the clams open (about 8 minutes for smaller clams and up to 15 minutes for large clams).

2   Remove the clams from the pot, take the clams out of the shells, and set the clams aside. Strain and reserve the cooking liquid.

3   In the large pot, cook the bacon until the pieces begin to get crispy. Remove the pieces with a slotted spoon and set them aside. Discard all the fat except a teaspoon or so.

4   Add the onion to the bacon fat, turn the heat to low, and cook the onions till they're soft but not brown (about 15 minutes).

5   In that same large pot, add the strained cooking liquid and the potatoes. Simmer the soup gently until the potatoes are cooked through — about another 20 minutes or so.

6   Add the clams, bacon, and cream to the soup, and add pepper to taste.

---

**PER SERVING:** *Calories 412 (From Fat 238); Fat 27g (Saturated 15g); Cholesterol 132mg; Sodium 316mg; Carbohydrate 18g (Dietary Fiber 2g); Protein 24g.*

---

**TIP:** To clean the clams, let them sit in fresh water for a few hours. Or you can rinse them in a few changes of fresh water, letting them sit in the water a few minutes between changes.

**VARY IT!** If you're gluten-free, you've probably seen restaurants serve clam chowder in bread bowls and figured those aren't for you. Well, try this: Heat your oven to 425 degrees and mix up a batch of gluten-free bread mix such as Chebe bread or Brazi Bites. Using ovenproof bowls as molds, press a layer of the dough about ½-inch thick into each bowl. Bake the bowls until the bread is golden brown, about 20 minutes. Peel the bread out of the bowl-mold and pour clam chowder into your bread bowl. See? You can have your bowl and eat it, too.

# Black Bean Chili

## INGREDIENTS

3 tablespoons cooking oil

1 pound lean steak, cut into 1-inch cubes

½ cup dry cooking sherry

1 small onion, chopped

2 stalks celery, chopped

2 carrots, chopped

Two 15-ounce cans black beans (drain most, but not all, of the juice)

One 15-ounce can chili beans (drain most, but not all, of the juice)

One 14.5-ounce can diced tomatoes (some have flavorings; choose if you want extra flavor)

One 4-ounce can diced green chilies

2 tablespoons brown sugar (doesn't matter whether it's light or dark)

2 tablespoons honey

1 tablespoon cumin

4 tablespoons chili powder

Red chili flakes to taste (optional)

## DIRECTIONS

1 Heat 1 tablespoon of the cooking oil in a large Dutch oven for about 1 minute on medium heat.

2 In a large pot, sear the steak cubes over medium-high heat in the cooking oil to brown the outside, leaving the inside rare. You may need to do this in two batches, depending on how large your pot is.

3 Add the cooking sherry and cook another minute.

4 Remove the steak-sherry mixture from the pot, place it in another bowl, and set aside.

5 Heat the remaining 2 tablespoons of oil in the same Dutch oven you used to cook the steak. Heat for about 1 minute on medium heat.

6 Add the chopped onion, celery, and carrots to the oil, and sauté for about 2 minutes.

7 Add the steak-sherry mixture that you had set aside to the chopped veggies in the Dutch oven.

8 Add the beans, tomatoes, chilies, brown sugar, honey, cumin, chili powder, and (if you like the heat) red chili flakes.

9 Stir and let it simmer on medium heat for 2 hours, stirring every 20 minutes or so.

10 Season with salt and pepper to taste.

**PER SERVING:** *Calories 280 (From Fat 79); Fat 9g (Saturated 1g); Cholesterol 29mg; Sodium 505mg; Carbohydrate 32g; Dietary Fiber 9g; Protein 19g.*

**TIP:** Most grocery stores carry a trio of chopped veggies, including onions, celery, and carrots. You may spend a tad more, but you'll save yourself some prep time by letting someone else do the chopping.

# Chapter **3**
# Delicious Dinners

Home-cooked dinners are one of life's great pleasures. But these days, many people are so busy that cooking home-made meals is a luxury. You may find yourself stuck in the rut of fixing the same three or four entrées each week.

Well, forget the broiled chicken and plain burger patties, friends! This chapter offers tips for how to create a calm and happy dinner atmosphere and shows you some great recipes that even picky eaters will want to try — well, maybe, eventually.

## Making Dinnertime a Pleasant Time with a Few Simple Tricks

TIP

Encouraging family involvement in planning meals, shopping, and preparing food helps make dinnertime a more enjoyable experience for the whole family. The following list offers some tips to help you get started.

>> **Build a colorful — not a full — plate.** This is probably the most important dinner planning tip you need to know. Incorporate a few different fruits and

veggies as well as some protein and healthy fat sources to get the most nutrition — and color — into your meals.

>> **Introduce topics that encourage dinner conversations.** Healthy conversation topics can include the food you're eating, the culture it came from, the high and low points of someone's day, and plans for the evening and the rest of the week. After a while, pleasant conversation will become more organic and natural at the table, and you can feel good that you're setting and promoting a positive lifestyle choice for yourself and others who share your dinner table.

>> **Have fun with dinnertime.** Think about creating theme nights (Mexican Fiesta or Trip to India, for example), or set an inviting table with a nice tablecloth, the good china and crystal, flowers, and candles.

# Whipping Up Yummy Dinners

The recipes in this chapter adapt well to (relatively small) changes. So use your favorite ingredients and flavors to create healthy and delicious dinners from the basic recipes included here.

# Slow Cooker Barley Stew

**INGREDIENTS**

1 cup uncooked pearl barley

½ cup dried brown lentils

1 large onion, chopped

3 cloves garlic, minced

3 carrots, sliced

1 cup sliced button mushrooms

1 cup sliced cremini mushrooms

8 cups vegetable broth

2 bay leaves

½ teaspoon sea salt

¼ teaspoon black pepper

1 teaspoon dried basil

1 teaspoon dried thyme

2 tablespoons lemon juice

**DIRECTIONS**

**1** Rinse the barley in a colander until the water runs clear. Place the barley and lentils in a 4-quart slow cooker. Add the onion, garlic, carrots, mushrooms, vegetable broth, bay leaves, sea salt, pepper, basil, and thyme and stir gently.

**2** Cover and cook on low for 7 to 9 hours, or until the lentils and barley are tender.

**3** Remove the bay leaves. Stir in the lemon juice, add more seasonings to taste, and serve warm with toasted whole-grain bread (gluten-free, if you like).

---

**PER SERVING:** *Calories 248 (From Fat 13); Fat 1g (Saturated 0g); Cholesterol 0mg; Sodium 837mg; Carbohydrate 50g (Dietary Fiber 12g); Protein 10g.*

---

**VARY IT!** You can add any of your favorite protein and vegetables to make this recipe your own.

*Delicious Dinners*

# Turkey with Caramelized Onion Apple Pecan Stuffing

| PREP TIME: 8 HR 25 MIN | COOK TIME: 5 HR | YIELD: 12 SERVINGS |
| --- | --- | --- |

### INGREDIENTS

8 slices whole-wheat bread, cubed

2 unpeeled apples, chopped

2 tablespoons lemon juice

1 cup small whole pecans

½ cup dried tart cherries

3 tablespoons butter

3 tablespoons olive oil

2 onions, chopped

2 eggs, beaten

¼ cup cold water

1 teaspoon sea salt

½ teaspoon pepper

One 12-pound turkey, giblets removed

2 tablespoons butter

1 teaspoon dried thyme leaves

1 teaspoon dried basil leaves

1 cup low sodium chicken broth

### DIRECTIONS

**1** Let the bread stand, uncovered, overnight to dry. In the morning, toss the bread with the apples, lemon juice, pecans, and cherries, and set aside.

**2** Preheat the oven to 325 degrees.

**3** In a medium skillet, melt the butter and 1 tablespoon of the olive oil over medium heat. Add the onions; cook and stir until tender. Reduce the heat to low and cook, stirring frequently, until the onions are dark brown. Do not let the onions burn.

**4** Add the onions to the bread mixture along with the eggs and cold water. Season with the sea salt and pepper. Stuff this mixture loosely inside the turkey's body cavity and neck cavity. Sew the cavities shut with kitchen twine. (You can also bake the stuffing separately in a casserole for 55 to 65 minutes at 325 degrees or until a meat thermometer registers 165 degrees.)

**5** Place the turkey in a roasting pan. Rub the turkey with 2 tablespoons butter and sprinkle with the thyme and basil. Drizzle with the remaining 2 tablespoons olive oil. Add the chicken broth to the bottom of the roasting pan.

**6** Roast the turkey for 4 to 5 hours for a 12-pound turkey, until a meat thermometer registers 170 degrees. The stuffing inside the turkey should be 165 degrees. If the stuffing is not at 165 degrees, return the turkey to the oven and cook for another 15 to 25 minutes until it reaches that temperature.

**7** Let the turkey stand at room temperature for 20 minutes. Cut and remove the kitchen twine, and then scoop the stuffing out of the turkey into a serving bowl. Carve the turkey and serve.

---

**PER SERVING:** *Calories 488 (From Fat 137); Fat 15g (Saturated 4g); Cholesterol 206mg; Sodium 468mg; Carbohydrate 20g (Dietary Fiber 3g); Protein 65g.*

---

**TIP:** The stuffing is delicious in chicken, too. Just cut the recipe in half to make enough for two 4-pound chickens. Put the stuffing into the chicken cavities. Roast at 375 degrees for 60 to 70 minutes, or until a meat thermometer inserted into the thigh registers 170 degrees. Remove the stuffing, carve the bird, and eat!

Delicious Dinners

# Chicken Chestnut Meatballs in Orange Sauce

| PREP TIME: 25 MIN | COOK TIME: 25 MIN | YIELD: 6 SERVINGS |
|---|---|---|

**INGREDIENTS**

3 tablespoons olive oil

4 green onions, minced

One 5-ounce bag roasted peeled chestnuts

1 egg, beaten

½ teaspoon sea salt

⅛ teaspoon white pepper

½ teaspoon grated orange zest

1½ pounds ground chicken, white and dark meat

2 tablespoons butter

1 cup orange juice

½ cup chicken stock

2 tablespoons lemon juice

2 teaspoons arrowroot powder

**DIRECTIONS**

1  In a large skillet, heat 1 tablespoon of the olive oil over medium heat. Add the green onions; cook and stir until tender, about 2 to 3 minutes. Remove the onions from the skillet and place in a large bowl; set aside the skillet and do not clean.

2  Add the chestnuts to the green onions in the bowl and mash with a fork until fairly smooth. Beat in the egg, sea salt, pepper, and orange zest. Add the ground chicken and mix with your hands until combined.

3  Form the mixture into 1-inch meatballs. Place on a cookie sheet, cover, and refrigerate for 1 hour until the meatballs become firmer.

4  When ready to eat, heat the butter and the remaining 2 tablespoons of olive oil in the same large skillet. Add the meatballs in two batches; cook just until browned, stirring occasionally, about 5 to 7 minutes, and remove.

5  Add the orange juice, chicken stock, lemon juice, and arrowroot powder to the skillet and bring to a simmer, stirring with a wire whisk. Return the meatballs to the skillet and simmer, stirring occasionally and gently with a wooden spoon, until the meatballs register 165 degrees on a meat thermometer and the sauce is thickened, about 8 to 12 minutes longer. Serve immediately over hot, cooked brown rice.

**PER SERVING:** *Calories 349 (From Fat 194); Fat 22g (Saturated 6g); Cholesterol 143mg; Sodium 353mg; Carbohydrate 17g (Dietary Fiber 1g); Protein 22g.*

# Butternut Mac and Cheese

PREP TIME: 25 MIN | COOK TIME: 1 HR | YIELD: 6 SERVINGS

## INGREDIENTS

1 small butternut squash

2 tablespoons butter

1 onion, chopped

2 cloves garlic, minced

2 cups vegetable broth

2 cups almond milk

2 cups finely chopped cauliflower

2½ cups whole-wheat or gluten-free pasta

1 cup shredded cheddar cheese

1 cup shredded Monterey jack cheese

½ cup grated Parmesan cheese

## DIRECTIONS

**1** Peel the squash, remove the seeds, cut into cubes, and set aside.

**2** In a large saucepan, melt the butter over medium heat. Add the onion and garlic; cook and stir until tender, about 5 minutes. Stir in the squash; cook and stir for another 6 to 7 minutes or until the squash starts to brown.

**3** Add the broth and almond milk to the saucepan and bring to a simmer. Lower the heat and simmer for about 20 to 25 minutes or until the squash is tender.

**4** While the squash mixture is simmering, bring another large pot of water to a boil. Add the cauliflower and simmer for 5 minutes; remove the cauliflower with a large strainer. Add the pasta to the water and cook until almost al dente, according to package directions; drain and toss with the cauliflower.

**5** When the squash is tender, mash right in the cooking liquid using a potato masher or immersion blender, or puree the squash, liquid, and vegetables in a blender until smooth. Stir in the cheddar cheese, Monterey Jack cheese, and ¼ cup of the Parmesan cheese. Then add the cauliflower and pasta.

**6** Preheat the oven to 375 degrees. Transfer the mixture to a 3-quart baking dish and top with the remaining ¼ cup of Parmesan cheese. Bake for 20 to 25 minutes, until the casserole is bubbling.

**PER SERVING:** *Calories 349 (From Fat 175); Fat 19g (Saturated 12g); Cholesterol 54mg; Sodium 547mg; Carbohydrate 29g (Dietary Fiber 5g); Protein 18g.*

**TIP:** Cauliflower is a healthy substitute for pasta. Most people won't be able to tell it's in the dish. This cruciferous vegetable adds great nutrition to this classic recipe.

# Ribollita

## INGREDIENTS

2 cups cubed whole-wheat bread

2 tablespoons olive oil, plus a little extra for drizzling

1 large onion, chopped

4 cloves garlic, minced

½ teaspoon sea salt

⅛ teaspoon white pepper

1 teaspoon dried thyme leaves

2 cups sliced mushrooms

3 carrots, sliced

3 stalks celery, chopped

⅓ cup chopped celery leaves

One 32-ounce box vegetable stock

2 cups water

6 plum tomatoes, seeded and chopped

Two 14-ounce cans cannellini beans, rinsed and drained

3 cups chopped kale

¾ cup grated Parmesan cheese

## DIRECTIONS

1 Preheat the oven to 200 degrees.

2 Spread the bread cubes on a baking sheet and bake for 8 to 10 minutes or until dry to the touch. Remove from the oven and set aside.

3 In a large soup pot, heat 2 tablespoons of the olive oil over medium heat for 2 minutes. Add the onion and garlic and sprinkle with sea salt and pepper. Sauté for 4 to 5 minutes or until vegetables are tender. Sprinkle with the thyme leaves.

4 Add the mushrooms, carrots, and celery; sauté for another 3 minutes, stirring frequently. Then add the celery leaves, vegetable stock, water, plum tomatoes, and beans, and stir.

5 Bring to a simmer, then reduce the heat to low, cover, and let simmer for 15 to 20 minutes or until the vegetables are tender. Stir in the kale and simmer for another 5 minutes or until the kale is wilted.

6 Stir in the bread cubes and simmer for another 5 to 10 minutes or until the bread has thickened the soup. Serve with the Parmesan cheese and drizzle each serving with some olive oil.

**PER SERVING:** *Calories 226 (From Fat 65); Fat 7g (Saturated 2g); Cholesterol 8mg; Sodium 653mg; Carbohydrate 31g (Dietary Fiber 7g); Protein 12g.*

# Tandoori Pork Tenderloin

| PREP TIME: 15 MIN PLUS MARINATING TIME | COOK TIME: 40 MIN | YIELD: 6 SERVINGS |
|---|---|---|

## INGREDIENTS

1 medium onion, finely chopped

6 cloves garlic, minced

2 tablespoons minced fresh ginger root

3 tablespoons lemon juice

1 tablespoon curry powder

1 teaspoon ground turmeric

1 teaspoon sweet paprika

1 teaspoon grated orange zest

½ teaspoon sea salt

¼ teaspoon white pepper

1 cup Greek lowfat plain yogurt

One 2-pound whole pork tenderloin

2 tablespoons olive oil

## DIRECTIONS

**1** In a blender or food processor, combine the onion, garlic, ginger root, lemon juice, curry powder, turmeric, paprika, orange zest, sea salt, and pepper, and blend or process until ground. Stir in the yogurt and transfer to a glass baking dish.

**2** Add the tenderloin to the baking dish and turn to coat. Cover and refrigerate for 8 to 24 hours, turning the meat once during marinating time.

**3** When ready to eat, preheat the oven to 425 degrees.

**4** Remove the pork from the yogurt mixture; discard remaining yogurt mixture. Heat 2 tablespoons olive oil in an ovenproof skillet and add the pork. Brown on all sides, about 5 minutes total.

**5** Put the skillet with the pork in the oven and roast the pork for 10 to 12 minutes or until a meat thermometer registers at least 145 degrees.

**6** Remove the pork from the oven, cover with foil, and let stand for 5 minutes before slicing to serve.

**PER SERVING:** *Calories 209 (From Fat 30); Fat 3g (Saturated 1g); Cholesterol 100mg; Sodium 292mg; Carbohydrate 7g (Dietary Fiber 1g); Protein 36g.*

# Spiralized Zucchini with Roasted Veggies

| PREP TIME: 20 MIN | COOK TIME: 40 MIN | YIELD: 4 SERVINGS |
| --- | --- | --- |

## INGREDIENTS

1 red onion, coarsely chopped

2 cups peeled, seeded, cubed butternut squash

3 tablespoons olive oil

12 cloves garlic, peeled

2 red bell peppers, seeded and chopped

6 plum tomatoes, seeded and coarsely chopped

½ teaspoon sea salt

⅛ teaspoon pepper

1 teaspoon dried marjoram leaves

2 pounds zucchini

2 tablespoons lemon juice

½ cup shredded Parmesan or Romano cheese

## DIRECTIONS

1 Preheat the oven to 400 degrees.

2 Combine the onion and squash on a roasting pan and drizzle with 1 tablespoon of the olive oil; toss to coat. Roast for 20 minutes.

3 Remove the pan from the oven and add the garlic, bell peppers, and plum tomatoes. Drizzle with 1 tablespoon of the olive oil and sprinkle with ¼ teaspoon of the salt, the pepper, and the marjoram. Roast until the vegetables are tender and start to brown, about 15 to 20 minutes longer.

4 While the vegetables are roasting, cut the zucchini into strips using a spiralizer, or cut into long thin strips. Toss with the lemon juice and the remaining ¼ teaspoon salt and set aside. Heat the remaining 1 tablespoon of olive oil in a large skillet and add the zucchini; cook for 2 minutes, stirring frequently, until tender. Put into a large serving bowl and cover to keep warm.

5 When the vegetables are done roasting, pour over the zucchini spirals in the serving bowl. Sprinkle with cheese and serve immediately.

**PER SERVING:** *Calories 281 (From Fat 135); Fat 15g (Saturated 4g); Cholesterol 11mg; Sodium 515mg; Carbohydrate 30g (Dietary Fiber 7g); Protein 11g.*

**TIP:** A spiralizer is a specialized tool that cuts vegetables into long, thin, curly strips that resemble pasta. This is an excellent way to serve a "pasta" dish if you're eating Paleo. You can substitute very thin slices of zucchini that you cut by hand. In that case, blanch the zucchini strips for 1 to 2 minutes in boiling water so they'll bend and look like fettuccine.

# Salmon Risi Bisi

**INGREDIENTS**

2 tablespoons olive oil

1 large onion, chopped

2 cloves garlic, minced

2 large carrots, cubed

1½ cups brown rice

2 cups water

1¾ cups vegetable broth

1 teaspoon dried thyme

½ teaspoon dried basil

½ teaspoon sea salt

⅛ teaspoon black pepper

Three 6-ounce salmon fillets

2 cups frozen baby peas, thawed

½ cup grated Parmesan cheese

**DIRECTIONS**

1   In a small skillet, heat the olive oil over medium heat. Add the onion and garlic; cook and stir for 5 minutes or until tender.

2   Place the onion and garlic mixture in a 4-quart slow cooker with the carrots and brown rice. Add the water, vegetable broth, thyme, basil, sea salt, and pepper. Cover and cook on low for 2½ hours.

3   Stir the mixture and test the rice. If it's still chewy, cover and cook on low for another 30 minutes. When the rice is almost tender, place the salmon fillets on top of the rice and vegetable mixture. Cover the slow cooker and cook for 35 to 45 minutes, or until the salmon flakes when you test it with a fork.

4   Break up the salmon with a fork and stir it into the rice mixture along with the thawed peas. Cover and cook for 15 minutes.

5   Stir in the cheese, turn off the slow cooker, cover, and let stand for 5 minutes. Stir gently and serve immediately.

**PER SERVING:** *Calories 416 (From Fat 103); Fat 12g (Saturated 3g); Cholesterol 54mg; Sodium 568mg; Carbohydrate 49g (Dietary Fiber 7g); Protein 29g.*

**VARY IT!** You can substitute chicken or pork for the salmon.

# Tequila-Lime Shrimp and Scallops

| PREP TIME: 2 MIN | COOK TIME: 10 MIN | YIELD: 4 SERVINGS |
|---|---|---|

**INGREDIENTS**

1 pound medium shrimp, cooked, peeled, and deveined

½ pound sea scallops

¼ cup lime juice

¼ cup lemon juice

¼ cup chopped fresh cilantro

2 tablespoons olive oil, divided

¼ cup tequila

2 teaspoons minced garlic (about 4 cloves)

2 teaspoons hot sauce

½ teaspoon ground cumin

½ teaspoon dried oregano

1 large onion, cut into thin wedges

1 green bell pepper, cut into bite-sized strips

1 red bell pepper, cut into bite-sized strips

4 lime wedges (for garnish)

**DIRECTIONS**

**1** If your shrimp or scallops are frozen, thaw and rinse them. If the scallops are as large as or larger than an egg cut them in half. Set the shrimp and scallops aside.

**2** In a large glass, ceramic, or stainless-steel mixing bowl, stir together the lime juice, lemon juice, cilantro, 1 tablespoon of oil, tequila, garlic, hot sauce, cumin, and oregano. Add the shrimp and scallops.

**3** In a large skillet over medium-high heat, cook the onion, green bell pepper, and red bell pepper in the remaining table-spoon of oil until they begin to get soft, about 4 minutes.

**4** Add the shrimps and scallops to the skillet, and bring every-thing to a boil. Cook and stir the mixture for about 3 minutes, until some of the liquid has burned off and the scallops are cooked.

**5** Serve the seafood over brown rice or whole-wheat pasta, or in the wrap of your choice, and garnish it with lime wedges.

**PER SERVING:** *Calories 397 (From Fat 205); Fat 23g (Saturated 10g); Cholesterol 181mg; Sodium 499mg; Carbohydrate 12g (Dietary Fiber 2g); Protein 36g.*

# Basic Roasted Chicken

| PREP TIME: 10 MIN | COOK TIME: 1 HR 15 MIN | YIELD: 4 SERVINGS |
|---|---|---|

## INGREDIENTS

¼ cup chopped onion

⅓ cup lemon juice

1½ teaspoons minced garlic (about 3 cloves)

2 tablespoons fresh, chopped rosemary

Salt and pepper to taste

4 tablespoons olive oil

1 tablespoon sesame oil

1 large roasting chicken

## DIRECTIONS

**1** Preheat the oven to 375 degrees.

**2** In a small bowl, mix the onion, lemon juice, garlic, rosemary, salt and pepper, olive oil, and sesame oil.

**3** Take the sack of giblets and the neck out of the chicken and discard (or save them for another recipe). Rinse the cavity with cool water and pat dry.

**4** Spoon about half the herb mixture into the inside of the chicken cavity. Use your hands to rub it around and coat the inside of the chicken. Rub the rest of the mixture on the outside of the chicken until the entire chicken is covered. Pat the chunks of onion and herbs from the mixture onto the chicken. Some of them will probably fall off while the chicken is cooking, but that's okay.

**5** Place the chicken in a roasting pan and cook it for about 1 hour and 15 minutes, until the breast meat reaches 170 degrees, or the juices run clear when you pierce the skin with a fork.

**PER SERVING:** *Calories 754 (From Fat 469); Fat 52g (Saturated 12g); Cholesterol 252mg; Sodium 337mg; Carbohydrate 4g (Dietary Fiber 1g); Protein 65g.*

**TIP:** Save the drippings. Let them cool and scrape the fat off the top. Then pour the drippings into an ice tray and freeze them. You can use the cubes later for soup broth or seasonings.

# Baked Lemon Mahi Mahi

| PREP TIME: 10 MIN | COOK TIME: 30 MIN | YIELD: 8 SERVINGS |
|---|---|---|

**INGREDIENTS**

Nonstick spray

8 boneless, skinned mahi mahi fillets

4 tablespoons lemon juice

3 tablespoons melted butter

½ teaspoon minced ginger

½ teaspoon minced garlic (about 1 clove)

½ teaspoon freshly ground pepper

¼ teaspoon paprika

¼ cup chopped cilantro

8 orange slices

One 20-ounce can crushed pineapple

**DIRECTIONS**

1 Preheat the oven to 375 degrees.

2 Using the nonstick spray, lightly grease two medium-sized baking dishes. Wash and pat dry the mahi mahi fillets and lay them in a single layer in the baking dishes.

3 Mix the lemon juice, butter, ginger, garlic, pepper, paprika, and cilantro in a small bowl. Drizzle this lemon juice mixture over the fillets.

4 Place an orange slice over each fillet. Drain and discard about ¾ of the juice from the canned pineapple and pour the crushed pineapple and remaining juice over the fillets.

5 Bake the fillets for about 20 to 30 minutes, or until the fillets are opaque. Don't overcook.

**PER SERVING:** *Calories 265 (From Fat 51); Fat 6g (Saturated 3g); Cholesterol 161mg; Sodium 187mg; Carbohydrate 14g (Dietary Fiber 1g); Protein 38g.*

# Chapter **4**

# Salads and Sides to Swear By

S
alads and side dishes can be just as important as the main meal itself. In fact, they can be the *meal* itself. But salads are often topped with rich dressings, and sides are sometimes seasoned with heavy sauces that make them off-limits to people who want a healthier lifestyle.

So does that mean you're stuck with boring salads of just lettuce and tomatoes? Nope. Are you limited to the old side dish stand-bys? No way. Check out this chapter, and you can be whipping up some scrumptious accompaniments to rival — or even serve as — the main course.

# Serving Up Healthy Salads and Sides

**TIP**

Salads are the ultimate healthy entrée as long as you follow a few basic rules, and a few sides together can serve as a nutritious meal too. Consider the following tips:

>> **Pack in as many vegetables or fruits as possible.**

>> **Make your own salad dressing and use only a small amount on your homemade salad.**

>> **Use greens that are as dark as possible in your salad for the most nutrition.**

>> **Add a protein source — like cubed cheese, nuts, tofu, beans, or cooked meats and seafood (such as chicken or fish) — to salads.**

>> **Add variety with a lot of little snacks and sides.** A few cubes of cheese, a handful of nuts, some fresh cut-up fruit and veggies, and perhaps some yogurt added to your salad or side make a great lunch that's easy to throw together.

# Mixing It Up with Salad and Side Recipes

Give the following recipes a whirl the next time you want a delicious yet nutritious salad or side dish. Don't be afraid to try something new!

# Clean Cobb Salad

**PREP TIME: 15 MIN PLUS STANDING TIME | YIELD: 4 SERVINGS**

## INGREDIENTS

½ cup lowfat Greek or regular yogurt

2 tablespoons sour cream

2 tablespoons buttermilk or soy milk

1 tablespoon lemon juice

1 tablespoon mustard

1 tablespoon minced flat-leaf parsley

1 clove garlic, minced or grated

2 tablespoons minced dill fronds

2 tablespoons minced chives

⅛ teaspoon black pepper

6 eggs

Water

4 cups torn romaine lettuce

2 cups baby spinach

2 ripe red tomatoes, cut into wedges

2 stalks celery, sliced

1 can cannellini beans, rinsed and drained

2 avocados, peeled and sliced

½ cup sliced almonds

½ cup crumbled blue cheese (optional)

## DIRECTIONS

1 In a small bowl, combine the yogurt, sour cream, buttermilk, lemon juice, mustard, parsley, garlic, dill, chives, and pepper; mix well. Cover and refrigerate.

2 Place the whole eggs in a 2-quart saucepan; cover them with cold water. Bring the water to a boil over high heat; boil for 1 minute. Then cover the pan, remove it from heat, and let the eggs stand for 12 minutes.

3 Drain the eggs and place them back into the pan; place the pan with the eggs in the sink. Run cold water into the pan until the eggs are cool to the touch. Carefully crack the eggs under the water and let them stand for 5 minutes. Then peel the eggs and cut them into wedges.

4 On each of four plates (or in four containers), arrange the romaine lettuce, spinach, eggs, tomatoes, celery, and beans. Drizzle the salad with the dressing you made in Step 1.

5 Top with the avocados, almonds, and blue cheese (if desired) and serve immediately.

**PER SERVING:** *Calories 451 (From Fat 263); Fat 29g (Saturated 7g); Cholesterol 324mg; Sodium 353mg; Carbohydrate 31g (Dietary Fiber 15g); Protein 23g.*

**TIP:** To make this salad ahead of time, omit the avocados and store the dressing, almonds, and blue cheese separately. When you're ready to eat, drizzle the dressing over the salad and top it with almonds and blue cheese.

# Fruity Coleslaw

## INGREDIENTS

⅔ cup lowfat Greek or regular yogurt

2 tablespoons olive oil

3 tablespoons apple cider vinegar

2 tablespoons lemon juice

2 tablespoons raw honey, or ¼ teaspoon stevia

½ teaspoon sea salt

¼ teaspoon black pepper

1 teaspoon dried thyme

3 cups shredded red cabbage

3 cups shredded green cabbage

3 stalks celery, sliced

2 Granny Smith apples, chopped

2 cups red grapes

½ cup dried cherries

1 cup pistachios or pecan pieces

## DIRECTIONS

1 In a large bowl, combine the yogurt, olive oil, vinegar, lemon juice, honey, sea salt, pepper, and thyme; mix well.

2 Stir in the cabbage, celery, apples, grapes, dried cherries, and pistachios until everything is coated with the dressing mix from Step 1. Serve immediately or cover and refrigerate for 2 to 3 hours before serving. Serve 1 cup per serving.

**PER SERVING:** *Calories 244 (From Fat 105); Fat 12g (Saturated 2g); Cholesterol 1mg; Sodium 179mg; Carbohydrate 33g (Dietary Fiber 5g); Protein 7g.*

**TIP:** Use this coleslaw as a condiment on chicken or beef sandwiches or stir in some leftover cooked salmon for a quick and healthy lunch.

# Fruity Chicken Pasta Salad

| PREP TIME: 15 MIN PLUS REFRIGERATING TIME | COOK TIME: ABOUT 10 MIN | YIELD: 6 SERVINGS |
|---|---|---|

## INGREDIENTS

½ cup lowfat Greek or regular yogurt

¼ cup lowfat sour cream

3 tablespoons buttermilk or almond milk

2 tablespoons apple cider vinegar

2 tablespoons mustard

2 tablespoons raw honey, or ¼ teaspoon stevia

1 teaspoon dried thyme

½ teaspoon sea salt

⅛ teaspoon white pepper

10 cups water

4 cups whole-wheat penne or farfalle pasta

3 cups cooked chicken, cut into 1-inch pieces

3 stalks celery, sliced

2 cups red grapes

1 cup blueberries

2 cups cubed cantaloupe

½ cup walnut pieces

## DIRECTIONS

1 In a large bowl, combine the yogurt, sour cream, buttermilk, vinegar, mustard, honey, thyme, sea salt, and white pepper; mix well to blend.

2 In a 4-quart saucepan, bring the water to a boil. Add the pasta; cook according to package directions until the pasta is just tender. Drain well and add the pasta to the bowl with the dressing you made in Step 1.

3 Stir in the chicken and celery until they're well coated. Gently add the grapes, blueberries, cantaloupe, and walnuts. Stir gently. Cover and refrigerate for 2 to 3 hours before serving.

PER SERVING: *Calories 492 (From Fat 129); Fat 14g (Saturated 3g); Cholesterol 68mg; Sodium 439mg; Carbohydrate 67g (Dietary Fiber 8g); Protein 31g.*

Salads and Sides to Swear By

# Fruit and Grains Salad

## INGREDIENTS

⅓ cup olive oil

2 tablespoons honey, or ¼ teaspoon stevia

¼ cup orange juice

2 tablespoons lemon juice

2 tablespoons Dijon mustard

¼ teaspoon sea salt

⅛ teaspoon black pepper

1 cup wheat berries, sorted and rinsed

3 cups plus 1½ cups plus 2 cups cold water

½ cup quinoa, rinsed well

¾ cup barley

2 apples, chopped

1½ cups cubed pineapple

2 stalks celery, sliced

½ cup dried cranberries or cherries

½ cup unsalted pistachios

## DIRECTIONS

1 In a large bowl, combine the olive oil, honey, orange juice, lemon juice, mustard, sea salt, and pepper; mix with a wire whisk. Refrigerate.

2 In a 2-quart saucepan, combine the wheat berries and 3 cups of cold water. Bring the water to a boil over high heat; then cover the pan, reduce the heat, and simmer for about 55 minutes or until the wheat berries are tender but still chewy. Drain well and add to the salad dressing you made in Step 1. Refrigerate.

3 In a 2-quart saucepan, combine the quinoa with 1½ cups of cold water. Bring the water to a boil over high heat; then cover the pan, reduce the heat, and simmer for about 25 minutes or until the quinoa is tender but not mushy. Drain well and add to the wheat berry mixture. Refrigerate.

4 In a 2-quart saucepan, combine the barley with 2 cups of cold water. Bring the water to a boil over high heat; then cover the pan, reduce the heat, and simmer for about 40 minutes or until the barley is tender but still chewy. Drain well if necessary and add to the wheat berry/quinoa mixture. Refrigerate.

5 Add the apples, pineapple, celery, dried cranberries, and pistachios to the grain salad. Stir gently to coat. Serve immediately or cover and chill for 1 to 2 hours before serving.

**PER SERVING:** *Calories 521 (From Fat 177); Fat 20g (Saturated 3g); Cholesterol 0mg; Sodium 247mg; Carbohydrate 82g (Dietary Fiber 13g); Protein 11g.*

# Quinoa Crunch

**PREP TIME: 15 MIN**                    **YIELD: 6 SERVINGS**

### INGREDIENTS

¼ cup lime juice

¼ teaspoon white pepper

¼ teaspoon freshly ground black pepper

¼ cup sliced marinated jalapeño pepper

¼ teaspoon coarse salt

¼ cup olive oil

1½ cups quinoa

3 cups water

¾ cup peeled, seeded, and diced cucumber

¾ cup seeded and diced tomato

¾ cup sliced red bell pepper

¼ cup sliced yellow bell pepper

¼ cup sliced green onions, white part only

¼ cup chopped flat-leaf Italian parsley

¼ cup chopped fresh mint

Salt and pepper to taste

### DIRECTIONS

**1** Make a vinaigrette by whisking together the lime juice, white pepper, black pepper, jalapeño, coarse salt, and olive oil. Set aside the mixture.

**2** Place the quinoa in a fine sieve and wash it under running water, rubbing it with your hands for a few minutes. Drain the water.

**3** In a large pot, combine the water and quinoa. Bring the mixture to a boil, lower the heat, and simmer it uncovered for about 10 to 15 minutes, or until the quinoa is barely tender. Don't overcook it. Strain the quinoa, drain it thoroughly, and let it cool. Don't rinse it.

**4** Mix the quinoa in with the cucumber, tomato, red bell pepper, yellow bell pepper, green onions, parsley, mint, and vinaigrette. Add a little salt and pepper to taste (you don't need much, because this dish has plenty of flavor). Serve it at room temperature or cold.

**PER SERVING:** *Calories 260 (From Fat 105); Fat 12g (Saturated 2g); Cholesterol 0mg; Sodium 240mg; Carbohydrate 34g (Dietary Fiber 4g); Protein 7g.*

**NOTE:** Quinoa contains all the amino acids your body can't produce on its own, so this grain can be the main dish. It also makes a power-packed side or salad.

**TIP:** Double the recipe because the leftovers are fantastic — this dish gets better each day as the flavors infuse the grain.

Salads and Sides to Swear By

# Rice Salad with Red Peppers, Garbanzo Beans, and Feta

| PREP TIME: 15 MIN | RESTING TIME: 1 HR | YIELD: 6 SERVINGS |
| --- | --- | --- |

### INGREDIENTS

½ cup lemon juice

2 teaspoons minced garlic (about 4 cloves)

¼ cup extra-virgin olive oil

Salt and pepper to taste

3 cups cooked brown rice, cooled to room temperature

One 15-ounce can garbanzo beans (chickpeas), drained

½ cup roasted red peppers

1 cup finely diced feta cheese

½ cup chopped fresh parsley

¼ cup chopped fresh dill

4 green onions, washed, ends removed, thinly sliced

### DIRECTIONS

1 Make the dressing by whisking together the lemon juice, garlic, olive oil, and salt and pepper.

2 In a large serving bowl, combine the rice, garbanzo beans, red peppers, feta cheese, parsley, dill, and green onions.

3 Pour the dressing over the rice mixture and mix well. Let it sit at least an hour before serving. Serve at room temperature or cold.

**PER SERVING:** *Calories 308 (From Fat 137); Fat 15g (Saturated 5g); Cholesterol 22mg; Sodium 561mg; Carbohydrate 35g (Dietary Fiber 3g); Protein 8g.*

# Sweet-Potato Potato Salad

| PREP TIME: 2 HR 15 MIN | COOKING TIME: 20 MIN | YIELD: 6 SERVINGS |
|---|---|---|

**INGREDIENTS**

2 pounds sweet potatoes, peeled

3 tablespoons canned chopped green chilies

½ cup chopped red pepper

2 tablespoons chopped cilantro

Dash paprika

⅓ cup mayonnaise

**DIRECTIONS**

**1** Dice the sweet potatoes. Steam them for 20 minutes or until they're tender but not mushy.

**2** In a large serving bowl, mix the sweet potatoes, green chilies, red pepper, cilantro, paprika, and mayonnaise. Chill the potato salad for at least 2 hours; serve it cold.

**PER SERVING:** *Calories 216 (From Fat 90); Fat 10g (Saturated 2g); Cholesterol 7mg; Sodium 112mg; Carbohydrate 30g (Dietary Fiber 3g); Protein 2g.*

# Chapter **5**

# Snacks, Desserts, and Nibbles

Yes, you can still eat tempting and tasty snacks and desserts on a healthy eating plan. But instead of grabbing a packaged candy bar or a carton of double-fudge ice cream to satisfy your sweet tooth, make some of your own desserts and snacks. This chapter provides plenty of ideas to get you started.

## Satisfying the Hunger with Healthy Snacks and Desserts

Great snacks and desserts consist of low-calorie, nutrient-dense foods in moderate portions.

**TIP**

Take some time every week to prepare small grab bags of fruits, nuts, and veggies that are all ready to eat. That way, when you're hungry, you can satisfy your cravings quickly the healthy way.

# Putting Together Tasty Desserts and Snacks with Some Easy Recipes

TIP

Don't think that eating healthy means you have to leave your favorite snack and dessert recipes in the dust. Instead, adapt your favorite recipes to make them healthy. Try the following:

>> **Add fruit purees, such as applesauce, to baked goods in place of some of the fat.** You can replace up to 30 percent of the fat in most recipes.

>> **Reduce the amount of sugar in baked recipes.** You can usually reduce the sugar by ⅓ to ½ without sacrificing the quality of the recipe.

>> **Substitute dark chocolate for milk or white chocolate.** Dark chocolate is a food that fits into a healthy eating plan. Look for dark chocolate with at least 70 percent cacao content.

>> **Look for baked whole-grain chips and dippers rather than the fried or processed varieties.** Make your own pita chips by cutting whole-wheat pita breads into wedges and baking them until crisp.

>> **Choose dessert recipes with lots of fruit in them.** A mixed fruit salad topped with nuts makes a great dessert, especially if you add a little plain Greek yogurt. Poached fruit is also a great snack or dessert.

When you come up with a winning recipe, just be sure to write it down so you can make it again!

# Sweet and Spicy Nuts

| PREP TIME: 15 MIN | COOK TIME: 30–40 MIN | YIELD: 16 SERVINGS |
|---|---|---|

**INGREDIENTS**

2 egg whites

Pinch of sea salt

2 tablespoons honey, or ½ teaspoon stevia

⅓ cup almond butter

2 tablespoons curry powder

¼ teaspoon cayenne pepper

½ pound raw almonds

½ pound raw pistachios

½ pound raw walnuts

½ pound raw pecans

3 tablespoons butter

**DIRECTIONS**

1  Preheat the oven to 325 degrees.

2  In a large bowl, beat the egg whites with a pinch of sea salt until soft peaks form. Gradually beat in the honey until the peaks are stiff.

3  Gradually add the almond butter to the egg white mixture, beating until combined. (The egg whites will deflate.)

4  Stir in the curry powder and cayenne pepper. Add the almonds, pistachios, walnuts, and pecans and stir to coat the nuts evenly.

5  Melt the butter and pour it into a 15-x-10-inch jelly roll pan; coat the bottom of the pan. Arrange the nut mixture in a single layer on top of the butter.

6  Bake for 30 to 40 minutes, stirring every 10 minutes, until the nuts are slightly toasted. Cool the nuts completely and store them at room temperature in an airtight container. Serve ⅓ cup per serving.

*PER SERVING: Calories 208 (From Fat 172); Fat 19g (Saturated 2g); Cholesterol 3mg; Sodium 13mg; Carbohydrate 7g (Dietary Fiber 3g); Protein 5g.*

**TIP:** You can serve this recipe straight as a snack or sprinkle it over some frozen yogurt or plain yogurt for a quick dessert.

Snacks, Desserts, and Nibbles

# Garlic Yogurt Cheese Dip or Sandwich Spread

| PREP TIME: 15 MIN PLUS REFRIGERATING TIME | COOK TIME: 45–55 MIN | YIELD: 18 SERVINGS |
| --- | --- | --- |

## INGREDIENTS

4 cups lowfat Greek or regular plain yogurt

1 large head garlic

1 tablespoon olive oil

¼ cup grated Parmesan or Romano cheese

½ teaspoon sea salt

½ teaspoon dried thyme

½ teaspoon dried marjoram

⅛ teaspoon black pepper

## DIRECTIONS

**1** Line a colander or strainer with four layers of dampened cheesecloth. Place the colander in a large bowl.

**2** Place the yogurt in the lined colander, cover it, and place it in the refrigerator for 24 hours.

**3** Preheat the oven to 350 degrees.

**4** Cut the garlic head across the center into two pieces, exposing the cloves. Drizzle the garlic with the olive oil and wrap it in foil.

**5** Place the wrapped garlic on a cookie sheet and bake it for 45 to 55 minutes, or until the cloves are soft when squeezed. Remove the garlic from the oven, unwrap it, and let it cool.

**6** Squeeze the garlic cloves out of their papery coating and place them in a medium bowl. Add the yogurt cheese, Parmesan cheese, sea salt, thyme, marjoram, and pepper and stir until blended.

**7** Place the yogurt cheese mixture in a serving bowl and chill for 2 to 3 hours before serving. Serve 2 tablespoons per serving.

**PER SERVING:** *Calories 174 (From Fat 68); Fat 8g (Saturated 4g); Cholesterol 15mg; Sodium 358mg; Carbohydrate 10g (Dietary Fiber 0g); Protein 18g.*

**TIP:** Choose Greek yogurt for a thicker texture and richer taste than regular yogurt.

**TIP:** The whey that drains out of the yogurt overnight (see Step 2) works great in soups or casseroles as the liquid.

**VARY IT!** You can flavor the yogurt cheese any way you'd like for either a dip or a sandwich spread. Omit the garlic and double the Parmesan cheese for a milder spread. For a fruity spread, omit all the ingredients except the yogurt cheese and mash 1 cup of strawberries; stir them into the plain yogurt cheese with ½ teaspoon of cinnamon. For a Tex-Mex spread, use the garlic but omit the Parmesan cheese, thyme, and marjoram; stir in 2 teaspoons of chili powder and 2 tablespoons of chopped jalapeño chilies.

# Sweet Potato Chips with Catalan Salsa

| PREP TIME: 15 MIN | COOK TIME: 20 MIN | YIELD: 6 SERVINGS |
|---|---|---|

## INGREDIENTS

2 large beefsteak tomatoes, seeded and chopped

One 15-ounce can artichoke hearts, drained and chopped

1 jalapeño pepper, minced

2 cloves garlic, minced

½ cup chopped almonds

½ cup chopped fresh flat-leaf parsley

¼ cup olive oil, divided

2 tablespoons lemon juice

1 teaspoon freshly grated lemon zest

2 large unpeeled sweet potatoes, scrubbed

½ teaspoon sea salt

## DIRECTIONS

1 Preheat the oven to 425 degrees.

2 In a medium bowl, combine the tomatoes, artichokes, jalapeño pepper, garlic, almonds, parsley, 2 tablespoons of the olive oil, lemon juice, and lemon zest, and mix gently. Set aside while you prepare the chips.

3 Thinly slice the sweet potatoes using a mandolin or a very sharp knife. Toss with the remaining 2 tablespoons of olive oil, spread in a single layer on two cookie sheets that have been lined with parchment paper, and sprinkle with the sea salt.

4 Roast the sweet potatoes for 18 to 22 minutes or until the edges are crisp.

5 Let the chips cool and serve with the salsa.

**PER SERVING:** *Calories 380 (From Fat 289); Fat 32g (Saturated 3g); Cholesterol 0mg; Sodium 365mg; Carbohydrate 21g (Dietary Fiber 5g); Protein 5g.*

**TIP:** A mandolin is the easiest way to make these thin and crispy potato chips. If you don't have one, use a very sharp knife and cut the potatoes into the thinnest slices you can.

# Chocolate Fruit and Nut Drops

| PREP TIME: 35 MIN | COOK TIME: 5 MIN | YIELD: 12 SERVINGS |
| --- | --- | --- |

**INGREDIENTS**

12 ounces dark chocolate (at least 60 percent cacao), chopped

1 ounce unsweetened chocolate, chopped

2 tablespoons coconut oil

1 cup chopped macadamia nuts

½ cup chopped walnuts

½ cup finely chopped dates

½ cup dried cranberries

½ cup unsweetened coconut

**DIRECTIONS**

1 Place the dark chocolate, unsweetened chocolate, and coconut oil in a large microwave-safe bowl. Microwave on high for 30 seconds, then remove and stir. Continue microwaving on high in 30-second intervals, stirring after each interval, until the chocolate is melted and smooth.

2 Stir in the remaining ingredients. Drop by spoonfuls onto parchment paper and let stand until set. You can refrigerate the candies if you'd like.

3 Store in an airtight container at room temperature.

**PER SERVING:** *Calories 339 (From Fat 241); Fat 27g (Saturated 12g); Cholesterol 2mg; Sodium 6mg; Carbohydrate 24g (Dietary Fiber 5g); Protein 4g.*

**TIP:** Dates can be purchased either dried or fresh. Any type of whole date works well in this recipe. Do not use the prechopped packaged dates that are covered in sugar, because they will be too dry for this recipe.

# Frozen Yogurt Bars

| PREP TIME: 15 MIN | FREEZE TIME: 3 HR | YIELD: 12 SERVINGS |
| --- | --- | --- |

## INGREDIENTS

2 cups lowfat Greek or regular yogurt

½ teaspoon stevia

2 cups frozen strawberries

1 cup frozen wild blueberries

1 tablespoon lemon juice

## DIRECTIONS

**1** Combine the yogurt, stevia, berries, and lemon juice in a food processor. Cover and process until well blended, stopping once to scrape down the sides of the processor.

**2** Pour ¼ cup of the mixture into a popsicle form, or fill it according to the package directions. Repeat for a total of 12 popsicle forms. Freeze the bars for at least 3 hours before serving.

**3** Remove the yogurt bar from the popsicle form and serve one bar per serving.

---

**PER SERVING:** *Calories 39 (From Fat 8); Fat 1g (Saturated 1g); Cholesterol 3mg; Sodium 12mg; Carbohydrate 5g (Dietary Fiber 1g); Protein 4g.*

---

**TIP:** The easiest way to make these bars is to use popsicle forms, which you can find at baking supply stores, hardware stores, and large supermarkets. If you don't have popsicle forms, you can use paper juice cups. Just pour the yogurt mixture into the cups, freeze them for 1 hour, insert a wooden popsicle stick into each cup, and then freeze them until the yogurt mixture is firm. Just peel the paper cup away before serving!

**VARY IT!** It's easy to change the flavor of this recipe; just use a different type of fruit! Peaches, raspberries, and bananas all work well and taste delicious!

# Apple Pear Cranberry Crumble

| PREP TIME: 15 MIN | COOK TIME: 2 HR | YIELD: 6 SERVINGS |
| --- | --- | --- |

**INGREDIENTS**

2 Haralson or McIntosh apples, chopped

2 firm pears, chopped

2 tablespoons lemon juice

½ cup dried cranberries

1 cup whole-wheat flour

½ cup old-fashioned rolled oats

½ cup chopped pecans

3 tablespoons coconut sugar

3 tablespoons butter

2 tablespoons coconut oil

2 tablespoons honey

½ teaspoon cinnamon

⅛ teaspoon sea salt

**DIRECTIONS**

1   Preheat the oven to 375 degrees. Grease a 9-x-9-inch glass baking dish with butter.

2   Combine the apples and pears in the prepared baking dish and sprinkle with the lemon juice. Top with the dried cranberries.

3   In a large bowl, combine the whole-wheat flour, rolled oats, pecans, and coconut sugar, and mix.

4   In a small saucepan, combine the butter, coconut oil, honey, cinnamon, and sea salt, and heat over medium-low heat until the fats melt.

5   Pour the butter mixture over the flour mixture and stir until crumbly. Sprinkle evenly over the fruit in the baking dish.

6   Bake for 30 to 40 minutes or until the apples and pears have softened and the topping is browned. Let cool for 25 minutes before serving.

**PER SERVING:** *Calories 387 (From Fat 162); Fat 18g (Saturated 8g); Cholesterol 15mg; Sodium 55mg; Carbohydrate 58g (Dietary Fiber 9g); Protein 5g.*

# Blueberry Cherry Crisp

| PREP TIME: 15 MIN | COOK TIME: 33-38 MIN | YIELD: 8 SERVINGS |
|---|---|---|

## INGREDIENTS

1 cup old-fashioned oatmeal

⅓ cup whole-wheat flour

½ cup chopped macadamia nuts

2 tablespoons coconut oil

3 tablespoons unsalted butter

2 tablespoons honey

1 teaspoon cinnamon

¼ teaspoon nutmeg

⅛ teaspoon sea salt

4 cups frozen cherries, thawed

2 cups frozen blueberries

1 tablespoon lemon juice

1 teaspoon stevia

## DIRECTIONS

1 Preheat the oven to 375 degrees. Grease a 9-x-9-inch glass dish with unsalted butter and set aside.

2 In a large bowl, combine the oatmeal, flour, and macadamia nuts. Set aside.

3 In a small saucepan, combine the coconut oil, butter, honey, cinnamon, nutmeg, and sea salt. Heat the mixture over low heat until the butter melts, about 3 minutes. Stir the oil and butter mixture and pour it over the oatmeal mixture. Stir until the mixture becomes crumbly.

4 Place the thawed cherries and frozen blueberries into the prepared glass dish. In a small bowl, mix the lemon juice and stevia and sprinkle it over the berries.

5 Spoon the oatmeal mixture over the berries. Bake for 30 to 35 minutes, or until the crisp is bubbly and the topping has browned. Serve 1½ cups per serving.

---

**PER SERVING:** *Calories 276 (From Fat 141); Fat 16g (Saturated 6g); Cholesterol 12mg; Sodium 40mg; Carbohydrate 34g (Dietary Fiber 5g); Protein 4g.*

---

**TIP:** This crisp is just as good cold the next day, so pack some in your lunchbox for a special treat.

# Dark Chocolate Bark

| PREP TIME: 10 MIN | COOK TIME: 15 MIN, PLUS STANDING TIME | YIELD: 24 SERVINGS |
|---|---|---|

**INGREDIENTS**

16 ounces dark or bittersweet chocolate (at least 60 percent cacao), coarsely chopped

water

⅓ cup dried wild blueberries

⅓ cup dried cranberries

⅓ cup coarsely chopped walnuts

⅓ cup coarsely chopped macadamia nuts

**DIRECTIONS**

1 Line a 13-x-9-inch cake pan with parchment paper and set aside.

2 Place all but ½ cup of the chocolate in the top of a double boiler. Fill the bottom of the double boiler with water and bring it to a simmer.

3 Place the top of the double boiler over the simmering water, making sure the bottom of the double boiler top doesn't touch the water. Heat the chocolate until it's melted and smooth, stirring occasionally.

4 Remove the top of the double boiler from heat. Carefully dry the outside of the pan. Add the reserved chocolate to the melted chocolate and stir constantly in one direction until it's melted and smooth.

5 Stir in the blueberries, cranberries, walnuts, and macadamia nuts. Immediately pour the chocolate mixture into the pre-pared pan and smooth it out until it's about ⅓ inch thick.

6 Let the bark stand at room temperature until it's firm. Cut the bark into 1-inch squares and store at room temperature in a tightly covered container.

**PER SERVING:** *Calories 137 (From Fat 77); Fat 9g (Saturated 4g); Cholesterol 1mg; Sodium 1mg; Carbohydrate 15g (Dietary Fiber 2g); Protein 2g.*

**TIP:** Dark chocolate is packed full of antioxidants and good fats, so eating one ounce (about the size of one 1-inch square) a day can be good for you.

# 6

# Staying Active After 50

# Contents at a Glance

# Chapter **1**

# Staying Active as You Age

While many people focus on saving money for retirement, changing their investment strategies as they age, they may forget to invest in their health and fitness, adapting their routines to their changing bodies. They may wind up with the financial means to explore the world and take up new hobbies but not the drive, the mental quickness, or the physical wherewithal.

This chapter explains why physical fitness is every bit as important as fiscal fitness as we age. If you're getting a late start on exercise, you'll find tips to help you get started safely. If you've already been exercising, you'll get advice on how to reset your routine and rethink your goals. Though after you hit the age of 50 you can still accomplish great physical feats, you may need to adjust what you do to ensure you don't get sidelined by injury or discouraged by trying to do too much. Find details to make sure your workouts are successful no matter how many candles are on your next birthday cake.

# Getting a Late Start: How to Begin

Even if you've never owned a gym membership or a pair of sneakers, it's never too late to begin exercising. Studies show that people of any age can benefit from getting in shape. Exercise can substantially reduce your risk of developing heart disease, arthritis, colon cancer, Alzheimer's disease, lower-back pain, and depression, and it can help keep you maintain your independence. If you saw a pharmaceutical advertisement that listed even half of those benefits, you'd be lining up at your doctor's office for a prescription. So here's your exercise Rx.

## Seeing your doctor for a checkup

**REMEMBER**

Getting an annual checkup can help keep you healthy, whether it's been ten weeks or ten years since your last doctor's visit. That's because your annual physical is the opportunity for your doctor to review every aspect of your health. Take this time to talk with your doctor about an exercise plan that will work for you. Your physician may be able to refer you to an appropriate health club, community center, or personal trainer.

Your doctor may even write a prescription for physical therapy (PT). A physical therapist is trained to help you correct muscle imbalances, rehabilitate injuries, and move correctly. In fact, if you start exercising and find yourself struggling, go back to your doctor and request a prescription for physical therapy. In most states, PT is covered by insurance for at least several sessions and can be just what you need to get your program off on the right foot.

## Starting cardio exercise

Be sure to proceed slowly when you start cardiovascular exercise—those activities that increase your heart rate. No one, regardless of age, should start their first treadmill workout at an all-out sprint. Try ten minutes the first day, and if that goes well, do ten minutes the next day, too. Gradually increase your workouts by no more than 5 percent (in terms of time or mileage) a week. Pay attention to what your body is telling you. If you feel a lot of creaking and groaning in your joints or if your heart and lungs have trouble keeping up, back off and wait for your body to catch up. Chances are you'll progress more slowly than someone younger, but you will progress.

**TIP**

Consider joint-friendly activities, such as walking, using the elliptical machine or stationary bike, or swimming. These activities allow your heart and lungs to build stamina without stressing your joints.

# Pumping some iron

You start losing muscle mass in your 30s. You need strong muscles to continue standing up straight, to maintain the strength required to do day-to-day stuff, like carrying in your groceries and unscrewing the cap of a childproof bottle of pain reliever, and to prevent injury.

If you've never lifted weights before, consider watching a how-to video, taking a class at a community center or gym, or hiring a trainer. It's fine to start with either free weights or machines; just begin with a low weight and add on slowly.

Concentrate on going through the full range of motion for each exercise so you take full advantage of the improved strength and flexibility you can gain. You can start with seated versions of moves, which require less balance and coordination than standing versions, until you build up your strength and confidence.

# Working on your flexibility and balance

Each year, one in four people over age 65 experiences a serious fall, which can lead to an injury that limits your mobility, sometimes permanently. Developing both flexibility and balance reduces your chances of falling and makes you more likely to catch yourself if you do fall.

If you've never worked on flexibility, consider joining a beginner's yoga, stretch, or tai chi class. Or find a video online. You can look for sessions that specialize in seated stretches, so you don't have to stand for too long or keep getting up and down off the floor (something that's hard to do when you lack strength and flexibility). If you're stretching on your own, start with seated versions or hold on to a chair or a wall for support.

**REMEMBER**

You should always warm up before you stretch. If you're especially inflexible, add an extra few minutes of warm-up to ensure good blood flow and pliability. Stretch every single day, even twice a day. You can fit it in when you're chatting with a friend, watching a show, or even brushing your teeth.

**TIP**

If you have extra income, consider having a trainer lead you in a stretching session. It will make you feel great and teach you a lot. Also consider taking up meditation, which can put you in a relaxed state of mind; this, in turn, can prime your muscles to be more receptive to stretching.

## FINDING A GYM

With a little research, you can likely find a gym that suits you well. When visiting local gyms, ask the following questions:

- **Does anyone on your staff carry a senior-fitness certification or other designation?** Several of the governing bodies that certify personal trainers offer training in senior fitness.

- **Do any of your classes specialize in senior fitness?** From water aerobics to Pilates, yoga to marathon-training groups, some health clubs offer special classes and group activities for older members. If your local gym doesn't offer special classes, check with your local YMCA, community health program, running or walking specialty store, and local houses of worship.

- **Do you offer senior discounts?** Hey, if you're paying 25 percent less for a movie, why not get a discount on your gym membership too? Don't be shy about asking for discounts. They may not be advertised, but if you ask, you may just receive a substantial discount on your membership fee.

# Adjusting Your Program if You're an Experienced Athlete

Sports headlines still express surprise whenever anyone over the age of 30 wins an important bike race, crosses the finish line of a marathon, or makes it on to an Olympic team. But the truth is, older athletes, both the professionals and those who simply exercise for the pleasure of staying in shape, are becoming smarter about how they train their bodies. Today's veteran athlete has access to more supportive shoes, more ergonomically designed equipment, and better protective gear, as well as solid, research–based training advice on how to prevent injury, eat for peak performance, and pack more quality training into less time.

What's more, many experienced athletes have been training since youth, so they're in tune with how their bodies should feel. For example, a seasoned 50+ runner likely knows the difference between a tweaked knee that should be rested for a few days and one that's simply a little sore from running extra hills. And regular exercise can certainly slow the aging process.

That said, 50+ athletes, no matter how experienced, still need to treat their bodies differently than when they were younger. As you get older, you probably don't snap back quite as quickly from hard workouts or injuries, and you may not race as hard or as often as you used to. This is because many of us lose muscle mass, our bones thin out, our hormone levels change, and our tendons shorten so we lose flexibility. So it makes sense that we may have to rethink our training priorities and our goals.

Here are some considerations for adjusting your fitness program:

>> Cardio exercise and competition: With training, you can continue to make gains in cardio. If you've been racing sprints, you may consider moving up your distances as you age, since runners lose about 1 percent of their speed per year after 40, and 2 to 3 percent after age 70, studies show. So older runners need to start their runs at a slower pace and build up to a faster one as they feel comfortable.

Older athletes routinely win endurance events. It's not uncommon to see a competitor over 40 break the tape of a major marathon. Even if you have no intention of going past the 5K mark, many competitions — walking, running, cycling, swimming, and skating — hand out age-group prizes so you can compete against people your own age instead of having to be lumped in with younger competitors.

**REMEMBER**

Listen closely to your body, which may tire more easily and require more rest days or shorter or less intense workouts than it used to. Consider a cross-training routine, if you haven't in the past, to help keep your body in shape.

>> Strength: If you didn't spend much time in the weight room in the past, head there now, or pull out those resistance bands. Stronger muscles not only help preserve your joints and prevent injury, but they also help you maintain balance, coordination, bone density, and a healthy ratio of muscle to fat. You'll also stand up straighter, have better posture, and look more youthful.

If you're a longtime lifter, add one or two warm-up sets into the equation to ensure your muscles are ready to move in the right pathways. As you age, your muscles are a bit slower to react. Warm-up sets help you avoid injury and post-workout achiness. Add extra sets for your thigh muscles (to protect your knees), your glutes (to protect your hips), your core (to protect your spine), and your shoulder muscles (to protect your shoulder joints).

>> Flexibility: Maybe you're accustomed to doing your cardio and then hitting the showers, never spending a single minute on stretching. This is a habit to reconsider if you want to keep active. Having flexibility will keep your movements more fluid. So if you're a runner, you may still be able to stretch out your legs and maintain your normal-length stride rather than the tight little shuffle recognizable in some older runners.

**TIP**

Yoga is an excellent activity to add to your repertoire, especially if you find you don't have the springiness you used to (see Chapters 2–5 in Book 6 for more about yoga). Consider taking a class that combines flexibility, balance, and agility, three skills that often require attention as the years click by. Look for classes with names such as On the Ball or Get in Balance; read the class descriptions, because names vary. Your gym may offer 15-minute stretch classes, a good entry point. You can find loads of worthwhile videos online.

## EXERCISING YOUR BRAIN

Exercise is so good for your brain that it almost makes the advantages to the heart, lungs, and muscles seem secondary. The brain uses the oxygen that is delivered through the bloodstream to fuel its various functions. During a session of cardiovascular exercise, such as running, swimming, or cycling, blood circulation speeds up and your lungs soak up a higher volume of oxygen from the air, which allows them to deliver significantly more oxygen to your brain. Working out on a regular basis improves blood flow all the time so the brain constantly receives more blood and oxygen. Research shows that people who participate in purposeful exercise show beneficial changes in brain structure and function. And it's never too late to start.

How much exercise you need to keep your brain fit isn't clear, but the Global Council on Brain Health, convened by AARP, suggests following current public health recommendations of 150 minutes of weekly, moderate-intensity aerobic activity and two or more days a week of moderate-intensity, muscle-strengthening activities. In addition to purposeful exercise, lead a physically active lifestyle throughout the day.

# Chapter **2**

# Yoga Over 50 Is Just Smart

Yoga is such a brilliant way to nurture your physical, mental, and spiritual health. The only thing you may need to do is make certain modifications to address any changing needs and keep you safely practicing yoga throughout your life.

The fact is, everyone's body is different. Everyone is born with certain innate abilities, as well as certain limitations. Additionally, whether you're in your thirties or in your eighties, age may also carry with it certain limitations. All humans may be similar in structure, but each person has very specific needs.

## Understanding the Benefits of Yoga

There are numerous benefits from doing yoga. Some benefits have been scientifically measured; others have yet to be medically proven. Regardless, most everyone who tries yoga or does yoga regularly often talks about having a better sense of overall well-being and having more energy. Best of all, there are many aspects of yoga you can use outside of a yoga class. Among them are better posture and balance, improved strength and flexibility, and breathing techniques that can calm down your system in stressful situations.

A lot of yoga offered today can be fast-paced, which may not work for you. On the other end is a chair yoga class or restorative yoga.

**REMEMBER**

You don't have to do the hardest version of a posture to receive the greatest benefits. Whether you're just beginning yoga or you want to continue practicing yoga throughout your life, you can make some modifications to allow you to start or to continue reaping the benefits of yoga, including

>> Reduced stress

>> Better sleep

>> Improved circulation

>> Improved strength and flexibility

>> Greater willpower and an overall sense of well-being

As your body continues to change with age, you need to pursue a type of yoga that adapts to those changing needs. Look for yoga classes or videos that embrace these sorts of modifications.

**WARNING**

If you look around your town at the yoga classes available to you, many may have the word *flow* in the title. This word may be your first red flag because flow classes are typically fast-moving by design. If you're new to yoga, it may be better to stay with introductory or level-one classes.

In today's world, people often have limited time for exercise, and they want a yoga class to have a cardio component. Unfortunately, the rapid tempo of some classes sometimes means you're rushed getting in and out of poses — and you don't have enough time to consider whether the pose is good for you in the first place.

The early yoga masters taught these same kinds of flowing classes, but it's critical to note that they were probably teaching young boys. And indeed, these young boys most likely had very different bodies than the one you're working with now.

It's also worth noting that these very same yoga masters started teaching differently when they began to work with middle-aged people who were not from India. Their students' needs were different and unique, and so are yours.

# Yoga at 50-plus

Yoga is good for your body, mind, and spirit. The truth is, yoga can be a great practice for anyone, offering you a multitude of benefits — if you practice the type of yoga that's right for your body. And, what's right for your body at age 20-something is probably very different from what is right at 50-something.

**REMEMBER**

At age 50 and over, yoga may help in these essential ways:

>> Keeps muscles, bones, and joints from losing density, length, and flexibility

>> Sustains mobility with greater ease of movement

>> Protects against falling down and incurring injuries

>> Guards against skin becoming thinner, looser, and more easily damaged

>> May speed recovery from some injuries

## Yoga reduces stress

The ability of yoga to reduce stress is widely known, and it may, in fact, be your No. 1 reason for beginning a new routine or wanting to continue your existing practice. The benefits of stress reduction can include

>> Lower blood pressure and heart rate

>> A decrease in muscle tension

>> Better sleep (including the ability to fall asleep)

>> Prevention or management of certain medical conditions that may be related to stress (including asthma, obesity, diabetes, migraines, and certain gastrointestinal issues)

The fact is that reducing stress can even slow down the aging process, which may be of particular interest to the 50-plus yogi.

## Yoga helps you breathe easier

Breathing is something you've been doing automatically since the moment you were born. But what if you changed it from something that happens without thinking to a process you guide with your conscious mind?

Shifting the process of breathing from something you don't think about to something you do gives your mind a target on which to focus. It helps focus a mind that's constantly flooded with an abundance of thoughts. And when your mind is focused on a positive activity, stress and anxiety may start to dissipate.

Timing your inhalations and exhalations with specific movements can help relax your body. Basically, try to inhale when you open up and exhale when you fold. If you follow this approach, your diaphragm moves more freely, and your stress level can be lowered because you're breathing more easily.

Chapter 4 in Book 6 offers some deep breathing routines designed to bring these feel-good promises to life for you.

## Yoga helps your body

Perhaps the best news about yoga is that it can help your body mature gracefully. Yoga can counter common events such as muscles starting to feel stiff and less flexible. Every muscle in your body is subject to these changes, and what specific muscles are affected is determined by how and how much you move on a daily basis.

With a regular yoga practice, you can guard against pulling your back while bending over to make a bed or straining your back picking up something off the floor.

### Movement

A lot of power can be derived from simple movement. In today's world, many people suffer from being too stationary. Sitting behind a desk or in front of a device may create physical or mental problems that you can often counter by easy movement. You don't have to do the most challenging poses to reap the physical benefits.

A focus on stretching will hopefully help increase both your flexibility and range of motion. These outcomes are particularly important to people 50-plus, who may be less flexible than they were years ago. More than that, inflexibility and a compromised range of motion can make you more prone to falling. The key then is to do yoga in a safe way.

### Balance

Throughout life, learning to balance is a challenge, but the rewards are great. As a baby, you learn to walk; as a child, you learn to ride a bike; in your teens, you may try skating, skateboarding, or skiing. Maintaining a good sense of balance is a must.

Yet balance takes practice at any age. Some yoga poses that require balance are in the rest of Book 6. Don't be discouraged if you're not particularly stable at first. Your body and your brain will learn. And just like walking or riding a bike took some practice, so, too, will balance poses. Stay safe (maybe stand near a chair or wall), and you'll get better with repetition.

## Chronic conditions

So many of the chronic conditions that plague us are caused or complicated by stress and a lifestyle that keeps people sitting in front of the TV or computer and not moving enough. Those conditions include

>> Back issues (upper and lower)

>> Breathing difficulties

>> Stress

>> Arthritis

>> High blood pressure

>> Obesity

>> Osteoporosis

>> Insomnia

>> Headaches

**REMEMBER**

Yoga can be a great tool in your toolbox for either preventing or managing many of these conditions by building strength and flexibility, improving the way you breathe, and reducing the amount of stress in your life. If you're just starting out or perhaps taking your existing yoga practice to a new level, you will want to practice yoga in a way that improves your health.

## Yoga for meditation and mental health

The health benefits of meditation for anyone at any age are well documented. While some studies suggest a meditation routine can actually delay the symptoms of Alzheimer's or dementia, simply reducing your stress may have a positive impact on things like your blood pressure or those conditions associated with increased stress and anxiety. Having a healthy emotional self may also help you maintain a healthy physical self.

In yoga, whether you're doing movements, postures, or breath work, the goal is always to steady the mind, control your breathing and heart rate, and provide a refuge of sorts where you can find some peace and tranquility. In fact, many yoga practitioners report better mental attitudes and better sleep, according to "The Use of Yoga for Physical and Mental Health Among Older Adults: A Review of the Literature," a study published by the International Association of Yoga Therapists.

### Check with your healthcare provider before you start

**REMEMBER**

Make sure you talk to your doctor before you start a yoga practice. Don't make the decision to try yoga without your doctor's knowledge and consent. And if you're currently not seeing a doctor but are dealing with acute pain, jumping into yoga is not the answer.

## Finding Your Place in the World of Yoga

If you're new to yoga, start slowly and gently — and most of all, be patient. Some poses will get easier with practice, and some will not. In the end, everyone has a certain body type with specific abilities and limitations. In starting a new practice, you'll discover both if you pay attention.

**TIP**

Modifications are the key to a lifelong practice. As your body changes, all you need to do is modify where necessary, and you'll be a practicing yogi for the rest of your life.

You may find it very helpful to ignore your ego and compulsion to compete (even with yourself!). Forget about what you used to be able to do! It is critical to remember that yoga needs to make you healthier, and you need to make choices that are smart for your body as it is today.

## Selecting the Right Place and the Right Teacher for You

When it comes to practicing yoga, you probably have a lot of choices, whether visiting a local yoga studio or viewing a video on your computer or smartphone. The most important thing is to choose a level of instruction that is appropriate to your current level of practice. If you happen to select a class that's too advanced or even too easy, you can easily get the wrong impression about what yoga has to offer.

**REMEMBER**

The bottom line is: Be selective. Make sure that the type of class is appropriate for your skill level and the teacher is good at keeping a roomful of people safe and informed.

## Yoga studios

Depending on where you live, you may find yoga studios on every other block. If so, you need to be selective. Choose your studios — and your classes — carefully.

Keep in mind that many of the flow or power yoga classes (see the later section "Gyms" for more on these types of classes) are designed for people who are looking for a more athletic experience — one that has an intense cardio component. The reality is that in today's world, people have only a limited amount of time for fitness, so — even in yoga classes — they are looking for a session that combines stretching and strength with routines that will get their heart rate up at the same time. These classes may not work for you.

Again, it's not about being less motivated; it's about being smart. You don't want to be in a class where the poses or the tempo require you to practice in a way that compromises your safety. You're there to get healthy, not injured.

**REMEMBER**

Although you may see yoga therapy-type classes that can address the specific needs of a particular population (for example, people looking for an emphasis on lower-back health), if you're dealing with a personal health issue, you should seek individualized yoga therapy.

Even general yoga classes are ideal when they're one-on-one because the yoga teacher can adapt the instruction to the very specific needs of the student. Private yoga lessons, however, are a bit too costly for most people.

Yoga has become so pervasive today that your choices on where to practice and whom to select as a teacher can seem infinite and definitely confusing. You can turn to a number of places where you'll find a comfortable setting and an encouraging and well-qualified teacher. The critical first step is to make a thoughtful choice.

Although no one place or teacher is right for everyone, you need both to be right for you. If you're a novice and you find yourself in a class that's designed for more experienced yogis, or if you discover your teacher is too aloof or perhaps lacking in knowledge, please move on to another option so you don't miss out on the many benefits yoga can offer you.

# Home

In addition to the wide range of in-person classes that may be available to you in your neighborhood, you've undoubtedly come across hundreds — maybe even thousands — of yoga online videos.

While many talented teachers and well-designed videos are at your disposal, your particular challenge is to find the ones that are just right for you — videos that will actually improve your health and fitness and not lead to injury. There are some great videos out there; you need to choose carefully — and choose wisely.

**WARNING**

Many videos are designed for what some call the young and restless. If you combine an inappropriately aggressive practice with the fact that you're in front of your computer or TV instead of in the actual company of an experienced teacher who is trying to keep you safe, you may be courting injury.

**TIP**

If you do try a video, you may want to look for something that is specifically designed for your age group. You may be able to determine this directly from the title. Also, look at the qualifications of the teacher. Ideally, that person will have some degree of expertise in adapting yoga to the 50-plus body.

# Gyms

Some very talented teachers, as well as some great classes, are at gyms. Again, just make sure the class offers the right approach for you.

People who come to the gym tend to have only a limited amount of time to dedicate to fitness. As a result, gyms may design their classes to provide a rigorous overall workout. People who come to these classes are often looking for a cardio component, so the yoga classes tend to be *flow classes,* which keep you moving rapidly, or *power yoga classes,* which emphasize strength and endurance.

If you're trying a class at the gym, talk to the teacher beforehand to make sure it's the right class for you.

# Houses of worship, community centers, and libraries

You can find some great classes and teachers in houses of worship, community centers, and libraries. Make sure the teacher is experienced and skilled, providing modifications for bodies of different abilities. And make sure the makeshift studio offers the right space and right props, or it's no bargain at all.

You may find that the yoga teacher is just renting space at any of these venues.

# Practicing without Injury

As the number of people attending yoga classes continues to climb, so, too, does the number of people going to emergency rooms because they got hurt in a yoga class.

You're probably completely on board with the goals of strengthening your body, increasing your flexibility and balance, reducing stress, and breathing more mindfully. But you'll want to add one more: avoiding injury. So listen to your body and trust your own instincts on what postures are beneficial and which ones are risky, and heed your pain signals.

Don't make the mistake of listening to your ego. Sometimes, people want to keep up with their hyper-mobile, 20-something teacher, or they want to show the people practicing next to them that they are just as flexible and just as advanced, or they want to do the moves they did when they last did yoga 20 years ago. And that is just plain foolish.

**REMEMBER**

Ignore how you look in a yoga pose, and certainly please do not compare yourself to how anyone else looks doing yoga. Listen to your body, listen to your intuition, and be smarter. If you're able to do this, you will discover how yoga can make you better, even healthier, than you are today. And there's a good chance you'll avoid injury.

# Playing It Safe

As previously mentioned, preparing your muscles and joints before moving in and out of various poses helps to reduce the possibility of injury, especially from over-stretching.

Moving in and out of a pose before holding it is referred to as the dynamic/static approach, which can also yield the benefits of PNF (explained in detail in this section).

So, then, there are a few reasons to move first before holding a pose: Mainly it lubricates your joints and helps you stretch further. You should not only come to expect this form of movement, but you may find you enjoy it!

**REMEMBER**

Knowing your own body and what it can do on any given day is essential. This book provides you with some important tips and guidance for modifying yoga to fit your particular needs. If you work with a teacher, find one who offers and demonstrates a variety of modifications of poses.

## Warming up

How often do you see athletes warming up before a game or runners stretching out before breaking into a sprint? It probably makes perfect sense to you. Before moving or stressing the body in a new way, warming up seems logical.

In yoga classes, you frequently start with a short warm-up sequence. A good teacher always structures the class so that one posture or movement prepares the body for what's coming next.

Our bodies benefit from preparing joints and muscles before each new posture. That is why some teachers frequently move students in and out of poses before asking them to hold steady. You should consider this approach as well.

One of the reasons yoga is such an effective routine for nurturing your body is that it tries to bring movement — often stretching, sometimes strengthening — to all areas of the body. That means, at some point in your practice, whether you're in a class or by yourself at home, nearly all of your muscles and moveable joints will be worked.

As far as your joints go, your goal is to warm them up in a way that focuses on specific movements (or ranges of motion). Just to be clear, your moveable joints include

>> Ankles

>> Knees

>> Hips

>> Spine

>> Neck

>> Shoulders

>> Elbows

>> Wrists

# Preparing the joints

If joints like your knees and ankles are designed to move, the joints themselves must be properly lubricated. Just like in your car, proper lubrication reduces the amount of friction between moving parts.

Moving in and out of a pose before holding it helps to distribute the lubrication (called *synovial fluid*) to all parts of the joint.

Take, for example, a simple hip rotation (see Figure 2-1). This movement is intended to focus on the hip joint — that big ball and socket where the top of your leg (your femur) fits into your hip socket. By rotating your knee in big circles, the joint is working in its full range of motion, distributing lubrication, and better preparing you for the movements to come.

**FIGURE 2-1:** Hip circles prepare the hip joints.

*Photo by Don Henry*

No wonder football players do this exact same warm-up before taking the field for a game.

# Performing magic with PNF

Another potential benefit of moving in and out of a posture is related to the concept of *Proprioceptive Neuromuscular Facilitation,* or PNF. This topic is somewhat complex, and fitness experts debate how PNF actually prepares the muscles and joints. Nevertheless, one of the most basic aspects of PNF is this: If you tense a muscle before you try to stretch it, it will relax more.

Typically, you can tense a muscle in two ways:

>> **Isometric:** Pushing against a fixed force

>> **Isotonic:** Tightening a muscle using gentle resistance

Isometric stretching in yoga usually involves a partner. For example, you can lie on the floor, with a straight leg lifted up and propped against your partner (see Figure 2-2). By first pressing the heel of the lifted leg against your partner, the muscles in your leg will tighten. After holding that press for approximately eight seconds, you can release the pressure and move the leg in the opposite direction. As a result of first tensing the muscles, they will now relax further than they would have had you not tightened them first.

**FIGURE 2-2:**
PNF with
isometric
resistance.

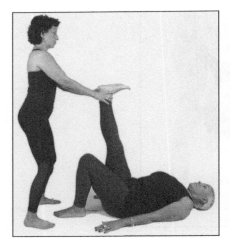

*Photo by Don Henry*

Of course, most of the time when you practice, no one is around to help you. This is where the dynamic/static approach comes in — moving in and out of a posture before holding it.

If you perform the same movement (see Figure 2-3) by lifting and lowering your leg yourself before holding the stretch, you're actually tensing your muscles; if you didn't tense your muscles each time you lowered your leg, your leg would come crashing to the ground with the force of gravity.

**FIGURE 2-3:**
PNF using isotonic resistance.

*Photo by Don Henry*

**TIP**

If the PNF concept of tensing a muscle before you stretch it ultimately allows it to stretch further, then moving in and out of a posture before holding may offer some of the same benefit.

# Chapter **3**

# Preparing to Practice Yoga

The prospect of adding yoga to your daily or weekly routine can be a bit intimidating. This chapter focuses on two of the reasons people use to avoid yoga: "I don't know what clothes to wear" and "I don't know what equipment to get."

The truth is, the clothes, mats, and props you choose should only serve to make your yoga routines safer and more effective. One goal of this chapter is to take away some of the mystery as you get ready to practice.

The other goal is to address what's known as sequencing — the order of poses. This chapter discusses the reasons behind placing postures in yoga in a particular order.

**REMEMBER**

Always talk to your healthcare provider before starting a new exercise regime, including yoga. And when you practice, have water on hand to help you stay hydrated!

# Keeping Yoga Equipment Simple

Unlike other physical activities, such as golf or scuba diving, you don't need a lot of expensive equipment to practice yoga. The following sections take a look at a few key items.

## Comfortable clothes

Yoga clothes may seem like a trivial topic to some, but some people feel like they need to spend a fortune on brand-name yoga clothing to be accepted into the yoga community. This assumption is decidedly not true.

You can find various name brands of yoga clothing. For the most part, the workmanship is great, and the clothing lasts a long time. Still, many people at all levels choose other clothing so long as it's comfortable. You don't need brand-name clothes to get good quality or to enjoy yoga.

REMEMBER

The only thing your clothing needs to do is make you comfortable and allow you to bend and stretch. Anyone who makes judgments based on what people wear on the mat — or, for that matter, even how flexible they may be — is completely missing the point of yoga in the first place. (That goes for self-judgment as well.)

WARNING

Note that it is considerate to choose yoga clothing that doesn't bring a blush to the cheek of the teacher or fellow students. You may see someone come to class wearing something that is not intended to be worn in inverted poses — and no one wants an impromptu anatomy class!

WARNING

Sometimes people leave their socks on in a yoga class because their feet get cold. But socks can be a real disadvantage, particularly in standing poses. If socks are slippery, it can make holding an already challenging posture even more difficult.

Bare feet in yoga is more than just a tradition. Doing yoga in bare feet is

>> Less slippery when moving in and out of poses (depending on your socks)

>> More stable for balancing poses (students often say that contacting the floor with their bare feet gives them a greater sense of stability)

>> More accommodating to muscles and ligaments as you move from posture to posture (stretch and strengthen)

There are nonslip yoga socks on the market. Some socks even have the toes exposed. While these socks are certainly safer, they are still a compromise.

**TIP**

If you wear orthotics — which can be particularly helpful during the standing portion of the class — you may want to leave your socks on during class and just slip your orthotics inside your socks. You'll definitely want to use nonslip socks, but this could be a way to wear your orthotics during a yoga class.

## Mats

Technically speaking, you don't have to use a mat to practice yoga. However, the investment has become so minimal (depending on the construction of the mat) and the benefits so numerous, it's highly recommended that you get one.

Where you practice determines how much padding you need — particularly because you'll be required to kneel or lie down. If you're doing yoga on a carpeted, padded floor, the thickness of your mat is probably not as important. If, however, you're practicing on a hardwood floor or some kind of stone tile — a thicker mat is sure to provide more comfort.

A mat can also provide you with a nonslip surface on which to build your yoga poses. Keep in mind, however, that mats can also be slippery, so take this into account as you consider price and construction. Yoga mats can range from $10 to $50 and beyond, depending on the thickness and design; some are bundled with props such as a block and strap.

Your process of selecting a mat should take into account the following potential benefits:

>> **Personal comfort:** A mat can be especially important on a hard floor.

>> **Designated space:** A mat establishes your own space (which may be particularly important in a group class).

>> **More stability:** A mat can provide you with a nonslip surface, which is useful in more precarious poses. Some mats can be better than others for this purpose; find out whether your mat has what is called a *sticky* surface, which is designed to help keep you from slipping.

## Blocks

Blocks can be very useful props, allowing you to go more deeply into a posture than you would be able to do on your own. They're often used to help you reach the floor, sometimes allowing your body to reap the benefits of a particular pose. (See Figures 3-1 and 3-2.) Years ago, most blocks were made of wood; now they are lighter, often made of Styrofoam. Although they come in all different sizes, the average block measures about 9-x-6-x-4 inches.

*Photo by Don Henry*

**FIGURE 3-1:**
Triangle pose
with no block.

*Photo by Don Henry*

**FIGURE 3-2:**
Triangle pose
with a block.

The first thing a block can do is bring the floor closer to you so that you can perform the most beneficial aspect of the pose. Here's an example using triangle pose.

>> Notice in Figure 3-1 that the model is touching the floor with her right hand, which, in turn, causes her left shoulder to rotate inward and downward.

>> In Figure 3-2, however, she uses a block to bring the floor closer to her and, as a result, is able to fully open her left shoulder, reaping the full benefits of the pose. Even with the block, this execution is definitely more advanced than in the previous figure.

Of course, you can modify the pose in other ways and still get the benefits. But if a block is available, you may want to consider how it can help you get more out of a particular pose.

You will also want to consider the block construction. The most common types are

>> Foam

>> Cork

>> Wood

Foam blocks are great for either lifting your hips, such as in a supported shoulder stand, or squeezing between your thighs to activate your inner-thigh muscles.

You can also use blocks for support or stability (again, look at Figure 3-2, where the block also provides support as the model leans sideways). For support, you may prefer a block made of a firmer material.

## Blankets

A good yoga blanket can be an essential tool. It potentially offers a

>> Cushion for your head when reclining

>> Cushion for your knees when kneeling or on all fours

>> Lift for your spine, with some added comfort, when sitting

>> Cushion for your pelvis (or even face) when lying on your stomach (prone)

Like most accessories discussed in this chapter, the quality of the material can be a factor. If it is too thin, it will be hard to fold it up enough to find true comfort. And it also needs to stand up to regular washing.

TIP

Consider a blanket when employing some kind of modification. For example, even in easy pose, a simple seated position, a blanket under the hips helps to make the spine straighter without being forced to engage certain muscles (see Figure 3-3). You sit taller, and it's easier on your back.

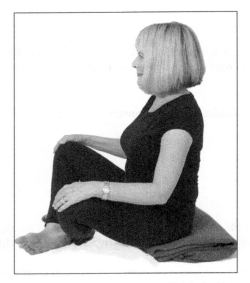

**FIGURE 3-3:**
Easy pose with a blanket.

Photo by Don Henry

You can also use blankets when you're lying down and your chin is tilted way back. A blanket is a great way to cushion the head and get the chin back to a normal position (see Figure 3-4).

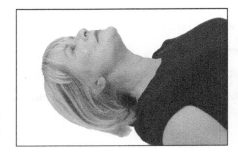 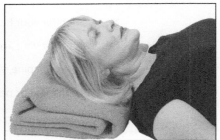

**FIGURE 3-4:**
Blankets help a tilted chin.

Photo by Don Henry

## Bolsters, cushions, and pillows

Bolsters are designed to provide you with comfort and support in various yoga poses. You may see bolsters used a lot in restorative yoga, in which you mostly stay seated or flat on the floor on your back. This type of yoga focuses less on movement and more on breath in comfortable positions.

A *yoga bolster* is essentially a cushion intended to provide you with additional comfort. Take child's pose, for example. If you think it's comfortable without using a bolster (or maybe you don't), try it with one (see Figure 3-5).

FIGURE 3-5: Child's pose with a bolster.

*Photo by Don Henry*

**TIP**

While some yoga studios may have bolsters on hand, you probably don't have one lying around the house. No worries. You can use a folded-up blanket or even a couch or bed cushion.

In any case, a bolster or pillow may be the perfect solution when you want something soft underneath you.

## Straps and other accessories

Straps are quite common in a lot of classes. You can use straps to stretch your hips and hamstring, or to constrain your arms in certain poses that tend to make your elbows want to splay open. Don't use one, though, unless you're being instructed by a teacher.

Because wrist problems seem more common in the 50-and-up population, a wedge can be a nice way to decrease the bending angle on certain poses. They are a relatively inexpensive prop and may be quite useful. A wedge works especially well when you're on your hands and knees (see Figure 3-6).

Preparing to Practice Yoga

CHAPTER 3 **Preparing to Practice Yoga** 425

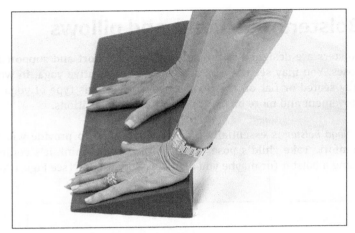

**FIGURE 3-6:**
Using a wedge.

Of course, if you have wrist issues, you can skip certain poses altogether — or perhaps try making fists with your hands instead of flexing your wrists (see Figure 3-7).

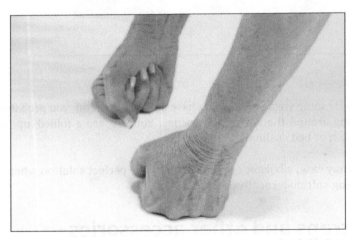

**FIGURE 3-7:**
Making fists.

You can check out all the other types of yoga accessories available to you and see what may be useful. Consider acquiring anything that will make it more likely for you to get on the mat and move.

# Preparing Proper Sequencing

If you're tempted to look at various yoga postures in the following chapters and create your own routine, be sure to give a great deal of consideration when creating any yoga sequence. You can use several approaches to sequence your practice or a class. For example, a sequence may lead up to what is called a *peak pose*. Or you may focus on a particular type of pose, such as hip-openers or twists.

Two questions to ask when creating a sequence of movements and postures are the following:

>> Can I prepare my body for what's to come?

>> Can I compensate for something I just did?

For example, in a particular sequence, you may choose a pose or movement designed to work the abdominal muscles — say, some kind of yoga crunches (see Figure 3-8).

FIGURE 3-8:
Yoga abdominal
crunches.

*Photo by Don Henry*

In a crunch, every time you raise your head and chest, you are shortening (or contracting) your abdominal muscles. Repeating these contractions over and over again is what helps to build strength.

Following these contractions, however, you have the opportunity to compensate for this movement. By putting the student into a bridge pose (see Figure 3-9), those very same abdominal muscles are now being lengthened and relaxed.

**FIGURE 3-9:**
Bridge pose.

*Photo by Don Henry*

Not only does this bridge pose provide some compensation for the previous abdominal work, but take a look at Figure 3-9 to see how the muscles around the neck and shoulders are stretching. The bridge pose is also preparing the neck for going into a supported half shoulder stand pose. So, the bridge pose is both compensating for the crunches and preparing the body for the upcoming inversion (see Figure 3-10).

While it may be unrealistic to think that every pose compensates for something that just happened or prepares for something to come (or both), every good yoga sequence is constructed with that thought in mind, in a logical way.

**FIGURE 3-10:**
Supported
shoulder stand.

# Chapter **4**

# Breathing through Your Yoga Poses

How many times have you heard the expression "take a breath"? Maybe your mother gave you that instruction when she wanted you to calm down before taking an impulsive action or making a hasty decision. Perhaps you say it to yourself now before reacting too fast to an inflammatory situation.

Even outside the yoga world, breathing and composure have a close relationship. Somehow a simple breath can decrease your level of stress and bring balance and self-control to a tense encounter or an emotional moment.

What makes yoga unique is that it sees the breath as a fundamental part of yoga practice and philosophy. It can be one of your most powerful tools.

## Benefiting from Breathing in Yoga

REMEMBER

The benefits of breathing exercises include the following:

» Reduced pain

» Reduced blood pressure

>> Slower pulse

>> Increased relaxation

You can achieve these outcomes just by paying attention to how you're breathing and starting to take control of the process.

# Leveraging Your Breathing

The thing about breathing is you've been doing it for a very long time, without thinking about it much. You have been breathing since birth, so your initial instinct may be that you certainly don't need to learn how to breathe.

**REMEMBER**

If you're going to leverage your breath as a tool, you don't need to learn how to breathe; you need to learn how to control your breath. Here are two critical points to keep in mind:

>> Yoga breathing exercises are about learning to take charge of the process. One way to do so is to practice different ways to breathe.

>> One of the overall goals of yoga is to achieve a state of calmness or peace — a steadiness of mind. You will not be working toward this goal if your breath work causes you anxiety. Don't try more difficult breathing exercises unless you are eager to learn and inspired by the challenge. You may have the option of working with a teacher, which can be a more effective way to learn the more advanced techniques.

## Breathing through the nose

The first thing to consider when you're thinking about your breath is the old yoga adage that says, "The mouth is for eating and the nose is for breathing." Inhaling and exhaling only through the nose definitely has some advantages — but only if you're able to do so comfortably.

**WARNING**

If you happen to have a cold, allergies, or some kind of obstruction (like a deviated septum), don't try to force anything. It's not a good time to breathe through your nose alone.

There are a few practical benefits of breathing through the nose, if you can. You employ the natural air filtration system that your body provides via nose hairs and the mucous lining. Also, taking in air through the nose provides temperature regulation. You can warm the air more efficiently, which is better for your lungs in any season.

While nasal breathing may have many other purported benefits, the simple fact is that the nasal passages are much smaller channels for the air to flow through than is your open mouth. As a result, you tend to breathe deeper and more slowly.

And slowing the breath — especially the exhalation — is the key.

## Extending the exhalation

Even the most ancient yoga texts talk about how powerful it is to extend your exhalation — or letting air out slowly — which can be a confusing concept. How can you expend more air than you take in?

You can't. But what you can do is lengthen your exhalation by expelling air more slowly than you took it in. If you're a singer, it's how you sing a long note; the same thing goes if you play a wind instrument.

TECHNICAL
STUFF

Some of the benefits of learning to extend your exhale are first recognized in what's generally considered to be yoga's foundational work, *The Yoga Sūtras of Patañjali* (Simon & Schuster) translated by Georg Feuerstein. In fact, Sutra 1.34, dedicated entirely to this subject, says that one way to quiet the mind and maximize joy is to extend the exhale: "[Y]ou can try lengthening the exhale and observe the pauses in between breaths to cultivate a calm and clear mind."

More recently, Tim McCall, M.D., explains, "Lengthening exhalation relative to inhalation reduces the 'fight or flight' impulse and maintains a healthy level of carbon dioxide in the blood, which helps you relax." You can see his complete discussion in the *Yoga Journal* at www.yogajournal.com/practice/buzz-away-the-buzzing-mind.

If you're not familiar with slowing down your exhalation, some of the breathing exercises in this chapter can help you practice just that.

Extending your exhalation ultimately sends a message to your brain, often resulting in

>> Slower heart rate

>> Lower blood pressure

>> Relaxed muscles and mind

>> Better digestion

This message stimulates your parasympathetic nervous system and says you are safe. As a result, your brain doesn't need to help you by producing the stress hormones (like adrenaline or cortisol) you would need if you planned on running away or staying and fighting. Instead, you relax.

## Breathing in four parts

It is customary to think of your breath as being in two parts: the inhalation and the exhalation. But, if you think about it, you really breathe in four parts:

>> Inhalation

>> Slight pause

>> Exhalation

>> Slight pause

To practice the four-part breath, your yoga instructor may ask you to increase the time it takes to inhale and exhale, and even increase the pauses. But if you're not accustomed to this type of breath work, the breathing may actually increase your level of anxiety.

Instead you can focus on the four-part aspect of your breathing — and that will be enough. In fact, it may also be easier to keep your mind focused if you're concentrating on a breathing pattern that you're not used to doing.

## Breathing and movement

Yoga philosophy stresses the relationship between the breath and movement. In fact, one translation for the Sanskrit word "yoga" is *union*, referring to the union between breath and movement.

It is important to keep in mind the following principles when yoga teachers instruct you to inhale or exhale as you move in and out of postures:

>> Breathe through the nose only (if possible), mouth closed, lips slightly parted.

>> Extend (lengthen) your exhale.

You'll also want to practice four-part breathing.

**REMEMBER**

Generally speaking, in yoga, the objective is very straightforward: Keep breathing slowly, no matter what pose you're doing.

**WARNING**

Holding your breath or breathing rapidly sends a different message to the brain. If trying to do a particular pose leads to this type of breathing, you should consider doing a less challenging (modified) version — at least until you are ready to do the pose with your breath under control.

The link between body, breath, and mind is essential. Without that link, yoga would just be another form of exercise. Yoga is unique because it brings breath, movement, and meditation together to bring the body into stillness.

**TIP**

It is definitely easier to inhale in certain positions and exhale in others. That is why it is important not only to keep breathing as you move, but to breathe in a way that works well with your physical posture. In yoga, you would typically take air in (inhale) when you open your body and extend (for example, raising your arms overhead). When you're closing your posture, you typically exhale (staying with the example, when you lower your arms back down). Coordinating your movement with your breath helps to ensure that your physical movements are compatible with your breathing process.

# Trying Three Ways to Breathe When Moving

If breath is truly going to surround your movements in yoga, it is worth paying attention to precisely how you're breathing. Consider taking one of the following three approaches:

>> **Focus breathing:** Breathe through the nose only, as discussed earlier in this chapter. This technique is probably the easiest and a good place to start.

>> **Belly breathing:** Breathe through the nose only and gently pull the belly in on the exhalation. In this approach, paying attention to the rising and falling of your stomach ensures your diaphragm is moving properly, which in turn provides stimulation to the surrounding areas, including the low back and pelvic floor. This approach is also a great way to help you relax.

>> **Chest-to-belly:** Breathe through the nose only and inhale first with your chest and then your belly. Focusing your inhalation into your chest causes your rib cage to expand and, when it does, your shoulders open. This opening or expansion counters the effects of everyday rounding (a phenomenon that increases with age and definitely impacts the posture).

# Chapter **5**

# 20 Great Postures for the 50-Plus Yogi

The obvious advantage of having a regular yoga program is that it requires you to move in ways that you otherwise would not move during the course of a normal day. And *movement* refers specifically to the stretching and strengthening that keeps your body flexible, straight, and strong, no matter your age.

But if yoga is to be a benefit and help you become healthier, you have to practice in a way that keeps you free from injury. If you start practicing yoga to become more fit and end up hurting yourself, you've already defeated the purpose.

Yoga needs to adapt to you and not the other way around. To that end, taking the time to understand the types of modifications you can choose as you bring your hard work to the mat can truly make all the difference.

# Remembering Function over Form

The expression "function over form" basically means that you should give top priority to how a particular yoga pose serves you and your body and not be so worried about how it looks.

The postures in this chapter are some of the most common in yoga practice — and they're also some of the safest, providing you modify them whenever needed.

**REMEMBER**

While you may receive numerous benefits from any given pose, including strengthening and stretching, your first objective is to enhance the health of your mind, as well as your spine.

But sometimes, for a pose to have the maximum positive impact, you need to choose a modification. What a pose does for your body is always more important than what it looks like.

## Listening to your body

Whether you're taking a class or practicing alone on your mat, keep in mind that you and you alone are in charge. Any good yoga teacher will try to keep you safe. But, in the end, only you know what's going on inside your body at any given moment, so pay attention to how you're feeling.

This chapter highlights some of the most common poses in a yoga practice. You're presented with both the traditional form as well as the same pose with modifications. The modifications may actually make the pose more accessible and pain-free. Please don't see the modifications as doing less.

You should also take note that one side of your body may feel differently than the other. This is understandable, since no human is symmetrical and you're probably either right- or left-handed, which indicates your dominant side. Moreover, the things your body needs to stay healthy and safe may vary from one day to the next.

## To modify or not to modify

Some movements or postures may be very easy for you, and you may choose to take a more traditional approach. Not everyone needs to modify every pose. Just don't be reluctant to modify any pose where needed. You may need to experiment a bit, just to see what feels best for your body. But please remember: "No pain, no gain" doesn't apply in yoga. If something hurts, try a modification. If it still hurts, stop. Even some of the seemingly easiest poses still may not be good for your body structure. For example, even the simplest inversion may not benefit you if you have high blood pressure or retinopathy, or suffer from GERD.

**REMEMBER**

As with any new physical activity, you should always consult your doctor before attempting any yoga pose.

## Focusing on the spine

You may have lost some ease of movement and grown a bit stiffer over time. One sign of this can be seen in your posture.

In the extreme, as muscles change, your spine may become less vertical, or less straight (see Figure 5-1).

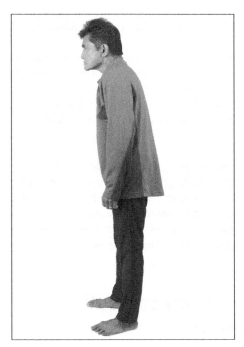

**FIGURE 5-1:**
The spine
becomes
less erect.

*Photo by Don Henry*

While you will certainly be strengthening some muscles in some poses and stretching and relaxing muscles in other poses, you will ultimately be standing straighter and walking taller as a result of adding yoga to your routine.

# Forgiving limbs

The traditional form of a pose or traditional alignment should not be your most important consideration. If you try to force your body into a posture that you see in a book or on a nearby yoga mat, you may be setting yourself up for injury.

**REMEMBER**

You need to be in a class, whether in person or via video, with a teacher who allows you to let yoga fit your body and can address exactly what you need at the moment. It makes no sense to force your body to fit a particular yoga class.

The key, then, is to adapt yoga to fit your body. And one of the primary ways you are going to accomplish this goal is by employing a concept called *forgiving limbs.*

Simply stated, the philosophy of forgiving limbs says that you're always, no matter what the pose, allowed and even encouraged to bend your arms and legs as needed. Bending prevents you from overstretching certain muscles (you can stretch a muscle or strain a muscle doing the same pose, if you're not thoughtful) and may allow you to keep your spine a bit erect — always a goal.

When you look at pictures in some yoga books or magazine covers, everyone seems to have the straightest arms and legs — often imitating the very traditional form of the pose. But you need to be smarter than that. You need to allow the function of the pose to take priority over the form. You need to let yoga serve you. In some cases, it may not be quite as pretty, but it will always be more effective, safer, even smarter.

Take, for example, a simple standing forward fold (see Figure 5-2). If you work to get your head toward your knees, giving gravity an opportunity to lengthen your spine and ease your vertebrae apart, it is very likely that your hamstrings (the back of your thighs) will object. However, if you put a nice bend in your knees, you will be able to get your head closer. As a result, you still get the benefit of letting the gravity decompress you — regardless of how much your knees are bent. This is *function over form.*

## Fascia (or what you can call your inner leotard)

Science describes *fascia* as a layer of connective tissue that runs throughout the body, supporting muscles, tendons, and organs. Think about it as an internal "leotard."

**FIGURE 5-2:**
Forward fold
(traditional and
modified).

*Photo by Don Henry*

Imagine a one-piece suit that extends from somewhere in your feet, all the way up to somewhere in your head. It's important to be aware of this because things that happen in the bottom of your body can actually impact what goes on at the top.

As just one example, a pain you feel in your neck may be caused by something happening in, say, your ankle. Again, that's because of your fascia — your leotard.

Keep in mind that your fascia likes to move and that it may be able to move more freely if you employ the forgiving limbs approach.

## Yoga is not a competition

The first time some people began running around the school playground or participating in a spelling bee in the classroom, they experienced an innate desire to stand out, to be better than the next kid. The sense of competition seemed almost instinctive.

When it comes to yoga, however, it's important to abandon any trace of a competitive nature.

Standing on your yoga mat, something still inside you — inside us all — may want to be better than the next person on the mat. More flexible. More graceful. Stronger.

Perhaps this instinct has been good for you. Maybe the need to excel has served you well throughout your life, in school, in sports, at work. But when it comes to yoga, it is essential that you learn to let go of that need to be the best. Yoga is not competitive — not even with yourself!

**REMEMBER**

The good news about being 50 and over is that, perhaps, it's just a bit easier to not let your ego drive your yoga practice. Comparing yourself to anyone else is a fruitless exercise. In fact, a successful yoga practice has only two measures, illustrated in the following two questions:

>> Are you moving in a way that nurtures your body and spirit?

>> Are you avoiding all injury and pain?

# Asymmetrical Forward Bend

The asymmetrical forward bend pose lengthens both the back and the hamstrings. This pose can be very challenging in its traditional form, particularly bringing your head toward your leg. You definitely don't want to ignore the most beneficial aspects of the pose by trying to make the pose look perfect.

**TIP**

**Modification:** Allow your forward leg to bend (instead of keeping it straight) to make it easier to stretch your back (see Figure 5-3). Notice in the modification how much closer the model can bring their torso to their leg just by bending their knee, giving them more space to lengthen.

**FIGURE 5-3:**
Asymmetrical
forward bend
(traditional and
modified).

*Photo by Don Henry*

# Bent Leg Supine Twist

You will generally do twists toward the end of a yoga sequence, when your muscles are warmed up and ready for stretching. The twisting posture continues strengthening and elongating those muscles that support your spine — all the way from the hips to the top of the spine.

This ultimately helps you stand straighter and walk more upright. Also, you prepare your back for sudden twisting movements that may happen when doing other things besides yoga.

**TIP**

**Modification:** When you bring the bent knee across your body, the traditional form would require you to bring that knee to the floor (see Figure 5-4). Instead, bring that knee toward the floor only as far as you feel a stretch, but not pain.

**FIGURE 5-4:**
Bent leg supine twist (traditional and modified).

*Photo by Don Henry*

# Boat Pose

Think of your abdominal muscles, your entire core, as being the front of your spine. Those muscles provide support for your back.

This concept becomes very obvious in people who have back issues. Often, back muscles are overworked because they're forced to do the work of abdominal muscles that are too weak to do the job.

The function of the boat pose, shown in Figure 5-5, is to strengthen the front of your spine. It's designed to strengthen your core.

Photo by Don Henry

FIGURE 5-5:
Boat pose
(traditional and
modified).

TIP

**Modification:** While traditional boat pose is done with your legs straight (see Figure 5-5), one of the ways to modify it is to soften your knees. If this pose is still too challenging, trying lifting one leg while planting the other foot firmly on the mat (with your knee still bent). This pose is a great way to build your core strength. It is critically important, however, for you to choose the appropriate modification (if needed).

# Bridge Pose

Like so many postures, traditional yoga equates numerous health benefits with the bridge pose. From insomnia and fatigue to anxiety and digestive issues, the bridge addresses a great deal.

Bridge pose variations are a way to compensate for abdominal work by integrating stability and control of the core. In addition to compensating for abdominal work, bridge poses also prepare the neck and shoulder muscles for a shoulder stand inversion.

TIP

**Modification:** For some people, raising the hips off of the floor is too challenging. The easiest modification is to leave your hips on the ground, but tilt your pelvis upward (see Figure 5-6).

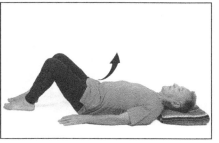

**FIGURE 5-6:**
Bridge pose (traditional and modified).

*Photo by Don Henry*

# Child's Pose

For most people, child's pose is calming, and most yoga classes treat it as a resting pose (see Figure 5-7).

**FIGURE 5-7:**
Child's pose (traditional and modified).

*Photo by Don Henry*

**TIP**

**Modification:** You can put your arms out in front of you or maybe alongside you (with your hands near your feet). Some people also find it easier to breathe if they open their knees instead of keeping them together.

# Cobra Pose

Cobra pose is probably the most common back-bending posture (see Figure 5-8). The primary function of this pose is to lengthen and strengthen the spine. You also stretch your arms and shoulders as you push upward and let your shoulders fall back. In any form, you need to keep your hips on the ground — and be careful not to over-arch your lower back.

*Photo by Don Henry*

FIGURE 5-8:
Cobra pose
(traditional and
modified).

TIP

**Modification:** One modification is to keep your gluteal muscles (your butt) loose. Your glutes are big muscles, and they will want to do all the work. If you keep them relaxed, you'll be forcing your low back muscles to take over instead. While the traditional cobra pose may allow you to use your gluteal muscles to help you lift, a more common technique requires you to keep your butt relaxed.

Yoga can help restore the natural lumbar curve in the lower back using the cobra pose without activating the gluteals. With too much sitting, adversely impacting general health, this technique is used more and more.

Also note in the modified version shown in Figure 5-8 that the model is doing this pose on their forearms (often called sphinx arms). This modification may be a good place to start if this pose is new to you.

# Corpse Pose

Corpse pose (see Figure 5-9) is a relaxation pose that is always a real favorite — especially at the end of a class or home session. Yet it's still a yoga pose, so you need to remember that at least some work needs to be done.

The primary function of corpse pose is rest. This pose is sometimes used at the beginning of class to help you relax and turn your attention away from what happened earlier or what may be on your agenda for later — or maybe just the grocery list. It's a pose that gives you an opportunity to steady your mind and connect with your breath.

At the end, the pose gives you an opportunity to make sure that you have relaxed all the muscles you used throughout the practice and once again find a place inside that is peaceful and stress-free.

FIGURE 5-9:
Corpse pose
(traditional and
modified).

Photo by Don Henry

TIP

**Modification:** The primary goal of this pose is to be comfortable, so feel free to make any adjustments that will help you relax. A common modification is to bend the knees with support.

# Downward Facing Dog

Like so many postures, the downward facing dog yoga pose (see Figure 5-10) offers a multitude of benefits. Still, the lengthening of the spine as it slightly arches, as well as the hamstrings, is readily apparent.

FIGURE 5-10:
Downward
facing dog pose
(traditional and
modified).

Photo by Don Henry

TIP

**Modification:** The problem with this pose is that you can put too much weight in your hands, creating issues for your wrists and shoulders. Bending your knees can help you distribute your weight more evenly and maybe even allow you to lower your heels closer to the ground. You can also try walking your feet slightly closer to your hands.

Keep in mind that your pelvis and femurs are designed to support your weight. Shoulder and arm structures are not, so find a balance of support.

# Easy Pose

The easy pose (see Figure 5-11) is clearly used for relaxation. But beware that, to sit straight and tall, you have to engage certain back muscles that actually strengthen as you hold the pose.

One school of thought in yoga philosophy believes all yoga postures are designed to stabilize your body so that you will be stable enough to sit in this position for long periods of time — particularly for meditation.

FIGURE 5-11:
Easy pose
(traditional and
modified).

Photo by Don Henry

**TIP**

**Modification:** If you want to make this pose easier, especially if you're staying in it for a few minutes, it helps to sit on something. It may be a stack of blankets, blocks, a bolster, or a cushion. Elevating your spine helps make it longer without using your own muscles to do it. You can also sit against a wall to support your back.

# Great Seal

In traditional yoga, the great seal pose (see Figure 5-12) is generally considered advanced because it requires doing all three of the locks or *bandhas*, as they're called in traditional yoga. In Sanskrit, *bandha* means to tighten or hold tight. The modified version of this pose offers a great way to relax and to strengthen the back muscles and the rest of the core.

**FIGURE 5-12:**
Great seal pose
(traditional and
modified).

*Photo by Don Henry*

**TIP**

**Modification:** In this more accessible version of the pose, don't add the locks (at least not right away). It still yields great benefits. Notice that in the modified version, you can soften the knee of the straight leg.

# Half Chair Pose

In a traditional chair or half chair pose (see Figure 5-13), your arms and legs are stretching and strengthening, which happens in the modified version as well (though, maybe to a lesser extent). But it's the extension of the spine that is the primary function.

**TIP**

**Modification:** You can make a number of modifications to this pose.

>> The first modification you can make is to widen your stance. It should feel more stable, more comfortable.

>> The next thing to think about is how straight you want to make your arms. Again, because the primary function of this pose is to put you into a slight backbend (extension), soften your arms if you feel any pain or discomfort when you straighten them up toward your ears.

>> Finally, pay attention to how your knees feel and decide how deeply you want to squat. Because it is a half chair pose, even the traditional version will go down only halfway. You may decide that, for you at that moment, less than halfway makes more sense.

FIGURE 5-13:
Half chair pose
(traditional and
modified).

*Photo by Don Henry*

# Half-Standing Forward Bend

Once again, the function of the half-standing forward bend pose (see Figure 5-14) relates to the spine. In each version of the pose, the back is slightly arched. Holding this pose not only lengthens and strengthens the back muscles, but it also targets the arms and shoulders.

TIP

**Modification:** Putting a slight bend in the arms makes this pose more accessible while still allowing for a slightly arched back. Also, notice that the feet are wider in the modified pose (instead of together), making for a more comfortable, sturdier stance.

FIGURE 5-14:
Half-standing
forward bend
pose (traditional
and modified).

*Photo by Don Henry*

# Knees-to-Chest

While the knees-to-chest resting pose may seem very basic, it is an important way to compensate the body after doing back bends and twists. It is a reset, of sorts, and a great way to massage your lower back (especially if you rock side to side). Bending your knees takes pressure off the back of your legs and lumbar area (see Figure 5-15).

FIGURE 5-15:
Knees-to-chest
pose (traditional
and modified).

*Photo by Don Henry*

TIP

**Modification:** One of the ways you can modify this pose is by positioning your hands behind your knees instead of in front of them or putting them on your knee caps with arms extended.

# Locust Pose

All you need to do is look at the photographs to know that the locust pose is primarily a back bend (see Figure 5-16). You have to use the muscles supporting your spine, including your gluteal muscles, to achieve an arch in your back.

FIGURE 5-16:
Locust pose
(traditional and
modified).

Photo by Don Henry

TIP

**Modifications:** You have the choice of several variations or modifications in this pose. Most of them have to do with what you do with your arms and legs. Modifications include

>> Both legs on the ground

>> One leg on the ground and lifting the other

>> Both arms in front of you, remaining on the ground as you lift

>> One arm lifts while the other remains down

>> One or both arms down at your sides

You should try various combinations in this pose to see what works best for you at the moment. (Don't strain your back by trying to create a bigger arch: Think long instead.)

REMEMBER

If your modification includes using just one arm and/or leg, be sure to do both sides. While the primary function of the pose may be a back bend, you're also strengthening your arms and legs as you lift, so you need to keep both sides even.

# Mountain Pose

Mountain pose is often used as a starting position. As you can see, it is a relatively easy pose, but keep in mind it should also be a strong pose — your muscles are engaged, even strengthened, in the process (see Figure 5-17).

 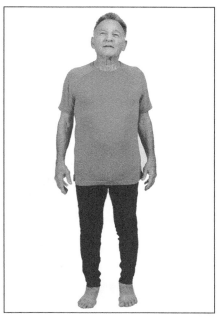

**FIGURE 5-17:**
Mountain pose (traditional and modified).

*Photo by Don Henry*

If, however, your first priority in any posture is thinking about what it's doing for your spine, this pose is no different. To that end, mountain pose is an opportunity for you to stand straight and tall, to improve and maybe even train your posture.

TIP

**Modification:** One modification you can make in this pose is to bring your feet to about hips-width apart, instead of standing in the more traditional way with your feet together. Bringing your palms forward requires your shoulders to open and to stretch your upper chest muscles (pectorals). Palms at your side is more relaxed.

Try this posture with and without modifications to decide what feels best.

# Revolved Triangle

Twisting poses like the revolved triangle have many reputed benefits in yoga, but the primary function in this pose is the lengthening of the back muscles (see Figure 5-18). Like all twists, this pose can provide some relief for low back pain — depending, of course, on what's causing the pain.

FIGURE 5-18:
Revolved triangle
pose (traditional
and modified).

*Photo by Don Henry*

TIP

**Modification:** The first way to modify this pose (as shown in Figure 5-18) is to put as much bend in your knees as feels comfortable. Just doing that will help you go into your twist.

Also, if it's painful for you to reach upward, you can wrap your hand around your low back (still keeping your shoulder up toward the ceiling).

# Seated Forward Bend

The seated forward bend pose (see Figure 5-19) is great for lengthening the spine and surrounding shoulder muscles, and traditional yoga even notes benefits relating to digestion, weight loss, anxiety, and insomnia. But another important, less positive result of this pose is injury.

The goal is to bring your head toward your knees. But most people's hamstrings will prevent that from happening.

WARNING

All too often, people try to compensate for tight hamstrings by increasing the bend using their spines, which may lead to a back injury. You need to be thoughtful when doing this pose.

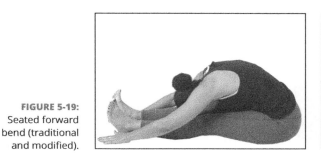

FIGURE 5-19:
Seated forward bend (traditional and modified).

*Photo by Don Henry*

TIP

**Modification:** The first modification you can make is to bend your knees. Again, the function of the pose doesn't relate to the legs — not even the hamstrings (even though they'll be challenged). If the focus is on the spine, bending your knees will allow you to bend forward more. If it feels okay, you can round your back; if it hurts to round, keep your back long.

# Standing Forward Bend

All day long, as you sit or stand, walk or drive, you remain upright, with gravity pulling your vertebrae together — in effect, compressing your spine (your discs are designed to help cushion that compression). The goal of the standing forward bend pose (see Figure 5-20) is to decompress your spine. You can see that the pull of gravity spreads your vertebrae apart. Your spine is lengthened and decompressed.

TIP

**Modification:** In the traditional form of the pose, you hinge forward from the hips, bringing your head toward your knees, keeping your legs as straight as possible. Of course, your hamstrings may have a different idea. Because the function of the pose is to lengthen and decompress the spine, softening your knees (bending your legs) is a totally acceptable way to get your head closer to your knees.

**FIGURE 5-20:**
Standing forward bend pose (traditional and modified).

Photo by Don Henry

# Supported Shoulder Stand

Doing inverted poses in yoga addresses many purported problems, including insomnia, digestion problems, menopause symptoms, and anxiety. The issue is that inversions are the category of yoga poses that causes the most injuries. The challenge is to find a version of the pose that is relatively safe, while still offering the benefits.

The supported shoulder stand (see Figure 5-21) offers most of the benefits of an inversion, while at the same time is safer than the more advanced inversions.

**TIP**

**Modification:** You can use any number of props, including a bolster, foam block, or stack of blankets, under your lower back to lift your hips. (If the pose is still too challenging, try putting your legs up a wall.)

In a yoga class, you often hear about reversing blood flow, but you know that your blood always flows in the same direction. You are, however, reversing the impact of gravity on your circulation. When you're inverted, gravity helps direct the blood back to your heart, making your heart work less to get it there and ultimately helping you to relax more.

FIGURE 5-21:
Supported
shoulder stand
(traditional and
modified).

*Photo by Don Henry*

# Warrior I

Like so many yoga poses, the Warrior I pose (see Figure 5-22) has numerous benefits. You're strengthening the front of the thigh (quadricep) of your forward leg and stretching the back of your other leg. But, as always, it's what's happening in your spine that is the most important aspect of this pose.

Coming into this pose requires you to arch your back. The muscles in your back that are supporting your spine are activated and strengthened.

**TIP**

**Modification:** How much you choose to straighten or bend your limbs is entirely up to you. If you need to bend your arms more or perhaps bend your legs less, make that choice — particularly if such modifications help you arch your back. Of course, if activating any of these muscles causes you pain, then bending a bit forward will allow you to find some relief and hopefully maintain some version of the pose.

Photo by Don Henry

**FIGURE 5-22:**
Warrior I pose
(traditional and
modified).

Chapter **6**

# Welcome to Your New Favorite Sport: Pickleball!

I t's the newest sport that's making headlines: Pickleball. You may have heard the pings of balls being hit across a nearby court. Former athletes are discovering pickleball and competing again for the first time in decades. Ordinary folks are finding themselves immediately welcomed into a community of people who share a passion for this quirky, addictive game. Those struggling with various health issues are finding pickleball to be a safe, accessible option for getting more fresh air and exercise (definitely way more fun than using a solitary elliptical!). Can pickleball save the world? Probably not, but research shows it can improve your health and well-being.

This chapter introduces you to the sport everyone's talking about: pickleball.

## Who's Playing Pickleball? Everyone!

Why, you may ask, would you want to get off of your comfy, custom-indented spot on the couch and go running around a tiny court chasing a plastic ball? Here's why: It's *fun!* Despite its silly name, it's an amazing game. It has action, patience, surprises, athleticism, power, finesse, strategy, trash talk (all in good fun), and so much more.

The rules of the game have made it perfect for players of all ages and all levels of ability. Does your shoulder no longer allow you to hit an overhead serve? No problem — the serve is underhand! Do you dislike running long distances? This sport is typically played as doubles on a small court, so you don't need to train for a marathon. Check out your local pickleball court and you may just find players of three different generations on the same court enjoying the game together.

The learning curve is short in pickleball, which makes it fun from Day One, but you can spend a lifetime trying to master it. You can pick it up in less than an hour and enjoy the challenge indefinitely because there is always more to learn. People play the game at swanky country clubs as well as small city parks, schools, and prisons. It's the same game, no matter where you play it.

Now, don't get us wrong; this sport can definitely be physically challenging, and it's played by elite athletes at the highest levels. Multiple professional pickleball tours take place with great players who constantly push the limits of the sport. Or you can just go out with a few pals and hit the ball around. Whether you want to excel or just have fun, welcome to your new healthful addiction!

In this chapter and Chapters 7–9 of Book 6, you dip just briefly into the origins of this sport and then get to know the basic rules and scoring. You also discover the burgeoning world of pickleball equipment, gear, and fashion. You get the low-down on the different kinds of courts, where to find them, and how to find people to play with. In short, you find all the information you need to get started in your new pickleball life.

## Looking at Pickleball in a Nutshell

REMEMBER

Created in 1965, pickleball is a hybrid of tennis, table tennis, and badminton. You play the game on a court with a three-foot high net, and the aim is to hit a perfo-rated plastic ball over the net with a paddle (about twice the size of a table tennis paddle) in a way that prevents your opponents from returning it. At first glance, it looks a lot like tennis on a miniature court. It involves less running than ten-nis, which is great if your knees don't like that sort of thing. Pickleball has unique rules that place a high emphasis on precision and strategy. The sport, which has a multigenerational following, can be fast-paced and competitive. Pickleball is a fast-growing sport all over the world, with more than 5 million players and counting.

Fun and accessibility were at the heart of pickleball from the very start. It was designed to be a game that everyone could play.

# Getting Everyone in on the Pickleball Act

Joel Pritchard was a member of Congress from Seattle who spent summers with his family and friends on Bainbridge Island, Washington. One summer in 1965, the kids were complaining of boredom. Joel and his friend Bill Bell felt there must be a way to get kids and parents to play together, so Joel set out to create a new game. Failing to find enough tennis rackets, he tried four table tennis paddles and a wiffle ball. The table tennis paddles didn't work so well, so the dads crafted some larger wooden paddles to use. They started to play on the old badminton court in the yard, and the kids lowered the net to waist height. Soon there was laughter, some shrieking, and a lot of rallying back and forth. They introduced the game to another friend, Barney McCallum, and made up some rules and a scoring system (with some inspiration from badminton). From there, the game has continued to evolve to this day.

**TECHNICAL STUFF**

There's more than one version of how the sport's unique name came about. One story from Barney McCallum claims that the game was named after Pritchard's dog, Pickles. Peggy Pritchard, Joel's daughter, points out that the dog came later, however. She says that her mother, Joan Pritchard (a competitive rower in college), came up with the name, loosely derived from the term *pickle boats* that college rowing teams use for the "odds and ends" members of their team. The "odds and ends" were much like the random pieces of equipment Pritchard had grabbed to play the new game. Whichever story rings true, the quirky name is as fun as the sport itself.

Here's a quick timeline of pickleball's evolution:

>> **1965:** Pickleball is created by Representative Joel Pritchard and his friends.

>> **1967:** The first "official" pickleball court is built on Bainbridge Island, Washington.

>> **1972:** A corporation is formed for the new sport.

>> **1975:** Articles begin being published about "America's newest racquet sport."

>> **1976:** The first known pickleball tournament in the world is held at South Center Athletic Club in Tukwila, Washington.

>> **1982:** The United States Amateur Pickleball Association (USAPA) is organized to encourage the sport's growth and advancement on a national level.

>> **1984:** The first official pickleball rule book is published.

>> **1990:** Growing exponentially each year, pickleball is now played in all 50 states.

- >> **1999:** The first pickleball website is launched.

- >> **2001:** Pickleball is introduced for the first time at the Arizona Senior Olympics.

- >> **2008:** The first mass-media exposure of the sport appears on ABC's *Good Morning America,* which airs a live, in-studio segment on pickleball that includes a brief demonstration.

- >> **2009:** The first USAPA National Tournament for players of all ages is held in Buckeye, Arizona.

- >> **2014:** The Pickleball Channel is launched.

- >> **2016:** USAPA reports 17,000 members and over 4,600 places to play.

- >> **2019:** The Sports Fitness Industry Association 2019 report indicates that pickleball continues to be one of the fastest-growing sports in the United States as participants reached 3.3 million.

- >> **2021:** Pickleball is featured on NBC's *The Today Show,* CNBC, BBC News, and *Live with Kelly and Ryan.* Stories are published in top-rated publications including the *New York Times, Vanity Fair, Forbes, Allure,* the *Boston Globe,* the *Economist, USA Today, Sports Illustrated, Parade,* and *Axios.*

- >> **2022:** More than 5 million people are playing pickleball all over the world. Washington State's Governor Jay Inslee signs a bill into law that makes pickleball the official state sport of Washington.

- >> **2023:** Some 36.5 million people played pickleball in the past year, according to the Association of Pickleball Professionals.

As this timeline shows, the sport of pickleball has grown gradually and steadily over the decades. As baby boomers started to retire, it grew faster, and then the pandemic hit in 2020 — and *boom!* The sport exploded. Each year, more and more people are playing pickleball all over the world.

# Discovering the Benefits of Pickleball

Many people assume that only older people play pickleball. Not true! People aged 4 to 100 are playing pickleball. About 30% of players are 18 to 34. Pickleball is being integrated into many schools' physical education programs, and a whole new generation of kids is growing up loving the game.

REMEMBER

The many good reasons to play pickleball start with its impact on body and mind. The health benefits of regular exercise are well documented, and pickleball is a relatively low-impact sport, easy on your joints, and yet provides a great workout. It provides a cardiovascular workout and helps improve balance, hand-eye coordination, and flexibility. Your body releases endorphins while you play, improving your mood. Keeping score and devising strategies to win are enough to keep your brain engaged for hours. The significant social aspect of the sport means that it's easy to meet lots of new people — and reducing isolation can boost your health and increase your lifespan! Your mental, physical, and emotional well-being are all connected, and pickleball checks every box.

REMEMBER

Here are some factors that make pickleball fun and easy:

>> **It's easier to start playing than most sports.** Sure, the scoring seems kind of quirky at first, but the barrier to begin playing is very low. Chapter 7 in Book 6 tells you everything you need to know to start playing real games your first time on a court.

>> **It's available year-round.** You can play the sport indoors or outdoors, in any season.

>> **You can find many places to play.** As Chapter 9 in Book 6 describes, you can already find courts in many parks, gyms, athletic clubs, and community centers, and many cities are busy converting basketball and tennis courts to pickleball this very minute. Resorts and residential communities are also actively adding more pickleball courts for their residents.

>> **You can easily find other players.** User-friendly online resources and handy apps help you find people to play with wherever you are, as you find out in Chapter 9 of Book 6.

>> **The sport is affordable.** No fancy gear is required — you just need a paddle and a ball. Playing is often free in places like public parks.

>> **You can improve your fitness.** The multidirectional movement in pickleball improves strength, balance, and agility. Quick bursts of play action provide interval-like training to boost your cardio fitness.

>> **The matches are often played quickly.** Pickleball is great for short attention spans, young and old. With quick games and rotating players, it's constant fun.

>> **It's a multigenerational sport.** Family and friends of all ages can play together. Hello, bonding!

>> **It improves social skills and boosts confidence**. Newbies are warmly welcomed onto the court to play. "We all started just like you!" can be heard on pickleball courts everywhere.

>> **You get to use your brain.** Strategy and placement rule over raw athletic speed and strength, so you can work on your pickleball game even while waiting in line at the grocery store or commuting to work.

>> **You get to channel your inner-kid.** Playing pickleball can be so much *fun!* Everyone needs more fun in their lives.

This chapter gives you many great reasons to start playing pickleball right now, so read on to find out how to play. A good place to start is Chapter 7 in Book 6, which, in addition to the rules, tells you about the layout of the court, how to serve, and a few basics to get you going.

# Chapter **7**

# Playing by the Pickleball Rules

Have you ever arrived at a party and wished you'd read the invitation a bit more closely? First you realize it's a potluck and you've brought nothing to share. Then you begin to see that it's quite obviously *not* a costume party. Worst of all, you talked about the party earlier in the day with the birthday girl, and now everyone is hiding behind the couches, ready to yell, "Surprise!" Oopsy.

This chapter is like the fine print on the invitation. It tells you the things you need to know to be safe, understand the pickleball court and its markings, keep score, and a few other essentials. After reading this chapter, you can arrive at the courts calm, cool, and collected because you'll know everything you need to start playing. Time to party!

**REMEMBER**

Don't wear out the pages in this section on scoring by nervously reading them over and over again. Scoring takes a little bit of practice, and the best way to fully grasp it is by trying it. Don't stress! In time, you will learn to keep score just fine. When you get on the courts and start playing, you'll quickly get the hang of it. At first, count on the other players on the court to help you figure out the score. In fact, you'll often hear it called out as a question rather than a statement.

# First Things First: Safe Pickleball Is No Accident!

Pickleball is a really fun sport. But nothing ruins the fun as quickly as an unexpected injury. The good news is that pickleball is considered a fairly safe sport. Plastic balls, lightweight paddles, and smaller courts make for a kinder, gentler way to play, for the most part. And although you won't see players falling very often, the court surface can feel pretty darn hard if you do take a tumble.

**REMEMBER**

Here are some safety tips you should know before stepping onto the court:

>> **Protect your peepers.** Pickleballs are made of hard plastic and fly at very fast speeds. Getting hit with a pickleball probably won't result in more than a small bruise for most parts of your body, but your delicate eyeballs are another story. Keep them covered at all times. Regular sunglasses or prescription glasses work just fine, or you can buy clear safety glasses at a sporting goods or hardware store. (You can find more information on protective eyewear in Chapter 8 of Book 6.)

>> **Wear court shoes.** Court shoes are built to provide lateral stability and movement. Running or walking shoes are designed for moving forward. There is a big difference! You find out more details on different types of court shoes in Chapter 8 of Book 6.

>> **Warm up properly.** To avoid muscle pulls and cramping, always stretch before you play, and do your full warm-up routine.

>> **Never run backward.** Not only is backpedaling a terribly inefficient way to move to the ball, but it's one of the leading causes of injuries in pickleball. If you do decide to chase down the ball, turn and run in the direction it's heading. Or you can always just say, "Nice shot." (If a ball is sailing high over your head, yell "YOU!" before your partner does — now you're off the hook!)

>> **Don't play on wet courts.** When testing a court to see whether it's dry, check the lines first — they are typically the slickest part of the court. Be aware of damp, shadowed areas.

>> **Call the ball.** If the ball is coming to the middle between you and your partner, be sure to communicate with each other. Yell out "Mine!" or "Yours!" Calling the ball prevents you and your partner from hitting each other while swinging simultaneously at the ball.

>> **Alert others when a stray ball goes on their court.** If you or someone on your court hits a ball that goes astray and is stealthily endangering a neighboring group of players who could step on it, please yell "Ball On!" repeatedly, until play stops. Failing to do so is not only dangerous but also a huge breach of pickleball etiquette that will earn you some wicked side eye.

>> **Stay hydrated.** Drink plenty of water, even if you don't feel thirsty or the sun's not beating down on you. If you perspire a lot or are prone to cramping, see if supplementing your water with electrolytes helps.

>> **Know your limits.** No question about it: Pickleball can be addictive. Even when you're already exhausted, you may feel the urge to play just one more game. This could be one game too many!

>> **Know where the first-aid kit and nearest AED (Automatic External Defibrillator) are located.** Take a CPR/first-aid class and encourage other players to join you. Learn to use an AED machine and have a plan for dealing with different types of emergency situations.

# Looking at the Layout of the Court

The pickleball court is laid out the same for both singles and doubles. It's a rectangle that measures 44 feet long by 20 feet wide. This is the same size as a doubles badminton court, or roughly one third the size of a tennis court. Along the outside boundaries of the court, you'll find the *sidelines* on the long ends and the *baselines* on the shorter ends.

The court is divided in the middle by a net that is 2 inches lower than a tennis net. The height relative to the size of the court can make the net difficult to get over.

On each half of the court is a 7-x-20-foot area directly in front of the net called the non-volley zone (NVZ), more commonly known as *the kitchen.* As the name *non-volley zone* implies, players aren't allowed to hit a volley (a shot hit before the ball has bounced) while in this zone. (Find out more about these rules later in this chapter.) Historians aren't sure how the kitchen got its nickname, but one theory claims that the term was borrowed from shuffleboard.

The court between the kitchen and the baseline is divided lengthwise into two service boxes by the *centerline.* The line that divides the kitchen from the service boxes is known as the *non-volley zone line,* or the *kitchen line.* Figure 7-1 shows the names and locations of the lines and zones on the court.

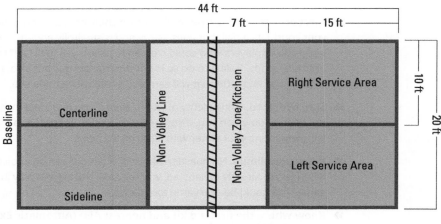

© John Wiley & Sons, Inc.

**FIGURE 7-1:**
The names and locations of the lines and zones of the court.

# Order on the Court: Learning the Basic Rules

As a general rule, you should learn the basic rules of a game before you attempt to play. An official pickleball rule book currently runs about 75 pages, but you don't need to commit all that to memory. The rules summary in this section helps you get out on the court and play your first few games today. Pickleball is a very social sport, so even if you don't know all the rules yet, there's probably another player on the court (or three) who are willing to help you. They were all beginners once, too, so don't be shy!

The following sections assume that you're playing doubles, which is by far the most popular format. Later in this chapter, you find out how singles scoring differs from doubles.

## Serving things up

**REMEMBER**

You can't start playing a game of pickleball until somebody serves the ball. Here are the basic rules you need to know to get started serving:

>> **You must serve diagonally (crosscourt) into the service box.** Your serve must clear the kitchen and bounce in the service box that's diagonal from you, on the opponent's side of the court. If it lands on the sideline, baseline, or

centerline, the serve is considered in. If it lands on the kitchen line, it's a fault. Figure 7-2 shows the path of a serve into the correct service box.

>> **The ball must go over the net.** If your serve goes into the net without going over, it's a fault. If your serve glances off the top of the net but still lands in the service box, it's good and must be played. If it touches the top of the net and lands out of bounds or in the kitchen, it's a fault.

>> **You must strike the ball below the level of your waist with a low-to-high motion.** You must serve underhand in pickleball, contacting the ball below your waist with an upward swing path. In addition, no part of your paddle may be higher than your wrist.

>> **If serving off the bounce, you may not add force to the bounce.** You can choose to hit the ball out of the air, before it bounces, by either tossing or dropping the ball with your non-paddle hand. Or you may choose to hit it off a bounce, but in this case you cannot apply any upward or downward force to the ball. This is called the drop serve.

>> **You must stand behind the baseline and between the imaginary extensions of the centerline and the sideline.** At the moment you strike the ball, neither foot can be inside the court boundaries, and at least one foot must be touching the ground behind the baseline (both feet can't be in the air). You can't stand way off to the side when you serve; you must be standing in the area behind the service box on your side of the court. Figure 7-2 shows where you must stand to legally serve.

>> **You get only one service attempt.** You have just one chance to hit your serve in. If your serve goes into the net or out of bounds, you lose your serve and do not get to try again until the next round.

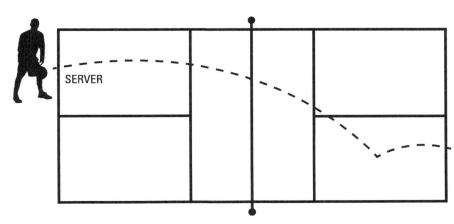

**FIGURE 7-2:**
The path of a serve into the correct service box.

SERVER

© John Wiley & Sons, Inc.

# The Two-Bounce Rule

After a player serves the ball, the receiver must let the serve bounce before they are allowed to hit it. (Otherwise, the world would be left wondering whether that serve was going to land in bounds.) When the receiver returns the ball to the serving team, that team must also let it bounce before they can hit. After those first two shots have been allowed to bounce, any player can legally *volley*, which means to hit the ball out of the air before it bounces.

The Two-Bounce Rule is one of the genius ideas that makes pickleball great. It prevents the "serve and volley" strategy commonly used in tennis, keeping players from blasting a huge serve and immediately running up to the net to volley the next ball. For this reason, in pickleball the serving team is not considered to be at an advantage at the start of each rally.

**TIP**

If you have trouble at first remembering to observe the Two-Bounce Rule, just count the bounces in your head: "One . . . two . . . game on!" Another way to think about this rule is that the ball must bounce *on each side of the court* before players may volley. So after you've watched the ball bounce on your side of the court, either on the serve or return, you can forget worrying about counting those darn bounces.

# Starting positions

The server is the only player required to stand in any particular place on the court when the point begins. (Actually, there is a rule stating that you must stand on your own team's side of the net, but that is obvious!) However, the Two-Bounce Rule clearly influences where the other three players should stand at the start of the point. Figure 7-3 shows the typical positions of each player when one player is serving.

Here's the breakdown for each player:

>> **The server must stand behind the baseline.** The rules state that the server must serve from behind the baseline and between the imaginary extensions of the centerline and sidelines.

>> **The server's partner should also stay behind or near the baseline.** Again, the Two-Bounce Rule requires the serving team to let the return bounce before they can hit it. In case the return is hit deep, both members of the serving team will want to stay back as far as possible so that they won't have to backpedal to hit the ball.

**FIGURE 7-3:**
The typical positions of the players when starting a point.

>> **The receiver stands behind the baseline.** The Two-Bounce Rule requires the receiver to let the serve bounce before they can return the serve. The receiver should also stay well behind the baseline in order to more easily deal with a deep serve.

>> **The receiver's partner stands up at the kitchen line**. Because the Two-Bounce Rule affects only the serving team and the receiver, the receiver's partner doesn't worry about the Two-Bounce Rule and instead focuses on being in the most offensive position at the kitchen line, ready to volley the next ball that comes to them.

TIP

If you're not sure where you're supposed to be standing, note that all players should ideally stand behind the baseline at the beginning of the point, except for the person standing directly across from the server. Also keep in mind that when it's your partner's turn to serve, they need you back there with them. It's their big moment! Stay back and support your partner when they're serving. Only the receiver's partner should be up at the kitchen line.

## At fault: Ways to lose the rally

A rally is over as soon as one of the players commits a fault, resulting in their team's loss of that rally. In basic terms, a fault occurs when a player

>> Hits the ball into (or under) the net

>> Fails to return the ball before it has bounced twice on their side

>> Hits the ball and it lands out of bounds

Many other types of faults can cause you to lose a rally, but don't worry: Even losing points can be tons of fun — it's still pickleball!

It's also considered a fault if a player

>> Violates any of the serving rules

>> Violates the Two-Bounce Rule

>> Contacts the ball with anything other than the paddle or the hand that is holding the paddle

>> Serves or returns as the incorrect player or from the incorrect side (see the later section "Knowing the Score")

>> Violates any of the kitchen rules (explained in the upcoming section "Non-volley zone: It's hot in the kitchen!")

>> Touches the net, net posts, or the opponent's side of the court. This rule applies to your paddle and clothing as well, which is why we've stopped playing in hoop skirts and parachute pants.

There are a few even less common ways to lose a rally, such as taking too long to return from a time-out in tournament play, but the faults in the preceding list are the main ones to worry about during recreational play.

## Non-volley zone: It's hot in the kitchen!

The non-volley zone (NVZ), also known as *the kitchen*, is another genius idea that makes pickleball different from other games. If players could just lean over the net and spike the ball directly into your face, that may impede your ability to enjoy this great pastime. The kitchen makes it so that players have to stay at least 7 feet away from the net if they want to hit the ball out of the air (a shot known as a *volley*).

If you think of the kitchen as its technical name, the non-volley zone, it tells you exactly what it is — a zone where you cannot volley. To be more specific, you cannot have any contact with the ball before it has bounced while you're in this zone. If anything about your volley starts, finishes, or takes place while you're in the kitchen, it's a fault. Note that the kitchen is a two-dimensional surface, not a three-dimensional space. In other words, it's perfectly legal to lean in and hit the ball out of the air from the area above the kitchen, as long as you are not touching its surface. The kitchen line and bordering sidelines are considered part of the kitchen. The out-of-bounds area adjacent to the kitchen is not.

TIP

If you see that a ball is going to bounce short in the kitchen and you can't reach it without going in, by all means *go!* You don't have to wait for the ball to bounce before you can go in — that's a common misconception. After you have gone in and made your shot, try to get back out of the kitchen as quickly as possible. Otherwise, your opponent may flick the ball right at you, forcing you to illegally contact it before it has bounced.

REMEMBER

Because the kitchen is unique to pickleball and the rules are frequently misunderstood, many new players are petrified of being anywhere near the kitchen. Try to let go of this irrational fear because it will only hinder your development as a player. Remember: The kitchen is not hot lava! Not only are you allowed to go in there, but you will absolutely *need* to go in there sometimes to retrieve the ball. The only similarity between the kitchen and your average lava field is that you don't want to camp out in there like the player in Figure 7-4.

**FIGURE 7-4:**
Don't hang out in the kitchen!

From Aniko Kiezel

You may hear pickleballers advising each other to "Stay out of the kitchen!" Although it's a cute turn of phrase, this advice is not entirely accurate. Instead of hanging signs in the kitchen that say "Keep Out," we'd prefer more helpful signs that say "No Loitering."

So now you know there's only one thing you can't do in the kitchen: contact the ball before it bounces. That doesn't sound so complicated, right? The confusing part for many players is understanding what qualifies as being "in" the kitchen, and in what situations it applies.

The rules define a kitchen violation (fault) as occurring when

>> **You hit a volley while any part of your body is contacting the kitchen.** Remember, the kitchen surface includes the kitchen line and adjoining sidelines. Even if just your pinky toe (the one that went "wee wee wee" all the way home) touches the very back of the kitchen line, it's a fault.

>> **You hit a volley and your momentum carries you into the kitchen.** If you initially strike the ball outside the kitchen but the momentum from the shot makes you step inside it, it's considered a fault. There is no time limit on this rule; that is, it doesn't matter if your opponents have already made their next shot (or three), or your partner smashes the next ball for a gold-medal, match-ending winner. If you haven't yet regained your balance from your earlier volley and you fall into the kitchen, it's a fault. After you have reestablished your balance, it is no longer considered part of the same shot, and you can go into the kitchen as you please.

>> **You hit a volley and touch the kitchen with your paddle.** If you lose your balance after hitting a volley and fall forward, try to avoid using your paddle to steady yourself. If your paddle makes contact with the kitchen during or after your shot, it's a fault.

>> **You hit a volley and your hat, glasses, or other gear falls into the kitchen.** If you hit a volley and your dentures fall into the kitchen, it's a fault for a variety of reasons (and one that your fellow players are unlikely to ever forget).

>> **You hit a volley and, in the process, knock your partner into the kitchen.** By contacting your partner in the midst of your shot, you made them a part of that shot. Nothing that you touch during the act of volleying can come in contact with the kitchen until after you have reestablished yourself outside it.

>> **After legally going into the kitchen, you hit a volley before reestablishing both feet outside the kitchen again.** This one's a little tricky to visualize, so imagine that you've stepped into the kitchen to retrieve a short, bouncing ball — knowing that you're perfectly safe because the kitchen is not hot lava — and you are contacting the ball after it has bounced. You return the ball, but as you are in the process of hustling back out of the kitchen, your opponent hits the ball right back at you. Unless you have managed to touch both feet outside the kitchen again, you may not contact the ball out of the air. Figure 7-5 shows examples of legal and illegal volleying.

**FIGURE 7-5:** A legal volleying example (left) and illegal volleying example (right).

*From Aniko Kiezel*

**REMEMBER**

The kitchen is a flat surface defined by its boundary lines and does not include the "air space" above it or the out-of-bounds area next to it. It's legal to volley while stepping or leaping over the corner of the kitchen, as long as your feet do not touch the in-bounds surface. This is called an *Erne*. (It's actually pronounced like "Ernie," and people may suspect you're a rookie if you don't pronounce it correctly.) If you want to show off, just tell them it's named after Erne Perry. The Erne is an advanced move, so don't worry if you can't hit one just yet — you'll at least win pickleball trivia night.

**TIP**

Be honest when you break the kitchen rules. Kitchen violations in recreational play are typically called by the player who made the violation or by their partner. The call usually sounds something like, "Oh wait, no, stop. Stop stop stop stop. I was in the kitchen." This declaration is often paired with a sheepish look, or in some cases a big smile, because smashing a ball from the kitchen feels really great — until you realize it didn't count! In tournaments with referees, the referees will call the kitchen violations. If you've been cheating a bit in recreational play, you will suffer in tournaments because referees are very good at spotting kitchen faults.

# Knowing the Score

Learning to keep score in pickleball can be a bit challenging at first. Although you may feel discouraged at first, we've never met anyone who quit the game because they couldn't keep score. You can do this! Scoring is a bit dry on paper but gets much easier when you start actually playing. It becomes second nature in no time.

**TIP**

If you don't know the score, the other players may! Even at the most advanced levels, players frequently forget the score and have to ask their partner or opponents. Don't ever be embarrassed about losing track of the score. If anything, it will help you fit right in!

## Doubles scoring: Easy as 0-0-2

In doubles, the score consists of three numbers. You're probably thinking. "Wait, wait, wait! The score has three numbers? But there are only two teams! This is crazy. I give up!" Here's how it works.

The first two numbers keep track of each team's score. Easy enough, right? The third number will always be either a 1 or a 2, and it keeps track of the player who is currently serving. Each team has two players and they each get chances to serve. That third number in the score is helpful for remembering whether you're the *first server* (1) or the *second server* (2) on your team because the server keeps changing throughout the game. Now that you're breathing again, you can get into exactly how this works.

Only the serving team can score points. At the opening of the game, the first team to serve is decided by chance. In recreational play, it's typically based on a venue's house rule (such as the team standing on a particular side of the court). In tournament play, the first team to serve is usually determined by guessing a number written on the back of the scorecard.

After the first team to serve has been determined, the player on that team who is standing on the right side of the court (when facing the net) becomes the first server. This player continues to serve as long as their team is winning the rallies (meaning that the other team is the first to commit a fault and end the rally).

When the serving team wins a rally, they earn a point. When you win a point, you and your partner trade sides of the court (right and left). You never serve in the same direction (or to the same opponent) twice in a row. To remember this, just think, "When you win, you switch." It's like a do-si-do in square dancing. (If you've ever square danced, that analogy should hit home for you.)

When the serving team commits a fault and loses the rally, the first server no longer gets to keep serving. Now it's their partner's turn to serve. (This rule has one big exception, which is introduced a little later in this section. For now, just roll with it.) This player is naturally referred to as the second server. Because the serving team didn't just win a point, however, the partners don't trade places but instead stay put. ("When you lose, you linger.")

The second server continues serving, alternating sides, until their team loses another rally. That team has now run out of chances to serve. It's the other team's turn to serve and try to win some points. Whenever the serve transfers from one team to the other, it's known as a *sideout.*

When a sideout occurs, the player who is standing on the right side of the court for the new serving team begins serving. They continue serving and winning points until their team commits a fault and loses the rally. Then their partner starts serving (from whichever side they happen to be standing on) until their team commits a second fault, resulting in a sideout back to the other team.

It is a rule that before you can serve, you must call all three numbers of the score. Call your own team's score first, your opponents' score second, and either a "one" or a "two," depending on whether you're the first or second server for that round. You'll often hear players asking each other, "Am I the 'one' or the 'two'?" This is just shorthand for asking, "Am I the first server or the second server?" If your team is ahead, be sure to call the score extra loudly for all to hear. If your team is behind, just mumble it under your breath.

**REMEMBER**

The first server is always the player standing on the right side of the court when the ball comes back over to that team to serve again. Just because you were the first server (the "one") a minute ago doesn't mean that you'll stay the "one" for the entire game. Don't get married to your number! It will change constantly throughout the game.

Just when this was all starting to make sense, the pickleball powers-that-be decided to create an exception to the aforementioned rules, just to drive pickleball players crazy. Note that at the opening of the game, the first team to serve was chosen at random. To make things more fair, that team gets only one chance to serve for that round, rather than the usual two. This rule prevents them from racking up a ton of points before the other team has had an opportunity to serve and score. For this reason, the opening score of a pickleball game is actually 0–0–2, not 0–0–1. As soon as the original serving team commits a fault, it's a sideout, and the other team gets to serve. From that point on, both teams get two chances to serve on every round.

Games are typically played to 11, but you must win by two points. So if it's 11–10, the game continues until someone wins by a margin of two points. Some games end at 20–18! In some tournament situations, games are played to 15 or even 21, but in recreational play, games to 11 are the norm.

**TIP**

When a game ends, players customarily come to the net and gently tap paddles, saying, "Good game!" This is an important part of pickleball etiquette, so always strive to be a good sport, whether you win or lose. See Chapter 9 in Book 6 for more details on pickleball etiquette.

## Singles scoring: Know your odds (and evens)

Keeping score in singles is quite a bit easier than doubles because the third number no longer applies. Whew! However, singles scoring does require you to know the difference between an odd number and an even number.

The game starts at 0–0, with the starting server on the right side of the court (facing the net). The right side is known as the *even side*. Because the server's score is 0, the server should be standing on the even side.

If the server wins the rally, their score becomes 1. Because this is an odd number, the server must switch to the left side, or *odd side* of the court, and serve from there. They continue switching sides as long as the server is serving and winning.

Unlike doubles, a "team" gets only one chance to serve, which is why you can ditch the third number altogether. If the server commits a fault, it's automatically a sideout and their opponent now gets to serve. The new server should begin serving from either the even or odd side, depending on whether their own score is even or odd. The receiver should line up diagonally from the server regardless of their current score.

So if you're serving and the score is 7–2, you will be serving from the odd side of the court. Your opponent will line up to receive the serve from their odd side as well. If you lose the rally and it's a sideout, your opponent will begin serving from their even side (because their score is 2) and you'll line up diagonally from them.

Just as in doubles, singles games are typically played to 11 points and you have to win by two, but the game can sometimes be played to 15 or 21 in tournaments, depending on the format.

## Rally scoring: Perhaps coming to a court near you

Much debate occurs these days about possibly changing pickleball over to a scoring system called *rally scoring,* which has every rally ending with a point scored, regardless of which team served. If your team wins the rally, you get a point, plus you get to serve next. If you were already serving, you just switch places with your partner and keep serving.

If the serving team's score is an odd number, they must serve from the odd side of the court, and vice versa for an even score. When a sideout occurs, the player standing on the side that matches their team's score (meaning either even or odd) will be the server. Similar to singles scoring, the score has only two numbers, not three.

This system has both pros and cons. Most people agree it would be simpler for new players to learn. However, the main reason for the consideration of rally scoring is that it makes match times more predictable, which helps with scheduling and televising matches. Of course, television coverage means more advertising money and attention coming to the sport. That makes for bigger pro tours, more prize money, and better odds of getting pickleball into large international events like the Olympics.

Rally scoring does make games tend to go a bit faster, which can be considered a pro or a con, depending on your point of view. Many people feel it takes away some of the strategic nuances of the game. For instance, with traditional scoring, a first server may decide to take bigger risks, knowing their partner has a chance to serve if they make a mistake. The main argument against rally scoring seems to be that it defies tradition and erases some of the uniqueness of the sport. Change is always hard, especially with a game so beloved for its many quirks.

# Making Line Calls

Calling the ball "in" or "out" as accurately as possible is very important in pickleball. When you call lines honestly, you help to improve the integrity of this great sport.

It's both your right and your responsibility to call the balls landing on your side of the court. Your opponents must call the balls on their side of the court. Even in refereed matches in professional tournaments, the players are responsible for making line calls. (Referees are primarily there to keep score and watch for foot faults. They will provide opinions on line calls only if asked, and most of the time they choose not to overrule the original call.) Spectators are not allowed to make line calls.

REMEMBER

Here's the golden rule for line calls: "If in doubt, you can't call it out!" In other words, if you didn't clearly see the ball land out of bounds, it's considered in. See Figure 7-6 for balls called both in and out. You need to be able to clearly see space between the line and the ball in order to call it out.

FIGURE 7-6:
A ball that should be called in (left), versus a ball that can be called out (right).

From Aniko Kiezel

If two partners disagree on a call, the ball is considered in. The benefit of the doubt should always go to your opponent. If you ask your opponents for their opinion, you must abide by it. But if you're so unclear that you're asking for third and fourth opinions, it means enough doubt exists that you cannot call it out. (Remember the golden rule.)

REMEMBER

If the ball lands on any line, it is in, except when the serve lands on the kitchen line. Because the kitchen line is technically part of the kitchen, the rule states that the serve must completely clear the kitchen, including the kitchen line.

You don't need to audibly call the ball in while the ball is in play. Just keep on playing and don't say anything. If it lands out, yell "out!" or signal that it was out by pointing your index finger straight up in the air.

Call the lines as promptly as possible, but not until the ball has actually bounced. Calling a ball before it bounces is considered player communication, rather than a line call, and you'll want to choose different words so as not to cause confusion. It's fine to call a ball out after you've already hit it, but be sure to call it before your opponents hit their next shot. It's extremely poor form to say, "Hey, remember that shot from five minutes ago? That was actually out. Looks like I won after all!"

# It's in the Rule Book! More Rules to Know

Every year, USA Pickleball (USAP) puts out a new version of its official rule book. The rules committee makes revisions each year, and keeping up with the latest changes is important. The proposed changes always generate a lot of lively discussion among players.

**TIP**

You'll probably want to carry an up-to-date rule book in your bag at all times. You can purchase an official rule book at USAPickleball.org. Read it all the way through at least once (perfect before bed, if you're having trouble sleeping!) to familiarize yourself with how the game is organized. Then hang on to it for reference in case you ever need to settle a rule dispute among friends. It's an investment in your game, plus it supports the governing bodies of the sport.

Here are some more interesting rules you should know about as you dive deeper into the game. Some of these situations sound strange, but almost all of them will eventually happen to you as you play more:

» **You are allowed to strike the ball twice on one hit (known as a carry), as long as it is unintentional and is one continuous motion.**

» **You can switch the paddle between hands when you're playing.** You can also hit the ball with both hands on your paddle. However, you can play with only one paddle at a time, so don't step out onto the court with a paddle in each hand!

» **Your paddle must be in your possession when it strikes the ball.** No throwing your paddle at the ball!

» **If your serve hits the receiver's partner before the ball bounces, it's your point.** This is sometimes called a "Nasty Nelson," after one particularly colorful player who was known for doing it intentionally.

» **The ball has to bounce to be considered out, so don't catch balls mid-air that you believe are flying out.** Doing so will be considered a fault on your team.

» **It's legal to hit the ball around the net post without the ball actually going over the net.** This is called an Around the Post (ATP) shot.

» **If the ball bounces on your side of the court, but a strong wind (or heavy spin) causes it to fly back over the net to your opponent's side of the court, you must touch the ball before it bounces again or you lose the point.** You may reach over the net to hit the ball, as long as you don't touch the net. If you're extremely talented, or lucky, you'll reach over and hit the ball straight into your opponent's side of the net to win the rally!

>> **Some portable nets have a horizontal crossbar along the bottom of the net.** If your shot goes over the net and hits the crossbar on your opponent's side of the net before it bounces in the court, the point must be replayed. (If it hits the crossbar on your own side of the net, it's a fault as usual.)

>> **If the ball hits the net post, ceiling, basketball hoop, or other permanent fixture before bouncing, it is considered out of bounds and is a fault on the team who hit it.**

>> **A ball passing through the net cords (between the net and the post) is a fault on the player who hit it.** The ball must either go over the net or around the side of the net post to count.

>> **Deliberately distracting your opponent while they are trying to hit, such as by yelling, stomping your feet, or waving your arms, is not allowed.** Although pickleball courts are rarely silent — laughing, trash talking, and strange grunts and noises are expected — there's a clear line between having fun and being a jerk.

# Chapter **8**

# Pickleball Equipment and Apparel

Curious about the pickleball "merch" currently available? Almost every major sports manufacturer and retailer has jumped into the pickleball market. You can now find countless paddle brands, clothing lines, and gadgets for pickleball enthusiasts. This chapter guides you through the aisles of the pickleball retail scene. You'll find out how to choose your first paddle, what types of balls to buy, and which other accessories are worth buying. Read on for the very best in pickleball retail therapy!

## You Can't Take the Court without a Paddle

Without question, your most important piece of equipment when taking to the pickleball court is your paddle. Although it may feel unfamiliar the first time you pick one up, you're about to form a close relationship with this inanimate object.

Beginners often ask more experienced players, "Which paddle should I buy?" This is a lot like asking someone else to pick out eyeglasses or shoes for you. It all comes down to finding "the one" for you (until something newer and better looking comes along).

WARNING

Friends don't let friends play with wooden paddles. They are terrible for your arm and your game. They do make excellent kindling for your pickleball club's next bonfire.

## Paddle standards: The long and the short of it

This section guides you toward choosing your first paddle, and in case things don't work out between you two, your next paddle (or five) as well.

REMEMBER

You can find hundreds of paddle models out there. Some players purchase only a USA Pickleball–approved paddle. All approved paddles must conform to certain technical and quality standards. These standards were primarily created to ensure fairness in tournament play. Even if you don't plan to compete in tournaments, you want a paddle that maintains the integrity of the sport by conforming to the standards. You'll also be comforted knowing it has passed tests for consistency and overall quality.

When determining whether a paddle meets their approval standards, USA Pickleball looks at the following characteristics:

>> **Material:** Paddles must be made of rigid, noncompressible material. Rubber-like materials aren't allowed. The paddle can't have any moving parts, springs, electrical, electronic, or mechanical features of any kind.

>> **Surface:** The paddle's hitting surface can't have any bumps, holes, or rough sandpaper-like textures designed to add extra spin on the ball, nor can the paddle have any reflective surfaces that could affect an opposing player's vision.

>> **Length and width:** The paddle length can't exceed 17 inches, including the handle. The combined length and width of the paddle can't exceed 24 inches. So if your paddle is especially long, it has to be a bit narrower, and vice versa.

>> **Thickness:** There are no restrictions on paddle thickness.

>> **Weight:** There are no restrictions on paddle weight.

# Understanding paddle technologies

As pickleball explodes in popularity, new models are being released every week. Comparing paddle features can be difficult because most brands use proprietary technologies, often with cryptic names and marketing language inevitably guaranteeing "More spin! Greater touch! Increased power! Six-pack abs! Financial independence in 90 days!"

Be careful of the hype. An expensive paddle won't magically take you from novice to pro, but the right combination of features can certainly make playing more enjoyable. It all comes down to trying different things and deciding what feels right for you.

**WARNING**

One material never recommended is wood. When pickleball was first invented, the paddles were made of wood. We're guessing you wouldn't try to play tennis in the 21st century with a wooden racquet — and the same goes for pickleball. "Beginner sets" made of wood are a waste of money, unless you're buying them for the kids to destroy, which sounds fun.

## The paddle's core

The first major factor to consider when testing paddle technologies is core construction. The *core* refers to the middle part of your paddle that is sandwiched between the two hitting surfaces. Cores can be solid or use a honeycomb structure. Honeycomb is popular because it provides strength while remaining lightweight. Turns out bees really know what they're doing. Solid cores offer a greater sense of touch, but they don't tend to have the same amount of "pop" (rebound), which some players prefer.

Here are the three most common types of core materials used:

>> **Nomex:** A type of cardboard dipped in resin, Nomex was the first material ever used in composite paddles and remains popular today. You get plenty of power and pop because this material is extremely hard, but it can make your shots a bit unruly.

>> **Aluminum:** Aluminum does not provide as much power but is preferred by some players for increased control and touch. One drawback is that aluminum paddles can dent easily.

>> **Polymer:** These cores are made from a plastic blend that is very durable. They tend to feel a bit softer and have a more solid hitting sensation. Polymer strikes a good balance between power and touch, and many new paddles coming out on the market today utilize this type of core.

### The paddle's surface

The second factor to consider is the hitting surface. Just as with paddle cores, each type of surface has its own pros and cons. You currently have three main options when choosing a paddle surface:

>> **Graphite:** An enduringly popular choice, graphite paddles are thin, light, and stiff. The stiffness offers a lot of feel down through your hand, and this increased sense of touch is why many players prefer them. The downside of graphite is that the sweet spot tends to be smaller, and this surface can crack or chip easily.

>> **Composite/fiberglass:** Composite paddles are softer than graphite and typically heavier. They do usually offer a larger sweet spot than graphite paddles and are more forgiving for beginners. Composite paddles are generally durable but can be prone to developing dead spots over time.

>> **Carbon fiber:** Carbon fiber is much stiffer than fiberglass and much more durable than graphite. Its high deflection rate can give you more precise control when aiming the ball. In addition, the "weave" of the fibers offers enhanced spin. Unfortunately, these paddles tend to be the most expensive.

You can also check out a few other technical features while shopping for a paddle:

>> **Edgeless paddles** offer more hitting area because they lack the protruding protective edge guard that most paddles have around their outside rim. The edge guard is there to protect the paddle from chips and cracks, so with an edgeless paddle, you need to be a bit more careful not to drop your prized possession.

>> **Unibody paddles** consist of a single molded piece of material rather than a separate paddle face and handle glued together. They offer high durability and increased feedback down through your hand.

>> **Vibration-dampening technologies** claim to reduce the risk of tendonitis by absorbing some of the shock of the ball hitting your paddle.

## Picking your perfect paddle shape and grip

After you've settled on your ideal core construction and hitting surface, think about the shape of your paddle. Within the USA Pickleball equipment standards, you can still find plenty of variety in paddle sizes and shapes. (Figure 8-1 shows some different kinds of paddle shapes.)

>> **Standard:** A paddle measuring approximately 16 inches long and 8 inches wide is considered to be standard shape. This shape offers a nice balance between reach and control, with an average-sized sweet spot located just

above the center of the paddle face. Within this standard category, you see some variation in how the corners are shaped — squared off, rounded, or angled — that affect its aerodynamics.

>> **Wide body:** A wide-body paddle is any paddle wider than the standard 8 inches. Consequently, the length will be shorter by the same amount. Wide-body paddles can be great for beginners because they provide a large, forgiving sweet spot. They won't feel very quick or aerodynamic in your hand, though.

>> **Elongated:** A paddle with a length greater than 16 inches is considered an elongated paddle. To have extra length, you have to sacrifice the equivalent width, which means a narrower sweet spot. Elongated paddles are popular with singles players because they provide added reach.

>> **Blade shape:** An extreme version of the elongated paddle, blades can be as narrow as 6 inches wide. To use one, you have to be pretty confident in your ability to strike the ball accurately in the center of your paddle every time. Some advanced players feel that the lever-like properties of this paddle help them to "whip" the paddle head at faster speeds.

>> **Oval:** Oval-shaped paddles are designed to mimic the shape of a tennis racquet. They have an aerodynamic feel and a centralized sweet spot. You may find you miss shots by not having any corners on your paddle, because sometimes hitting off the corner is the best you can manage!

FIGURE 8-1:
Some different paddle shapes.

*From Aniko Kiezel*

CHAPTER 8 **Pickleball Equipment and Apparel**

**REMEMBER**

Just as important as the shape of your paddle face is the size and shape of the handle (known as the *grip*). You want a paddle that feels comfortable in your hand. If you pick up a paddle for the first time and it doesn't feel comfortable, immediately put it back down!

Choosing the right size and shape of grip can also help prevent stress injuries to your hand or elbow. The wrong-sized grip, either too small or too large, can cause you to resort to improper technique. If you're purchasing your first paddle and want to err on the side of caution, go for a smaller-size grip. You can always replace the grip wrap with a thicker one (described later in this chapter).

When looking at grips, keep these four factors in mind:

>> **Size (circumference):** When referring to a grip's size, manufacturers are talking about the circumference. Most grips are between 3⅞ inches and 4½ inches in circumference. You should select one based on the size of your hand. (Figure 8-2 illustrates how to measure your hand.) Measure from the tip of your ring finger to the middle crease in your palm, and choose a grip that matches this length. Again, this measurement is just a general guideline; the most important gauge is that it feels comfortable in your hand.

>> **Length:** Paddles with elongated faces have proportionately shorter handles, and vice versa. If you use a two-handed backhand, you'll likely want a paddle with an extra-long handle.

>> **Shape/bevel:** Grip shapes vary from more flat and rectangular to more square to more rounded-off beveling. Some paddles have a larger "butt" at the end to anchor the bottom of your hand against. As far as shape, it's entirely a matter of personal preference.

>> **Wrap:** Paddle handles are typically wooden, so a rubberized wrap is added for comfort (who wants splinters?) and to help prevent your hand from slipping. Some are made from thin, smooth material, some are extra thick for added cushioning, and some have ridges (known as a contour grip) for your fingers to settle into. If you don't like your paddle's original grip wrap, you can always swap it out; see the later section "Grasping at grips, gloves, and overgrips" for more on replacement grips.

## Weighing your options

When choosing a paddle, there's one more topic to weigh in on, and it's an important one: paddle weight. Here's the good news: The difference between the lightest and heaviest paddles out there is only around 2 ounces. That's about the same as 12 pieces of paper, or two AA batteries, or a large egg.

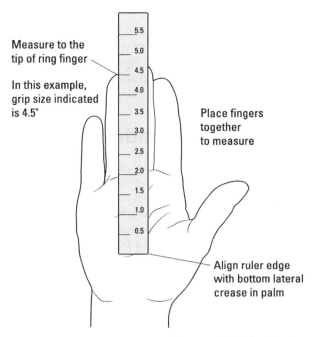

Measure to the tip of ring finger

In this example, grip size indicated is 4.5"

Place fingers together to measure

Align ruler edge with bottom lateral crease in palm

**FIGURE 8-2:**
How to measure your hand for the right paddle grip.

© John Wiley & Sons, Inc.

Although the weight of an egg is hardly going to make or "break" your pickle-ball career, many players do have a clear preference in paddle weight. Before you shell out your hard-earned money for a new paddle, consider the following weight categories:

» **Lightweight paddles fall in the range of 6.0–7.2 ounces.** They are slightly quicker at the net and offer good control. On the down side, you will struggle to get a lot of power when swinging a light paddle. Many beginners like to use a light paddle until they build up their strength.

» **Midweight paddles range from 7.3–8.3 ounces.** This is the most popular weight range because it offers a balance of control and power.

» **Heavyweight paddles are above 8.4 ounces.** You'll get tons of power swinging one of these beasts, but they are harder to control and can be fatiguing for your arm.

Individual paddles of the same make and model will have slight discrepancies in weight due to the manufacturing process. The difference typically equates to about the weight of three pennies. Only highly advanced players would be able to detect such a difference. If you're concerned, some manufacturers offer a "guaranteed weight" option when ordering.

## Choosing your first paddle

Armed with all the information in the previous sections, you may feel both empowered and overwhelmed. Spending weeks exploring every possible option before purchasing your first paddle is not realistic. You have to start somewhere, and it's completely normal to purchase your first paddle with plans to upgrade in a few months. As you develop your personal preferences, the choices will start to narrow. Or, most likely, you'll demo a friend's shiny new paddle one day and develop an acute case of Paddle Envy. At that point, you've made up your mind — nothing else will do!

TIP

Here are some tips for choosing your first "starter" paddle:

>> **Try some demo paddles, if possible.** By far the best way to choose a paddle is to test different models and pick the one you like the best. Paddle demo programs are often available through local pickleball/tennis shops, paddle brand reps, and online retailers.

>> **Don't assume that expensive is better.** The price of a paddle can be influenced by a lot of things, and not all of them reflect its playability. You may end up hating everything about your pricey paddle and be stuck with it while you save up for a new one.

>> **Match the paddle to your personality.** Are you an aggressive competitor who enjoys pushing the limits of strength and speed? You may gravitate toward the power game. Are you a thoughtful, strategic person who prefers to be patient and wait for your moment? You may enjoy more of a controlled, soft game. Choose a paddle accordingly.

>> **Avoid extremes.** As a new player, you'd be smart to start with a midweight, standard-shaped paddle. That will give you a baseline to work from so that you'll have an easier time deciding which direction to explore next — heavier, lighter, softer, stiffer, and so on. The other advantage is that you can customize your very "average" paddle to test different characteristics. For example, adding lead tape to the outside edge will increase the overall weight and change the paddle dynamics.

>> **Make comfort your first priority.** As a newbie, you can expect to develop a few blisters and feel sore in muscles you forgot you had — no need to add to the pain by using a paddle that isn't comfortable to hold.

# Pickleball Is Nothing without Pickleballs

In describing the game to the uninformed, you may say that it uses a plastic ball with holes in it, similar to a wiffle ball. When the game was first invented, it did in fact use a wiffle ball. However, a modern pickleball is quite different, from the shape of the holes down to the type of plastic.

## Ball standards: It's not a wiffle ball!

Pickleballs are highly engineered and must conform to strict standards to be USA Pickleball–approved. Manufacturers have spent a lot of money on research and development to try to come up with the perfect pickleball.

An approved pickleball must have between 26 and 40 holes. It's made of plastic that's molded with a smooth surface and free of texturing. It must be one uniform color except for identification markings. The most common colors are yellow, neon green, white, and orange. In recreational play, players typically write their name or initials on their balls with a permanent marker.

To receive the USA Pickleball Approved stamp of approval, balls must weigh between 0.78 and 0.935 ounces and measure between 2.87 and 2.97 inches in diameter. This is just slightly larger than a tennis ball. Bounce height and compression are also important because these greatly affect playability, and they are measured under highly specific conditions.

## Counting the holes: Indoor versus outdoor balls

Balls are manufactured a little bit differently for indoor play versus outdoor play. (See Figure 8-3 for a look at both.) When playing outdoors, you have to deal with wind and more abrasive court surfaces, usually asphalt or concrete. Indoor courts are typically very smooth, wooden gymnasium floors. These tend to absorb more energy from the ball.

Some indoor venues, such as indoor tennis courts, have outdoor surfaces. In those venues, the outdoor balls usually perform better than the indoor balls.

The main differences between indoor and outdoor balls are the number of holes, type of plastic, and total weight. Table 8-1 explains these and other differences between indoor and outdoor balls.

FIGURE 8-3:
An indoor ball
(left) versus
an outdoor
ball (right).

From Aniko Kiezel

**TABLE 8-1**

## Comparing Outdoor and Indoor Balls

| Outdoor Balls | Indoor Balls |
|---|---|
| Slightly heavier (~0.9 oz) | Slightly lighter (~0.8 oz) |
| Slightly larger in diameter | Slightly smaller in diameter |
| Harder plastic | Softer plastic |
| Smaller holes, and more of them (usually 40) | Larger holes, and fewer of them (usually 26) |
| Easier to hit hard | More difficult to hit hard |
| Harder to control | Easier to control |
| More painful when it hits you (duck!) | Less painful when you take a shot to the body |
| More breakable; prone to going out of round (that is, losing its shape) | Less breakable |
| Noisier | Quieter |

WARNING

Don't store your pickleball gear, especially balls, in your garage or car. They are greatly affected by temperature. Heat can cause them to melt slightly and go out of round. Severe cold makes the balls brittle. To be safe, keep your pickleball gear indoors.

# Getting touchy feely: Hard versus soft balls

Some pickleballs are harder than others. The past decade has seen a great debate about using harder, less forgiving balls versus softer, easier-to-control balls. Some high-level players find that the slicker, harder, faster ball makes the game more challenging. Other players prefer the slower pace and extra "touch and feel" provided by softer balls.

Here are examples of "hard" outdoor balls currently on the market:

>> CORE

>> Dura Fast 40

>> Engage Tour

>> Franklin X-40

>> Selkirk SLK Competition

>> TOP

Examples of "soft" outdoor balls currently on the market:

>> ONIX Fuse G2

>> ONIX PURE 2

>> Penn 40

>> Selkirk SLK Hybrid

>> Wilson TRU 32

# Deciding which balls to buy

Pickleballs typically cost between $2 and $4 each. You have many brands of balls to choose from, with more coming out all the time, but don't feel overwhelmed! The easiest answer is to just purchase the same ball the players around you are using.

Indoor venues often provide the balls, but this isn't always the case, so be prepared with at least one indoor ball in your bag.

If you want to purchase your ideal ball for recreational play, choose a ball that pairs nicely with your style of play. If you struggle to control the ball, or enjoy slower-paced games, you may want to pick a softer ball. If you prefer faster-paced rallies, choose a hard ball. If you're on a tight budget, consider purchasing softer balls because they will last longer. Many players in cold climates purchase harder balls in the summer and softer balls in the winter because the cold temperatures cause the hard balls to break easily.

WARNING

Consider buying only balls that have been tested and approved by USA Pickleball. Many cheap imitations out there just won't bounce right or stay round for more than a game or two.

TIP

If you're getting ready to compete in a tournament, find out ahead of time what ball will be used so that you can practice with that brand.

# Pickleball Fashion (an Oxymoron?)

There are no strict guidelines for pickleball fashion, and you'll find more about that wacky world here. Safety and comfort are a must, of course.

## From the catwalk to the courts

Although celebrities are playing and falling in love with pickleball in growing numbers, you probably won't see Anna Wintour of *Vogue* promoting the fashion of the sport anytime soon. The beauty of pickleball lies in its simplicity, and that principle also applies to "What do I wear to play?" As with any sport, it's important to wear clothing with safety in mind.

Pickleball apparel has two requirements: 1) comfort and 2) climate-appropriateness. In addition to T-shirts and shorts, you often see tennis or golf-style clothing and other athletic wear with wicking properties. Hats, visors, and sweatbands can complete your ensemble. If it's cold, sweatpants, sweatshirts, light jackets, and puffy vests are totally acceptable. In tournament play, doubles teams may wear matching outfits. This is meant as an intimidation tactic to make you think, "That team really has it together!" It's also just fun to be matchy-matchy with your buddy.

REMEMBER

A rule we're glad to see incorporated into the rule book is Rule 2.G.2, which states, "Depictions, graphics, insignias, pictures, and writing on apparel must be in good taste." Remember, courtesy is important.

In addition to the apparel basics, get ready for the wide, wacky, and wonderful world of pickleball fashion. This is a world where crazy T-shirt puns, bright shoes, silly socks, and zany visors are fairly common. Just imagine neon shorts with bright-green pickleballs all over them, paired with a T-shirt that says *Pickleball Ninja,* topped off with a tie-dyed bucket hat (ninjas love tie dye) and, well, you get the idea. Once spotted: "Adulting can wait. Let's play pickleball!"

As you can see from the previous "fashion" examples, pickleball is all about playing safely, comfortably, and then hitting the courts and having tons of fun!

## Sliding into suitable shoes

How well you move on the court is directly related to the shoes you wear. A well-fitting, quality court shoe will help you glide effortlessly across the court. All court shoes offer heightened durability, stability, and comfort compared to a typical athletic shoe like training or running shoes. Proper court shoes are stiffer, more stable, and specifically designed for those tricky lateral moves that are inherent to pickleball play.

WARNING

Running shoes are designed to only go in one direction — forward. Attempting to zigzag around the court in running shoes can cause you to roll an ankle or otherwise trip and fall. And never, ever play in sandals, knobby-soled shoes such as hiking boots, or bare feet.

The soles of court shoes are designed to grip court surfaces better, which is useful for quickly taking off in any direction. Speaking of soles, make sure that you get indoor court shoes if you're playing on wooden gymnasium floors. Indoor court shoes usually have a beige gummy sole that helps grip ultra-smooth floors. Unfortunately, those gummy indoor soles wear down very quickly on abrasive outdoor courts. So if you play on both types of surfaces, you should definitely consider getting dedicated pairs of indoor and outdoor shoes.

TIP

If you're playing indoors on a wooden floor, you'll find that the dust on the floor can build up on the soles of your shoes. The way to make them grippy again is to moisten them. If you aren't a dainty type, just wipe your sweaty palm on your soles and they will immediately become grippy. If you are more refined, keep a lightly damp towel courtside.

For outdoor play, look for tennis, pickleball, or outdoor basketball shoes. Suitable indoor court shoes may be sold as badminton, racquetball, indoor basketball, or volleyball shoes. Don't assume that the brand you bought last year still fits exactly the same this year; manufacturers constantly change sizing and fit.

## Headwear for form and function

Pickleball headwear ideally needs to be lightweight, breathable, and washable. Many styles include wicking for maximum comfort while you're sweating out your big match. Some players prefer visors over hats, but either way, headwear is primarily about protecting your eyes from the glare of the sun (or indoor court lighting). If you're playing outdoors on a sunny day without sunglasses or a hat, you're basically wearing a sign that says, "Please lob me!"

Hats and headbands are also useful for keeping hair and sweat out of your eyes when playing. Windy days are bad enough for pickleball without your hair repeatedly whipping across your face. Then there's the dreaded "sunscreen-induced blindness" caused by sweating off the sunscreen you so responsibly applied to your forehead that morning.

WARNING

Please, wear sunscreen. And if you're without hair on top of your head, choose a hat over a visor or headband. Skin cancer is no joke.

You'll see hats in every color of the rainbow, or even the whole rainbow on one hat. Baseball caps, bucket hats, beanies, and floppy sun hats are all very common. Headwear is a great way to create a signature look that makes you recognizable everywhere you play.

## Protective eyewear: Still cheaper than your co-pay

Wearing protective eyewear while playing should be nonnegotiable. Pickleball players have gotten hit in the eye and suffered permanent damage because of it. Typically, it's not a ball hit directly by your opponent, but one ricocheting off your own (or your partner's) paddle that finds its way to your face.

To avoid injury, simply cover your eyes with protective eyewear, sunglasses, or corrective glasses. Sporting goods stores sell athletic eyewear in the racquetball, pickleball, or shooting sections. Some come as a set with interchangeable lenses in different tints. If you're on a really tight budget, you can pick up safety glasses from a hardware store for under $10. Any kind of sunglasses, from cheap drugstore ones to designer frames, will protect you as well. Just keep those eyeballs covered!

If you wear prescription lenses, eyewear manufacturers offer custom sports glasses in many styles. Many players play in their everyday glasses, including bifocals and trifocals. Some can play with them just fine, but if you find that you're struggling to strike the ball on the sweet spot of your paddle, the problem may be your glasses.

**TIP**

If you sweat a lot, you may need glasses that have extra ventilation and don't fit super snugly against your face to reduce fogging. You may also want to throw some anti-fog glasses cleaner and a cleaning cloth in your bag.

**WARNING**

Some players wear eyeglass frames with the lenses popped out. Although this approach is probably better than nothing, it doesn't offer full protection for your delicate eyeballs. Whatever glasses you get, they need to be comfortable so that you won't be tempted to play without them. Consider investing a little more in a stylish, high-quality pair that you don't mind wearing (and that won't negatively affect your game). Please be proactive and protect your peepers.

# Going Gaga for Gadgets and Accessories

As with most sports enthusiasts, pickleball players tend to love their gadgets and gear. You can make pickleball a very inexpensive sport to play, or you can spend every available dime on more equipment. It's totally up to you! (If you have a significant other, they may have an opinion on this as well, but that's between the two of you.)

## Bag it up

You'll definitely want a bag of some sort to carry your gear to and from the courts. Players use all types of bags — totes, backpacks, sling bags, and tennis or racquetball bags. There are even pickleball-specific bags you can purchase.

Here are some features you may want in a pickleball bag:

>> **Multiple pockets of varying sizes:** Nobody wants to spend ten minutes digging through a cavernous bag to find the asthma inhaler. Most of us appreciate having multiple pockets so that we can easily find things.

>> **A padded paddle compartment:** A padded compartment is the perfect way to keep your precious paddles safe without needing separate paddle covers. You also get the satisfying feeling of slipping your paddle into its "holster" at the end of a hard play session.

>> **A separate and vented shoe compartment:** These keep your smelly shoes away from your less smelly stuff.

>> **An insulated area to keep your cold stuff cold:** If you're planning any long days or hot afternoons at the courts, an insulated area in your bag for snacks and drinks is a great feature.

>> **A hook to hang your bag on the fence:** If your bag doesn't come with a hook but has some sort of top loop or handle, you can always add your own carabiner.

TIP

Get a bag that is just big enough for what you actually want to carry to the courts. If you get a giant bag, you will most likely fill it with things you don't really need. And a heavy bag means more wear and tear on your body every time you have to hoist that thing like a soldier in boot camp. A smaller bag also makes stuff easier to find. For tournament play, though, a larger bag can be very helpful. You may need clothing changes, towels, food, an extra paddle, and room for all your medals.

## Grasping at grips, gloves, and overgrips

The original factory grip on most paddles is just fine. It will get you going and stay nice and tacky — until it doesn't anymore. Friction from repetitive use, sweat, and dirt will cause your grip to become less tacky over time.

TIP

Instead of tossing your paddle, try one of these solutions:

>> **Replace the original factory grip.** You can purchase either the same or a different grip for around $10. Some great videos online show exactly how to replace your old grip. If you purchase from a local tennis/pickleball shop, ask them to wrap it for you.

>> **Try a contour grip.** One option to consider is to replace your grip with a contour grip. This is a style of grip that has raised ridges to fit your fingers into. Many players like the feel of the contour grip because it helps give them a more consistent hand position.

>> **Add an overgrip.** The most popular and economical way of dealing with slippery grips is the addition of an overgrip. They are thin wraps that go over your regular grip. They absorb sweat and add tackiness. You can find videos online that show you how to apply an overgrip.

>> **Wear a glove.** Many players choose to wear a glove to keep their hand from slipping. Others find that wearing a glove sacrifices some of the "feel" you need to finesse your shots. If you do wear a glove, make sure it fits well, tending toward being slightly tight. Shop for pickleball, racquetball, or golf gloves.

>> **Try a grip-enhancing product.** Many products are on the market that help absorb sweat and improve tackiness. You can use a liquid or powder grip enhancer, such as those used by gymnasts and weight lifters. You can also try a tacky towel, much like what woodworkers use to remove sawdust from their projects.

# Unpacking the world of portable nets

If you're playing on a court that doesn't have a permanent net installed, you'll need a portable net. These can range in price from $100 to over $2,000. Check out models from Douglas Premier, PickleNet, and SwiftNet 2.1.

When shopping for a portable net system, consider the following features:

>> **Weight:** If you're carrying the net to the courts every time you play, you want a lightweight net. If the net will be left up all the time, you want a sturdier, heavier net that won't blow over with the slightest breeze.

>> **Dimensions:** If you plan to use the net for regular games on a standard-sized court, double-check that the net you're buying is regulation width (22 feet). Mini or half-court nets are available if you're just using them for practice sessions.

>> **Frame construction:** Almost all nets are made of powder-coated steel or aluminum. Most nets have horizontal crossbars along the bottom, but the shape and placement vary. Almost all regulation-sized nets have a solid vertical center rod that maintains the 34-inch net height in the center.

>> **Assembly time:** When shopping for a portable net, you see that nearly all of them claim to be quick and easy to set up. Generally, the fewer parts, the better.

>> **Wheels:** If you're looking for a net that will be left inside a gym or other multiuse facility, get one with wheels on it. With luck, the nets can be easily moved out of the way when not in use. Wheels add weight (as well as cost and assembly time), so if you're setting up and taking down the nets frequently, don't get one with wheels.

>> **Replacement net availability:** Nets take more abuse than you may think. Between all the setup and takedown, balls pummeling the nets at high speeds, players running into them, and harsh outdoor elements, you will need a replacement net long before the frame wears out. A temporary net left permanently outdoors will be looking pretty sad after about a year. Find out whether the manufacturer of your net system sells replacement nets and, if so, how much they cost.

# Buying Equipment Locally and Online

Now that you have a serious wish list going for pickleball gear, where do you buy it?

A good option for purchasing gear is to support local small businesses. You often get the best-quality service, and your dollars stay in your community. There are most likely players and dealers in your area who represent various brands and allow you to purchase paddles from them directly on the courts. Small tennis/paddle sports shops are a great place to shop, too, because they usually have demo paddles to check out. They are also fine places to try on and buy court shoes.

Large sporting-goods chains are starting to clue in to the pickleball craze and are offering more equipment. See if these chains carry multiple brands, or your selection will be limited.

Obviously, if you don't live in an area with brick-and-mortar sporting goods stores, you'll probably need to shop online. The major online retailers are Amazon, Fromuth Pickleball, Pickleball Central, Pickleball Galaxy, and Total Pickleball. You can also purchase directly from the manufacturers' websites. Some online retailers will let you try paddles or offer you a free return if you don't like the paddle you bought.

**REMEMBER**

You can spend as much or as little as you want on gear. Pickleball is a very affordable sport. If you have a decent paddle, a ball or two, good stable court shoes, and eye protection, you are ready to hit the courts!

# Chapter 9

# Heading to the Pickleball Courts

As a beginning player, you are totally focused on getting the ball over the net. This chapter, however, aims to broaden your view of the sport and help you understand the different kinds of courts to play on, the etiquette of pickleball, and some particularities (or maybe peculiarities) of this sport.

Depending on where you live, you might have dozens of different venues to choose from when you start to play. It can seem overwhelming at first to figure out where to play, at what time, and with whom. On the other hand, your town may have only one or two established clubs, and you may feel intimidated about being the newbie. As a new player, finding your niche can sometimes take a little time. The good news is that with the exploding popularity of the sport among people of all ages, genders, backgrounds, and athletic abilities, you're sure to find a community (and build some amazing new friendships along the way).

Through familiarizing yourself with pickleball etiquette and culture, you'll gain the confidence to visit new venues and become a pickleball chameleon, ready to mingle and fit in with all kinds of groups. (Or at least you'll know, "It's not me, it's them" if you aren't digging the vibe at certain courts.) The global pickleball community is full of wonderful, friendly people with an enthusiasm for sharing the game they love. Don't be scared to jump in with both feet!

# Comparing Different Courts

Now, armed with your paddle and ball, you want to find a court so that you can actually play. But you may find it helpful to understand the differences in courts — whether the court is indoor, outdoor, dedicated, multiuse, public, or private. The topic really is not that complicated, and the following sections simplify it so that you can find the right court environment that works for you. There are plenty of pickleball players who will play on any kind of court, anytime — just to play!

**REMEMBER**

Keep in mind that no matter the court, some elements of the game remain the same:

>> The court dimensions are always 20 feet wide by 44 feet long.

>> The net height is the same: 36 inches at the sidelines and 34 inches at the center.

>> The rules are the rules — they always stay the same.

See Chapter 7 in Book 6 for more information on court specifics.

## Playing on outdoor courts versus indoor courts

There are three main (and fairly subtle) differences between outdoor and indoor courts: the environments, the balls used, and the court surface. Although playing on both kinds of courts involves a learning curve, making the transition back and forth between them becomes easy after you understand the different characteristics of each.

>> **The physical environment of the courts is different.** On outdoor courts, the sun, wind, haze, mist, dampness, shadows — you get it — can affect play. Even a gentle breeze can affect how and where the ball travels, despite your best intentions. With the wind behind you, for example, you barely have to hit the ball to send it sailing to your opponents, or worse, beyond their baseline. If it's blazing hot, you need sunglasses and a hat or visor, and you need to make sure you stay properly hydrated. Assess the weather factors each time you set out to play.

On the other hand, some people prefer playing on indoor courts because the experience is more consistent. The lighting is usually bright, and none of those pesky weather conditions is an issue. Depending on the acoustics of the indoor courts, playing indoors can be much louder than outdoor play. The biggest complaint about playing indoors is that gymnasium-type facilities have their floors lined for basketball, volleyball, badminton, and pickleball. That's a lot of lines! It can be quite difficult to call the lines when you're looking at a court like that. Finding and holding your position at the kitchen line with so many other lines nearby can also be a challenge. Just remember that it's the same game, so have fun!

**WARNING**

Never, ever, ever play on wet courts; they are a hazard for slipping and falling. Yes, you can sing in the rain, but please, please don't play pickleball in it!

The best you can do is to be aware of the variations in playing pickleball outdoors and indoors. The availability of outdoor and indoor courts will vary too, of course, depending on where you live or travel. Always pack your paddle!

>> **The pickleballs used outdoors versus indoors are different.** Outdoor balls, engineered to minimize wind disruption, are harder, heavier, and have 40 holes. On the flip side, indoor balls are softer, lighter, and have 26 holes that are slightly larger than their outdoor cousins'.

>> **The surfaces differ on outdoor and indoor courts.** An outdoor court has an asphalt or a concrete surface. The ball tends to bounce lower and move faster, which means that you have to react more quickly and bend your knees more to make good returns. On indoor courts, the surface is usually like a basketball court with a more flexible wooden surface that is kind to your knees. These same gentle floors can also be quite slippery, glossy, and reflective. You'll want a nice "sticky"-soled indoor court shoe to avoid slipping; see Chapter 8 in Book 6 for more details about shoes. Playing on an indoor court means slower-moving balls and longer rallies back and forth; also, the shots will travel exactly where you send them because of the lack of wind.

A rare find is an indoor facility that has an outdoor surface. Basically, this is an indoor area where the facility has installed asphalt tennis, Futsal (a type of soccer), or, better yet, dedicated pickleball courts. If you happen to find one of these gems, use an outdoor ball because it will perform better on the more abrasive surface.

As a budding pickleball player, you likely have plenty of options on where to play. You'll quickly discover whether you prefer playing pickleball on outdoor or indoor courts, or maybe you are fine with both. Read on to discover the differences between dedicated and multiuse courts, and public versus private courts.

## Playing on dedicated versus multiuse courts

Dedicated courts are always the ideal place to play because you don't have to compete for time with other sports (tennis and basketball, for example), and the lines are clearly marked and easy to see. After you have played on a dedicated pickleball court, it's hard to go back.

On multiuse courts, players can sometimes find all the different lines confusing. Many multiuse courts require you to bring your own net (see Chapter 8 in Book 6 for tips on buying one). Others use the existing tennis net, which you can lower using an adjustable strap in the center. Most parks provide these on multiuse courts, or you can purchase a net height adjustment strap from a pickleball equipment supplier.

The advantage to multiuse courts is accessibility. Many local parks and recreation departments choose to include multiuse courts in their facilities so that they can appeal to a wider audience playing different types of sports. Because the pickleball craze is relatively new, it's much quicker and cheaper for them to simply paint lines on existing tennis or basketball courts. You can go just about anywhere these days with your pickleball paddle and ball in hand and find a lined court to play on. If not, it should be a relatively easy sell to ask your local park to paint pickleball lines on a seldom-used tennis court.

## Joining in at public versus private venues

Because the popularity of the sport of pickleball is sweeping the nation, you need to learn the ins and outs of playing at both public and private courts. Connecting with other players, signing up for pickleball clinics, and taking a lesson or three from a certified coach are all great places to start. The internet will certainly open up a world of pickleball playing possibilities (say that three times fast) near you. Later in the chapter you can read more on finding places to play.

Many community parks have pickleball courts, although they are most likely multiuse courts. Pickleball courts are a popular amenity for newly built communities because they don't take up a lot of space and offer family- and senior-friendly recreation for residents. Sometimes there is a reservation system, and sometimes it's just a matter of knowing that certain groups play at certain times. Check with your community or local parks and rec department to see whether groups exist for you to play with, or just go to a court and talk to the players who are there. You're likely to find folks who are eager to share the info you need to play in that area.

TIP

Don't worry if you haven't found a group to play with yet. All you need is three more people who want to learn as you do. Many sports stores and facilities rent paddles for a limited time if you're just figuring out what kind of paddle you like or whether you like playing in the first place.

Private venues have memberships to play at gyms, sports clubs, country clubs, and other sports facilities. The costs of membership vary greatly, or nonmembers may have to pay a daily drop-in fee. The advantage of membership is knowing you have a place to play, other players are there wanting to play, and you can reserve a court, stop by a drop-in clinic, or join designated play times. Many private venues are used only for residents of particular communities. So the next time you're ready to move, be sure to check out the pickleball situation. Some communities have dozens of dedicated pickleball courts just for their residents.

# Wanna Play? Finding Courts and Players Near You

After you know all the different kinds of courts and places to play, you have several options to find courts and players near you. The following websites and organizations are dedicated to helping players connect and play everywhere.

## Referencing Places2Play

Places2Play is a helpful database created by USA Pickleball that helps you find courts and clubs near you. It's very easy to access online at `www.places2play.org/`. The map is also an app — just type in your location, and all the places to play pickleball in your community come right up. In the "Comment" section, details about each location, drop-in times, and so on appear. Although the tool is free to use, USA Pickleball encourages you to become a member.

TIP

One factor to keep in mind about Places2Play is that not every venue keeps its information current at all times. If a contact number or email is given, it's wise to reach out first before turning up somewhere new with your paddle in hand.

## Using PlayTime Scheduler

PlayTime Scheduler (`playtimescheduler.com`) is another free online tool that can be extremely useful in finding courts and play sessions in your local area. It's a community-driven website through which players invite others to join them by posting sessions for a specific time, place, and skill level. You can RSVP by simply clicking a button to add your name to the list. After at least four players sign up, it's game on! PlayTime Scheduler makes it easy to see where your friends are playing on any given day, or to meet new players with similar skill levels and schedules. You can even sign up for email notifications so that you never miss a game!

Some players use the "invite only" feature to create private sessions for their friends, ladder leagues, or other groups. Keep in mind that PlayTime Scheduler is an invitation system, not a court-reservation system. Most public parks do not allow you to reserve courts, and private venues use different systems for reservations.

PlayTime Scheduler is a great resource when traveling because you can easily hop between different cities and check out the action on the local calendar. Although some cities are more active than others, the site is used on six continents across the world and is growing in popularity every day.

## Reaching out to USA Pickleball Ambassadors

USA Pickleball has created an Ambassador program to promote its organization and the sport of pickleball. Ambassadors are volunteers who pledge to promote the sport in the local area that they represent. They work directly with communities, clubs, and other recreational facilities as advocates and guides to help build pickleball programs for all to enjoy. Ambassadors work together within their designated districts as well as across multistate regions to enhance the development of USA Pickleball and pickleball in general.

TIP

To contact the Ambassador for your area, go to `usapickleball.org/get-involved/usa-pickleball-ambassadors/`. This resource can quickly get you plugged into what's happening in your local community.

## Searching social media

Tapping into social media to search for players and courts is another way to connect. Most local pickleball clubs have Facebook groups, making it easy to connect with other players in your area. There is a huge amount of enthusiasm from players on Facebook, Instagram, and X (formerly Twitter), and you could easily spend all day scrolling through pickleball content of all kinds.

USA Pickleball (usapickleball.org/) promotes events and tournaments through social media channels as well. When Nationals and other big tournaments are being played, it's a great way to find out what's happening in real time — both on the court and behind the scenes.

Most upcoming tournaments are listed on www.pickleballtournaments.com/. You will find no shortage of opportunities to compete if that becomes your thing.

# Picking Up on Pickleball Etiquette

Anytime you try a new sport, you may notice a certain etiquette that players follow. These are the unwritten rules of the game that aren't set in stone in any rule book. In pickleball, proper etiquette is very important because it's such a social, inclusive game. If you find yourself on the court and aren't sure what to do, just ask a more experienced player. They will be happy to help. The following sections give you some good guidelines to follow, both on the court and on the sidelines.

In addition to understanding the etiquette, the following sections shed some light on the quirks of pickleball culture, as well on how drop-in play works and the ins and outs of playing with new people.

## Striving to be safe, courteous, and honest

When you're new at playing pickleball, chances are you're focused on the rules and mechanics of playing. Getting to know the etiquette of the sport, however, is equally important. Sometimes safety, honesty, and courtesy may seem like common sense, but it's still good to understand the "manners" when in a new social setting. Pickleball is definitely an inclusive, considerate sport, in which integrity is key.

TIP

Here are a few guidelines for good pickleball etiquette:

>> **Wait until all players are ready before you serve.** Sometimes random balls from other courts roll onto your court, or one person has some other distraction. Wait until everyone is focused to begin to play.

>> **Call the score clearly.** Call the score loudly enough for everyone playing to hear it before serving the ball. It's easy enough to lose track of the score, but if you haven't been able to hear your opponent call it for three points, good luck!

>> **Say, "Nice shot."** Congratulate and encourage not only your partner but also your opponents when they make a great shot. Pickleball players like to encourage each other — keep in mind that you're having cooperative fun. (You can still want to win, too!)

>> **Be aware of the time when you are using the court.** If many people are waiting to play, be aware and respectful. Don't stand there chatting for ten minutes. You can do that off the court. If you have played a bunch and people have been waiting, maybe sit out a game after you've played two or three. Different clubs and venues have their own rules, usually posted by the courts. Use common courtesy and treat others the way you would want to be treated.

>> **Don't walk through someone's game to get to another court.** Instead, wait for a break in the action and then quickly get to your court. Your foursome should all go together so that the players don't have to stop their game multiple times.

>> **Call "Ball on!" loudly when your ball ends up on another court.** You immediately and safely alert the players about a ball on that court so that they won't trip and fall. The play is stopped, the ball is politely retrieved, and the rally on that court is replayed. If your ball is not in any danger of injuring anyone on the other court (for example, it's up against the back fence) and the players haven't noticed that your ball is on their court, wait until they finish their point and then ask for your ball back. "Better safe than sorry" is the rule here, so it's always better to stop play than put anyone at risk.

>> **Don't coach other players unless they've asked you for advice.** Pickleball players like to help each other, and nothing is wrong with that. If you want to share your wisdom with another player, ask them first; for example, "Would you like some advice about your backhand?" Don't be offended if they decline your advice. Often players would prefer to work with an actual coach, or they may not be in the mood to work on their strokes that day. Also, please don't delay games by doing an extended coaching session, especially if others are waiting for a court.

>> **If an opponent has restrictions, don't deliberately lob a ball so far behind them that they can't possibly get to it.** That's just not nice, and it's a cheap shot. Intention is what makes the difference. If you're playing with someone who is older or injured and unable to move quickly, don't take advantage of that when playing recreationally. Be kind. Now, if it's a tournament, that changes things a bit. That player entered the tournament and you are all there to win. So, players will play to that end.

>> **Walk to the net after every game and tap paddles with the other players.** It is customary after the game has been played for the players to approach the net and gently tap their paddles, saying things like "Good game!" and "That was fun!" (Some people prefer to tap their paddle handles instead because they don't want to scratch the face of the paddle, but either way is fine.)

>> **Lose and win graciously.** No one likes a sore loser or a gloating winner, and we want you to be liked! Pickleball is supposed to be fun, and nothing sucks the joy out of the room like players who take themselves way too seriously.

>> **Bonus tip: If you are a new player, there's good news for you.** Almost everyone makes a point to play with new players. "It's how we learned to get better," other players will tell you enthusiastically as they insist you join in. Patience, encouragement, and kindness are hallmarks of this game.

## Understanding pickleball culture: OMG! (One more game!)

Almost universally, people are surprised by two prominent features of the sport. First, it's easy to play, even the very first time you try. Most people, despite their level of athleticism, can hit the ball and rally the first time they play. You can easily improve within a few weeks of playing regularly, or with a lesson or two.

Second, pickleball can be an inviting, inclusive, and courteous sport. You don't need to be a big-time jock to enjoy it. It's not segmented by a player's size, strength, gender, or age. As mentioned earlier in this chapter, public courts are readily available everywhere — in parks, schools, community centers, churches, and new housing developments. Courts are popping up at private clubs like crazy because of the sport's exploding popularity. People are even building courts in their backyards.

You might notice, when you pass a pickleball court, lots of smiles and laughter, kindness, and positivity. Players develop friendships. It's not unusual to see an experienced player happily going over the rules with a first-timer who is just learning to play.

Sure, pickleball has a funny name. It's a sport that was created in the 1960s. (See Chapter 6 in Book 6 for a brief history of pickleball.) Now it's one of the fastest growing sports in the country. Who knows — one day, pickleball may be in the Olympics.

TIP

The culture of pickleball has deep roots in fun and camaraderie. Here are some ways to familiarize yourself with this growing sport even further:

>> **Find your community:** If you want to play once a week just for laughs and a little exercise, you'll find your group. If you want to meet more regularly for a game or three, you'll find your people. Or if you want a more competitive environment, most likely you can find tournaments going on in your local area all year-round.

>> **Dive into media:** You can watch professional players on TV. ESPN, CBS, Fox Sports, and Tennis Channel have regular broadcasts. *Pickleball Magazine* is the official magazine for USA Pickleball, and there's also a high-end magazine called *InPickleball*.

>> **Travel the world:** You can find pickleball camps and resorts all over the world for intense instruction and enjoyment. Even major cruise lines now offer "pickleball cruises."

## Knowing even more reasons why you should play pickleball

Pickleball is much more than just a sport; it's a community. It's social. Chatting with your partners and competitors during a match is expected. Good sporting conduct and courtesy are key elements of the game and experience.

By playing pickleball, you will likely improve your physical fitness and have a more positive mental state of mind all at the same time.

Civility, as mentioned, is a big part of the game. Players typically do their best to make honest line calls. It's not uncommon to see players calling a fault on themselves when they find that they were in the kitchen while volleying. For many players, winning or losing is secondary. It's a unique sport that way. Many people find fun and friendship are at the core of the experience. Pickleball brings back recess for adults!

## Navigating drop-in play rotation

Pickleball encourages players to play in organized drop-in games, or *open play.* Open play allows strangers to meet and play together. Some open play sessions are organized by skill level, whereas others aren't, giving beginners a chance to learn from more experienced players. Pickleball aims to be truly inclusive, which makes the play more fun. Even if you are an advanced player, you can mix with other levels occasionally — it can be a lot more fun than you may think!

Venues that offer drop-in play typically use some kind of rotation rules or organization system to help manage court traffic. Some common methods include

>> **Paddle line-ups and paddle racks:** Whether people simply hang paddles on a fence or use a specially designed paddle rack, most courts have a system for determining who's next in line.

>> **Four on, four off:** In this common rotational system, a foursome finishes their game and all four players come off the court. The next four waiting in line then take the court.

>> **Winners stay and split:** In this case, only the losing team rotates off the court, and two new players come on to replace them. The winning team splits up so that they each play with one of the oncoming players.

>> **Winners stay together:** Often referred to as a Challenge Court format, winning teams stay on and continue to play together as long as they keep winning. After each game, the losing team exits and two new "challengers" come on to face the winners.

>> **King/Queen of the court:** In this format, courts are designated from the lowest to highest level. As teams win their games, they move "up" to a higher court, sometimes splitting partners. The losing team moves "down" to a lower-level court, or back to the waiting area if they are already on the lowest court.

These are just a few of the most common court rotation methods. Each venue has its rules for rotating onto the courts. The rules are usually posted in writing, but if not, just ask the friendliest person you see. After you join in open play a few times, you'll see a welcoming rhythm to it.

**WARNING**

When leaving or entering your court, make sure you don't cross the back of a game in play. You don't want to distract other players or possibly injure yourself.

**REMEMBER**

With drop-in play, communication is key. Don't be afraid to ask questions if you're unsure of how the rotation is going — pickleballers love to help new players. It's the nature of the game!

## Playing nice: Being a good neighbor

You may find pickleball courts nestled into quiet neighborhoods. In that case, it's important to keep your noise level in mind (as when shouting "Wahoo!" at the top of your lungs when you score, for example) and not offend the nearby neighbors. Make note of the set hours of play that are posted and honor those guidelines. Think about it: The people living in homes near pickleball courts may not even play pickleball, and they have to hear *a lot* of dinking and wahoo-ing most days.

**REMEMBER**

Be sure to leave the courts clean and the gates closed when you leave. Please don't ever toss broken pickleballs onto the grass at your local park. With just a few simple acts, you can help to make sure that neighbors welcome pickleball, not fight against it. Plus those balls can jam up lawn mowers.

If you are considering building your own private court, how close you live to other neighbors will be a significant factor to consider. Sure, pickleball players may love the sound of a good "dink-dink-dink" rally. Your neighbors — not so much. So before you sink a bunch of money into building a court, consider working with the neighbors on sound and traffic levels well in advance. Who knows? Maybe you will turn your neighbors into pickleball fans and players as well.

TIP

Consider installing soundproofing windscreen material to reduce the pickleball noise. Some manufacturers say their soundproofing can reduce the noise up to 50 percent. (This will not apply to the loud whoops every time Uncle Larry wins a point.)

# Index

# R

relocating *(continued)*

mobility and accessibility, 246–247

moving, 255–265

mailing address, 256–258

transportation, 258–261

unpacking, 263–265

utilities, 261–262

packing list, 224

renting versus buying, 239–240

researching, 211

testing location, 212

to-do list, 223

types of housing, 248–252

Remitly, 307, 338

remote work, 123–125, 175–176. *See also* nomad lifestyle

appeal of, 176

considerations regarding, 176

defined, 271

history of, 272–273

opportunities, 124–125

safety, 123–124

Remote Year, 328

rental income, 16

*Résumé Magic* (Whitcomb), 135

résumés, 129–141

essential qualities, 130–132

communication skills, 131–132

innovation, 132

lifelong learning, 132

problem solving, 131

self-starters, 130

technology skills, 130–131

getting help with, 141

getting noticed, 132–137

automated screening systems, 137

CAR stories, 135–136

contact information, 133

education and training, 136

formatting, 133, 137

gaps in history, 135, 139

short and simple, 132–133

work experience, 134–135

highlighting distinctions, 138–139

interviews, 148–149

LinkedIn, 94, 99, 131, 133

omitting imperfections, 139

tailoring, 139–141

changing careers, 140

job boards, 140

key word searches, 141

returning after extended absence, 141

targeting openings, 140

turnoffs, 137–138

retail sector, 119

RetiredBrains, 68, 115

retirement funds, plans, and accounts. *See also* Social Security

asset inventory for wills, 47

benefits of staying in the workforce, 62

comparing, 172

contributing to, 23

employment in financial sector, 120

income from, 13

Roth options, 23

self-funded, 13

target-date funds, 21

retirement visas, 320

RetirementJobs, 115

returnships, 89–90

Revolut, 307, 338

revolved triangle pose, 453–454

Ribollita recipe, 368

Rice Salad with Red Peppers, Garbanzo Beans, and Feta recipe, 382

Rix, Sara, 70

Roadsurfer, 329

Roasted Veggie Hummus Pitas recipe, 356

## S

salads and sides, 375–384

Clean Cobb Salad, 377

Fruit and Grains Salad, 380

Fruity Chicken Pasta Salad, 379

Fruity Coleslaw, 378

Quinoa Crunch, 381

Rice Salad with Red Peppers, Garbanzo Beans, and Feta, 382

Sweet-Potato Potato Salad, 383

tips for, 376

salaries, 170–171

interview questions, 157, 159

researching, 170–171

starting pay, 171

Salary.com, 113, 171

Salmon Risi Bisi recipe, 371

Salmon Salad Sandwich with Peach Salsa recipe, 358

Salvation Army, 312

Sasquatch Mail, 314

savings

decision to downsize, 190

goals for, 14

scams

housing reservations and booking, 338

investing, 21–22

do's and don'ts, 22

warning signs of, 21

phishing, 117

Social Security *(continued)*
   life expectancy, 30–33
   selecting the right time to begin, 25, 37–39
   spousal benefits, 34–36, 38
   working later, 36–37
   Supplemental Security Income, 13
   survivors benefits, 13, 36
Social Security Disability Insurance (SSDI), 13
*Social Security For Dummies* (AARP), 13
Society for Human Resource Management (SHRM), 65, 132–133, 146
soft skills, 80–83
   analytical thinking, 81
   communication, 81
   confidence, 81
   cooperation, 81
   creativity, 81
   decisiveness, 81
   defined, 80
   flexibility, 81
   honesty, 81
   integrity, 81
   leadership, 82
   learning, 82
   listening, 82
   literacy, 82
   organization, 82
   patience, 82
   people skills, 82
   planning, 82
   positive attitude, 83
   problem solving, 83
   punctuality, 83
   reliability, 83
   resilience, 83
   resourcefulness, 83
   self-management, 83
   transferrable, 85
sororities, 72
Special Needs Trusts Fairness Act, 54
special-needs trusts, 55
Spiralized Zucchini with Roasted Veggies recipe, 370
Sports Fitness Industry Association, 462
spousal benefits from Social Security, 34–36, 38
   monthly reductions, 35
   selecting the right time to begin, 34
   survivors benefits, 36
springing durable powers of attorney, 45
SquareMouth, 313
SSDI (Social Security Disability Insurance), 13
SSI (Supplemental Security Income), 13
standing forward bend pose, 455–456
starting date, 182
Stoller, Jane, 225
storage spaces
   decluttering, 233
   estimating living space, 245–246
straps, for yoga, 425
strong passports, 317–318
student visas, 320
studio apartments, 249
   truck size needed for moving, 259
Sublet.com, 333
*Success as a Mediator For Dummies* (Pynchon and Kraynak), 125
supervised probate, 51
Supplemental Security Income (SSI), 13
supported shoulder stand, 429, 456–457
survivors benefits, 13, 36
Swapalease, 312
Sweet and Spicy Nuts recipe, 387
Sweet Potato Chips with Catalan Salsa recipe, 390
Sweet-Potato Potato Salad recipe, 383
switching costs, 290–292
   money-related costs, 290–291
   time-related costs, 290–291
synovial fluid, 415

## T

Tandoori Pork Tenderloin recipe, 369
Taproot Foundation, 91
TaskRabbit, 332
Tax Policy Center, 52
taxes
   estate taxes, 52
   gifts, 52
   nomad lifestyle, 309–310
   property taxes, 253–254
   on side gig income, 17
   states with no income tax, 204
TED, 91
*Telecommunications-Transportation Tradeoff* (Nilles), 273
telecommuting, 272–273. *See also* nomad lifestyle; remote work
Teleport, 289
temporary nomads, 270. *See also* nomad lifestyle
Tentrr, 329

## Publisher's Acknowledgments

**Senior Acquisitions Editor:** Tracy Boggier

**Senior Managing Editor:** Kristie Pyles

**Compilation Editor:** Georgette Beatty

**Development Editor:** Linda Brandon

**Copy Editor:** Christine Pingleton

**Proofreader:** Debbye Butler

**Production Editor:** Tamilmani Varadharaj

**Cover Image:** © PeopleImages/Getty Images; © filadendron/Getty Images

Printed and bound by CPI Group (UK) Ltd, Croydon, CR0 4YY

09/06/2025

14685924-0001